Margarita Fischer

For Bill

Margarita Fischer

*A Biography of
the Silent Film Star*

THERESA ST. ROMAIN

McFarland & Company, Inc., Publishers
Jefferson, North Carolina, and London

The present work is a reprint of the illustrated case bound edition of Margarita Fischer: A Biography of the Silent Film Star, *first published in 2008 by McFarland.*

LIBRARY OF CONGRESS CATALOGUING-IN-PUBLICATION DATA

St. Romain, Theresa, 1980–
Margarita Fischer : a biography of the
silent film star / Theresa St. Romain.
p. cm.
Includes bibliographical references and index.

ISBN 978-0-7864-6933-8
softcover : 50# alkaline paper

1. Fischer, Margarita, 1886–1975. 2. Motion picture actors and
actresses — United States — Bigraphy. I. Title.
PN2287.F477S7   2012   791.4302'8092 — dc22   [B]   2007051999

BRITISH LIBRARY CATALOGUING DATA ARE AVAILABLE

© 2008 Theresa St. Romain. All rights reserved

*No part of this book may be reproduced or transmitted in any form
or by any means, electronic or mechanical, including photocopying
or recording, or by any information storage and retrieval system,
without permission in writing from the publisher.*

Cover photograph: Studio portrait of Margarita Fischer, around
1917 (photograph by Melbourne Spurr) courtesy of the Margarita
Fischer Papers, Special Collections and University Archives,
Wichita State University Libraries

Manufactured in the United States of America

*McFarland & Company, Inc., Publishers
Box 611, Jefferson, North Carolina 28640
www.mcfarlandpub.com*

Table of Contents

Acknowledgments	vi
Preface	1
Introduction: *The Girl Who Dared*	3
1 *The Girl Who Couldn't Grow Up*	7
2 *Where Paths Meet*	19
3 *The Land of Promise*	28
4 *The Rose of California*	39
5 *Mlle. La Mode*	53
6 *The Dangerous Talent*	70
7 *In Love and War*	87
8 *The Lure of the Mask*	98
9 *When Queenie Came Back*	112
10 *Uncle Tom's Cabin*	122
11 *Beach of Dreams*	133
12 *Her Heritage*	150
13 Conclusion: *Any Woman*	159
Filmography	165
Chapter Notes	175
Bibliography	193
Index	199

Acknowledgments

This book began life in a much shorter form as my master's thesis for Wichita State University's Department of History. Mike Kelly, former curator of the Department of Special Collections at Wichita State University's Ablah Library, first introduced me to Margarita Fischer and her papers, for which I owe him a great debt of gratitude. The Fischer Papers and Pollard Papers held in the Department of Special Collections served as the foundation for this work. Current curator Dr. Lorraine Madway and library assistant Mary Nelson were incredibly helpful throughout the lengthy research process for this book; I literally could not have done this without them. Additional thanks go to my thesis committee members, Dr. Judith Johnson and Dr. Christopher Brooks, and particularly to committee chair and constant encourager Dr. Jay Price.

Margarita Fischer's family was an excellent source of information about the actress. Gina Laitinen first opened this door by corresponding with me. Margarita Kotselis, the actress's great-niece, graciously consented to an interview and was helpful, patient, and thorough in responding to my many questions. I greatly value her feedback and insight into Margarita Fischer's personality and family life.

Many thanks to Robert Birchard for sharing the interview he conducted with Margarita Fischer. Thanks, too, to Geoff Williams for corresponding about Charles Pyle and the Fischers as he researched his own book. Others who provided much-appreciated guidance, information, or a nudge in the right direction were James Cozart, Jerry Hatfield, F. Gwynplaine McIntyre, Dr. Craig Miner, David Pierce, Paul Spehr, and the staff of Margarita Fischer's former home, the historic Rancho Buena Vista Adobe.

Finally, I want to thank my family and friends for their unfailing encouragement throughout the prolonged process of research and writing. My husband, Bill Head, was especially supportive.

Preface

This work traces the life and career of Margarita Fischer, leading lady on the stage and silent screen, whose fame spanned the first three decades of the twentieth century. Those were decades of rapid change in both American society and the American film industry. As Margarita matured from teenaged ingénue to bona fide star, she altered her public image in order to remain relevant and appealing throughout these changes. She headed her own theatrical company as a teen, using her youth and innocent appearance to lend respectability to her profession. When she entered film in 1910, she combined the flexibility gained from years of theatrical touring with a savvy understanding of the nature of her own appeal to audiences. By 1914, she headed the American Film Manufacturing Company's Beauty brand of films, and fans of her work outnumbered those of Mary Pickford.

Margarita remained popular for the remainder of the decade by updating her image from that of a becurled innocent to that of an accessible star and sophisticated fashion icon (once she embarked upon feature filmmaking). She made both risky, innovative pictures and formulaic romantic comedies, although the former strained her marriage to the intensely private director Harry Pollard, and the latter frustrated her artistically. Always devoted to her family interests—indeed, she supported her immediate family from the time she began touring at the age of twelve—she retired from the screen in 1921 to support her increasingly alcoholic husband and save her failing marriage. When her marriage and Pollard's career both grew more secure, she returned to the world of film, making three more pictures in the mid–1920s. Margarita continued to shepherd her image and always presented a gracious, glamorous front, but she never regained her former stardom. After playing a leading role in Universal's prestigious but financially disappointing *Uncle Tom's Cabin* (1927), she retired for a second and final time at her husband's request. She supported him emotionally as he directed Universal's *Show Boat* (1929) and built a body of work for MGM before his final illness in 1934.

Following her retirement from film, Margarita enjoyed a brief return to the local stage, then spent the remaining decades of her life quietly—traveling, caring for her relatives, and becoming increasingly active in local humanitarian work. Silent for years on the subject of her illustrious past, she regained an interest in her cinematic legacy late in life, and before her death in 1975 she attempted to safeguard it through correspondence, interviews, and publicity. Despite her efforts, her film career remains largely forgotten today, a victim of poor film preservation as well as changing tastes in entertainment.

This work began life as a thesis completed for a master of arts in history degree, with an emphasis in public history, at Wichita State University in Wichita, Kansas. The author has always maintained an interest in early film history, and the happy presence of the extensive Margarita Fischer Papers and the Harry Pollard Papers at Wichita State University's Ablah Library, Department of Special Collections, provided an excellent avenue for research into this subject area. These collections of papers comprise personal letters, fan mail, studio contracts, scrapbooks of newspaper clippings and magazine articles, and hundreds of still photographs from both Margarita Fischer's and Harry Pollard's films. Donated by Margarita Fischer's niece and heir, the collections provided the foundation for all research into the lives and careers of this couple.

Additional sources offering a wealth of information on Margarita Fischer include an interview conducted by Robert S. Birchard with the then-elderly actress herself around the year 1970, and an interview conducted by the author with Margarita Fischer's closest living relative, Margarita Kotselis, the actress's namesake and great-niece, who lived with the elder Margarita as a child and remained close with her until her death in 1975. Ms. Kotselis's willingness not only to be interviewed but also to correspond with the author regarding various questions provided an invaluable window into the actress's personal life.

Margarita Fischer has been virtually ignored by film historians since the end of her career, and no full-length work (and few brief works that address her more than peripherally) has ever been published on her life and career. Over the course of her stage career and her subsequent seventeen-year stint on the silver screen, however, she worked with a wide variety of performers, studios, and directors that are today better known. As a result, many outstanding secondary sources are available to contextualize the biographical content available through the primary sources of family papers and personal interviews. For example, Claudia D. Johnson's *American Actress: Perspective on the Nineteenth Century* uses numerous anecdotes to illustrate shifts in American attitudes towards the stage and the women who acted upon it. Authors Kalton C. Lahue, Timothy James Lyons, and I.G. Edmonds have examined the work of some of Margarita's film studios in, respectively, *Motion Picture Pioneer: The Selig Polyscope Company*; *The Silent Partner: The History of the American Film Manufacturing Company, 1910–1921*; and *Big U: Universal in the Silent Days*. Biographies and autobiographies of Margarita's close contemporaries provide additional insight into the progression of early film careers, including Kelly R. Brown's *Florence Lawrence, the Biograph Girl: America's First Movie Star*; Sally Dumaux's *King Baggot: A Biography and Filmography of the First King of the Movies*; Eve Golden's *Vamp: The Rise and Fall of Theda Bara*; Gloria Swanson's *Swanson on Swanson*; and several excellent biographies of Mary Pickford and Charlie Chaplin.

Any biographer's task is, in a sense, detective work, for any source left behind is insufficient in itself to provide more than a partial understanding of some aspect of the subject's life. It is the author's sincere hope that the breadth of sources drawn upon for this work has resulted in a biography that does justice to the accomplishments of Margarita Fischer. Her fame in the early twentieth century indicates the degree to which the American public embraced her as a representation of their values and desires. Bridging the traditional and the modern, she was, in many ways, an ordinary woman who happened also to be a world-famous actress. Margarita Fischer's life and work present a window into the developing American film industry, shifting roles within American society, and the stunningly familiar choices of a woman balancing the everyday obligations of family and career nearly a century ago.

Introduction: *The Girl Who Dared*

The youthful actress seemed to have all the good things in life as she welcomed the reporter to her comfortable, elegant bungalow on the main street of Santa Barbara, California. Blithe and beautiful in a white organdy dress, her curly dark auburn hair pulled into a loose knot, she met her interviewer on her wide porch (well-used, judging from the comfortable wicker furniture scattered across its length) at dusk following a long day at the studio. Her wide green eyes may have been tired from an early morning studio call, but they snapped with wit and good humor as she introduced the other members of the household, her older sister and their widowed mother, to the admiring member of the press. The journalist eagerly took in the cozy rockers, the piles of stylish cushions tossed around to make comfortable reading spots, the manicured lawn in front, the war garden in back — which had grown under the young actress's care from a patriotic duty to a beloved hobby during these times of the Great War. Yes, the star seemed entirely content as she moved about her well-loved home and yard, chatting casually as she shifted between work and home duties, sorting out potential scripts for her next film and demonstrating her infallible technique for determining a pumpkin's ripeness (she shook it and listened for rattling seeds).

Eventually, the three women drew up chairs with the interviewer around the living room hearth, the fire banked low for the balmy evening. With frequent interjections from her laughing elders, the diminutive star gleefully recounted family picnics, fishing trips, adventures on location shoots, and one infamous day when her young niece dumped her off of the child's tricycle. When her sister teased her to grow up, she retorted playfully, "That isn't one of my ambitions." Yet the seemingly carefree actress was also savvy and socially conscious — with the greatest war the world had ever seen raging across Europe, she grew "everything from roses to squash" to help support her family, while her mother — the household's accountant — pinched pennies to buy ever more war bonds. The reporter eventually came to the topic of the young star's recent career and successes, naming several popular romantic, dramatic, and comic movies she had made over the course of the late 1910s. Did she have a favorite type of role or film? No, she valued their variety, she explained. Her mobile face tensed with resolve as she replied, "I don't intend to fall in a rut, making just one sort of picture."[1]

The actress, Margarita Fischer, was already known for her versatility. Since her stage debut at the age of eight, she had developed a reputation for her great adaptability as a performer, as well as her willingness to take professional risks, most of which paid off. She moved inevitably from the stage to the new world of the movies in 1910. In 1914, a few years before she gave the above interview, she had been voted the nation's most popular actress in a fan magazine poll, and a thriving studio had created a brand of one-reel films especially for her

INTRODUCTION

to star in. When the film industry moved inevitably to the production of longer, feature-length pictures, she and her actor/director husband, Harry Pollard, set up their own production company to tell more challenging stories. As the leading lady in all of the couple's films, Margarita demonstrated great range and flexibility during this time. Over the course of 1916 and 1917 she played such diverse roles as a depraved woman, an innocent child, an exotic islander, a sailor, an opium addict, a carnival dancer, and a heedless heiress.

Motivated by the need to financially support her widowed mother, divorced sister, and young niece, Margarita Fischer kept a keen eye on ever-shifting public tastes, and she strove to maintain a fashionable and appealing image in order to safeguard her impact at the box office. Sometimes her desire to remain appealing to filmgoers conflicted with her own artistic standards, which had been honed to prefer roles of variety and substance ever since the actress's youth on the stage. When the strains of running a production company (combined with her husband's increasing dependence on alcohol) began to erode her marriage, she returned to the security of contract employment with a studio and eventually began filming a series of unremarkable romantic comedies to pay the bills. She and Harry Pollard separated anyway, and her mother, sister, and niece set up household with her instead. The warm, cheerful interview recounted above took place in 1918, around the time of the collapse of her marriage, and shortly before she fell into the very career rut she feared.

Throughout professional and personal changes, however, Margarita Fischer remained a shrewd manager of her image, and she owed the longevity of her popularity to this gift. Never maintaining a publicist, she herself shaped her physical appearance, her screen persona, and her "private" self for the theatergoing and filmgoing public over the course of more than three decades. She cultivated friendly and courteous manners for her public and for the media, charming the press into focusing on her carefree appeal and easy glamour while hiding the less sunny (though perhaps more universal) truth of her family difficulties. She and the troubled Pollard eventually reconciled, and under his direction she made her final film, a big-budget epic Universal Studios version of *Uncle Tom's Cabin*, in 1927. Margarita Fischer retired from the screen afterwards at the age of forty-one at the request of her increasingly frail husband and, after a brief stint on local stages, relaxed into a quiet, prosperous retirement in the company of family and friends. Harry Pollard died in 1934, and Margarita never remarried. She herself passed away in 1975 at the age of eighty-nine.

This work relates a narrative of Margarita Fischer's life and acting career while keeping in mind the broader issues informing her personal and professional decisions. Chapter 1 begins the story of her long life, recounting her youth on the stage and her rise to fame as a theatrical performer. Chapter 2 follows the development of her professional reputation as an independent stage artist and her (reluctant) decision to make films. Chapter 3 examines the infant film industry and the beginnings of Margarita Fischer's film career, as well as her marriage to fellow performer Harry Pollard. Chapter 4 looks at the growth of the actress's film stardom and her versatility as a performer. Chapter 5 recounts the time of her greatest stardom — with the American Film Manufacturing Company — placing this within the context of changes within the film industry and the beginning of the feature film era.

In Chapter 6, the actress begins her creative phase, the intense period in the late 1910s when she and her husband took great artistic risks within their own production company, Pollard Picture Plays. This decision eventually required too much personal sacrifice, and the

Introduction

actress chose to safeguard her family's financial security and her own popularity at the expense of greater artistry — and, unwittingly, of her marriage. Chapter 7 follows Margarita Fischer's return to studio filmmaking as the Great War broke out, and her patriotic activism during the war. Chapter 8 traces her reinvention as a comic actress, and her growing dissatisfaction with the formulaic roles assigned by her studio. As the film industry entered another period of transition (into the "flapper era"), Margarita retired as an actress for the first time and reconciled with her husband. His career renaissance and Margarita's subsequent return to the screen are described in Chapter 9, while Chapter 10 describes her most expensive and ambitious film, Universal's grandiose adaptation of *Uncle Tom's Cabin*, which proved to be the actress's final screen appearance, as the sound era transformed filmmaking. Chapter 11 recounts Margarita's transition to private life, as, for the first time in their marriage, Harry Pollard's career eclipsed her own. He became a successful director of sound movies for Universal and MGM before retiring in 1932, two years before his death. In Chapter 12, the widowed actress focuses on her private life, centered on her extended family, and then attempts to recover the legacy of her once-great career before the end of her life. Chapter 13 concludes the narrative with an examination of Margarita Fischer's significance and the wider issues of social history and film history that are raised by her life and work.

Throughout her career, Margarita Fischer saw her profession and her country change a great deal, and she changed her image in response, maintaining her popularity as a performer for more than three decades. Like so many other silent stars, she has long been forgotten, but in her own time she was famous and beloved. As an actress, she epitomized both Hollywood glamour and public appeal; her fans felt as if they knew her, even as they admired her unattainable life. In private, however, Margarita held everyday values and made difficult but very modern decisions in an attempt to balance her personal life with her career. Hers is the fascinating story not only of one woman's life, but also of the nascent film industry and of American society in the early twentieth century.

1

The Girl Who Couldn't Grow Up

Margarita Fischer was born into a different world than the one in which she died. In the year of her birth, 1886, the Civil War was still a raw memory, and the internal combustion engine was an obscure novelty; in 1975, when she died, the Vietnam conflict was winding down, and men had walked on the moon. Social attitudes and expectations had changed to the same degree as had technology, seeing women advance from the hearth to the polls to the boardroom. In the early twentieth century, social roles for women were in continual flux, and shifts in attitudes and social expectations throughout Margarita Fischer's life both enabled the career actress to attain great professional success, and bound her—albeit willingly—by personal obligations.

The United States in the final years of the nineteenth century was, in the words of historian Thomas J. Schlereth, "a country in transition," in which "migration and movement, mobility and motion characterized identity."[1] The Industrial Revolution had arrived in full force, and communication and transportation were easier and faster than ever before for Victorians. In 1880, Americans had 50,000 telephones; only ten years later the number had risen to 800,000. Railroad track mileage increased by 150 percent between 1876 and 1900, making bulk shipping around the country much quicker. As convenience and speed increased, the cost of industrially produced and transported staples of life, such as food and clothing, dropped in the last three decades of the 1800s.

Technology was changing individual lives and social demographics on a broad and unprecedented scale as the 1800s came to a close. For the first time in American history, the 1870 census found, farmers made up less than half the population of the nation. The number dropped to twenty-seven percent by 1920 even as farm acreage increased. With the passing of the age of the yeoman farmer, Americans moved in increasing numbers to rapidly industrializing cities, holding positions in manufacturing, construction, transportation, and commerce. Industries consumed raw materials such as lumber, coal, and iron ore in huge quantities, and they produced, along with finished goods, a prosperous class of owners and a large working class of hourly employees that for the first time included many women. In working-class families, women and children often contributed to the family's income, along with men; by 1900, one-fifth of all women worked outside the home.[2]

The same energy, change, and movement that characterized the United States as the nineteenth century drew to a close also influenced Margarita Fischer's early life. She began life in a world that was beginning to shift both economically and socially, and she had the good fortune to be born to creative, bold, and loving parents who embraced the new opportunities opened by social change. Her parents, John and Kate Fischer, did not hail from theatrical backgrounds, but the couple's ambitious bent guaranteed them a life outside of common work in factories or on farms. John Fischer was the strong-willed, inventive, entrepreneurial Wisconsin-born son of German-speaking Swiss parents. It was probably in Iowa, in the early 1880s, that he met and married the devoutly Catholic Iowa native Katherine Heagney, the game, robust daughter of a New England Scotch–Irish Civil War veteran turned farmer.[3] The newlyweds settled in Iowa after their marriage, and that state became the birthplace of their first child, Dorothy (nicknamed Dottie), in June 1884. Margaret, the couple's second and last child, was born in Missouri Valley, Iowa, on February 12, 1886. A dainty child, she was at once nicknamed "Babe," and was always known as such within her family. Three years after her birth, the family moved to Silverton, Oregon, to be closer to relatives of John's who lived in Salem, about thirteen miles away.[4] Town life suited the young family well; here John and Kate bought and managed a hotel in town, and their daughters began to attend school.[5] They might have learned their lessons from their aunt Anna, their father's sister, who taught at the Salem school and eventually served as its principal.[6] Certainly the two little girls, especially Babe, developed a close relationship with their affectionate unmarried aunt during their youth which would last for the rest of Anna Fischer's life.

The Fischer family was introduced to the theatrical profession purely by chance and financial misfortune. In 1894, a would-be theatrical agent (supplementing his income working for a piano company, the Fischer girls observed) ran up a large board bill with his touring company at John Fischer's hotel. Completely without the funds to pay the bill, he and his out-of-pocket company put together a charity performance of the Adolphe d'Ennery play *A Celebrated Case* to raise the money owed. Needing a child actress for the part of five-year-old Adrienne in the play's lengthy "prologue" (about one-third of its length), he judiciously cast the doe-eyed younger daughter of the hotel manager to whom he owed his payment.[7] Dorothy was too old and was well-grown for her age, but Babe, with her long, dark auburn curls and wide green eyes, was a small, pretty child who could easily pass for younger than her eight years. Her opportune appearance changed the course of her family's life.

A Celebrated Case was a forceful choice for the charity performance, as the period drama begins with a marital reconciliation, a jewel theft, a case of mistaken identity, an impulsive murder, and a wrongful conviction. The character of Adrienne overhears her mother's murder and wrongly blames her father, setting in motion the dramatic conflict of the play.[8] The small town of Silverton had probably never seen anything like it. "My father was always stage-struck, so he fell for it," the newly minted actress later remembered of the plans for the charity performance.[9] John Fischer's aspirations aside, Babe also had a natural affinity for the stage.

The young girl had a great deal of both sprightly and emotive dialogue to remember in her role as Adrienne, and she evidently handled her demanding scenes with a natural ease and skill. As she remembered later, "My father decided then and there that he would make a star of me"—evidently not dismayed by the financial straits of the profession, as evidenced by the need for a benefit performance.[10] Babe herself took advantage of the presence of the theatrical company to learn music and dance from a young girl among its ranks, demonstrating a talent for these performing arts as well. She learned, by her recollection, "skirt dancing, acrobatic dance, sailor's horn pipe, the sword dance, the serpentine dance, and ballet. I also learned to play the violin (not well)."[11]

Dottie (left) and Babe Fischer, around the time of Babe's first appearance on stage at age eight in 1894. Photograph by W.L. Jones (courtesy the Margarita Fischer Papers, Special Collections and University Archives, Wichita State University Libraries).

After seeing her budding talent and her acclaimed work in other local plays, John Fischer succumbed to the lure of the footlights and sold his hotel to manage his daughter's promising theatrical career.[12] Although it was her parents' decision to pursue the acting profession, the actress later said of this time: "I loved the life. I was on the stage when I was so young, and I loved it."[13] Babe Fischer's natural gifts won steady work for her, and the Fischer family began touring around the western United States as stage performers once Babe reached the age of twelve and could take on a larger variety of roles. This marked the end of the Fischer sisters' formal education (not at unusually early ages for the time) and the beginning of the family's full-time professional careers as actors.[14]

The family's decision to go on the road and on the stage was a bold one, as the life of touring actors at the turn of the century was financially unstable and often of uncertain respectability. In a society of still–Victorian mores and notions of propriety, actors were "social pariahs," and the theater itself was seen as "a place of evil, a breeding ground for sin that all decent people avoided."[15] Indeed, until the 1870s, many playhouses truly did trespass against the family-centered morality of the time by reserving a "third tier" of seats in which prostitutes congregated for the purpose of finding customers.[16] Even after this custom died out, theaters retained their seedy reputation due to their association with "vice"— not only in the third tier, but also upon the stage. Plays often dealt with controversial topics, presenting murder (as in *A Celebrated Case*) and overt sexuality or making light of religion. The immediacy of this live entertainment form made its scandalous messages, in the eyes of contemporary clergy, particularly dangerous and convincing to susceptible audience members.[17]

Vaudeville began in the late nineteenth century as a family-friendly alternative to the "legitimate" theater, at least nominally sanitizing racy material in order to appeal to middle-class audiences. A disjuncture often existed between the "clean" acts that were publicized and the actual acts that performed, however; the greatest draws in these skit-oriented variety shows were often scantily clad women.[18] Other common acts included animal performances, comedians, magicians, singers, and one-act plays. This combination of the prurient and the proper — all for an inexpensive ticket — turned out to be incredibly popular. Although "legitimate" performers often viewed it as an inferior form of entertainment, many of them also performed on vaudeville stages in order to capture the attention of such large and enthusiastic audiences.[19] Despite its eclectic appeal, the lifespan of this entertainment medium was only about fifty years, from the first use of the term "vaudeville" in the 1880s until the end of the 1920s, when the moving pictures that vaudeville had popularized in their infancy proved to be the American public's cheap entertainment of choice.[20]

The Fischer touring company's timing was fortunate. They blended both types of theater, performing full plays, with vaudeville-like acrobatics and dances between acts, at a time when vaudeville was in its prime and the reception given to "legitimate" actors was less daunting and derogatory than it had been in previous decades. With the closing of "third tiers," the gap between the morality of theaters and of society had begun to close as well. Pitfalls still abounded for a young woman embarking upon a stage career, though. Female morality and reputations have historically been more valuable and more vulnerable than those of men, and both were automatically questioned when a woman chose to act in public. According to author Claudia D. Johnson, an actress became "the antithesis of ideal womanhood" by leaving the domestic sphere and abandoning the traditional modesty and demureness so valued

1. The Girl Who Couldn't Grow Up

by the late Victorians.[21] Apart from the possibility of public censure, the daily life of a traveling player was physically difficult for actors of both sexes, as they maintained a grueling rehearsal schedule in order to keep up with their audiences' constant demand for new material.[22]

During Babe Fischer's stage career, her family dealt with both of these challenges through a judicious management of both image and material. She and her sister Dottie began their careers inconspicuously and modestly, as befit their mother's firm religious convictions. Her father formed a stage company in partnership with another actor, and three years after the Fischer family began touring, the season playbill for Fischer and Van Cleve's Players listed John Fischer first out of twenty performers, while Kate, Dottie, and Babe were respectively billed a demure fifteenth, sixteenth, and seventeenth, indicating the small size of their roles.[23] As a performer, however, Babe quickly began to eclipse her relatives. In contrast to the stockier Dorothy, whose firm, pleasant features resembled her mother's, the younger sister had grown into a haunting, delicate beauty who her father's theatrical company began to feature in increasingly prominent roles.

Due to her youth, her small size (she was thin and barely five feet tall), and her lack of formal schooling, Babe initially felt self-conscious about both her appearance and her knowledge when her performances began to receive more attention within the touring company and from audiences. For her time on stage, she molded her small frame into a voluptuous hourglass with "symmetricals" (costume padding, especially for legs) to play adult women, including Mary Magdalene. Onstage, she was transformed, becoming her characters with the ease of a natural talent. As soon as the young teenager stepped off the stage and into the real world again, her confidence diminished. Rather than bowing to discouragement or insecurity, though, she determined to change herself for the better. "I spent every moment thinking, reading, trying to make myself fit to associate with clever people."[24] Her determination, her desire for self-improvement, love of books, and thirst for education and knowledge were lifelong traits fostered during her youth as a touring performer.[25]

Despite her personal shyness, Babe intuitively grasped the importance of managing her professional image. Realizing that her youthful sobriquet was out of keeping with the more sophisticated roles into which she was transitioning, she decided to select a more appropriate stage name for herself. During a sojourn back in Oregon at the age of fourteen, she explained,

> I told Papa that I didn't want to be called Babe anymore, that I wanted a more dignified name. So one of the traveling men that came to Silverton wrote out my name in all different languages — French and Spanish, and, you know, many others. And he wrote it out Margarita — M-A-R-G-A-R-I-T-A — and I chose that. And that is the Spanish and Mexican way of spelling Margaret.[26]

This teenaged whim proved to have lasting effects. Margaret Fischer would always remain Babe to her family and closest friends, but to her public — and, eventually, on all legal documents — she was known as Margarita for the remainder of her life.

The newly named Margarita adjusted to her growing fame quickly over the next few years in now-forgotten melodramas and drawing room comedies with titles like *Nugget Nell*, *The Great Blue-grass Derby*, *The Fatal Scar* (during a production of which, coincidentally, she once cut her hand quite badly), *Mother and Son*, and *A Bachelor's Romance*. She also appeared

Babe, already a proficient actress, hints at her dancing talents in this photograph, probably taken in 1899. She would soon take the professional name of Margarita and become the major draw of her father's theatrical touring company. Photograph by W.L. Jones (courtesy the Margarita Fischer Papers, Special Collections and University Archives, Wichita State University Libraries).

in perennial favorites such as *Uncle Tom's Cabin* (playing the part of Eliza) — a story and role that proved important in her later film career — and *East Lynne* (as Lady Isabel), a popular play adapted from a nineteenth-century novel of the same name by Mrs. Henry Wood.[27] This role in particular was a dramatic victory for the teenaged actress; the play's plot concerns the domestic and romantic struggles of the inhabitants of an English manor house. Lady Isabel is a melodramatic, mature character for a teenager to play; she is first tormented by an interfering sister-in-law, then convinced by a rogue (with whom she later elopes) of her husband's infidelity. She eventually learns of the rogue's deception, returns home in disguise, witnesses the death of her child, and then dies in the presence of her husband and his new wife.[28]

Margarita relished these roles, though as her career as a leading lady began, she found that her natural histrionic instincts were not infallible. One early reviewer commented on her obvious talent, but noted, "She sometimes overestimates the sentimental and plays it up too strongly. Emotion is all right and justly appreciated in its place, but plain, natural acting sometimes makes the greatest impression. Miss Fischer has the power to do this without dragging through her part."[29] Margarita carefully read and saved such evaluations of her performances, and she took them to heart. Over time, she honed her talent and learned to express herself effectively but with a greater, more natural restraint. She and the other company players also gained versatility during these years. Although solid dramatic acting constituted the backbone of their performances, the touring life also required great flexibility, sometimes literally, from the company players. Margarita later recalled the frantic pace of the stock company, in which "fiendish" quick changes of scene forced her to "[drift] from dancing into acrobatic performances, and I had to give some of them between the acts of *East Lynne*. Imagine working as Lady Isabelle [sic] and then turning somersaults between the acts!"[30]

Offering their blend of vaudeville and "legitimate" drama, the company appeared in small towns, cities, and even mining camps in much of the western United States, including Oregon, Idaho, and California. Sometimes they moved on after only a few days, but at other times the pace slowed, and the players remained in one town for several weeks and performed the same play for multiple audiences. In 1902, for example, the players spent over a month in Idaho, performing their old stalwart, *East Lynne,* in Boise's Sonna Opera House. While there, they organized a "benefit" for John Fischer (possibly due to an illness or debt) consisting of comic skits, a "splendid dramatic recitation," and numerous songs, including some sung by the ever-versatile Margarita.[31] Margarita also made friends with a local couple, William E. Borah and his wife. Borah was a striking, strong-minded man who would be elected to the United States Senate in 1906, but it was his youthful wife Mary, sixteen years older than Margarita, who made a real impression on the teenaged actress. More than sixty years later, she still remembered fondly the kindness of the older woman, as well as Mrs. Borah's "beautiful home — having tea with you — and ... your taking me for delightful rides in your lovely rubber tired carriage."[32] As Mrs. Borah recalled in return, there was also a young man present who was "very much interested in you" — which may have made the day yet more pleasant and memorable for the sixteen-year-old.[33] Margarita appreciated the chance to spend time in these congenial everyday activities, which were not encountered very often in the touring life. Mary Borah's warmth also gave Margarita a taste of the community and friendships she and her family missed by living constantly on the road.

In addition to sacrificing social relationships outside of the touring company, the Fischer players sometimes made sacrifices of their health. The endless activity wore on their constitutions at times, but the show always had to go on, despite illness. One local review noticed approvingly that "the health of Miss Fischer is much improved over what it was on [the company's] last trip" through the town.[34] Becoming accustomed to the grueling schedule of the touring performer, Margarita developed tremendous physical stamina and strength of will at a young age. When she came down with a severe case of tonsillitis, she had her tonsils taken out between performances with no anesthetic, then returned to the stage.[35]

Not surprisingly, in later years Margarita remembered her family's touring era as a time of frequent privation. Her father served as manager, salesman, promoter, and script scout, as well as performer, and solvency often hung by a thread. "It was a hard game," she recalled later, "for many times we didn't know where our next meal would come from. Then would come several good nights and we would eat again."[36] She may have romanticized some stories about the family's slow rise to financial security; there is a touch of Dickens in Margarita's anecdote about "staring in bakery windows, sniffing at hot roll scents wafted up from the basement ovens, and wishing I could afford to buy enough for a satisfying meal."[37] She admitted that "The company didn't have it as hard as we did, for father always looked after them first. We were the shoemaker's children who went without shoes.... But times changed. We were just getting on well when father died."[38]

In truth, renown, if not wealth, came early to the personable young actress. Talented, as well as blessed with striking looks, Margarita had a unique ability to connect with her audience even as a teenager, and she gained such attention within her father's joint touring company that it was renamed "The Margarita Fischer Company" before she was fifteen years old. As she gained command of her craft, reviewers repeatedly singled out her performances for praise, calling her "a talented emotional actress," and "an actress of far more than ordinary ability," one who could deliver "a portrayal that was finished, intense, natural and extremely forceful."[39] She demonstrated talents for music, comedy, farce, and romance, but she seems to have particularly enjoyed strong melodramatic roles, such as that of *East Lynne*'s Lady Isabel or the title character in *Leah, the Forsaken*. Of her portrayal of the Jewish woman who is maligned and abandoned by a faithless lover, one reviewer noted, "Miss Fischer's work was something long to be remembered. She gave to the character of Leah, a living, breathing, praying and cursing personality." (Her male lead didn't come in for the same share of praise; the reviewer huffed that "had she been supported by a capable 'Rudolph' the play would have been as brilliant as any Cleopatra drama ever put on the local stage.")[40] Such spirited roles offered Margarita a freedom onstage that, as an unmarried, underage woman, she would never have been allowed offstage.

In 1904, at the age of eighteen, Margarita Fischer was in a still unusual but increasingly common role: that of a working woman. By 1900, one-fifth of all women worked outside the home, often encountering institutionalized sexism in the form of low wages and overt discrimination. The mores of the late Victorian era still defined a middle-class woman's most fulfilling and natural role as that of a wife and mother, and many working women simply bided their time until they could move from their father's house to a husband's. At the same time, economic demands changed the way many men worked, pulling them out of the home for longer periods of time and placing the burden of child-rearing almost completely on women. The "cult of domesticity" arose as a result of this arrangement; women in such a situation were financially dependent on their male providers, and, out of necessity, they focused on and idealized their families and children, the only spheres that remained nominally under their influence.[41]

Yet the same moral expectations that kept some women trapped within the supposed purity of the family circle offered a new freedom to the bold, ambitious, and unconventional. Seeking training for edifying professions, such as teaching and doctoring, women entered colleges and medical schools in ever-increasing numbers before the turn of the twentieth century.[42] Growing numbers of educated and professional women made great strides in occupation during the final decade of the nineteenth century, participating in 360 of the 369 types of employment recorded in the 1890 census.[43] With the expansion of roles for women came a rejection of some of the values of the cult of domesticity; the birth rate fell by half over the course of the 1800s, and the divorce rate more than tripled between 1860 and 1900, both signs of increasing female autonomy.[44] Inevitably, some of these women, especially those seeking economic advancement, had moved onto the stage, enticed by the parity of pay and the artistic freedom enjoyed by the most talented actors and actresses.[45]

Margarita Fischer, both living and working within the family circle, benefited from the freedom of the theater as an avenue for portraying spirited, "cursing" personalities. She still relied on her father's shrewd marketing to help her bridge the gap between traditional and progressive feminine roles. The Margarita Fischer Company, under John Fischer's continued management, advertised its leading lady's face as well as her name, using her beauty to draw attention, and her youthful, innocent appearance to impart respectability, to the troupe's productions. The troupe's official advertising pamphlets nicknamed her "The Nonpareil" (French for "incomparable" or "unequaled") and listed her "combination of rare gifts of Talent, Temperament and appearance guided by a soul which strives for the attainment of artistic ideals." Aware of the impact that a little glamour could have in the small towns of the Pacific Northwest, the pamphlet also carefully explained that in "Miss Fischer's Wardrobe will be found creations of beauty and elegance and each part will be correctly dressed."[46] Now a very youthful adult, Margarita Fischer (advertised at this point as "the Youngest Leading Lady on the American Stage"— whether or not this was actually the case was immaterial) had the good fortune to exactly suit the dark-haired, shapely standards of beauty of the time, especially with the help of her "symmetricals." Her fortunate appearance perhaps explains why she, rather than the older but "funny, chubby" Dorothy, a pleasantly pretty but not striking young woman, was nurtured into the company's leading lady.[47] The irreverent second daughter did not always take seriously the undeniable advantage of her good looks, once presenting her elder sister with a wistful, glamorous portrait inscribed, "Your ugly young sister, Babe."[48]

Indeed, the family associations of the young actress's career afforded her a unique respectability, but they also presented her with the unusual challenge of professional sibling rivalry. The younger sister had overshadowed the elder since being fortuitously cast in *A Celebrated Case*, and her success had eventually inspired the entire family's move to the stage. Dorothy played character and supporting parts to Margarita's leading roles throughout the seven years the family toured the nation together, which created no end of contention between the teenaged sisters. Born only twenty months apart, "we were too near an age to give way to each other," Margarita remembered later. "I liked to impress my 'leads' upon my sister, which was very ungenerous of me.... We used to say quite rude things to each other and eventually mother had to come and sit in the dressing-room with us to make us behave ourselves." The rivalry went on until one performance of *Jerry the Tramp* when Margarita's character had a "pathetic" scene and was supposed to cry on Dorothy's shoulder. "We would not touch each other," she remembered wryly, "[until] father took us in hand and gave us a good lecture."[49] The sparring sisters might have been typecast in their performances of *The Great Blue-grass Derby*, in which a reviewer remarked that Dorothy played "to the slightest detail" the part of the "hateful enemy" of Margarita's plucky character.[50]

Dorothy had been married three months before this performance, in September 1905, to the Fischer company's ambitious young business agent (and sometime minor company player) Charles C. Pyle.[51] Even as the sisters entered adulthood, though, they remained competitive. In fact, Dorothy may well have married Pyle to start a family of her own and be recognized in her own right. If so, this backfired terribly, as Dorothy herself later admitted that the Machiavellian Pyle had married her mainly to gain reflected glory and financial advantage from having a famous sister-in-law.[52] Still, despite the competition of their upbringing, the sisters formed a deep bond in their unusual childhood that persisted through adulthood, when they dropped the rivalries of their younger days to become devoted friends and periodically share a household. Years later, when Margarita eventually transitioned into film, Dorothy's daughter Kathie became a child star under her aunt's tutelage.

The sisters' competitive streak aside, the Fischer company members seemed to enjoy working with their leading lady. On February 12, 1906, for her "nineteenth" birthday (actually her twentieth, but Margarita's youth was a key part of her image), they presented her with an engraved watch, accompanied by a note signed by company members as a "token of respect and appreciation."[53] At the top of the list were the signatures of Margarita's parents and sister, and of Charles Pyle, who had drafted the gracious letter to his famous new sister-in-law. At this time, the touring company had been performing at the Girton Theatre in Eureka, California, for a generous six weeks and were booked for another three, and they took advantage of their relative stability to celebrate

This wistful portrait of the teenaged Margarita was circulated on her theatrical company's promotional materials around 1903. Although her good looks were a great boon to the company, Margarita inscribed this portrait to Dottie from "Your ugly young sister, Babe." Photograph by Baker studio (courtesy the Margarita Fischer Papers, Special Collections and University Archives, Wichita State University Libraries).

their leading lady's birthday in grand style. The company gave a special birthday performance of the play *Sex Against Sex* to a packed house of invitation holders, then enjoyed a whimsical private dinner party at the nearby Hotel Grand, where they feasted on dishes such as "Consomme a la Margarita," "Patties of Chicken Liver, Manager Style," "Asparagus Tips, Mama Fischer's way," and "Banana Fritters a la Dot" [*sic*].[54] John Fischer "had risen from his sick bed" to be present at the event, noted one article, an occasion that warranted much toasting of his health.[55]

Such celebrations were undoubtedly a welcome respite from the difficult life of traveling players, and this one must have seemed all too brief, for change, loss, and family friction soon marred the company's sojourn in California. Shortly after Margarita's "nineteenth" birthday party, Charles Pyle gave up his position with the Fischer company, which he had held at least since July 1904. He immediately embarked upon a new career as a theatrical manager in partnership with F.W. Parker, a journalist and the manager of the Hotel Grand's banquet facilities. The departure was amicable, as the pair established the "Theatre Margarita" in Eureka in honor of Pyle's elegant sister-in-law, and invited the Fischer company to continue their stay in that town by inaugurating the theater's opening with a booking there in June 1906. Reflecting its managers' gift for publicity, the theater was touted as "one of the most modern and best-equipped little play-houses on the Pacific coast... [B]urlesque, comic opera, vaudeville — all kinds of shows — will be presented from time to time to furnish a pleasing variety for the theatre-going public."[56] John Fischer, planning ambitiously, bought the rights to a new play for the company, selecting one in which both of his daughters were to have a role (despite her marriage, Dorothy had not yet made any plans to leave the stage). For the first time, the Fischers were going to tour the entire nation, and John Fischer was looking forward to leading them all the way to the East coast. "He was going to start from Eureka and do one-night stands to New York City," where he would introduce Margarita to David Belasco, the star-making theatrical producer, she remembered.

Dorothy Fischer Pyle, probably around the time of her marriage in 1905. Photograph by Moore (courtesy the Margarita Fischer Papers, Special Collections and University Archives, Wichita State University Libraries).

"He thought I was the world's wonder. It's wonderful to have parents that think of you that way."[57]

Sadly, John Fischer died in the spring of 1906, probably shortly before Parker and Pyle's invitation, and the planned cross-country tour never came to be. Although all of the players must have grieved for their beloved manager, the loss was particularly wrenching for his widow and daughters, who missed his vision and cheer within the family circle as well as on the stage. Margarita had lost the support of her father's unconditional love and belief in her talent just as she was on the brink of a career-making journey that had the potential to ensure her fame and the financial security of the family. Without his guidance, she did not know what to do next. She, perhaps even more than her mother or sister, reeled from John Fischer's death.

The bewildered Fischer players coasted for a time on the bookings their late manager had arranged. They first fulfilled their obligation to Parker and Pyle, though the joyous inauguration of the theater had now turned melancholy. When they assembled for their initial performance of *Under Two Flags* at the Theatre Margarita on June 14, 1906, the players must have been struck hard by the fact that they were playing without the familiar label of their company name and were under the control of a director other than John Fischer. The second play the company members put on at the theater, *Two Orphans*, cast the Fischer sisters in the title roles — a terrible bit of irony.[58]

Only one day after this play closed, the remains of the Margarita Fischer Company moved on to a different theater to perform a new show, *La Belle Marie*, without Dorothy or her husband.[59] This may have been a one-time performance, for the distressed players also continued performing at the Theatre Margarita for another two weeks. When the young leading lady, anxious for some stability, attempted to negotiate a longer engagement for her company, she evidently presumed too much on Pyle's family ties, and in return received a terse letter from Parker and Pyle informing her that "we hereby deny that there was an agreement for an extension of that time." The letter closed with the statement, "We hereby notify you that on the evening of July 4th, 1906, your engagement with us will cease and all relations between us will terminate."[60] Charles Pyle tactfully had his partner sign the notice, but its brusque tone informed his sister-in-law that her players would have to find a way to earn their own living, despite their bereavement. Margarita, deeply affected by this rejection, preserved this letter carefully with her other stage memorabilia, perhaps as a sign of the constant struggle of the life she had chosen.

2

Where Paths Meet

A life on the stage "meant everything" to John Fischer, and he had pulled his family along for the ride.[1] When he died, Margarita was devastated. Headlining for her family since her early teens, and living on the road for much of her life, her creative, ambitious, supportive father had represented one of the few stable elements in a demanding and constantly shifting world. She had depended on his faith in her as an actress as well as a daughter, trusting that he would find opportunities to guide her career for the good of the family. His loss was therefore a professional threat as well as a personal sorrow — if, indeed, the two can be separated. Over the course of her teens, Margarita had become the family breadwinner, and her family's well-being was dependent on the success of her career. John Fischer had organized and guided this career, though, and without his leadership her touring company dispersed after the final engagement at the Theatre Margarita. "We were all lost for a time," she later recalled. "Father had always done everything in the world for us, and I dreaded going to managers, and, indeed, I dreaded business of any kind."[2]

Charles Pyle's new managerial career offered Dorothy a permanent home, so she chose to retire from the stage following her father's death. The younger Fischer sister had no such domestic situation, and, despite her "dread," chose to continue acting. She may have been unfamiliar with business, but this she did know, though barely twenty years old: her survival, and that of her mother, depended on her talent, her face, and her ability to appeal to audiences. The young actress took to heart her family responsibilities and determined to promote these qualities as advantageously as possible. This determination, and the need from which it sprang, forever after shaped her approach to her career.

The Fischer women were helped temporarily by a benefit endorsed by the Woodmen of the World, a fraternal order to which John Fischer had belonged that had a tradition of helping the relatives of deceased members.[3] The papers Margarita saved from this time are regrettably sparse, but she took care to preserve a fan letter from a thirteen-year-old "little girl who loves you," received during the months of struggle while she sought the security of an individual acting contract with a theatrical company.[4] Such an affectionate note, which declared boldly that "we enjoy your playing better than that of any other actresses," must have been a boost to the grieving, financially worried young woman. Perhaps another small consolation during this unstable time to the increasingly image-conscious Margarita, responsible (like all actresses) for providing her own costumes, was the fact that the *San Francisco Dramatic Review* described her as "one of the best dressers among our leading women."[5]

Margarita Fischer's other papers dating from 1907 and 1908 show her struggle to find work during the months after her father's death, but the young woman they reveal is no stereotypical shrinking violet. As she began to manage her own career, her financial need helped her shed the youthful shyness that had dogged her teenage years, replacing her "dread" of business with a tough-minded courtesy. Her years as the nominal leader of a touring company must have provided her with plentiful examples of contract negotiations, and she now embarked on her own negotiations for the first time. It took her a while to learn the dance of offer and counter-offer, and at first her ambition (or perhaps desperation) in these matters sometime outstripped what the market would bear. Besides her unsuccessful effort to negotiate more time at the Theatre Margarita in 1906, she lost an engagement in April 1907 because she was committed elsewhere and was unable to open the play on the chosen date, though she found sporadic work in San Francisco later in the year.[6] When the opportunity arose, she jumped at a chance for greater stability. By late October 1907, she had formed a connection with Walter Sanford, a San Francisco theatrical manager interested in hiring Margarita to play roles "of the sweet sympathetic class." Sweetening the offer, he assured her that "you would be under little expense for dressing them"—an important consideration to a cash-poor actress just striking out on her own.[7] Despite his interest in hiring the young player, though, Sanford firmly refused her bold request for a salary of sixty-five dollars a week.

In making this salary demand, Margarita may have been driven in part by a desire for professional advancement, but she was also increasingly motivated by familial need. The three Fischer women, mother and both daughters, were extremely close-knit after John Fischer's death, and all were aware that by now the Pyles' marriage was in serious trouble. Begun on questionable terms, Dorothy and Charles's two-year-old marriage had quickly soured due to a combination of financial struggles and personality clashes. Dorothy's husband could be volatile within professional circles, including the management of the Theatre Margarita, which had begun so promisingly. Pyle often conflicted with actors booked by the theater, and he was once arrested for making repeated death threats against one who had also threatened to tar and feather him (the altercations were euphemistically attributed to "dissentions existing between actors and management").[8]

Within the home, Pyle proved no more stable or dependable than he was at work. The process of Margarita's salary negotiation with Sanford was hindered by the actress's preoccupation with her sister's "illness," as the theatrical manager tactfully called it. The petite Dorothy—at less than five feet tall, she was even smaller than her diminutive younger sister—had given birth to her first and only child, her daughter Kathrine (nicknamed Kathie by the family), just two months before, on August 21, 1907. Dorothy's constitution had been permanently weakened by the difficult labor.[9] Possibly due to his continued involvement in business ventures of varying success, Pyle was financially unstable, and the Pyles' tenuous living situation was aggravated by the expense of Dorothy's extended recovery after Kathie's birth. "It wasn't a match made in heaven, and he pretty much deserted her after my mother was born," recalled Pyle's granddaughter, Margarita Kotselis. "[He] left her in the hospital with my mother. He didn't pay the hospital bill, so my aunt [Margarita Fischer] had to take care of it." Pyle also tended to womanize, further undermining the couple's relationship.[10]

These unpleasant events exacerbated the family tension that had been present since the Pyles' marriage, and tension finally flared into outright hostility when the widowed Kate Fischer, protective of her namesake baby granddaughter, had her son-in-law twice arrested for failing to support Dorothy and Kathie. Charles Pyle was able to convince the judge to release him both times, defending himself by mentioning the extenuating circumstance of Dorothy's refusal to let him live with her, a euphemism for the end of the couple's sexual relationship (no doubt motivated by the severe toll that childbirth had taken on Dorothy's health).[11] He may also have used this development as the justification for his infidelity. The two court encounters proved the beginning of an extended falling-out between husband and wife, during which Margarita took on the role of provider for her mother, sister, and niece—a role she kept thereafter. Charles and Dorothy Pyle finally divorced in 1910.[12] The couple never regained friendly terms with one another, though Kathie—the only child Pyle ever had—sporadically reconnected with her father in her adulthood.[13]

In the midst of these family struggles, Margarita and Walter Sanford finally did work out a satisfactory contract, and Margarita accepted a ten-month employment period as a "leading actress" for Sanford's San Francisco company at a salary of fifty dollars per week. She was firm about settling down with her family, at least temporarily, as all clauses in the contract dealing with travel were struck out. Sanford did retain some control over the actress's performance schedule, however; the contract contained the stipulation that she not appear at any theater other than his "Empress" venue in Vancouver for three months after the San Francisco contract ended on September 11, 1908.[14] Margarita raised no objection to these terms; it was surely just a relief to have a guaranteed regular income for the first time in more than a year.

Although she no longer had to deal with the rigors of constant touring, Margarita learned at once that her new employer maintained as furious a performance pace as her family's stock company ever had. She was put to work at once, appearing in a production of *Behind the Mask* with the Sanford players within a week of her contract's beginning on November 11, 1907.[15] The content of this play, performed at San Francisco's Globe Theatre, is not known; there were several different productions of that title in the early twentieth century. The cast, however, would prove quite notable: Margarita played alongside a twenty-one-year-old Al Jolson, a vaudeville performer who eventually developed a singing career of virtually matchless popularity. Known as "The World's Greatest Entertainer," Jolson would achieve cinematic immortality for his starring role in the first feature film to use synchronized sound, the groundbreaking 1927 movie *The Jazz Singer*.

Another fellow performer more relevant to young Margarita's personal life was Harry Pollard, a quietly determined, charming, and handsome Kansas-born actor seven years her senior. Pollard (not to be confused with silent film comedian Harry "Snub" Pollard) came from even less of a theatrical background than did Margarita herself: he was descended from several generations of Illinois and Kansas farmers.[16] Within a few years of Harry's birth, the Pollards had moved to California and continued to make their living from the land by maintaining an orchard near Fresno, but young Harry soon began to pursue a more dramatic lifestyle than that of his family. Precocious and well-spoken, he won a medal at the age of eleven for an essay and speech in favor of Prohibition—which, as a supposedly "dry" adult with alcoholic tendencies in the 1920s, he ruefully called "a great farce." Encouraged by his father to become a lawyer, he began at age thirteen to travel around Fresno County delivering Populist speeches written by his father, soon becoming known as "the silver-tongued boy orator." Never enthusiastic about entering the legal profession, after his father's death the younger Pollard felt released from these expectations. After his graduation from high school, Harry Pollard traveled to nearby San Francisco to pursue his own dream of an acting career.[17]

He quickly found work at San Francisco's Alcazar Theatre, beginning in non-speaking roles (including, as he remembered, "chief spear-carrier" in the play *Bonnie Prince Charlie*) for three dollars and fifty cents per week, but he was "ambition and energy personified," as he later described himself, and memorized other players' speaking roles in order to work his way up to understudy.[18] The young hopeful finally got his break during a performance of *The School for Scandal* when the actor in a minor speaking role failed to show up. The well-prepared Pollard impressed manager Charles Bryant by "reel[ing] off the part from memory," winning the right to the role thereafter.[19] He became a sort of protégé of the manager, who appreciated the would-be actor's work ethic and intelligence. Bryant, Pollard later explained, "[turned] me loose in his marvelous library of stage books and ordered me to study everything pertaining to the stage. I spent most of my time in Bryant's library and I all but lived on books, for, with only $3.50 a week to live on, I all but starved."[20] This time of study nurtured in the youth a deep and abiding appreciation for stage acting which no other profession would ever supplant.

He also developed extremely high standards for his own work, and he had little patience with fame for its own sake, valuing it only as a means to greater financial security or artistic freedom. Bryant eventually bumped the young Pollard into the role of "juvenile" for a touring company at the comparatively generous salary of $12.75 a week, which was as hard-earned as was Margarita Fischer's livelihood as a touring performer. After a long hazing of frequent travel and empty pockets, he moved up through the ranks of various touring companies for the next few years.[21] He married briefly and unhappily to a fellow stage player, quickly divorcing before returning to act in San Francisco in the spring of 1906. Coming back to this friendly city, he must have thought things were finally looking up for his career, but his return fell only one week before the cataclysmic 1906 earthquake.[22]

The great San Francisco earthquake began on April 18, 1906, touching off a series of fires that dramatically increased both the loss of life and the property damage inflicted by the quake. By the time the fires were brought under control three days later, more than three thousand people had lost their lives, and $500 million worth of property (in 1906 dollars) had been destroyed. The Alcazar Theatre, where Pollard had planned to act, was among the buildings destroyed.[23] Although he was safe, his promising livelihood was destroyed along with the theater, and he must have been discouraged, despite all his "ambition and energy." This cataclysmically determined career change turned out to be a professional and personal boon, though. The young actor at first made ends meet by working as a laborer in the quake's aftermath, but he still wished to work on the stage and jumped at an opportunity offered by Charles Pyle for an engagement at the Theatre Margarita in Eureka in mid-1906. Pollard later recalled that he first met "the beautiful girl" Margarita Fischer at this time. Pyle thus served as "indirectly the unwitting agent of Cupid" for the couple, as a later article explained, by permitting the initial introduction of his young sister-in-law to Harry Pollard just before the Fischer company was brusquely dismissed.[24] This meeting must have been very brief, and Margarita almost certainly

The versatile young stage player in a newsboy-style outfit, probably around 1907. On the stage, young women like Margarita enjoyed freedoms unknown in everyday life — including the freedom to wear pants (courtesy the Margarita Fischer Papers, Special Collections and University Archives, Wichita State University Libraries).

Dapper "legitimate" actor Harry Pollard, probably around the time he and Margarita Fischer first met in 1906 (courtesy the Harry Pollard Papers, Special Collections and University Archives, Wichita State University Libraries).

had no contact with Pollard in the year and a half that passed before they were reacquainted in San Francisco in late 1907. If she remembered him at all, though, the struggling young woman was surely glad to see that her leading man in the Sanford Company had a familiar face.

Once in the same company, the pair strengthened their connection. "That's where the romance started," Margarita remembered.[25] The relatively prosaic story of their meeting was much sentimentalized in film magazines of the next decades. One of the more breathless (and inaccurate) accounts of the couple's first meeting contorts chronology and geography to tell the story of a "baby girl" whose father died when she was 13 — seven years distant from the truth — and who then "came to New York with her mother, wide eyed and afraid" and met her future husband in a theatrical company, where he looked out for her and her mother until "engagements separated them"; but they eventually met again, "practically starved," in Chicago and embarked upon the rest of their careers together.[26] The fear and hunger were undoubtedly present to some degree, but, in truth, the beginning of the romantic relationship between Margarita Fischer and Harry Pollard was quiet and subtle. The reserved pair took great care to hide its development from the theatergoing public, and possibly also from their fellow players.

Despite her new romance and the supposed security of her employment with Sanford, Margarita continued to seek a more lucrative position due to the financial pressure of supporting her mother, her sister, and her rapidly growing baby niece. Impressed by Margarita's reputation as a leading lady, the manager of the Los Angeles Grand Opera House solicited her for "leading business in melodramatic stock" in May 1908. Her response was rejected, though, as "the salary you state is more than we care to pay."[27] Hoping for expanded opportunities nonetheless, the cash-strapped actress chose not to renew her contract with Sanford when it expired four months later, and she moved immediately into her contractually required three months of exclusive work for the Empress Theatre in Vancouver.

Again benefiting from her good looks, she appeared on the front page of the theater's bulletin as "a Popular Member of the D. S. Lawrence Players" within two and a half weeks of the end of her contract with Sanford.[28] "Margaret [sic] Fischer is so very decorative that it is always a pleasure to see her on the boards," applauded one reviewer, appreciating the way she "wears beautiful clothes very beautifully and queens it all over the stage."[29] Despite this cheerful publicity, she evidently soon regretted her decision to leave the Sanford company, perhaps because she missed Harry Pollard, or possibly because financial insecurity was drawing near. She signed a second contract with Sanford's troupe in Vancouver on October 12, 1908, at a slightly improved salary of fifty-five dollars per week.[30] This weekly salary gave her an annual income of almost three thousand dollars, which was comparable to that of a professor of the time. The income would have been quite comfortable for one, but as the young actress continued to support three other family members financially (and possibly at times her sister's nominal husband as well), funds were extremely tight.

Margarita continued to play with various "legitimate" theater and vaudeville companies, managing her own career with growing success in these itinerant years after her father's death. She had always held a high profile within her touring company, but the negative aspects of renown were still unfamiliar to her in August 1909, when the *Oregon Daily Journal* published a purported interview with the hometown girl making a name for herself in the theatrical world. Margarita clearly felt misrepresented by the article, which recounts the actress's single-minded pursuit of stardom; various points in the preserved account bear her good-natured handwritten comments of "Ha! Ha! Ha!" and "I never said it." "I never said one word of this," she dashed across the top of the article. "At first I was boiling mad — then I laughed."[31] To an actress still accustomed to the friendly publicity of her father's management and wide-eyed small-town reporters, a manufactured article portraying her as grasping was something of a shock. The reporter may have meant to do her a favor by publicizing her name — and, after all, the article included a large, attractive photograph of its subject — but Margarita resented the ease with which others could shape her image. Interestingly, one of the fabricated comments that bothered her most was that she held the ambition to become a theatrical star by having a great part written for her: "I think I might set all Broadway agog with such a part." Margarita's ambition came from her family's needs, not for the sake of her own stardom, and this article may have seemed improper to her in the forward, self-serving quotes attributed to its subject. The piece might have fostered her determination to communicate a sympathetic self to her public. When the young actress did talk to the press in the future, it was nearly always with candor and graciousness, as well as the same light humor she indicated in her response to the "Ambitious" article.

In November 1909, soon after this encounter with the perfidy of the press, Margarita accepted a contract with T. Daniel Frawley's Canadian theatrical company at her previous Sanford salary of fifty-five dollars per week.[32] Harry Pollard, her fellow actor in the Sanford troupe, was also a member of this company, almost certainly not coincidentally. The Frawley actors remained in Winnipeg through January 1910, performing in the "Romantic Comedy Drama" *If I Were King*, in which Margarita Fischer, for the first time since her touring company took her name a decade previously, did not receive special billing.[33] This slight could have motivated her move soon afterwards to the Grace George company in Chicago, with which she played for a season at the city's Grand Opera House. Grace George's company was a great leap forward for the career-minded young actress, headed as it was by the illustrious performer whose Broadway career eventually spanned more than half a century. Grace George was one of the most famous and respected actresses of her day, and "when I was asked to play with Grace George, I thought my cup would run over, especially as I got a good salary," Margarita explained. The elder actress was as generous as her name would indicate, for "she told me after the first night, 'You've made a *personal* hit — I am very pleased with your acting.'"[34]

Margarita then joined Joseph Medill Patterson's company in spring 1910, perhaps due to the end of the Grand Opera House season. Once again she performed in a leading role, this time in the dramatic play *By Products* at the Windy City's Studebaker Theatre. Unfortunately, the play was "a complete failure," a later article stated, and the players soon found themselves jobless and without theatrical prospects in a strange city. Completely out of funds, Margarita borrowed ten cents for a taxi fare to check out the other prospects for actors in Chicago. "That dime was the turning point in my career, for it carried me out to the Selig studio, where I secured my first position before the camera. Just think of it! Falling so low as going into the movies!"[35] Margarita signed on with William Selig, the eponymous head of the Chicago-based studio, to enter films for the first time.[36] His generous offer of eighty dollars a week decreased the sting of the failure of *By Products*, and Margarita jumped at the chance for greater financial security for herself and her family. "When they wanted to offer me a continued engagement with Miss George ... I felt like a Croesus as I waved them away with my eighty dollar contract."[37]

2. Where Paths Meet

It was inevitable that such an accomplished performer should be noticed by the burgeoning film industry. In 1910, at the age of twenty-four, Margarita Fischer was an experienced professional who had been acting for two-thirds of her life. She had supported her family, she had gained the respect of her peers, she had managed her own career, and she had negotiated her own finances. She was an uncommon woman who had conquered the theatrical world while still adhering to society's ideals of femininity. She was now ready to bring to a new type of acting career the beauty, talent, and determination that had always served her so well.

3

The Land of Promise

In early 1910, under the aegis of the Selig Polyscope Company, Margarita Fischer entered the world of the movies for the first time. The burgeoning film industry of the early twentieth century sought out many stars of theater and vaudeville to make moving pictures, and the beautiful, talented, hard-working Margarita would have been particularly attractive to studios eager to create a successful product. The United States had made its first forays into true film only fifteen years before Margarita Fischer initially appeared on celluloid, but already studios had diversified, grown competitive, and had begun to create the star system.

The earliest true films had emerged in France in 1895 when the Lumière brothers first combined a camera with a projector, allowing them to display moving pictures on a screen rather than within a single-person viewing device.[1] Thomas Edison, the inventor of one such earlier device, the Kinetoscope, brought the French brothers' technology to an American public, projecting the first films in this country in 1896.[2] Early films were often simply captured from everyday life — scenes such as sneezes, trains entering a station, or the action on a street — and were seldom longer than a minute or two. They were instantly popular, though, and fascinated audiences around the world demanded a constant supply of new and increasingly sophisticated material. Filmmakers began to experiment with different ways of presenting material and telling a story; newsreels, comedies, and special-effects films were all born within the first few years of cinematic history.

Litigiousness plagued the development of early American films, however, and competition and patent disputes led beleaguered startup film companies to consolidate into larger ones. Thomas Edison at first regularly initiated litigation against other filmmakers, suing for copyright violations of "his" film projection technology, but he soon determined that greater financial success would come from working in tandem with other companies. By 1908, the Motion Picture Patents Company, also known as "the Trust," had been set up by ten early filmmakers (two foreign and eight domestic companies, including Edison's studio and Margarita's first employer, the Selig Polyscope Company) to regulate film production. The Trust negotiated an exclusive contract with Eastman Kodak for film stock and refused to exhibit the films of member studios in theaters that also showed the films of studios outside the Trust. This resulted in a monopoly that drove almost all competitors out of business and effectively limited the legal production of film to less than a dozen major studios for several years. On a positive note, however, the Trust also placed the industry on a firm financial base and offered maverick members like director D. W. Griffith the funding to begin experimenting with storytelling techniques and developing the idea of film as art.[3]

When Margarita first appeared on film for the Selig Polyscope Company in mid–1910, the Trust was at the height of its strength, and the Chicago-based Selig studio was prospering. William Selig, a former minstrel show operator, founded his studio in 1896. Edison had sued him for patent infringement from 1905 to 1907, but after Selig was brought into the fold of the Trust, his studio flourished. Selig was able to open a second production facility in California in 1909, thus making his namesake studio the first to make a film entirely in California. Possessing both foresight and a wariness of further litigation, Selig made connections with well-known authors and genre writers to provide his filmmakers with a constant supply of creative — and not previously copyrighted, and therefore legally usable — material. He built up a company of stock players at the same time, most of whom, like Margarita Fischer, had formerly acted on the stage. In early 1910, when the film entrepreneur hired Margarita, the Selig studio was thriving so well that both its Chicago and California studios were undergoing a significant expansion of production and studio space.[4]

By the time Selig recruited Margarita for his stable of actors, the movies had gained enormous public appeal and played to huge numbers of Americans each day. A 1909 article noted that Selig productions "are witnessed by some 300,000 people daily in Chicago, and by as many more in country towns."[5] Films were democratic, initially appealing to immigrants and the working classes; at a time when the average ticket to a theatrical production cost two to six dollars, a movie ticket cost no more than seventy-five cents.[6] By the early 1910s, middle-class audiences were also drawn in, especially when films were combined with live vaudeville performances.[7] Middle- and upper-class patrons of movies initially tended either to be fans of the theater looking for more realistic sets and effects, or people who had rejected the perceived immorality of the legitimate theater but were eager to sample a new entertainment form.[8]

The same cross-class appeal that led to the burgeoning of the film industry also drew the vigilant eye of Progressive reformers. The United States was in the extended throes of social reform in the late nineteenth and early twentieth centuries. Grouped under the label of Progressivism, improvements came in response to the crushing human cost of industrialism, which tended to further marginalize the already poor. Progressive reforms were generally advocated by young, educated, optimistic middle-class whites who often lived apart from social problems but nevertheless attempted democratically to solve them — including such issues as public health difficulties, political corruption, crises in the education and prison system, and the unequal treatment of the sexes.[9] Progressive ideals pervaded American society, including its popular culture, and, beginning in the first decade of the twentieth century, filmmakers came into contact with censor boards that believed in the instructive power of the cinema and attempted to guide the content of film in accordance with the mainstream values of the white middle class.[10] In 1909, Progressive reformers collaborated with members of the film community to create the National Board of Censorship in New York City. Within only a few years, the board's power waned due to its inability to effectively regulate the distribution of controversial films; but by that time state boards had been set up across the country to judge movies according to their individual standards.[11]

The individual theater booker was concerned with little of this, though; the main attraction of "moving pictures" was their economy. Short films of one reel or less, rather than feature films, were the standard cinematic offering until the second half of the 1910s. A reel, or a thousand feet of film, was generally projected at sixteen frames per second during the silent era (as opposed to sound film, which is shown at twenty-four frames per second) and lasted about fourteen minutes at that speed. Movies could be mass-produced and shown repeatedly to multiple audiences per day; thus, theater owners could entertain fifteen times the number of people for one-fifth of the cost of booking live performances.[12] Film was also immediate; regardless of their native tongue, audiences were able to connect with the close-up emotions of a silent film actor as they never could with someone on stage. The concept of entertainment in general began to expand to include film as a full and vital component as stage actors increasingly looked to the screen for employment. Many stars of theater in 1910 and 1911 went on to make names for themselves in film, including such future cinematic luminaries as Douglas Fairbanks, Helen Hayes, George Arliss, and Billie Burke.[13]

The world of filmmaking in 1910 was, for Margarita Fischer and for other former stage actors, a familiar one, despite the complex technology involved. Film at the beginning of the 1910s was still dominated by melodramatic one-reel productions composed according to theatrical staging methods, and the material presented by studios at this time was instantly accessible by both former stage actors and audiences accustomed to live entertainment.[14] Indeed, film historian Richard Koszarski points out, "There were good reasons for melodrama to take hold so firmly in the pre–1914 cinema. As a dramatic style, it dominated the American stage at a time when Ibsen, Shaw, and even Pinero were considered too radical for the mass audience. Less sophisticated filmgoers could hardly be expected to patronize more subtle entertainments at their local nickelodeon."[15] Early cinema owed an enormous debt to the "legitimate" theater, therefore, and not only for its actors and story material. The new form of entertainment borrowed the storytelling methods of late nineteenth-century melodrama, cutting between scenes from different story lines and relying on wordless action to propel the plot.[16]

Actors, however, remained the greatest—and initially most elusive—commodity the stage had to offer to filmmakers. Pioneering film historian Terry Ramsaye, writing in 1926, recalled that "the motion picture had no respectability then [just after the turn of the century], and actors were scornful"—as, indeed, Margarita Fischer had been at "sinking" to performing in the movies. Those theatrical notables who took part in filmmaking at this time did so anonymously, hoping not to damage their professional reputations. According to one colorful early account, the Edison studio actually employed a sort of recruiter who searched the haunts of stage performers who were between jobs, knowing that these financially desperate, vulnerable people were most likely to accept work with a film studio.[17] As recalled by ground-breaking movie director D. W. Griffith's wife, actress Linda Arvidson, the experience for a stage actor having to work for "those terrible moving picture places" was "humiliating":

> We were always conscious of the fact that we were in this messy business because everything else had failed—because nobody had seemed to want us, and we just hadn't been able to hang on any longer.... Real actors and actresses ... would work a few days and disappear. They had found a job on the stage again. The better they were, the quicker they got out. A motion picture surely was something not to be taken seriously.[18]

Indeed, film and its players at this time suffered from many of the same prejudices that the "legitimate" theater and its own actors had dealt with only a few decades earlier.

A strong-featured young Canadian actress with the unlikely name of Florence Lawrence helped to change these attitudes by becoming one of the first film players to be publicized by her real name and inadvertently become the first movie star.[19] In the first years of the twentieth century, the public felt curiosity about, and devotion to, the anonymous actors they enjoyed onscreen, yet films were sold and marketed by studio or brand (for example, "the new Selig") rather than individual title or actor. Lawrence, known from 1908 only as "the Biograph Girl" after the studio for which she worked, was one of the American Mutoscope and Biograph studio's most consistently popular actors.[20] Through a dramatic publicity stunt worthy of a modern-day public relations team, Lawrence's popularity helped to overturn the tradition of anonymously acted films.

Carl Laemmle signed the actress away from Biograph to his Independent Moving Pictures Company (known as "the Imp" or "the IMP"), a small studio scraping along outside the folds of the Trust, in 1910. He then gained renown for both Lawrence and his own studio by planting an article in a St. Louis paper stating that she had died in a streetcar accident. After allowing a day for public grief, Laemmle denounced this "cowardly" and "silly" story and produced the living actress, now identified by name, to a cheering Missouri crowd.[21] The event was, says film historian Richard Dyer, "the first example of the deliberate manufacture of a star's image. Equally ... it is the first example of the producers of films responding to public demand, giving the public what it wanted."[22] This publicity stunt was also a major victory for an independent studio over the power of the Trust: Lawrence's popularity ensured that the IMP remained solvent, which helped to break the Trust's stranglehold over film production and eventually strengthened the position of all independent studios.[23]

The dramatic response to Florence Lawrence's "resurrection" showed industry leaders that the public wanted to identify, and to identify with, the figures onscreen, and studios scrambled to sign suddenly more tractable "known" actors and create stars of unknowns.[24] Film stardom was an entirely new type of fame: rather than idealizing the film actor, as they had with famous performers of the past (such as Sarah Bernhardt or even Harry Houdini), early audiences wanted to identify with and feel as if they knew the performers acting out scenes from daily life on a flickering screen.[25] Actors were initially skeptical of this new type of fame, just as they had been of film itself. Within four years of Laemmle's stunt, however, author Robert Grau noticed that attitudes had changed to such a degree that film had become even more popular with actors than theater. "No one believes that there is the least danger of the motion-picture play replacing the spoken play as an entertainment," he wrote in 1914, "but that the former has routed off the boards all but a few of the traveling companies and has driven cheap melodrama entirely from large and small cities alike, is admitted; and now ... the rosters of the film studio include more well-known players than the speaking stage."[26]

Margarita Fischer benefited from this attitude change, moving successfully (if, at first, unwillingly) into the world of film as smoothly as she had stepped onto the stage in her childhood. She intuitively possessed the power to engage her audiences in a comfortable way — as one young fan later wrote to the actress, "You remind me of a typical high school pal."[27] The actress herself was motivated by qualities other than fame, however; the young head of her family saw in the deep pockets of the film industry the promise of her own prosperity and stability. "I saw that some of the players had real homes, with some chance to enjoy them," she remembered wistfully.[28] Although she at first felt the indignity of the failure of *By Products*, which made filmmaking seem like a poor second choice to the stage, she was naturally of a curious mind and optimistic disposition. "I was always attracted by [the movies], and the splendid monetary offer made me by the Selig Polyscope Company settled it for me," she later admitted, recalling that she "played leads with this company in Chicago for nine months."[29]

Margarita's romance with the "silver-tongued" Harry Pollard continued through the time of her employment with Selig; Pollard, in fact, acted for the studio as well.[30] The couple needed money, so the remuneration of film work was the main reason Harry Pollard "reluctantly" entered Selig's employ, since Margarita later described him as "a typical legit [stage actor]" who "scoffed" at the picture business.[31] The actor himself recalled, "I didn't care about going into pictures so I boosted my salary way above what I had ever gotten before, thinking that he wouldn't pay it." When Selig agreed, "There was nothing for me to do but accept the job."[32] The studio's high salaries did not necessarily imply glamour; Pollard helped build stages for sets, and he and Margarita had their dressing rooms in the former stalls of a converted barn.[33]

Many former theatrical players needed a period of adjustment to get used to working in front of a camera. As Selig director Otis Turner explained, "To get an effect with moving pictures there has to be plenty of action. With the average actor repose is one of the strongest methods of obtaining an effect, but it's exactly the opposite here. The gestures have to come quick, and the expression of the features has to change rapidly to convey the idea we wish to."[34] There is no evidence that Margarita's own transition to this new style of acting was difficult or prolonged, however. She may have been assisted by a document entitled "Pointers on Picture Acting," released by Selig in 1910, which included such helpful tips (obvious now, but not then) as "When the director gives you the word for action at the start of the scene, don't wait and look at the camera to see if it is going," and "Use your eyes as much as possible in your work. Remember that they express your thoughts more clearly when properly used than gestures or unnatural facial contortions."[35]

In 1910, the Selig studio was fresh and energetic, a groundbreaking member of a similarly vigorous industry just learning its way. Although the company had already established a California filmmaking satellite, its main base of operations was still in Chicago — in fact, Selig and fellow Chicago studio Essanay made the Windy City a bustling center that produced one-fifth of the world's films in 1910. The same year, Margarita saw Selig's new, three-story studio complete construction in that city at a cost of $75,000, and in March 1910 she began her nine-month contract and became one of two hundred employees to work there.[36] Documentation of her early work is scanty, but Margarita probably first stepped before the Selig movie cameras in April or May 1910.[37]

Few of the Selig studio's films have survived to the present day, but the survivors include among their number an example of Margarita Fischer's earliest work on film: a 1910 version of *The Merry Wives of Windsor*, which was released on November 24, about eight months into the actress's nine-month Selig contract. The film attempted a true rendition of the Shakespeare play of the same name, which focuses on the financial woes of Sir John Falstaff and his attempts to woo two wealthy merchants' wives (played in the brief film by Margarita and fellow Selig leading lady Kathlyn Williams) in order to get money from them. Once they become aware of his stratagem, they and their husbands work both together and separately to trick Falstaff, and the play ends with his humiliation in a "fairy glade." The Selig adaptation is fairly true to the source material and would be easily followed by anyone who knew the play, although plotlines were severely truncated to fit the one-reel length within which films were framed at the time. A contemporary reviewer noted that "it jars upon the nerves of one who is familiar with Shakespeare"—yet it was "markedly appreciated by the audience."[38]

As a youthful Mrs. Page in this early movie, Margarita appears natural and gleeful in her gestures and behavior, and her wide eyes, dark hair, and ready laugh draw the eye of the viewer. Within the confines of the brief film, she received a generous amount of screen time, and her scenes of conspiracy with Kathlyn Williams against the luckless Falstaff are pivotal and well-played. Margarita and Kathlyn would become two of the Selig studio's most famous alumnae, and this early pairing shows the easy screen presence of both actresses. The film also provides a fine example of the Selig studio's dedication to pictorial quality through its realistic Elizabethan costuming, natural performances, and varied staging in both exterior scenes and carefully designed sets (visually expanded with painted backdrops, but these are realistically done in great detail).[39] Despite the film's unavoidable narrative sins against the Bard, it is a well-produced picture, and was one of many American-made Shakespeare shorts that received a positive reception in Great Britain in the early 1910s.[40]

Most silent movies no longer survive, and the film titles may be all that remain of Margarita's other 1910 work for Selig. Even these provide hints of the same chameleon-like range she displayed as a young stage player. The newly minted movie player's work for Selig included melodrama, romance, and even modernized as well as period Shakespeare in films such as *For Her Country's Sake*, *The County Fair*, *Rival Dramatists*, and *Romeo and Juliet in Town*.[41] This final film was a one-reel contemporary translation of the basic plot elements of the play: Romeo Brown and Juliet Smith fall in love and reconcile their estranged families.[42] Margarita also played quite a different, and much less wholesome, role in *The Vampire*, an early adaptation of the Rudyard Kipling poem of the same name that more famously inspired the feature-length "vamp" picture *A Fool There Was* in 1915.

Most frequently, however, the novice film actress performed in a spate of Westerns, with titles like *The Trimming of Paradise Gulch*, *The Cowboy's Stratagem*, *The Wilderness*, *The Early Settlers*, and *The Red Man's Way*. She made at least the first of these, and probably more, with Tom Mix, a thirty-year-old former soldier turned cowboy who moved from trick riding into filmmaking, eventually becoming one of the film world's first and greatest cowboy stars. For these Selig Westerns, actors performed alongside actual cowboys and ranchers who were paid about five dollars a day for their efforts—a worthy salary, except in comparison to the contract pay of the actors, some of whom made as much as one hundred dollars per week.[43]

The Selig Polyscope Company was a great proving ground for Mix's talents and those of other Western players like Margarita Fischer, as the studio all but invented the Western as a genre. It was helped in no small part by its Chicago-based production center (and, by 1909, its California studio), which permitted ready location shooting on rugged and varied landscapes unavailable to East Coast filmmakers. The Selig style of Western filmmaking would have been quite palatable to "legits" like Margarita Fischer and Harry Pollard. As Andrew Brodie Smith noted in his study of the silent Western, the Selig studio sought to improve the status of film as an art form, as well as to create films of high quality: "Selig's films prefigured the epic Western and established the notion that the genre should convey a sense of history and celebrate American nationalism."[44] The studio did more than establish a filmmaking genre. By the time Margarita Fischer made her first Western, this type of film—led by the efforts of the Selig studio—was defining the mild climate and varied landscape of California as an ideal home for filmmaking, and was also helping to define the United States culturally in the eyes of filmgoers around the world.⁴⁵

At the studio, Margarita often came into contact with the best-known people of the day and received a new lesson in the vagaries of fame. As she recalled:

> They used to have visiting celebrities come, and Enrico Caruso came. And they had a big backyard — it was two blocks long — where they had horses and they had a little baseball top for us to play on.
>
> So this lovely big blonde girl and I were playing out on there, handball, back and forth, when Enrico Caruso came out from the main office, and stepped in and played with us. Oh, my goodness, we were all so thrilled. But in a minute or two ... this big blonde girl, this luscious-looking girl, and Caruso were just playing ball together and they just left me out of it!
>
> And then, oh my, I ran off the field and ran upstairs to the dressing room and just cried and cried, made such a noise, and Harry [Pollard] ... came to the door and said, "Babe, what's the matter?" And I said, "Caruso won't play ball with me." And that was quite a joke around the studio for a long, long time.⁴⁶

Perhaps she didn't enjoy being a studio joke — or perhaps the young actress, who had hopped so frequently between touring companies over the last few years, was simply ready to move on to greener pastures, at least figuratively. In December 1910, even before the last of

Harry Pollard and Margarita Fischer in Arizona, working on a Western for the American Film Manufacturing Company. This photo is inscribed on its back "To Dot from Babe/Taken in Tucson Arizona/January 1911" (courtesy the Margarita Fischer Papers, Special Collections and University Archives, Wichita State University Libraries).

her Selig releases reached theaters, she began a two-month stint making films in Arizona for the American Film Manufacturing Company. This independent studio had released its first films only one month before, and the studio intended to distinguish itself by focusing on Westerns.[47] American was typical of contemporary studios in its employment of several stock companies who filmed at multiple locations simultaneously in order to keep up with the public's voracious appetite for entertainment. To Margarita and other former actors in touring theatrical companies, the experience of "trooping around the United States to make moving pictures" was nothing new.[48] Still, she was as yet uncommitted to the new medium, making only five one-reel pictures for American. These would have held no surprises for her due to her experience in Westerns for Selig, and she quickly completed *Two Lucky Jims, An Arizona Romance, Bertie's Bandit, The Mission in the Desert,* and *The Squaw and the Man* (not to be confused with 1914's famous *The Squaw Man,* the Cecil B. DeMille picture often named as the first feature-length movie made in Hollywood). Harry Pollard appeared with her in at least one of these, *Bertie's Bandit.*[49]

In February 1911, the versatile young player "went back to my old love for a time" and "played leads" for the Lloyd Ingraham Stock Company in Omaha.[50] Her decision to drop a promising and lucrative film career and once more become a member of a local theatrical company that probably did not pay as highly is surprising from a professional standpoint. From a personal standpoint, though, it was inevitable. Harry Pollard "detested" the filmmaking life, thinking it "beneath his dignity."[51] Just as deeply, though, he loved Margarita, and she returned his feeling. The courting couple eventually married in secret on July 9, 1911, in Golden, Colorado (today a suburb of Denver), following their Omaha sojourn with the Ingraham company. Margarita changed her last name legally but continued to use her maiden name professionally, and although the couple worked together in the meantime, they continued to hide the fact of their marriage until the following spring.[52]

The couple's careful concealment of their true wedding date from their peers initially allowed them each to maintain their own individual fame and continue to appeal to the romantic fantasies of their audiences. Evelyn Scott, a memoirist of early twentieth century plays and film, noted that "stock companies counted, for a part of their receipts, on the yearnings of the female audience towards their leading men. Yearnings in the early 1900s in the Middle west had their moral code. Leading men were expected to be bachelors."[53] The men who attended the young couple's performances were no less passionate in their "yearnings" than were the female audience members. The benefit of being publicly single in order to continue to appeal romantically to fans must have been driven home by a passionate letter Margarita received only a month before her wedding, in which an Omaha fan wrote for three pages about the "strangely beautiful" impression she made during a performance of the historical play *The Road to Yesterday.* The letter closed dramatically with a compliment to the young woman's "perfect" acting, and added that she was "sweeter than the lids of Juneau's [sic] eyes."[54] As their careers progressed, their private marriage also allowed the couple to claim varying wedding dates, as befitted their changing but ever-youthful images. Later publicity articles assert a variety of different marriage dates for the husband and wife, as Margarita repeatedly revised her age.

Margarita Fischer and Harry Pollard played in a variety of roles at Omaha's Gayety theater during their spring and summer with the Ingraham company, winning the usual

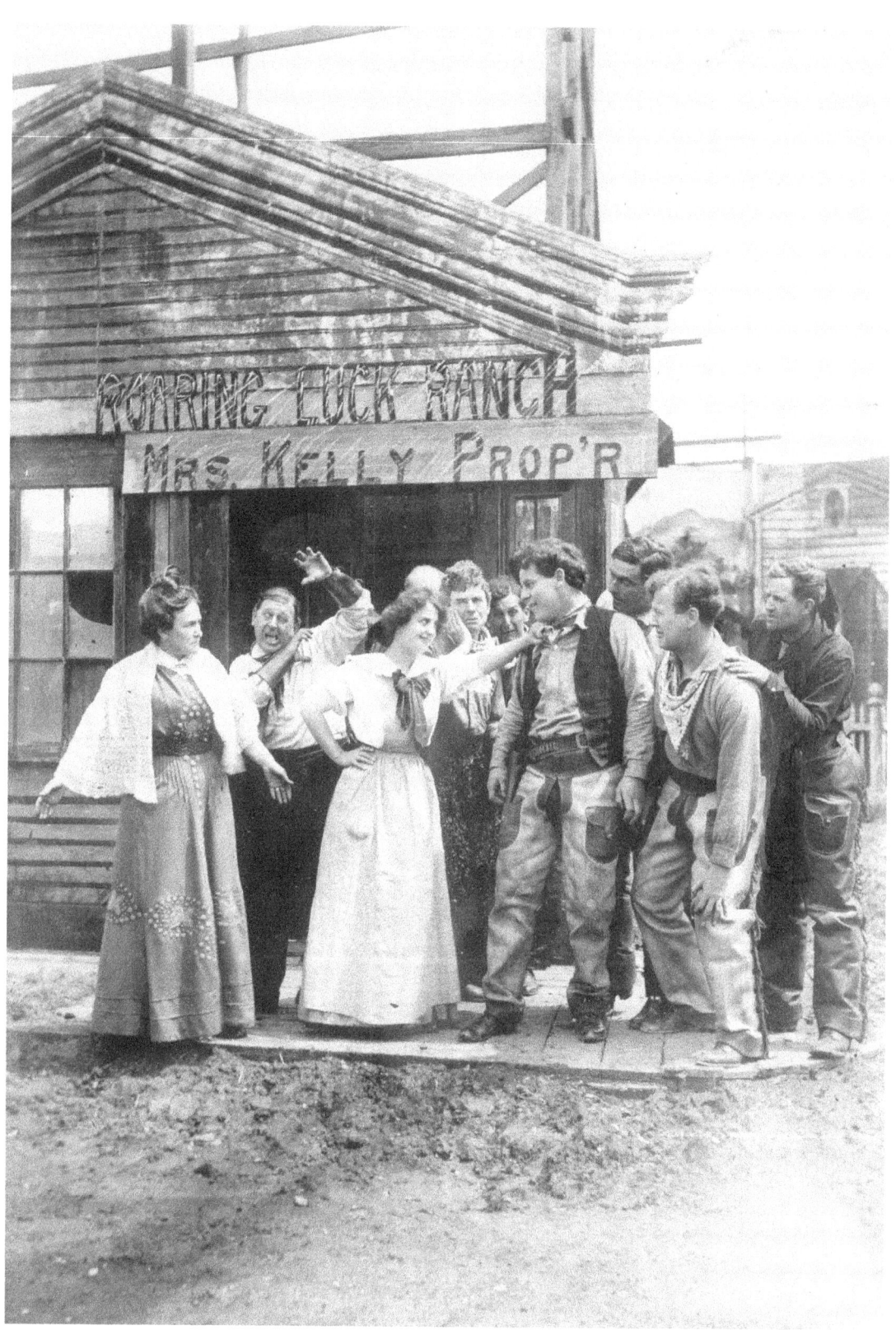

plaudits for their work. The first play the company put on was *The Spenders*, performed to an enthusiastic packed house. The young performers acquitted themselves well. Despite the fact that Margarita was saddled with the part of, as a reviewer noted, "one of those conventional, nearly colorless heroines that even good acting cannot vitalize," she was applauded for a "demurely effective" performance that made a "very pleasing impression."[55] Pollard, said the same critic, showed himself likely to "play his roles with masculine vigor and thus remove himself from the catagory [sic] of those sweet, dear boys who become matinee idols."

The Ingraham players added quickly to their repertoire; in the dreamy English historical drama *The Road to Yesterday*, most cast members played both present-day and Stuart-era roles.[56] The play itself was a "swashbuckling" and energetic affair involving two couples. Through dreams, one couple discovers that they have conflicted in a past life and must be reconciled in the historical era before they can build a life together in the modern day.[57] The other couple—which included Margarita's role—fall in love in both past and present after being distracted by unsuitable, stuffy partners. Margarita played her part with "romance and vitality ... girlish buoyancy and grace." Pollard, not surprisingly, played her romantic interest "with intelligence and skill."[58]

Perhaps influenced by the vaudeville tradition of focusing on the female form, Omaha reviewers paid a great deal of attention to the young actress's physical beauty, as well as her dramatic talent. The issue of her costuming in the title role in the Ingraham company's next play, *The Return of Eve*, excited as much speculation as did the plot of the show. When she came onstage for the first performance of the play, wearing, as a critic noted, a "primitive gown of autumn leaves over mink hides, sleeveless and décolleté at both top and bottom," the "gasp of admiration" and "prolonged applause" of the audience could only have been in response to her appearance, which contributed much to the success of the play.[59] In an article about the Gayety's new "iced air" cooling system, the author notes that it worked so well that Margarita "complained that she was covered in goose pimples" as she performed "clothed only in leaves"—perhaps as big an enticement to audiences as the comfortable temperature of the theater.[60] Margarita's costuming actually created so much buzz that it almost overshadowed her performance. One fashion-conscious reviewer quickly praised Margarita's "poetic interpretation, touched with roguishness and that indefinable quality known as charm," but then added helpfully, "One questions ... some details of her sartorial embellishment. Why a dress of autumn leaves, when all the setting of Eden is the opulent green of summer? Mosses and green and a coronet of flowers might seem quite as picturesque, and certainly less incongruous."[61]

After a few months of this personal and professional affirmation, the Ingraham company's summer season was over, and the newly wed Margarita and Harry Pollard made preparations to return to filmmaking. Margarita marked the beginning of her wholehearted commitment to her film career by signing an eleven-month contract with Carl Laemmle's IMP studio on

Opposite: Still from *Bertie's Bandit* (American), released on January 26, 1911. Margarita Fischer and Harry Pollard appear at center (Margarita's hand is on his shoulder). The American Film Manufacturing Company was a very new independent company seeking to build a reputation as a producer of Westerns (courtesy the Margarita Fischer Papers, Special Collections and University Archives, Wichita State University Libraries).

November 27, 1911. Witnessed by Laemmle himself, the contract set her salary at ninety dollars a week for the first five months of her employment, with a raise to one hundred dollars a week for the final six months. The contract also included an option for another year, with the weekly salary for the second year of work set at $125.[62] In comparison to the lean years on the stage, "we had everything. We thought we were rich," Margarita recalled of these newlywed days as film players.[63]

This contract represented her highest rate of pay to date, and she began earning her keep immediately. Her first movie for the studio, *Over the Hills (to the Poorhouse)*, was released only three days after her contract was signed — indicating that she had actually been working for the studio for several weeks prior to that time, and had probably won the contract due to Laemmle's recognition of her work ethic and talent.[64] Pollard also joined the IMP by the year's end and costarred with his wife (as her hunchbacked surgeon sweetheart) for the first time in January 1912 in the romantic *The Worth of a Man*.[65] From this point, Margarita Fischer's personal and professional lives were irrevocably intertwined. She was publicly an actress and privately a wife, and as Pollard was often her leading man in both spheres, the roles sometimes strengthened one another and sometimes conflicted over the coming years.

4

The Rose of California

In signing on with the Independent Motion Picture Company, Margarita Fischer and Harry Pollard were aligning themselves with a studio perhaps more inextricably linked with its founder even than William Selig was with his studio. The IMP was the brainchild of the self-made, single-minded, German-born Carl Laemmle, a warm-hearted pixie-like figure who had opened his first theater in 1905 as a step toward what he hoped would be financial independence. Laemmle combined a financial talent strengthened by a bookkeeping career with a shrewd eye for advertising and public appeal, and his single theater quickly expanded into two. Frustrated by a lack of reliable film product and delivery for his theaters, he created the Laemmle Film Service to distribute and purchase films from manufacturers across the country. By 1909 his characteristic professionalism had grown this into the nation's largest exchange, an agency that rented films to movie theaters (a more successful system than the early one of having theaters buy prints outright, as the prints ceased to draw crowds after a short period of exhibition and then became useless to theater owners). Laemmle began film production the same year when his exchange's product was jeopardized by the Trust after he refused to join the Trust itself, due not to the cost of a Trust license, but to his self-made man's dislike of monopolies and outside control.[1] Laemmle quickly developed a sense of the production end of the new industry — including a shrewd idea of what would appeal to cinema fans, as evidenced by his dramatic stunt involving the supposed death of actress Florence Lawrence in 1910.

Laemmle's studio was a good match for the similarly self-made Pollards. Initially, in the world of film, Margarita's career advanced much more rapidly than that of her less fashionably attractive husband. After being tested in a small part in *Over the Hills (to the Poorhouse)* and winning her IMP contract, she took the female lead in *The Girl and the Half-Back*. This, her first major performance for the IMP, was indeed a familiar role to one who had spent her theatrical career playing roles of "the sweet, sympathetic class."[2] In this light romantic drama, she portrayed Alice, a coed who loves the captain of the college football team until he is blamed — by a romantic rival for Alice's affections — for giving opposing teams the play signals. Alice discovers and reveals the truth, and the restored hero wins the game for the team.[3]

Both the twenty-five-year-old actress and her thirty-two-year-old co-star, King Baggot, were a bit past the age to portray college students, but contemporary audiences probably took no notice of this fact. Baggot, though virtually forgotten today, was in late 1911 the foremost male actor of the IMP, a handsome St. Louis–born actor and brightening star who was eventually known as "King of the Movies."[4] He was incredibly versatile, having (like Margarita) honed his acting skills in stock companies before moving into film. His onscreen roles eventually included upper-class characters, ethnic characters ranging from Chinese to German to Turkish, specialized occupations such as detective, gold miner, sea captain, and race-car driver, and one of the earliest film portrayals of Dr. Jekyll and Mr. Hyde.[5] In 1914 he was still a revered IMP star, admired for his professionalism and talent as well as his appearance; that year, contemporary film historian Robert Grau said of him that "at this writing he is one of the six most idolized favorites of the screen.... As usual, there is little cognizance taken of the fact that this man is what he is to-day because of the seriousness with which he invests his work, because he is a prodigious worker, and finally because he has remained steadfast to the organization [the IMP] which he joined as an experiment."[6]

Margarita was fortunate to be paired with such a proficient and popular actor in only her second outing with a new studio. She could appreciate Baggot's work ethic and versatility, and the two probably got along well, for she and Baggot appeared together in four of her first six major performances for the IMP, released in a whirlwind five weeks from November 30, 1911, to January 4, 1912. Eager to familiarize the public with this new leading lady, the studio put forth her films *A Pair of Gloves* and *The Portrait* in the ten days following the release of *The Girl and the Half-Back*. The IMP then paired her with Baggot again in *A Lesson to Husbands*, in which she played a con artist and temptress, and in *The Trinity*, wherein she played a more wholesome young woman who attracted a young artist and unwittingly threatened his friendship with an older man before bringing the whole trio closer together.[7] These roles allowed Margarita to stretch her screen persona for the first time since she had played the title role in *The Vampire* for Selig. *A Lesson to Husbands* offered her a chance to play a seductive and grasping character, although the film itself did not represent a departure from melodramatic storytelling, as traditional morals and family structures were vindicated in the end. The young actress was pleased with these roles, despite the speed with which her films were produced. Attempting to reconstruct her own filmography around this time, she noted, "I like the Imp pictures I have been in better than all the rest."[8]

The fast pace of Margarita Fischer's filming schedule was characteristic of the industry as a whole, for the world of film was rapidly changing. During perhaps no other time except the later years of the transition to sound was there such upheaval in the movie business. The early 1910s marked the beginning of studio conglomeration, at first in order to break the power that the Edison-led Trust held over the distribution of films. The General Film Company distributed the films of the Trust studios beginning in 1910. By 1912, the power of the Trust was seriously undermined due to the efforts of independent filmmakers such as Carl Laemmle and William Fox, who refused to pay the Trust's licensing fees and opened court cases against them. Fox won a case against the Edison studio in 1912, and the following year the federal government itself sued the Trust as an illegal monopoly.[9]

In the meantime, the American Film Manufacturing Company (Margarita Fischer's second studio employer) had joined three other studios to distribute their pictures through the

Opposite: Margarita Fischer, as Alice, exults with King Baggot (right) after a chastened William E. Shay's (left) plans to separate the pair are foiled in *The Girl and the Half-back* (1911). This was only Margarita's second film for the IMP; it was a great vote of confidence for her to be cast with an esteemed actor like Baggot (courtesy the Margarita Fischer Papers, Special Collections and University Archives, Wichita State University Libraries).

4. The Rose of California

Mutual Film Corporation in competition with the General Film Company. Carl Laemmle, head of the IMP, responded to Mutual's organization by forming the Universal Film Manufacturing Company in June 1912 to distribute the releases of five additional studios, and in the following years even more studios joined the Universal fold.[10] This process of merging continued throughout the decade until, by the end of the 1910s, many of the pioneering film companies were experiencing serious financial difficulties due to competition from newer, larger studios with deeper pockets.[11] Filmmaking was becoming a serious business, and with rare exception large producers rather than stars held the power. The Selig Polyscope Company was a notable casualty of this process. The innovative, eclectic studio declined in the years following Margarita Fischer's departure due to a combination of competition, reorganization, and loss (to death or to other studios) of key figures before finally closing in 1918.[12]

The early 1910s also marked a shift in the location of film production from the East Coast to the West. Southern California's varied geography and pleasant climate granted studios the opportunity to film most of their pictures on location yet remain within striking distance of a central production facility.[13] Margarita Fischer had not yet made a film on the West Coast when she signed with the IMP, although she had worked in most other parts of the country. The Selig Polyscope Company had maintained a satellite production center in the Los Angeles area since 1909, but Margarita had made pictures at Selig's Chicago center during her tenure with the studio. She had worked in Arizona for American, and she probably made her first films for the IMP in New York. Soon after completing her first films with King Baggot, however, she became a part of the film industry's westward movement. On December 30, 1911, the day *A Lesson to Husbands* was released, Margarita, Harry Pollard, and a group of other IMP players and producers began a railway journey to California to set up the "Western IMP Company" in a Los Angeles subdivision.[14] This subsidiary studio's first production, in which both Margarita and her husband played parts, was the appropriately titled short film *The Rose of California*, released on February 29, 1912.

Margarita must have been pleased to return to California, for although it may have brought back memories of her father's death, it was also the state in which she had met her husband and in which her niece, Dorothy's daughter Kathrine, had been born in August 1907. Besides her family associations, Margarita would have soon seen that California was also a land of opportunity for women. In this young, energetic state, the "New Woman," an independent, athletic, educated creature, had increased freedom to move outside of the male-dominated status quo. By the 1910s, her comparative financial and sexual freedom had redefined ideas about women's proper roles in marriage, family, and work.[15] Because femininity still represented decency and respectability to the American public, enterprising women in California could use both their reputable images and their newfound social freedoms to move to the forefront of the movie industry as it sought to gain credence as an art form.[16]

Behind and in front of the camera, women in early Hollywood enjoyed a level of power that remains unmatched to the present day. They wrote for and edited fan magazines, painted color onto film, ran cameras, handled publicity, cut films, reviewed films, cast films, and even managed studios.[17] Witty, prolific Frances Marion, a former reporter, came to Hollywood as a screenwriter the same year Margarita Fischer arrived; within five years, she was the highest-paid writer in the film industry. Marion was not the only woman who shaped the stories that the biggest stars acted out; female screenwriters scripted fully half of the films produced between 1911 and 1925.¹⁸ Another influential woman was Mary Pickford, a close friend of Marion's, who had come to California as a teenaged actress for the Biograph Company in 1910. She gained popularity and power quickly, earning four thousand dollars per week by 1915 and thereby becoming the world's highest-paid woman at the age of twenty-three.¹⁹

Among Margarita Fischer's own accomplished peers under the umbrella of the Universal studios was Lois Weber, a respected director, producer, screenwriter, and actress, and a courageous, determined activist whose films frequently took on complex and controversial moral issues.²⁰ Universal provided a particularly friendly environment for groundbreaking women; the conglomerate employed more female directors than any other studio during the silent era, having nine on the payroll at one point. Weber was the foremost of these, for she was skilled as both a director and writer, and her experience as an actress allowed her to coax sensitive and naturalistic performances from her casts. She was a constant voice for social change through her films, advocating an end to capital punishment and the need for greater respect for teachers, noting the harmful effects of racial prejudice and religious hypocrisy, and continually campaigning for the right of women to access birth control.²¹ Lois Weber's reputation grew steadily from the time Margarita first encountered her in California in 1912 until author Carolyn Lowrey applauded her "fearless" production methods and her "indubitable position" as "one of the best directors of the screen" in 1920.²²

The offscreen power of Hollywood women was often reflected in the roles actresses played onscreen. Film fans of the early 1910s — a majority of whom were women — appreciated seeing trailblazing female-centered stories such as those shown weekly in the increasingly popular serial format. Serial films were premiered by the Selig Polyscope Company in 1913 with Kathlyn Williams (Margarita's fellow "merry wife of Windsor") as lead player, and they quickly proliferated. Serials tended to focus initially on the escapades or travails of a central female character; the most lastingly famous one, *The Perils of Pauline*, centered on Pearl White's character's repeated attempts to safeguard her life and inheritance from the depredations of a male villain.²³ Such films, says historian Nan Enstad, both reflected contemporary women's entry into the workplace in increasing numbers and offered escapist relief from the limitations placed upon them in this new sphere.²⁴ More traditional melodramas also remained popular with women, as they upheld the still-entrenched Victorian ideals of femininity and domesticity, but even these were usually performed with a contemporary twist. The most famous and popular actresses of 1912 — Mary Pickford and Florence Lawrence; the dimpled, pixieish Lillian Walker; the fragile, dark-haired Gish sisters, Lillian and Dorothy — frequently played traditional roles, but spiced them with a youthful, piquant energy.²⁵

The often-contradictory images of women were, argues author Miriam Hansen, finally "submerged in the consumerist discourse that had enabled the public articulation of competing models of female identity in the first place."²⁶ This "consumerist discourse" was best shown by the proliferation of film-related magazines. The filmgoing public was fascinated by the stars and stories they saw onscreen, and their voracious appetite for information about these figures led to the establishment of fan magazines to meet public demand. *Motion Picture Story Magazine* (later *Motion Picture Magazine*), founded in 1911, was the first of several publications to publish prose summaries of film plots (complete with dialogue), often illustrated with production stills and drafted by respected fiction authors.²⁷ This periodical was actually organized by the Trust, and offered much information about film plot lines but little about actors, who initially remained unidentified within its pages.[28] However, the publication soon introduced a popular feature called "The Answer Man," actually scripted by a woman, which provided a forum for fan inquiries about the work and eventually the private lives of their favorite stars.[29]

Moving Picture World, which was founded in 1907, began life as a plain, scrappy weekly magazine in New York, but its technical insight and cogent recommendations for improving cinematic products quickly transformed it into an influential, well-respected trade magazine with national influence.[30] *Photoplay*, founded in 1912, was the first true fan magazine in its focus on names and tidbits of news; it also printed some of the most unbiased reviews of the era's films. Unlike modern tabloids, explains film historian Kevin Brownlow, *Photoplay* "was a forthright, hard-hitting, well-balanced, and highly entertaining publication" which "set the standard for film journalism."[31] Within the next few years came similarly titled periodicals, such as *Feature Movie Magazine, Picture-Play, Movie Pictorial, Movie Weekly,* and *Photo-Play World*.[32] The theatrical sections of newspapers, as well as the pages of publications formerly dedicated solely to actors of "the legitimate," also provided the public with information about new films and favorite stars. Most notable among these in the 1910s were the *Morning Telegraph,* a New York newspaper that began printing film industry news in 1909, and *Billboard,* a theatrical publication that became the first to print advertisements for movies.[33]

Some of the information in these periodicals was insipid and studio-concocted; indeed, some fan magazines were actually owned by studios and merely reprinted their publicity. *Moving Picture Stories* was an egregious example; it simply fronted for the Universal publicity department once it began publication in 1913.[34] Author Richard deCordova notes that publicity information varied very little from actor to actor, and stardom was as often a result of the studio publicity machine as it was the outgrowth of a performer's actual gifts.[35] Yet, as author Gaylyn Studlar counters, fan magazines also offered much genuine information on performers, films, and the filmmaking process, and over time became a conduit for a sophisticated discourse on the nature of fame and stardom.[36] Within that environment, even the most flagrantly fabricated articles offer information to the modern scholar about how stars wished to be perceived, and, in turn, about what appealed to film audiences of the time.

The rapid introduction of a flock of publications focusing on film stardom represents a similarly quick shift in the way film performers were perceived. A dichotomy arose between the ideas of actor and star. While both terms were used to describe stage performers — indeed, both were used at times to describe Margarita Fischer — the distinction was more revealing (sometimes unintentionally so) when applied to the world of film. By one definition, an actor was a performer recognized for talent, personality, and malleability, while a star's appeal lay in physical desirability and in "filling roles tailored to a carefully cultivated image."[37] At this early point in the development of the film industry, most well-known performers were still solid actors — but some, like Florence Lawrence and Mary Pickford, were becoming stars as well. These players inspired interest in their private lives and, over time, also fostered the fan preference to see them looking and behaving in a manner consistent with audience expectations both onscreen and off. Within just a few years — by the beginning of 1916 — the concept of stardom and the star system was already so entrenched and familiar that it was ripe for self-referential parody. The Mack Sennett–produced short film *A Movie Star,* through the bizarrely mustachioed persona of Mack Swain as "Handsome Jack," teases both the public for its fascination with celebrity and the self-involved actors who can't resist giving the public what it wants.[38]

Such expectations never arose to the same degree for stage performers; although Margarita had cultivated a distinct image as the "Youngest Leading Lady on the American Stage," she was not responsible for maintaining it in the presence of constant media interest and the eager eyes of thousands of audience members a day. As her film career developed, however, Margarita would embrace both the actor and star aspects of her career, sometimes at her own behest and sometimes at that of her studio. At times she built her image as a versatile performer, while at others she became for her public a star who truly embodied the most appealing qualities of a certain role type.

To Margarita Fischer, who had been conflating feminine roles since her teens, the positive blend of images permitted by fan magazine articles seemed like a wonderful way to tap into her largest audience yet. Over the course of the 1910s, she skillfully used the forum of fan magazines to shape her persona in the public mind. Due to Harry Pollard's reservations, neither he nor his wife had a personal publicist, so Margarita's sympathetic development was probably more authentic and individualized, as well as more limited in its scope, than that of many stars. Her studios did, of course, publicize her films and at times place personal "news items," but Margarita had no publicist to speak for her or seek special opportunities for promotion of her work or image. Therefore, personal interviews with the actress, although at times a bit flowery, are generally factually accurate (or at least as much as the actress wished them to be) and have the ring of authenticity.

While Margarita valued the fame that she developed over the course of her acting career, viewing it as both pleasant and necessary for the continuation of her career, Harry Pollard was always impatient with the trappings of stardom that came with film acting. The role of a publicist was the main aspect of fame that he scorned, but it was hardly the only one. He was "a very private person" who "didn't believe in big parties, didn't believe in the Hollywood scene," stated the couple's great-niece, Margarita Kotselis.[39] In later life, Margarita Fischer joked about this, recalling that her husband "wouldn't even hire a press agent.... Everyone said, 'You should have a publicity man,' and he said 'What for? Just to tell the public that I think I'm great?' So we didn't have any. Neither one of us. And, of course, it's very necessary."[40] Harry Pollard disagreed, however: stardom simply interfered with carrying out one's vocation as an actor.

When she began her California filmmaking career in 1912, Margarita could have had little inkling of the way it would develop over the course of the decade. She arrived for work at the Western IMP Company as a well-respected member of the company, but still as a relative unknown with the filmgoing public, who might never have seen her publicized by name. If hard work alone could have made the young actress a household name, she would have been instantly famous; after the release of *The Rose of California* on February 29, 1912, she and her husband filmed and released five short films in five weeks. Only the characters' names from these films are known, but even from this small bit of information it is clear that in two of them—*The Baby* and *Where Paths Meet*—the real-life married pair played onscreen lovers or spouses. In another, *Better Than Gold*, Margarita had a dual role as a mother and daughter. The plots of the other two films, *Squnk City Fire Company* and *The Dove and the Serpent*, are less easily deduced, though Margarita's role in the latter as "Tortola, the dove," and co-star Edward Lyons's portrayal of "Luis, the serpent," indicate both a melodramatic plot and one of the first of the actress's ethnic characterizations.[41]

The young Margarita's appearance, described later in her life as "a lovely brunette of a Spanish type" (perhaps recalling these early roles), was as great a boon to her in the world of silent filmmaking as it had been in her theatrical days.[42] The standard of beauty of her own teenage years had been closely tied to the work of artist Charles Dana Gibson, who drew energetic, modestly dressed women with piles of hair, straight noses, and large, intelligent eyes.[43] Though fashionable clothes and hair became sleeker through the years, beauty in the following decades continued to be defined in similar terms to those Gibson had promoted. Margarita's curly dark hair, large eyes, and compact form were beautiful to film audiences of the 1910s, just as they had been to theatergoers of the 1900s. Although she actually had dark auburn hair, green eyes, and "a very light Irish complexion," the orthochromatic (red-insensitive) film stock used through the 1910s tended to polarize colors.[44] Blue eyes showed up very pale or even white, while medium-colored eyes, such as Margarita's, appeared to be darker, and red-tinted hair such as hers photographed much more dark than it actually was. On orthochromatic film, Margarita appeared to have what technical film writer Austin Lescarboura would call in 1919 a "camera face" of "dark, regular features and dark eyes," which, combined with her fair skin, was more striking than any other combination of coloring.[45]

Such a complexion also gave Margarita Fischer the freedom to play any race in an industry where white actors regularly played characters of all ethnicities. By the end of 1914, after less than two years in California, she had played a gypsy in *Draga, the Gypsy*; a Mexican woman in *The Land of Promise*; the African-American Topsy in *Uncle Tom's Cabin* (Harry Pollard played the title role); an "Oriental princess" in *The Diamond Makers*; an Italian girl in both *The Sacrifice* and *Italian Love*; and a Hispanic character named "Carmelita" in *The Legend of Black Rock*.[46] From a modern-day perspective, the industry practice of casting white actors in diverse roles was clearly ethnocentric, but at the time, Margarita would have merely seen these as opportunities to expand her range. Although racism is today commonly associated with blackface performance, there is no evidence to suggest that Margarita herself, who performed in blackface as Topsy, was racist in her attitudes. In fact, although the film itself has been lost, surviving stills from this early version of *Uncle Tom's Cabin* show Pollard's Tom to be a character of scholarly dignity and soulful mien, while Margarita's Topsy is typically playful and impish. (She may actually have been too restrained for her time; a *Variety* reviewer was disappointed that her performance was not of the entertaining "low comedy" sort.[47]) It is more likely that the couple simply thought the roles would be both fun to play and — never a small consideration — central to the production. Margarita seemed always to regard the quality or prominence of a role, rather than the character's race, as the most important consideration for a film performance. She was willing to alter her appearance as needed, such as when playing Topsy, but she tended to restrict her physical alteration to the bare minimum — such as a wig and, of course, costume — and fill in the visual gaps with the character of her performance. At the end of her career, when she played *Uncle Tom's Cabin*'s Eliza onscreen with appearance unaltered save for a long black wig (not a phenotypic impossibility for that role), she was offended when her race rather than her performance occasioned remark from a reviewer.[48]

Besides these diverse portrayals, the versatile Margarita played a wide variety of characters of her own race during her time with the Universal studios. A newspaper article attested

4. The Rose of California

Margarita Fischer and Harry Pollard played Topsy and Uncle Tom in the 1913 IMP version of *Uncle Tom's Cabin*. (The film title and players' names are scrawled across the image.) Blackface performances such as these were common in the world of early film, where white actors regularly played characters of all races and ethnicities (courtesy the Harry Pollard Papers, Special Collections and University Archives, Wichita State University Libraries).

to the flexibility of the increasingly famous actress, avowing that "there was never a more pathetic 'poor girl' on the screen, or a sweeter 'old lady,' when the opportunity presents itself."[49] This malleability was common to many of the greatest film players of the time, and as author Paula Marantz Cohen noted, it seemed to be rooted in their upbringing:

> The most prominent stars to emerge during the silent period were possessed of an unusual plasticity of character and …they followed the cues of public response to shape themselves along the lines that the public wanted. Almost all had come from relatively poor backgrounds, had had no settled homes or consistent influences, and had lived from an early age in the public eye.… Movies were uniquely designed to cast these performers in roles that reinforced a particular structure and style for their personalities.[50]

That is, besides Margarita's fortunate appearance, her childhood on stage and the demands of her early performing career had combined to make her remarkably suited to succeed in the new world of film.

Draga, the Gypsy, a one-reel film released in 1913, is one of Margarita Fischer's few surviving early works and offers hints as to both the ways in which the actress shaped her image for the camera and the type of film in which the actress was appearing for Universal. The hoary but popular romantic plot involves a rich young man (Robert Z. Leonard, who also often worked as a director) and an itinerant gypsy chief's daughter (Margarita Fischer) meeting by chance, falling in love, and eloping. The difference in their social classes separates them first from their families and then, when the gypsy proves unable to fit into her husband's genteel world, from each other. The tearful Draga determines to return to her tribe, but as she packs her things, she interrupts her wild younger brother in the act of robbing her husband's house, where the couple lives with his critical and suspicious mother, a recipe for marital strife if ever there was one. Draga protects her brother by taking responsibility for the theft, and she is then cast out of the house by her husband and mother-in-law. Her brother confesses, however, and the joyful husband, the scales fallen from his eyes, runs to the gypsy tribe to take his wife back. He encounters her on the brink of ritual suicide (her father having advised her that "death alone brings back — she who marries an alien to our race") and confesses his error, and the young couple is finally reunited.[51]

This is a fabulous amount of storytelling for a scant fifteen minutes of screen time, and the one-reel film is well-paced and generally well-acted. Not much is demanded of any of the performers except for Margarita, who gets to run the gamut of emotions from shy to enamored to frustrated to terrified to resigned. As the young woman caught between two worlds, she is almost always effective, imparting her mannerisms with a subtle exoticism as well as the boundless energy that so often characterized her screen performances. She veers into overstated theatricality as she wildly bemoans her decayed marriage before determining to return to the gypsy way of life. She is entirely natural and believable, however, as the willful gypsy maiden coyly darting her eyes away from Robert Z. Leonard's captivated face, or as the new wife energetically pumping her mother-in-law's hand upon meeting her for the first time, or throwing a temper tantrum — and books — upon completing a stultifying literacy lesson and failing to get her husband's attention, or tripping over her unfamiliar long skirts as she attends her first society party. Her appearance lends itself well to the role as well; with long, free-flowing hair, kerchief, and peasant blouse, she is the picture of a cinematic gypsy, and the contrasting severity of her upper-class clothing and hairstyle is an apt visual representation of the strictures she experiences in her new life.

In such idealistic romances and melodramas, Margarita parlayed her name recognition into genuine film celebrity. She had proven herself an accomplished professional by the end of her first two years in California, working in a wide variety of roles and with a large swath of the film industry. Besides acting for notable directors of the day, such as Lois Weber (for whom she made three films in 1913), Otis Turner, and sometime costar Robert Z. Leonard, Margarita worked alongside such future luminaries as master of the grotesque Lon Chaney, then a bit player for Universal who appeared in Margarita's *Shon, the Piper*, 1913; Frank Borzage, later an Academy Award–winning director, but the father of Margarita's character in 1913's *When the Prince Arrived*; and Wallace Reid, who, after acting with Margarita in 1912's *The Tribal Law* (which he co-directed with Otis Turner) and *An Indian Outcast*, and 1913's *Fires of Fate*, went on to become one of the most appealing leading men of the late 1910s. Bringing together her two acting worlds of stage and screen,

Margarita, at left, in the title role of *Draga, the Gypsy* (Rex, 1913), looks warily at her husband (Robert Z. Leonard) and mother-in-law (unidentified) when they find the bag of goods they think she stole (courtesy the Margarita Fischer Papers, Special Collections and University Archives, Wichita State University Libraries).

Many of Margarita's IMP pictures had a historical or multicultural aspect. In forefront, Robert Z. Leonard, as *Shon, the Piper* (101 Bison, 1913), and Margarita celebrate the disguised title character's revelation of his nobility. Future "man of a thousand faces" Lon Chaney had a bit role in this film (courtesy the Margarita Fischer Papers, Special Collections and University Archives, Wichita State University Libraries).

Margarita also made a few films alongside her former stock director Lloyd Ingraham in 1912.[52]

Her most frequent leading man was Harry Pollard, not surprisingly, and although he made some films without his wife, he most frequently performed as her costar. Margarita grew into a much better-known player than Pollard during their first year in California, possibly because he became more interested in working behind the camera. The "typical legit" may have come to enjoy directing because it drew less unwanted press attention than acting, or his curious mind may simply have wanted to understand more completely the technology supporting his new vocation. He still acted opposite his wife, but beginning with the one-reel *Nothing Shall Be Hidden* in June 1912, he occasionally directed her as well. As the diversifying Pollard recounted later, "I'll frankly admit that I was a tough actor to handle for, right or wrong, I had my own ideas of how a character or a situation should be played, and I was determined to do it my way or not at all. Carl Laemmle will tell you that it was in self-defense that Universal let me have my way" and permitted the opinionated actor to embark upon a directorial career.[53]

4. The Rose of California

The Pollards did not remain exclusively with the IMP for the full eleven months of Margarita's contract; once the Universal distributorship was established in June 1912 (seven months into the contract), IMP players were free to work for other Universal member studios.[54] Margarita began working for the Universal subsidiary studio Rex in July 1912 and remained there until the end of 1913, also completing the occasional project for the IMP or Universal subsidiaries Nestor, 101 Bison, or Crystal Films.[55] Her husband, too, moved between Universal member studios in 1912, but in 1913 he split his time between acting for Universal studios and directing for the American Film Manufacturing Company, an independent outside of the Universal fold which distributed through the rival Mutual Film Corporation. At the end of 1913 — after less than two years in California — Pollard was gaining the experience he craved as a director, and Margarita was one of Universal's most bankable young stars, along with King Baggot, Laemmle's early recruit Florence Lawrence, and sometime director Lois Weber.[56] Margarita had made nearly three dozen one-, two-, and three-reel pictures, an average of three films every two months. While an impressive output, this shrank in comparison to the amount of work she put out in the next year; in 1914 alone, at the peak of her output, she starred in forty-two pictures.

Of Margarita's massive body of work from the early 1910s, only one film is available for home viewers: the 1913 Crystal Films short *How Men Propose*, from which the original intertitles have been lost. This contemporary comedy, in which Margarita plays the bright "Grace Darling," was produced and probably directed by the skilled Lois Weber. Released only three weeks after *Draga, the Gypsy*, Margarita's middle-class American role provides an excellent contrast to her ethnic role as Draga, and her performance offers another tantalizing glimpse of the rising star's appeal to early twentieth century audiences. She does not appear glamorous — her hairstyle is conservative, her clothing a simple shirtwaist and skirt — but the twenty-seven-year-old Margarita is nonetheless vibrant as her character encourages three very different men to propose marriage to her. No intertitles are necessary; the actress's magnetic eyes and expressive face tell the story as she glances knowingly at the camera, her wry smile inviting the viewer in on the joke on these three rather ridiculous men — that she is merely "writing an article on how men propose," and has no personal interest in the suitors. In the

Harry Pollard in a 1912 IMP studio portrait. Although he was initially unenthusiastic about the movie industry, he quickly became interested in working behind the camera. Photograph by the Universal Film Manufacturing Company (courtesy the Harry Pollard Papers, Special Collections and University Archives, Wichita State University Libraries).

final moments of the film, she blithely leaves the scene and gives a maid a form letter to deliver to each man that tells him the truth, offers him back his ring, and invites him to keep his picture of her.[57] *How Men Propose* is a playful, energetic assertion of female power in which Margarita shows herself to be a gifted actress, entirely familiar with the unique requirements of performing on film.

As *Draga, the Gypsy* and *How Men Propose* indicate, Margarita was effective in a wide variety of roles, and her growing reputation drew the attention of other studios. At the end of 1913, the American Film Manufacturing Company wooed her away from Universal, perhaps at the encouragement of her husband, who had now been directing films for American for some months. This rival of Universal's, run by co-presidents John R. Freuler and Samuel Hutchinson, had changed somewhat since Margarita's short sojourn with it in Arizona in late 1910 and early 1911. American still maintained an Arizona facility, but, cognizant of trends in film production, had by late 1913 closed its two original Chicago production companies (though the company maintained its printing and manufacturing center there) and added one in Santa Barbara, California, instead. "One of the owners would come out [from Chicago] about every three or four months, and stay for a while to see what was going on and make corrections and improvements," Margarita remembered.[58] The Pollards were recruited as one of these "improvements" to the Santa Barbara studio. Margarita was hired to join American's California production company, which focused on creating the contemporary dramas and social comedies in which she had proven herself so able for Universal. Harry Pollard accompanied her to American, enticed by the promise of an expanded directorial career.[59]

5

Mlle. La Mode

Later in her life, Margarita Fischer recalled the Santa Barbara of late 1913 as "a delightful town to live in. Such a nice atmosphere, and of course the studio was all new."[1] Open only since the summer of 1913, the American Film Manufacturing Company's Santa Barbara branch boasted large, Spanish-style studio buildings with tiled roofs, which provided a pleasant and comfortable contrast to the converted barns of the Selig studio in Chicago.[2] The bright, fast-growing Southern California coastal town seemed suffused with buoyant energy, and the move to American appeared to be an auspicious one. At this time a thriving independent studio, American — nicknamed "Flying A" in film periodicals due to its winged logo — at once brought the full force of its publicity machine to bear on the image of its promising new acquisition, Margarita Fischer. Her face within an American Beauty rose (the most popular and prevalent strain of the time) was adopted as the symbol of American's California company, which also took the name "Beauty" for its brand of contemporary pictures.[3] In countless photos, publicity articles, and reviews, Margarita was touted as "the American Beauty," inextricably identified not only with the studio but also with a quintessential all–American attractiveness and appeal.

When she signed on with American's California studio, Margarita enjoyed her first taste of the star treatment through a studio's promotional machine. As the face of and main performer in an entire line of the studio's films, she was suddenly extremely important to its livelihood, and American therefore allocated a great deal of resources for producing and promoting her work. "I must say, they treated me wonderfully.... They made it a very happy engagement, and I was treated royally," the actress stated of her time with the young company.[4] Even before the release of the first Beauty film, the one-reel *Withering Roses*, on January 14, 1914, both it and Margarita were publicized in the most flattering terms. In one authoritatively worded article, the actress (erroneously dubbed "Margaret") was described as "the beautiful and famous exponent of the art of pantomime" who

> is ranked with the highest experts in the art of silent expression. Being far beyond the experimental stage, and having acquired perfection in technique, she is in a position to enter her new duties with her mind free to consider the ultimate possibilities of the parts assigned to her, and to bring out all there is in them.
>
> Miss Fischer shines particularly strong in romantic roles, but has also advanced so far into the realm of emotional work and tragedy that she must be considered among the leaders in that branch of the pantomimic art.[5]

Margarita's appearance received positive exposure as well, for a photo of her smiling, dramatically hatted face above an armful of pale roses (American Beauty, no doubt) often accompanied

The American Film Manufacturing Company used this rosy 1914 portrait to introduce Margarita Fischer as the star of the studio's new Beauty brand. Photograph by Witzel (courtesy the Margarita Fischer Papers, Special Collections and University Archives, Wichita State University Libraries).

such articles, and one news item called her "one of the most beautiful and charming actresses ever engaged for moving pictures."⁶

Advance hype for the first Beauty film itself, which costarred and was directed by Harry Pollard, was no less glowing, even if not the most creatively phrased. One article breathlessly stated, "Word just comes from the American studios that Harry Pollard's first production under the 'Beauty' brand is one of the most beautiful ever turned out, and the acting of Harry and the beautiful Marguerita [sic] Fischer is beautiful, too — all beautiful for the 'Beauty' brand, which is as it should be."⁷ The plot, another piece noted, was "a delightful fantasy" and "essentially an artistic production" in which a "selfish man [is caught in a] struggle between the machinations of his evil spirit and the refining influences of his sweetheart."⁸ Once *Withering Roses* was released, an item crowed that "Harry Pollard and Margarita Fischer of the Beauty brand are delighted with the reception accorded their first release.... It is doubtful whether any new brand has ever been so unanimously received as has this single reel, with its beautiful story and delicate handling."⁹ This first Beauty picture also featured a curious bit of stunt casting that drew additional attention; the couple's niece, Dorothy's daughter Kathrine Pyle, appeared in *Withering Roses* in the role of a crippled child under the name "Kathie Fischer."

No print of *Withering Roses* survives, so the film's lasting merit cannot be judged. In general, such brief films tended to be hastily produced (Margarita's filmmaking schedule for American in 1914 permitted little more than one week be given to each picture's production), and as such they may have possessed entertainment value but no lasting quality. Certainly, the temptation plot of *Withering Roses* sounds similar to that of other romantic dramas in which Margarita had performed in the past. However, Pollard, in his newly prominent role as director, apparently had an astute eye for presentation that set this film apart to some degree. News items noted the profuse use of flowers in the picture to create a romantic, dreamlike atmosphere, while Margarita's dual roles as Pollard's character's sweetheart and a fairy in a vision would have required the director to demonstrate a great deal of technical skill.¹⁰ Despite the quick filmmaking schedule, American gave its new stars the financial support and artistic license to add an extra spark of creativity to Beauty's one-reel productions. The young pair approached their work with an energy and enthusiasm that fairly leaps out of still photos and must have lifted these tales out of the realm of rote mediocrity when they were first screened for audiences.

Although the Pollards did not maintain their own press agents, their work was still promoted by the studio, and Margarita also sought to promote herself through news items and interviews. Additional items may have appeared independently of her efforts, due to her growing fame and fan interest in her — although never so many as those featuring stars who maintained a publicist. During the time she made one-reelers with Beauty, Margarita's publicity stressed her youth and glamour as well as her everywoman appeal, often resulting in decidedly unsubtle prose. One article informed its readers that "Margarita Fischer possesses one of the most lovable personalities on the screen. She has not one trace of snobbishness and is kindness personified — a charming little lady.... She is very popular and deserves her popularity."¹¹ Another, perhaps reacting to some recent news of contention, asserts, "Margarita Fischer of the American 'beauty' brand is now known as the 'American Girl,' and surely no more beautiful or delightful example of American femininity could possibly be found. If Margarita has any enemies, we do not know of them."¹² At the end of 1914, after artist Harrison Fisher

In this still from *Withering Roses* (1914), the first American Beauty film, Harry Pollard (left) is torn between the influences of Joe Harris as the "evil spirit" and Margarita as an angelic fairy (courtesy the Margarita Fischer Papers, Special Collections and University Archives, Wichita State University Libraries).

announced his ideal feminine beauty for 1915, an article appeared stressing the ways in which Margarita fit the standards of that famed illustrator of beautiful women. Her solemn portrait in a heart-shaped outline accompanied the somewhat muddled text pointing out her "perfect heart shaped face," her "round, oval chin," and her "even nose." "Miss Fisher [sic] fits perfectly the type of beauty described ... by the famous illustrator," the piece triumphantly concluded.[13]

The barrage of positive publicity drew a great deal of public attention to the actress, but the quality of her films kept the public's eye on her. American was known for the excellence of its comedies even before the Beauty brand was founded, and Beauty only solidified this reputation, as its films maintained the energy of earlier comic pictures but portrayed more complex characters and plots. The one-reelers released under this brand were sufficiently profitable to allow American to add a second Beauty production company to its fold.[14] The Pollards were key to the initial popularity of Beauty, since they exclusively personified the primary Beauty brand for almost a year. Margarita appeared in, and Harry Pollard directed (and often acted in), every film released under that brand from January to October 1914 — nearly forty pictures.[15] Margarita's and Beauty's reputations were captured in Robert Grau's 1914 history of filmmaking, *The Theatre of Science*, which ended with a short chapter on "Photoplay stars, authors, and directors — Interesting incidents in their stage and film careers." Margarita Fischer is one of the limited number of players profiled in this section; Grau recounts her life and career briefly, and commends her for her "flattering offer from the American Company and their alliance with the Mutual program under the new brand known as the Beauty series of film."[16]

As Margarita Fischer continued to put forth films on an almost weekly basis, the studio's positive publicity came true; she became a nationally familiar and beloved actress over the course of her early months with the studio. When *Photoplay* printed the results of a readers' poll of favorite stars in June 1914, Margarita Fischer was the winner of "Photoplay Magazine's greatest popularity contest," with 318,100 votes, more than forty thousand more than the runner-up, Selig's Kathlyn Williams. Mabel Normand and Mary Pickford ranked third and fourth in the final results, close behind Williams in numbers of votes. "The wonderful enthusiasm shown by movie fans made this a victory worth winning, one that indicates the great loyalty of photoplay lovers for their favorite actress," noted the poll's accompanying text. The contest "was won for Miss Fischer by her friends, and for their loyalty she is deeply grateful."[17] Margarita received double publicity from this issue of the popular fan magazine, as her image also appeared on the cover of the magazine in the form of the Beauty logo, her face within a rose. These poll results are all the more impressive not only because of Margarita's lack of a personal press agent to create ballyhoo, but also in comparison to Pickford's popularity at that time: since the March 1914 release of *Tess of the Storm Country*, the high-earning actress had been featured as "America's Sweetheart," and the film had given her stardom a great boost.[18]

Affectionate fan letters flooded in for Margarita from men and women alike — some analyzing her talent, some admiring her onscreen presence, others merely odd. One appreciative man who had followed her career for years wrote the actress, "Your most wonderful talent attracted my attention when you were on the legitimate [stage].... Kindly allow me to say that you are the most beautiful actress in the films, today. I do not think that there is any one who can surpass you in character parts. You are so natural in every part you portray before the camera."[19] The young daughter of a theater owner congratulated Margarita on her lead in the *Photoplay* contest and added, "They certainly named you correctly when they call you the American Beauty. I think you are the most beautiful actress on the motion picture screen.... The nights we have [your films showing] means a couple hundred more people than the ordinary."[20] Besides commenting on her looks and talent, Margarita's fans felt close personal connections with her; one older female fan noted, "I know you are kind, for it shows in every action."[21] At this stage of her career, Margarita still read each fan letter and even commented on some. One of the more bizarre letters she saved eagerly demanded a reply, not just once but three times, and explained:

> I had a dream of you last night, I was looking into your eyes and they were of a hazel color & your hair was dark. My eyes are hazel, & my hair is auburn in color. Dreams come true sometimes & I think that what I saw in that dream was true, I mean about the eyes & hair.[22]

Having received fan mail since her teenage touring days, Margarita treated this lightly, scrawling jokingly across the top of the letter, "I think this must be my affinity, ha! ha! ho! ho! he! he!" Most fan mail she took quite seriously, though, often replying personally to questions, and sending signed photographs in response to frequent fan requests — which represented a substantial investment, since stars had to pay for their own stills.[23]

Not surprisingly, Margarita also took a personal interest in the way her work was publicized for moviegoers, particularly in the California theaters that also boasted a connection to her days on the stage. The manager of San Francisco's Grand Theatre, a familiar sight from her touring days in the area, sent photographs of the theater's front in response to the actress's request to see how her publicity stills and film posters were being displayed. He added, "You and the Beauty films are growing more and more popular every day with our patrons."[24] The canny star jumped on the opening offered by this cordial note and sent the manager what he described as "two very fine enlargements of yourself" that he thought "will be an added attraction to our lobby display."[25]

These early months with American must have been a happy time for Margarita Fischer; she was constantly portrayed and perceived as talented and beautiful, and she was working with her husband, making popular films that allowed them to take some creative stretches. Harry Pollard almost certainly did not mind that his wife was better known than he was; besides his preference for stage acting and his growing interest in the technical aspects of filmmaking, he and Margarita enjoyed a modern type of marriage, a "companionate" union of equals in which each maintained an individual identity along with their individual names. Though fans knew of their marriage and commented on it in letters, attention was never drawn to it in their film publicity, and Margarita was always referred to in the press as "Miss Fischer."[26] The quantity of their work indicates that the pair truly enjoyed making movies together. Whenever the husband appeared in a Beauty picture, it was as the wife's leading man. By August 1914 he had married her or fallen in love with her on film in, among others, *The Wife, The Sacrifice, A Flurry in Hats, Her Heritage, The Professor's Awakening,* and *The Courting of Prudence*.[27] In *A Modern Othello,* the pair gleefully revisited Shakespeare, though with even less faithfulness than in Margarita's 1910 Selig picture *Romeo and Juliet in Town*: author Robert Hamilton Ball describes this one-reeler as merely "a comedy of modern life involving a jealous husband."[28]

Filmmaking at Beauty's Santa Barbara home was also a delightful change for the young couple from the bitterness of Chicago winters and the pressing heat of Arizona. Santa Barbara enjoyed a perpetual spring, only a mile from the California coast, and actors longed for the location shooting that represented an excuse to get out into the beautiful weather and sometimes even shoulder into the nearby millionaires' mansions for a look at their exotic possessions. "There were so many beautiful homes there," Margarita explained impishly. "They all had caretakers, and they would open their mansions and let us go in. And we could roam all over. One man was a bachelor, and he had a little room on the top, a round room, with a round sofa in it, and pillows and everything — very much the Turkish style."[29] American's management actually developed a rule against location shooting by 1917, since, according to the actress, its directors "didn't work as hard when we were out on location. They didn't finish as quick as they did [when shooting in the studio] because everybody left to go and it was a picnic, really."[30] Overall, "we played more than we worked" in Santa Barbara, and "there was plenty to do for entertainment," including viewing the productions of touring theatrical companies not unlike those with which Margarita had begun her career.[31] On days off, the press reported, the Pollards liked to go "motoring" in Margarita's "beautiful automobile" — a growing fascination of hers now that the pair enjoyed financial security — and enjoyed more of the sights of Southern California.³² As American was geographically set apart from other California studios, "that was a holiday when I went down to Los Angeles," the actress explained.³³

Working for American in the mid–1910s was a unique experience in the filmmaking world, which as a whole had been competitive since the formation of the Trust. American was known in trade circles for its "spirit of cooperation" and "fair treatment of every employee" (as trade magazine *Moving Picture World* noticed), and Margarita valued this congenial atmosphere.³⁴ She found most members of the studio's leadership to be "very nice people," and would remain friendly with general manager R. R. Nehls for years after leaving the film industry. Among her fellow players at the studio, despite the unavoidable competition for parts and publicity, "I never remember any ugliness of any kind with any of the stars. There was never any *mean* jealousy, ever."³⁵ Working off of the principle that "Most people are good if you're good to them," Margarita was gleeful and effortlessly energetic as she and her husband turned out their increasingly popular pictures.³⁶

Family ties made the Beauty filmmaking process still more pleasant for Margarita. Dorothy, divorced since 1910, settled with her daughter in Santa Barbara and began building a new life in connection with Margarita and her husband. By 1914, the devout Dorothy had found a Catholic church in Santa Barbara for herself and her child; Kathie actually marched

Family connections made filmmaking a joy for Margarita Fischer. She was joined in *A Midsummer's Love Tangle* (American [Beauty], 1914) by her husband (center), her niece Kathie, and her sister Dorothy (made up to look matronly). About to throw the book at them all is actor Fred Gamble as the father of Margarita's character (courtesy the Margarita Fischer Papers, Special Collections and University Archives, Wichita State University Libraries).

in the boys' band there (the church had no girls' band) and eventually went to convent school, with tuition paid by Margarita.[37] Under Margarita's guidance, mother and daughter entered pictures as well. The actress's sister and niece appeared with her and Pollard in *A Modern Othello*; in fact, Margarita worked with them continually throughout much of 1914. After Kathie's successful turn as the crippled child in *Withering Roses*, the six-year-old appeared with her aunt whenever a child's role needed to be filled. She played Margarita Fischer's young sister in the second Beauty picture, *Fooling Uncle*; two weeks later she acted the part of "a naughty little girl" in the slapstick romantic comedy *Peggy's Elopement* (retitled *Sally's Elopement* upon release).[38] Kathie demonstrated as precocious a talent as had her aunt; in *The Sacrifice*, released on February 18, 1914, she won praise for her "really remarkable and wholly natural" performance as the son of a poor Italian couple (played by her aunt and uncle) who sent their child away to be educated by affluent relatives.[39] She again played a waifish child in *Her "Really" Mother*, leaving a negligent parent and finding a true "mother" in the person of a neighbor woman, a lonely writer.[40]

Not all of Kathie's contributions to her aunt's films, however, were as smooth as they appeared to be on film — for either the child or her relatives. As an Italian child in *The Sacrifice*, she had to be made up quite a bit — not just to look like a boy, but to cloak her pale coloring (rather than inheriting her mother's black hair and gray eyes, Kathie had her father Charles Pyle's blonde hair and blue eyes, both of which appeared even lighter on film).[41] The first time she played a boy's role, too, she had trouble acting "boyish" enough. Attempting to help the child get into character, her beloved uncle Harry told her to "spit in her hands and fight like a man." The young child, misunderstanding her uncle's unaccustomed toughness, spit in her hand with such force that "she had all the spit running out of it," Kathie's daughter Margarita Kotselis recounted.[42] Later, when filming *The Divinity of Motherhood* in the fall of 1914, Kathie played the role of Cupid and sat on a rooftop for day after day of filming with wings taped to her back. "When they took the tape off, she was sunburned so badly it would rip the skin off, and then she'd go back and do it again the next day," said Kotselis. "As young as she was, she remembered [that]" in later years.[43]

Dorothy Fischer Pyle probably began her own Beauty career in an unidentified role in *Sally's Elopement* under the stage name "Mary Scott."[44] Two and a half months later, she played the mother of her younger sister's character in *A Flurry in Hats*, and over the next five months she played other matronly characters.[45] While Kathie's relationship to her famous aunt was stressed by her stage name, Dorothy's even closer relationship to Margarita was hidden. The name "Mary Scott" was certainly chosen to hide her identity, perhaps so that her daughter could more easily become identified with the famous Margarita Fischer. Oddly enough, Dorothy's ex-husband would also become a part of the film industry before the end of the decade. Charles Pyle worked for the short-lived Commonwealth Pictures in 1917 before eventually moving into the sales and sports promotion that would eventually bring him his greatest renown.[46]

It seems extremely unlikely that Dorothy, not even two years older than Margarita, could have appeared her mother or even much her elder without stage makeup, but the determined youthfulness of Margarita's own casting hints at her emergent concerns about aging. In mid–1914, her thirtieth birthday loomed less than a year and a half away, and she had been acutely aware of the unforgiving, youth-focused nature of the acting profession since celebrating her "nineteenth" birthday for the second time eight years before. Her former IMP costar, King Baggot, stated in a 1914 interview that "One of the greatest fears that a person in my profession has, it that of old age. The motion picture camera is heartless.... To the hero of the movies, there is an element of tragedy in the public's insistant demand for a youthful idol. Age dims the glamour, which has been built up around him [sic]."[47] Lying about one's age was a common practice among actors, perhaps exacerbated by the unforgiving camera. As Lillian Gish wrote later, "The camera was heartless; it exaggerated.... [S]ometimes the harsh cameras made a fourteen-year-old seem an old hag." As a result, "Children of fourteen and fifteen often played parts far beyond their experience or understanding" and thus became competition for older actresses — no doubt only intensifying the preoccupation with age that film actors developed.[48] Margarita understood and shared this concern with youthfulness, and she took particular pains to shape her publicity after inquiries about the relationship between Margarita and Kathie Fischer began to appear in fan magazines. One item that must have appeared in a "letters to the editor" column of such a periodical stated that "Kathie Fischer of the Beauty Company is Margarita Fischer's niece, not her daughter. Mercy, Margarita isn't old enough for that."[49] The actress gradually revised her age over the next year; by March 1915, when her first feature film was released, she had dropped five or six years from her age and was "23 or 24" in publicity material.[50]

Margarita's unsettled feelings about her age could have been amplified by changes in the film industry in 1915 and by pressures from her studio. Thanks in part to the success of her Beauty brand, American had prospered. By the fall of 1915, the studio had built a firm reputation on comedic and dramatic shorts, releasing eight or nine films every week and reaching a size second only to that of Universal.[51] Beginning in the spring of 1914, though, Harry Aitken, the co-president of American's distributor, Mutual (he shared those duties with John Freuler, who also served as co-president of the American studio with Samuel Hutchinson), had begun personally bankrolling what had become an expensive white elephant titled *The Clansman*, directed by D. W. Griffith.[52] Mutual's board of directors had been nervous about the unprecedented scale of the film — planned for twelve reels, it would be more than double the length of most films being produced — and declined to finance it, so Aitken provided the initial estimated budget of $25,000. Indeed, the picture's cost eventually spiraled to $61,000, plus $30,000 more for printing, advertising, and distribution, though Griffith raised the difference needed since, according to the film's star Lillian Gish, he was too embarrassed to ask Aitken for more money.[53]

This decision to finance a film personally may have opened or exacerbated a rift between Aitken and the similarly risk-taking Samuel Hutchinson, who, as a studio head of American, was at this time developing American's first feature-length film. Titled *The Quest*, the picture boasted Margarita Fischer and Harry Pollard as stars, and Harry Pollard as director. The picture was probably shot and completed in the latter half of 1914, but Harry Aitken refused to allow its release. He explained, "It's risqué.... Our policy is clean pictures for clean people. I've written Hutchinson that if he doesn't clean up his pictures, we'll refuse to distribute them through Mutual."[54] American's famed "spirit of cooperation" may well have remained present among its staff of actors and crew, but it now began to crumble between studio leaders. Hutchinson's response to this slight against his judgment was to foster a rumor of Aitken's financial insolvency among the studio staff. This inevitably created hostility between Aitken and the American Film Manufacturing Company, which was further intensified when the cautious John Freuler, a partner to both Hutchinson through American and Aitken through Mutual, declined to take any mediating steps. As a result, Harry Aitken formed an entirely new distributorship, Epoch, in partnership with D. W. Griffith, in order to shepherd the release of their pet project, *The Clansman*.[55]

Aitken's and Griffith's financial gamble, now entirely separated from American and Mutual, paid off with an unimaginable degree of success. In February 1915, the release of Griffith's epic — soon to be retitled *The Birth of a Nation* — shook up the film industry and forced a drastic revision of the medium's capabilities. The lengthy film starred familiar faces from Griffith's earlier pictures (such as Lillian Gish, Mae Marsh, and Robert Harron) and boasted high production values and a huge cast in its heart-pounding battles, touching reenactments of the events surrounding Lincoln's death, and star-crossed but ultimately triumphant North-South romances.[56] Audiences, as well as critics, were in awe of the sheer scope of the three-hour film. "The hand of Griffith overshadows all," breathed a reviewer in the *New York Dramatic Mirror*. "Telling his story fearlessly and masterfully, at times he cuts deep beneath the skin, till one must question the brutality while praising the art.... If there is to be a greater picture than *The Birth of a Nation*, may we live to see it."[57] While criticized today — and even by some contemporaries, including the NAACP — for portraying African-Americans negatively and romanticizing the Ku Klux Klan, the film remains technically brilliant, so far ahead of its time in terms of directing and editing methods that its construction still appears essentially modern after more than nine decades. Contemporary audiences were stunned by the film and turned out to see it in record-breaking numbers. According to star Lillian Gish, the epic made back its entire cost in two months at a single New York theater, and grossed $3.75 million in New York City alone by the end of 1915.[58]

"*The Birth of a Nation* was cinematic revolution," wrote film historian Kevin Brownlow in later years. "No well-informed person could allow himself to ignore it. The intelligentsia ... conceded at last that the film had value. With critics and writers embroiled in controversy, the middle classes went to see for themselves. And more important still, the men who controlled the business grew ambitious again."[59] *The Birth of a Nation* was far from the first feature film (one of at least five reels); studios had been regularly producing films of this length since 1912.[60] Still, its unprecedented length inspired other studios to expand the scope of their storytelling. Recognizing the public's ready appetite for unique and ambitious films, American, too, again turned its eyes toward feature filmmaking. The studio had produced films longer than one reel since 1913, although its first attempt at producing a feature film, *The Quest*, had initially proved fruitless.

However, with the release of *The Birth of a Nation* and its attendant expansion of the scope of cinematic storytelling — as well as the exacerbation of the breach between Aitken and the leadership of American — Samuel Hutchinson took another look at *The Quest* and decided that it could be released after all. The completed film was slated to become the first of a series released under the brand name "Masterpictures" in order to evoke D. W. Griffith's nickname of "the Master." Harry Aitken still remained opposed to the film's release, and after a battle of wills between the heads of American and Mutual, Mutual released *The Quest* in March 1915 and forced Aitken out of Mutual's presidency, electing a new president in May.[61] This left the distributor under more harmonious but less ambitious leadership, and also hurt it financially, for when Aitken departed, he took with him from Mutual the right to distribute the films of American's sister studios. The distribution company sought but failed to keep additional talent to fill this gap, and over the next two years it came to depend heavily on American's films to keep it afloat, placing great strain on the studio's production staff.[62] Aitken, meanwhile, formed the instantly respected Triangle Film Corporation with directors D. W. Griffith, Mack Sennett, and Thomas Ince. Based in New York, the successful studio drew its actors in part from the pool of theatrical luminaries in the area, and it released hundreds of films over the next few years (until it disbanded in 1920), including Griffith's *Intolerance* and many more popular Lillian Gish pictures.[63]

Margarita Fischer and Harry Pollard were probably intimately familiar with these studio machinations, since their work was so closely connected to the conflict between Hutchinson and Aitken. *The Quest* may have merely been a convenient excuse for these too-similar personalities to clash openly, but once a split had taken place, much rode for American on the success of the Pollards' film. They could not take this success for granted from a technical standpoint: Austin Lescarboura, a film writer who scripted a book-length analysis of the technical aspects of filmmaking only a few years later, noted, "Of the hundreds of leading players of the films, one can count on the fingers of one's two hands the players who can play in and direct their own productions."[64] Pollard had been balancing the two roles with agility for some time, but *The Quest* was of unprecedented length and scope, and it had tested his abilities to a new degree. *The Quest* revisited the themes of cross-class love and warring impulses used in earlier shorts such as *Withering Roses* and *Draga, the Gypsy*. The feature told the story of John Douglas (Harry Pollard), a world-weary millionaire who survives a shipwreck and comes ashore on an unspoiled island. He falls in love with Nai (Margarita Fischer), a chieftain's daughter, and they elope (perhaps the plot point Aitken found "risqué," since the elopement would of necessity take place without benefit of conventional clergy). The couple lives in peaceful seclusion until John's friends arrive to "rescue" him and his bride. Back in civilization, John sees the harm and degradation that come to Nai in the polite society of his world. Fortunately, this return journey proves to have been a dream, and, much relieved, he determines at last to live always with Nai's tribe.[65]

Filming *The Quest* proved to be an adventure, and not merely because its running time was to be twice that of any other film the Pollards had yet made. The role of Nai's exotic tribal home was played by rugged Santa Cruz Island, approximately 20 miles off the coast of Santa Barbara. As Margarita explained later, a good location like Santa Cruz was difficult to find, since California's natural scenery had been so well-catalogued over the last half-decade of filmmaking that "almost every place that lends itself to picture background has been shot to death."[66] Santa Cruz island, however, was as yet still fresh, rarely filmed, "wild and mountainous," unsettled, and blessed with tropical-looking plant life, dramatic waterfalls, and placid lakes. The optimistic cast and crew soon found the island to be even more untamed and rugged than they had expected. Margarita had to be tied to her husband and his assistant director for safety when climbing a mountain for the shoot, and the crew had to live "primitively" due to the island's lack of lodging. In order to pad out the provisions they had brought, they fished and shot some of the island's numerous feral pigs. "All in all," concluded an article about the film's production, "the entire company was glad to get back to civilization."[67]

Studio upheavals aside, the results of this trying shoot were well worth the effort, for the picture received uniformly positive reviews upon its release. *The Quest*, stated a reviewer from the illustrious trade magazine *Moving Picture World*, boasted three major strengths: the first was "the surpassing natural scenic beauties of the exteriors, the second was the continuous grip of the story, and the third — though not at all subordinate to either of the preceding ... — was the talented acting of the principals in the cast." Besides Pollard's careful direction and set design (which had been created with "artistic taste"), he was judged to have performed "the best photodramatic work I have seen him do." Margarita herself was lauded for her versatility after a year of Beauty's light comedies, with her "bewitching" and natural performance noted (in a somewhat back-handed compliment) as "proof positive that she is an actress of much greater ability and versatility than had been supposed." Singled out for particular praise was a scene in which the innocent, frightened Nai knocks the shipwrecked John Douglas unconscious with a rock upon meeting him, and a later scene in which she frantically attempts to remove the Western clothes in which she has been dressed.[68] Critics did disagree over the "twist ending" of Nai's trip to society being revealed as a dream, a favored method of the Pollards for representing alternate courses of action, beginning with *Withering Roses*. This trick was much-loved by *Moving Picture World*, which found it to involve "both art and good judgment," but was disliked by more ethnocentric reviewers, one of whom had, perhaps, not grasped the parameters of the dream sequence, and thus found it "wofully [sic] disappointing" that "the two characters who have won your sympathy and admiration elect to forego civilization and return to the tribe and savagery."[69]

Serendipitously, among the long catalogue of Margarita Fischer's lost performances, a single reel of *The Quest* survives, including the pivotal section where the innocent Nai first encounters the shipwrecked Westerner. This fragment permits a glimpse of American's production values in this "Masterpicture," as well as another very different characterization by Margarita and one of Harry Pollard's few surviving performances as an actor. Margarita does not have a taxing job in this early portion of the film; her Nai prances athletically around her rugged island home with a crude harp, taking delight in her surroundings — the fresh sea breezes, the texture of sand, a decorative rope of seaweed. She is the pet of the village, a credibly large grouping of grass-roofed huts peopled by bearded men (looking somewhat Nazarean, with long hair, robes, and sandals), long-haired women, and happy, tunic-wearing children — including Kathie Fischer as an assistant to the tribal priest in a protective ceremony for the tribe's hunters. Greatly aided by the dramatic landscape, the film maintains a consistent primitive look — Biblical, with touches of the tropical in its grasses, jewelry, and fruits. Indeed, the tribe's English-speaking status and maintenance of a priest suggests a mainland Christian background, although these possible origins are not explored in the surviving portion of the film (though if they were touched on in other parts of the feature, it would seem to undermine Harry Aitken's objections to the film's immorality).

A common thread of joy runs through this, as well as Margarita's earlier performances for Selig or Universal. While always remaining in character, her delight welled up from within and shone out of her eager face; she simply enjoyed making films. Nai's wide-eyed glee and innocence are so believably established that her reactions to the appearance of John Douglas seem only natural: she first tries to rescue the exhausted man, but when he emerges from the surf, she is unnerved by his unfamiliar appearance and flees from him. When he pursues her,

5. Mlle. La Mode

Still from *The Quest* (American, 1915), Margarita Fischer and Harry Pollard's first feature–length film. Margarita as Nai, the chieftain's daughter, shows her father (Joseph Singleton, at left) and several curious villagers the mysterious shipwrecked stranger (Harry Pollard), whom she has just subdued with a rock. Kathie Fischer is peering over her aunt's shoulder at right (courtesy the Margarita Fischer Papers, Special Collections and University Archives, Wichita State University Libraries).

she reacts instinctively to protect herself by knocking him unconscious; but once he is lying still and is again nonthreatening, she wishes once more to help him. The prone shipwreck victim is brought into the village, and Nai watches curiously but secretively over him as he recovers, again fleeing every time he begins to pursue her. In the role of her would-be lover, Harry Pollard fairly shines with good humor. For a millionaire shipwrecked on a deserted island, he displays no temper (perhaps because he is occupied with thoughts of his "dream girl," Nai), but rather remarkable inventiveness as he figures out how to shave without razor, strop, or mirror. He repeatedly reaches out to Nai admiringly and without hurt at her fear of him. Douglas may not have tested Pollard's skill as an actor very much, but he probably preferred the directorial side of making *The Quest* anyway — and as the director, he led the picture in leaps all over Santa Cruz Island, taking full advantage of the craggy, exotic island to tell his fish-out-of-water love story.[70]

Margarita had begun her career playing ingénues, and at the age of twenty-nine — or "23 or 24," according to her publicity — she still generally based her screen reputation on wholesome, elegant, sympathetic characters. This type of work continued to find favor with film critics; *Moving Picture World*'s glowing review of her presence in *The Quest* is evidence of that.[71] Margarita's publicity material, too, remained high-profile and positive. A lengthy fan magazine cover article in mid–1915 described her as an accomplished actress "with the ability to excite tears as easily as she can command distinction in the heaviest dramatic roles," as well as a beautiful, magnetic, fashion-conscious, and somewhat conventional young woman, "blessed with a happy disposition," "not a great reader" or athlete, who made "clean, clever comedies," did not like "morbid pictures," and was most fulfilled when she "[did] a great good in a modest, artistic and womanly manner."[72] While this seems a bit of an exaggeration for the determined Margarita, the article's conclusion seems quite apt for her varied screen portrayals: "The secret of the bold Miss Fischer" concluded the author, "is that she is HAPPY and wants to disseminate happiness, and to see her is to make those about her happy, too."[73]

Happy she was, as she and her husband had built enviable careers at a respected studio. In early 1915, however, at about the time American's leadership came into serious conflict with Mutual's, a new type of female role began to dominate the screen. Margarita's wholesome image was no match for the heated publicity surrounding the film industry's newest fixation, the mysterious and extremely modern Theda Bara, who had burst onto the screen in January 1915 as "the Vampire" in Fox studio's *A Fool There Was*. Bara's was a new kind of stardom. Rather than building her name gradually through a series of popular films, as had Margarita Fischer, her persona was created out of whole cloth and marketed to the public before she ever appeared in a movie. Producer William Fox "exposed" her (fictitious) exotic and decadent offscreen life and sent the actress on a publicity tour in late 1914; by the time *A Fool There Was* found room in theaters, Bara was already a familiar face to moviegoers, irrevocably tied to an illicit, seductive image.[74]

The film was almost an afterthought to the hype, a somewhat hastily made six-reeler inspired by a Rudyard Kipling poem entitled "The Vampire" (which Margarita had filmed five years before as a one-reeler for Selig). *A Fool There Was* told the story of a sensual, evil woman who debases a series of lovers. During the opening minutes of the movie, a shattered lover cries, "You have ruined me, you devil, and now you discard me!" and commits suicide while traveling with her on an ocean liner. The Vampire at once turns her attention to another passenger, a diplomat, who quickly and eagerly abandons his family and succumbs to her exotic charms. In the film's characteristic final scene, the unrepentant Vampire strews her lover's decrepit form with rose petals during his dying moments.[75] Bara's turbaned, heavy-lidded countenance urged audiences to "Kiss me, my Fool," and people across the country flocked to see her ambitious, sexual, evil characterization. The film was generally well-reviewed and proved one of 1915's most popular pictures, doing enough business to pull the fledgling Fox studio out of debt.

Bara—who, like Margarita Fischer, was by the mid–1910s shaving a few years off of her true age—continued to play similarly wicked characters throughout her short film career, unwittingly introducing into the American lexicon the word "vamp" as a term for a seductive, predatory woman.[76] "The vamp was a woman gone astray, a parasite woman who could feed off the solid stock of America, destroying the vital future it should have," says author Janet Staiger. "The character of the vamp seems almost to be merely a foil for an extensive examination of the power of sex, women's rights in this new age, and the crumbling belief in the assertion that some nineteenth-century notions of the family's behavior were still pertinent for twentieth-century America."[77] This new way of depicting womankind proved to be extremely popular. Tempting, sinful female characters appeared in films through the remainder of the silent era, played by such high-profile actresses as Alla Nazimova in *Salome* (1922), Nita Naldi in *Blood and Sand* (1922) and *The Ten Commandments* (1923), Margaret Livingston in *Sunrise* (1927), and Greta Garbo in *The Temptress* (1926) and *Flesh and the Devil* (1927).[78]

Margarita Fischer's comment about disliking "morbid pictures" could well have been a direct response to the success of *A Fool There Was* and its imitators. To embrace the wicked new persona would have required her to retool her image, for though she was known for her great range, she had hardly ever played such an unredeemed character. Besides her own role in *The Vampire*, the closest she may have come to playing a "vamp" role was probably that of the con artist in the early IMP short *A Lesson to Husbands*. Her temptress in that film was financially motivated rather than preternaturally cruel, though, and family values were firmly validated in the end. The actress's screen portrayals in the mid–teens were more similar to those of Mary Pickford, who, though bested by Margarita in the 1914 *Photoplay* popularity poll, was building her reputation as "America's Sweetheart" through scrappy and sweet performances in the spirited, youthful title roles of films such as *Tess of the Storm Country* (1914), *Cinderella* (1914), *Mistress Nell* (1915), and *Rags* (1915).[79]

Margarita Fischer, the "American Beauty," followed her own portrayal of the innocent Nai in *The Quest* with the Pickford-esque role of the teenaged "Samanthy, an orphan" in another Masterpicture, *The Lonesome Heart*. A two-page ad for the film, directed by future Paramount notable William Desmond Taylor, featured photographs obviously playing on the Pickford image, though American's star looked credibly youthful in the role. On one page, a grim-faced matron scowls down at a grinning, oblivious Margarita giving a "horsey ride" to a younger orphan (played by Kathie Fischer) who uses the older actress's long braids as reins. On the other page, a wistful, daydreaming Margarita in braids and ill-fitting gingham leans on a mop that symbolizes the drudgery of her life.[80] Margarita offered a revealing comment about the pressures of these films in a small publicity article: "Now that I have appeared in my second Masterpicture, ... I look back with some amusement on our trepidation over undertaking the first.... I am as proud as I can be over being the first star to appear in one."[81]

Her next film was yet another Masterpicture, the cross-class love story *The Girl from His Town*.[82] In this film, Margarita left Pickford's territory and returned to an adult role, playing a small-town girl with a wonderful singing voice who is lifted to fame and fortune after an influential agent hears her performing at a church social. Always beloved by the scion of her hometown's wealthiest family, she can only accept his true devotion (not exactly a bitter pill to swallow) after she gains recognition in her own right — and after friends step in to help her realize her own feelings for him. Margarita and the other cast members had great fun making this picture, which called for her "diva" to perform throughout the film and required director Pollard to shoot in an actual theater. Los Angeles's Republic Theater stood in for London's Gaiety, host to the film's pivotal performance. The cast and crew, with the help of the chorus of the show "Champagne Belles" and a theater full of audience member volunteers, shot from nine at night to 4:30 in the morning. Margarita herself enjoyed being up on a stage in front of a live audience again, and shooting was hindered only briefly by the panicked escape of her resentful bow-bedecked bulldog, Peter the Great.[83]

This film also gave Margarita an opportunity to demonstrate the dancing skills developed in her vaudeville days. Ads featured her prominently in ballerina dress, and one article singled out the technical excellence of a unique double exposure in which Pollard blended

images of a speeding car's polished body with the "terpsichorean movements" of "sprightly" Margarita.[84] *Moving Picture World* found this film to be "the hit of her film career thus far." Stated reviewer James McQuade (who had also reviewed Margarita's performance in *The Quest*), "If you ask me to commend to you a clean, absorbing photodrama, with not one, but several punches of the virile kind in it, and with a star that is not only bewitchingly beautiful from toes to finger tips, but endowed with photodramatic talent that enables her fairly to live the part, I need go no farther than *The Girl from His Town*."[85]

Still, Margarita could not compete directly with the popularity of Mary Pickford. Although her fan support had exceeded that of the doe-eyed, golden-curled actress the previous year, it was clear by the end of the summer of 1915 that Pickford, six years younger than Margarita, had become film audiences' preferred ingénue. Her characters' combinations of "cuteness," wholesomeness, and optimism in downtrodden circumstances resounded with the public's "nostalgic ideals of femininity," in the words of film historian Gaylyn Studlar.[86] At the 1914 release of *Tess of the Storm Country*, Pickford had been billed on a marquee as "America's Sweetheart" for the first time. The film was a huge success, and its star soon began earning two thousand dollars per week for her subsequent portrayals of spirited Tess-like child-women. Within a year, the success of Pickford's movies justified the doubling of this salary to an unprecedented four thousand dollars weekly.[87] Margarita, who worked under contract for a studio whose leadership was currently in upheaval, earned less than one-fourth of Mary Pickford's salary in 1915.[88]

"[Pickford] is Everywoman much more wholeheartedly than her lesser rivals," observed film writer (and, eventually, first film curator of New York's Museum of Modern Art) Iris Barry a few years later. "She is not an actress but an incarnate idea, the flame round which every woman's desire circles mothlike. Indeed her only rivals are the Bad Women."[89] Margarita decided not to "circle mothlike" around Mary Pickford anymore. Nor, however, did she wish to play an unredeemed "Bad Woman" type in the vein of Theda Bara, although looks that appeared dark on film, as hers did, had become associated with the sensual exoticism of the vamp. While she did not cultivate this association, it undermined her ability to draw attention in the light, youthful roles upon which both she and Pickford had built their careers.

Too dark to be an ingénue in Pickford's mold, but too wholesome to play a vamp, Margarita Fischer stood at a crossroads in her career in 1915. She had found that she was highly successful—both in creating a good product for critics, and deriving satisfaction from the moviemaking process—when she made movies that suited her creative, versatile persona, such as *The Quest* and even *The Girl from His Town*. With the boundaries of filmmaking being pushed ever farther, with roles for women diversifying, with films growing in length and prestige, she had the opportunity to change the type of work she was putting before audiences—a risky but necessary move if she wanted to remain relevant as an actress. After releasing *The Girl from His Town* in early August 1915, Margarita prepared to deepen her image, making changes in her acting career that shaped it as much as had her decision to leave the stage five years before.

Opposite: In *The Lonesome Heart* (American, 1915), Margarita attempted the type of scrappy orphan characterization that so often meant success for Mary Pickford, though she soon became interested in pursuing more dramatic stories. Here she gives a "horsey ride" to a younger orphan (Kathie Fischer) while Lucille Ward looks grimly on (courtesy the Margarita Fischer Papers, Special Collections and University Archives, Wichita State University Libraries).

6

The Dangerous Talent

"'The movies' have become the most popular entertainment of the country, nay of the world, and their influence is one of the strongest social energies of our time," asserted psychologist Hugo Münsterberg in 1916. "Nobody can foresee the ways which the new art of the photoplay will open, but everybody ought to recognize even today that it is worth while to ... make the art of the film a medium for an original creative expression of our time."[1] Münsterberg's observation was inspired by the same issues that, only a year earlier, prodded Margarita Fischer to alter the course of her career — that is, technological innovation, audience response, and the changing nature of onscreen appeal. Both actress and academic reached the conclusion that despite these changes in filmgoing habits — or perhaps because of them — film had a unique power to instruct its eager viewers. "The social reformer," stated Münsterberg, "ought to focus his interest ... on the tremendous influences for good which may be exerted by the moving pictures."[2] With Bara the vamp and Pickford the sweetheart respectively entertaining the public with sexuality and innocence, Margarita Fischer chose to set herself apart from both, taking the "new art" in a new direction by investing herself in fewer, more complex, and more controversial films with strong social messages.

She had first shown an interest in exploring moral issues when making Beauty pictures in 1914. Although these dealt mainly with light romantic subjects, one short film, *The Divinity of Motherhood*, incorporated anti-abortion principles based on Margarita Fischer's Catholic beliefs into its plot. Released in November 1914, the picture recounted the tale of a young wife who is horrified and distraught to find out that she is pregnant, fearful of the life changes to come. She dreams, though, of her child being raised in an environment where he is not wanted, growing up bitter and resentful and blaming his mother for his wasted life "as a result of rebellion against her duty," as publicity material said. The wife wakes, repents of her reluctance, and gives her husband the news of their impending parenthood.[3] Despite its unusual subject matter, *The Divinity of Motherhood* received no special attention among the Fischer-Pollard Beauty shorts, probably because the film's subtle pro-life message was watered down by the picture's heavy sentimentality and euphemistic symbolism. Stills from the film show the couple meeting in "The Garden of Love" and being watched over by Cupid; at the film's end they connect through Cupid to a telephone switchboard of baby names.[4]

The film's subject was trenchant nonetheless; the distribution of contraception became illegal in the 1870s, and abortion became illegal at around the same time, but the "New Woman" of the 1910s desired freedom from the frequent pregnancies and high mother and child mortality rates endured by previous generations. The national birthrate declined in the first decades of the twentieth century, demonstrating that women did indeed use various contraceptive methods, but the illegality of such practices often resulted in ignorance, secrecy, and poorer medical treatment.[5] Public health nurse Margaret Sanger distributed information about contraception beginning in 1912 with the hope of decreasing birth rates in a manner that would not compromise women's health, and in 1916 she opened the nation's first family planning clinic, although it was quickly closed by police.[6]

These and other percolating social issues recaptured the Pollards' attention in late 1915, when their careers had taken a permanent turn into feature-length filmmaking, and motivated them to make the first of their more challenging films. The September release *Infatuation*, a romantic melodrama that hinted at the destructive effects of alcoholism, displayed a budding social consciousness that provided experience for more incisive pictures to come. In a plot foreshadowing his own eventual career path, Pollard starred opposite his wife as an actor who develops a drinking problem and cannot find work. Margarita played the daughter of a strict railroad president, who loves the self-absorbed actor and tries to bring him back to health. The film's message about the destructiveness of alcoholism was undermined by a contrived happy ending in which "the girl's purity and genius for loving transforms the man of common clay into a real hero."[7] (Only a few years later, the couple would themselves be faced with this problem, and they may have looked back in envy at the film's tidy ending.)

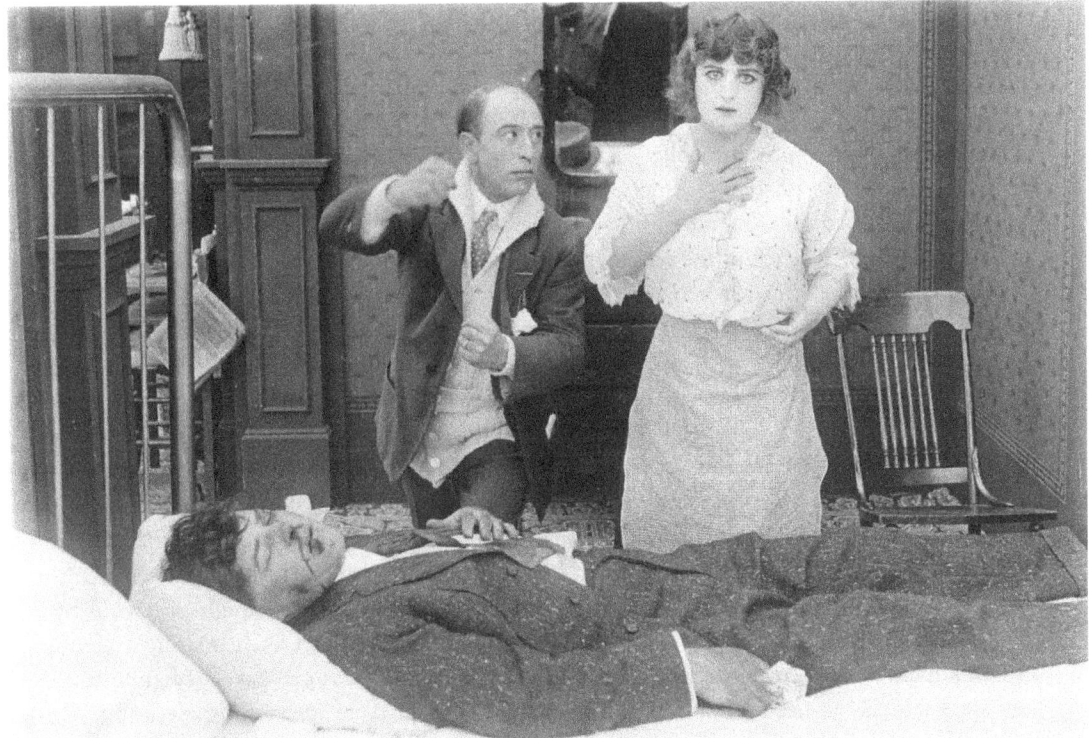

The alcoholic Cyril Adair (Harry Pollard) lies unconscious after a drunken brawl in the unfortunately prescient *Infatuation* (American, 1915) (courtesy the Margarita Fischer Papers, Special Collections and University Archives, Wichita State University Libraries).

Perhaps without meaning to, Margarita began laying the groundwork for her next picture well before *Infatuation*'s release. The warm-hearted actress, who may have been remembering her own straitened childhood, "adopted" fifty or so children from an orphanage near American's Santa Barbara headquarters. She visited the building every week for several hours, and she became quite a favorite with the children, who knew she always carried coins enough for all to buy treats. By the time *Infatuation* reached theaters, she had been carrying out these visits for several months, explaining:

> Being an "imaginary" mother is something new to me, but I enjoy it immensely, and, what is more, I know the kiddies do too. You can find a great amount of happiness in helping those poor little unfortunates to a few hours of pleasure. It's a sure cure for the blues, and I would advise all those so afflicted to try it.[8]

She continued these visits at least into 1919, when she played hostess at a fete for 130 young inhabitants of St. Vincent's Orphanage. "In addition to giving the orphanage a check," reported the *Los Angeles Times*, "Miss Fisher supplied ice cream cones and candy for each of the 130 children, all of whom are now of the firm belief that she is no less a personage than Santa Claus' grandchild."[9]

In her next feature film, the "imaginary mother" demonstrated her investment in children, as well as her family's religious underpinnings, through a role closely identified with motherhood. Again under the directorship of her husband, this was Margarita's fifth consecutive "Mutual Masterpicture," indicating substantial studio investment in these films. Titled *The Miracle of Life*, the film was released on October 21, 1915, and it offered Margarita her first adult role in a non-romantic story since she had embarked on feature filmmaking. She must have welcomed the chance to play a different sort of character even as she communicated a message that was important to her, as she revisited *The Divinity of Motherhood*'s anti-abortion subject matter with more subtlety. The plot is similar to that of the earlier Beauty short, but the film's greater length allowed more character development, and its more experienced star and director avoided much of the sentimentality, if not the heavy symbolism, of the earlier film.

In *The Miracle of Life*, when a wealthy young wife (Margarita Fischer) first learns of her pregnancy, she is "horror-stricken" and repelled by her husband (played not by Pollard but by actor Joseph E. Singleton). She is frightened of the changes to come in her life and is desperate to be "[restored] to the condition in which she may enjoy to the fullest limit the follies which society offers." She drinks an abortifacent provided by a friend, at once faints, and revives to find the deed done, a doctor at her side, and her sorrowful husband hurt and alienated from her. He divorces her and eventually remarries and has children with his new wife, while Margarita's character lives a luxurious but lonely life with "an emptiness that funds cannot fill." In her old age she has a vision of being barred entrance to heaven and sent to "the region of everlasting punishment," then another vision of being led through the world by a child who shows her repeated instances of the "happiness which attends the rearing of young. All this happiness ... is denied her through the act of her younger days." Naturally, this unhappy fate has all been a vision within a dream — that favorite storytelling method of Pollard's. The scene shifts back to an image of the young wife lying on her bed with the "deadly potion" in her hands. She tosses it aside, where it kills a bed of flowers, and tells her husband the news of her pregnancy, and "both are happy in the joy which is to come." The film ends as the "little life completes its long journey and arrives at the home it is to bless."[10]

6. The Dangerous Talent

In this still from *The Miracle of Life* (American, 1915), hedonistic Grace Catherwood (Margarita Fischer) receives a solution to her unwanted pregnancy from a questionable friend (Lucille Ward) (courtesy the Margarita Fischer Papers, Special Collections and University Archives, Wichita State University Libraries).

The Miracle of Life was well-received by critics. Louis Reeves Harrison of *Moving Picture World* called it a "triumph of motion picture art," noting its "strong motif and artistic treatment" and its "softening and humanizing influence upon all who see it," as well as the high quality of its technical execution, such as lighting, tinting, and double exposures.[11] It reminded some reviewers of the social message in the film *Damaged Goods*, a feature about the horrors of syphilis which had been released by American only a few weeks before. Another critic called the Pollards' picture "one of the most unusual dramas ever seen on the screens.... A powerful attack through beautiful pictures is launched on the cardinal sin of modern society." "Of necessity," the critic admitted, "a large part of the picture is of an allegorical nature."[12] A final review of the film observed, "Race suicide is a subject that must be handled most gingerly in motion picture drama. *The Miracle of Life* handles it with delicacy and power."[13] Margarita and her husband may have been driven to visit and revisit this topic because of their own continued childlessness after more than four years of marriage, which eventually presented the couple with a difficult moral choice.

As Vachel Lindsay wrote in the contemporary treatise *The Art of the Moving Picture*, "The moving picture goes almost as far as journalism into the social fabric in some ways, further in others."[14] The truth of this statement was demonstrated when, inevitably, the moral and social issues surrounding abortion and other forms of birth control drew the attention of other Progressive-era filmmakers. Of these, Margarita's former Universal cohort Lois Weber treated these subjects most thoughtfully in her powerful 1916 feature *Where Are My Children?*, which looked at the harmful effects of abortion on an upper middle-class marriage. The critically and financially successful film attacked a society that, by making birth control illegal, forced women to manage their family size furtively and often by using harmful methods. Weber believed that the most destructive of these, to families as well as to women, was abortion, as she demonstrated through the film's characters of a district attorney (played by Tyrone Power, Sr.) and his high-living wife (Helen Riaume, Power's real-life spouse at the time). The husband prosecutes an abortionist whose client dies; the wife periodically goes to the same abortionist to terminate unwanted pregnancies without telling her husband. The estranged, secretive couple is brought closer together when they learn the truth about the other's activities, but they then discover that they can never have children. At the film's end, a series of haunting images shows the cheerless couple growing old together, accompanied by the maturing ghosts of their never-born children.[15] Appearing as it did seven months after *The Miracle of Life*, it is likely that Weber's grittier, less circumspect film was nonetheless influenced by the trailblazing work of the Pollards.

Weber's film draws fire from modern feminists for its firm anti-abortion stance, but, in fact, her views, like those of Margarita Fischer and Harry Pollard, were progressive, unusual, and risky in the 1910s. Such divisive topics as birth control and family planning (whether by contraception or abortion) invited the risk of censorship, although by the time Weber's film was released, the film industry had set up the sympathetic National Association of the Motion Picture Industry (NAMPI) to police the content of pictures, and censorship then became less of a concern for filmmakers. In 1914 and 1915, however, when the Pollards made their first socially conscious films, Congress was debating a bill that would allow the federal government to censor film content (though it never passed), and state boards censored films according to individual and sometimes very strict standards.[16] American, through Mutual, was particularly sensitive to censorship issues: in 1915, the United States Supreme Court had actually ruled in the case *Mutual Film Corporation* v. *Industrial Commission of Ohio* that films were not protected as free speech because they were merely commercial products.[17] Margarita Fischer and her husband were therefore more cautious and euphemistic than was Weber in treating contentious issues, though they did allow *The Miracle of Life* to be referred to as a "birth control picture" in later months.[18]

The Miracle of Life proved to be the Pollards' last joint film for American. There is no evidence that they left on unpleasant terms; their contracts may have been up, and they may have been looking for new opportunities or simply a higher salary. They moved on, even before the release of *The Miracle of Life,* to work with Essanay, a Chicago-born Trust member studio that had just opened a new Los Angeles studio for feature production oriented around the studio's primary star, Charlie Chaplin.[19] Essanay had lured Chaplin from Keystone (home of the famous slapstick Kops, as well as the studio for which Chaplin had first developed his iconic Tramp character) with a signing bonus of $10,000 and a then–shockingly high weekly salary of $1,250. The Essanay period represented a time of creative development for Chaplin, as he shed many of the cruder mannerisms he had honed on British music hall stages and instead began developing the complex, pathetic/romantic films which would eventually cement his legend. Although later regarded by Chaplin as a minor, contentious period in his career, his year with Essanay turned him into the world's most famous star, in large part due to the marketing efforts of the studio.[20]

The Pollards were drawn by Chaplin's glittering stardom and the chance to take part in his maverick filmmaking methods—news items even hinted that Pollard fancied himself a budding comedian—but they were awakened to the reality of Essanay studio life almost at once. The studio's aggressive publicity alone would have bothered the reserved Pollard, but he also ran into trouble with golden boy Chaplin, who soon began to tarnish in the eyes of studio leadership. Chaplin was writer, director, editor, and star, and would eventually even compose his own films' scores. He supervised and dictated every step of the formation of his pictures with a painstaking, even obsessive, care that conflicted with the studio's established cost-cutting practices, such as projecting original negatives and reissuing footage, policies that eventually led to legal tangles with their former star.[21] A onetime collaborator of Chaplin's recalled, "He did everything five thousand times. [He was] a real perfectionist."[22] A news item about the Pollards' collaboration with Chaplin was an odd mix of enthusiasm and apprehension: "Marguerita Fisher [sic] is hard at work with the Essanay, and her first release with that brand is anxiously waited for. Her hubby, Harry Pollard, is with the Chaplin aggregation. We pity him!"[23]

Even more than Chaplin's tightly regimented production methods, which effectively eliminated any chance for the continuation of Pollard's promising directorial career, Margarita and her husband clashed with the Little Tramp's creator on personal grounds. "They were extremely, extremely moral people," explained the couple's great-niece, Margarita Kotselis. "I think that's one of the reasons why my uncle [Harry Pollard] wanted to keep away from the Hollywood crowd.... At that time there was a lot of carousing, a lot of stuff going on, that he totally did not approve of."[24] Chaplin was soon to become notorious for his promiscuity and his pursuit of extremely young women: his first and second wives were both sixteen years old at the time of their marriage, and both weddings took place due to pregnancy—a hoax by his first wife, but real in the case of his second.[25] Pollard's new comedy mentor became, in his eyes, a startling example of the immorality of the film industry soon after his move to Essanay. "He couldn't stand Charlie Chaplin because he thought he was crude.... He considered Charlie Chaplin really disgusting.... So I think that's why he kept himself and my aunt away from that scene," said Kotselis.[26]

Not surprisingly, the pair's sojourn at Essanay proved short-lived. Their departure was never attributed to Pollard's personal distaste for Chaplin, which probably was only one of several contributing factors. Instead, while Harry Pollard came in for a share of criticism from one wry magazine article, fault was also assigned to the "tough Chaplin gang":

> A few months ago, Harry considered himself a comedian, and joined the Chaplin Essanay Company. Pollard is not a comedian, nor an acrobat, and what they didn't do to him out on the coast with that tough Chaplin gang of players was a caution. Well, anyway, to make a long story short, friend Harry grabbed his wife sternly by the wrist—she was playing with Essanay at the time—and fled with her to the Equitable. He has never been the same since, and I am certain that he doesn't think that he has any possibilities as a comedian now. If Harry was really serious about learning if he could make good as a comedian, he ought to have gone to the Keystone Company and applied for a job.[27]

Margarita and her husband never released a film for Essanay, but instead moved on, chastened, to a studio as different as could be: one based in New York which would primarily focus on the dramas with which they were, after the Essanay debacle, more comfortable. Chaplin himself left Essanay in February 1916 to oversee his own independent studio through Mutual, also staying there only a year before moving on up the ladder of stardom.[28] Essanay trudged along for a while after his departure and that of the Pollards, but finally went under in 1918.[29]

Still before the October 1915 release of *The Miracle of Life*, the at-sea Pollards had completed their hazing with Essanay and had signed on with the Equitable Motion Pictures Corporation.[30] This New York–based studio was just starting up, and it welcomed such well-known figures as Margarita Fischer and Harry Pollard into its fold as it tried swiftly to build a reputation for prestigious feature-length films. An ad in *Moving Picture World* in September 1915 touted the studio's upcoming slate of releases with the following copy:

> When the United States Rubber Company began making auto tires, they did not sell one tire until they had proven by research and test that their entire output would be equal.... They did not sell the first good one and trust to the Almighty that all others would be just as good.
> EQUITABLE follows the same principle. We are stocking up with good pictures before releasing one. Thus are the exhibitors assured of quality and consistency.[31]

The ad lists Margarita's upcoming feature *A Big Play* (spelling her last name "Fisher") alongside the work of similarly well-known stars, such as stage actress-turned-leading lady Clara Kimball Young and character actor Robert Edeson.

Margarita and her husband began their careers at this new studio with the usual positive publicity; in late September *The New York Review* printed an attractive portrait of Margarita, along with a prominent news item titled "Three New Stars of the Screen Just Captured by Equitable," and described the actress as "without the shadow of a doubt, one of the most beautiful personalities on the screen" whose "popularity gained with every release."[32] The article revealed that "In preparation for her work with the Equitable Motion Pictures Corporation, Miss Fischer and her director, Mr. Pollard, have been searching the fiction markets for the past three weeks for suitable vehicles for her appearance, and it is now found in a dramatic success."

This "dramatic success" was not, in fact, *The Big Play*. Margarita Fischer's first and only feature for Equitable was *The Dragon*, which was released through Equitable's distributor, the World Film Corporation. Directed by Pollard and released on January 3, 1916, the five-reel film was at least as unusual, emotionally demanding, and technically difficult as anything else the pair had ever done. In criticizing extremist politics, *The Dragon* required Margarita to play the dual roles of a dissipated mother and an innocent daughter. In the role of the young daughter, Messalla, Margarita returns from a convent to live with her emotionally broken father in Washington Square, an address that carried hints of socialist leanings for contemporary audiences.[33] The family's tragedy stems from the father's business failure and the subsequent departure of Messalla's mother, Elizabeth (also played by Margarita), who has abandoned her family for "the dragon" of Fifth Avenue and its worldly delights. Against her father's wishes, Messalla seeks to be reunited with her mother; as she travels the city she unwittingly brings down destruction upon those who conspired to ruin her father. At the film's end, Messalla finds and is menaced by her mother's seducer, but Elizabeth's timely intercession saves her daughter and reunites the family—just in time, too, as the seducer's home is destroyed by a bomb Messalla unknowingly brought to it.[34]

Studio publicity attempted to instill the idea that this was "a production of the highest class" which "shows that the law of compensation some times works out in a peculiar way."[35] The film's message was not always so well-received by critics, however. One said that "the manner in which the story has been transferred to the screen is generally deserving of praise," but that the film "does not ring true. In theme it seems more the effort of a writer to evolve the sensational than to adhere to the verities." The same critic noted the "impossible task" of playing both mother and daughter, praising Margarita's "superb" performance as the amoral Elizabeth but grumbling that "she fails to convince as the child who would be unable to recognize beans if the bag were open.... [O]nly a very young child or one mentally deficient would in life walk up and down Fifth avenue asking policemen ... if they could direct her to the Dragon."[36] The dissatisfied critic did, however, note Pollard's skill at managing the tricky special effects and double exposures necessitated by Margarita's dual roles. Flush with independence, and perhaps confident in his wife's ability to overcome an unpolished story, the director had chosen to focus his energies on the technical aspects of filmmaking that he found truly compelling.

Other Equitable pictures may have received similarly mixed reviews, in part explaining the studio's short life. It existed so briefly (1915–1916) that it is hardly ever mentioned in film histories. Industry conglomeration and financial straits also contributed to its demise; studios at this time often got into bidding wars for the talents of the most popular stars, since there was a much greater public demand for the work of this elite pool of players than could possibly be supplied. The cost of filmmaking grew as a result, squeezing small studios and start-ups such as Equitable out of the market.[37] Politics and power struggles among industry leaders also helped to bring about the studio's failure. The contentious Lewis J. Selznick (father of producer David) served as vice president of Equitable and its distributor, the World Film Corporation. When he conflicted with the powerful Carl Laemmle, head of Universal, he was eased out of the leadership of Equitable and World. Selznick responded to this slight by forming his own production company featuring Equitable's most prestigious star, Clara Kimball Young.[38] Without his guidance, the studio dissolved, and the World Film Corporation also declined in prestige and lost its major names over the next few years.[39]

Taking a cue from Young and Selznick, Margarita Fischer and Harry Pollard responded to the dissolution of Equitable by returning to California and marshalling support for their own production company, Pollard Picture Plays, to be based in San Diego's cultural mecca, Balboa Park.[40] They won financial backing from a local millionaire, then negotiated with Mutual for film distribution, thus reconnecting indirectly with fellow Mutual supplier and recent employer American.[41] The process of setting up a production company took much of the year, but by early September 1916, notices of upcoming pictures starring Margarita Fischer were appearing in trade journals and fan magazines. "Wanted — Handsome Men," proclaimed one ad, which sought for Pollard Picture Plays "the college bred, solid gold young type" of man to "adorn" the "fascinating photoplays in which the beautiful Margarita Fischer plays the leading roles."[42] *Moving Picture World* also placed the star rather than the director at the forefront when it printed the notice on September 2, 1916, that "a special series of Mutual Star Productions featuring Margarita Fischer" were in the works, adding as a sidenote that "These Fischer Mutual Star Productions will be directed by Harry Pollard."[43]

The Pollards' new production company announced an ambitious schedule of six Fischer-Pollard features — *The Pearl of Paradise, Miss Jackie of the Navy, The Butterfly Girl, The Knight of Tarquizzi*, *Birds of Passage*, and *The Light of Heaven*— to be released between November 2, 1916, and March 22, 1917.[44] The first of these was released on schedule to much fanfare in trade journals and newspapers — which, in the absence of press agents, may have been drafted and distributed by the director and star themselves. Every aspect of the adventure-romance's production was reported in the press, from the attention-grabbing scenes in which Margarita's "lithe young figure," as an article described it, appeared nude "in strong and supple silhouette, graceful as the wild creatures of the hills," to the offscreen adventures of the cast, who performed a scene from the production company's next film during a costume ball for "prominent society people" at the luxurious Hotel del Coronado.[45] The cast and crew yielded even more dramatic copy when they were caught for more than a day in a "harrowing" windstorm while filming shipboard scenes around Santa Cruz and Santa Rosa islands. Trapped for thirty-six hours with no food and a cursing parrot, a weary Margarita understandably described this at the time as the most "nerve-testing" and "adventurous" experience of her life.[46]

Upon completion, *The Pearl of Paradise* more than justified the peril and tension of its production. According to Timothy James Lyons, who has studied American and Mutual in detail, *The Pearl of Paradise* is "a complex tale of intrigue and adventure" worthy of inaugurating the Pollard Picture Plays schedule; it is also, due to "Pollard's treatment of plot, subtle acting by all the characters, and close attention to lighting and composition ... a film advanced beyond the standard fare released from the American studios."[47] The Pollards had learned well about location, plot, and characterization during their time with that studio. The basic plot of the film was similar to that of *The Quest*: an innocent young woman, Yulita (Margarita Fischer), is raised in peace by her father on a tropical island until she falls in love with an American man who is shipwrecked on the island (played by Pollard in one of his final roles as an actor). However, *The Pearl of Paradise* complicates matters by menacing Yulita with a villainous Dutch suitor, providing Pollard's character with a cultured fiancée, and using flashbacks to fill in the tragic story of Yulita's mother (also played by Margarita).[48]

In *The Pearl of Paradise*, Pollard Picture Plays had created something both risqué and heartfelt, unusual and very appealing. The Pollards must have felt optimistic about the reception of their next scheduled picture, *Miss Jackie of the Navy*, which attempted to recapture the adventurous style and sex appeal of *The Pearl of Paradise*. Unfortunately, *Miss Jackie* lacked the previous film's strong storyline; the plot simply involved Margarita Fischer's wild rich girl impersonating a seaman in order to win the heart of the naval captain she loves. Pollard Picture Plays had assigned itself a too-rapid release schedule, and after lavishing so many resources on its previous picture, *Miss Jackie* was probably written and produced too hurriedly. Even so, its release date was pushed back for several weeks.[49] The production company attempted to promote itself into a success; Margarita went on record as saying of the picture, "I like it better than anything else I ever did."[50] The film's publicity underscored its visual style rather than its narrative quality; selling points included "Margarita Fischer all dressed up like a sailor boy," "The ceremonial dance to the snake god of Voodoo worship," and "A 'flivver' that can do 69 miles an hour."[51] Photos of a smiling Margarita in naval uniform grasping a giant snake accompanied suggestive text such as "Margarita Fischer insists on ... doing a love-scene with Samson, a twenty-eight foot python."[52] Even this amount of salesmanship was insufficient to garner good reviews for the picture, though; one critic called it "One of the most tiresome and monotonous of plays. Margarita Fischer is the whole thing, and her attempts to appear

6. The Dangerous Talent

Margarita as the exotic Yulita dances for her father (Joseph Harris, left) and an appreciative John Weldon (Harry Pollard) in *The Pearl of Paradise* (Pollard, 1916) (courtesy the Margarita Fischer Papers, Special Collections and University Archives, Wichita State University Libraries).

vivacious and coquettish overshadow what little plot there is. There is not enough continuity of anything to hold the interest."[53]

This must have been a major disappointment for both director and star. Fortunately, the next two Pollard Picture Plays were very different from *Miss Jackie*. *The Butterfly Girl*, released on January 8, 1917, was directed by Henry Otto rather than Harry Pollard, who may already have been looking ahead to the company's next picture. This third Pollard Picture Play gave Margarita the chance to make use of her youthful background in dance by portraying a carnival dancer who escapes a predatory manager and finds love with a kind and wealthy young man. This feature was filmed and set on the grounds of the San Diego Exposition (ensuring its hometown popularity), and involved a colorful backdrop of showmen and fairgoers, some genuine and some portrayed by actors.[54]

Rather than follow this film with the pictures originally planned—*Knight of Tarquizzi*, *Birds of Passage*, and *The Light of Heaven*—the behind-schedule production company scrapped these ideas and embarked upon a startlingly ambitious single film. *The Devil's Assistant*, released three months after *The Butterfly Girl*, was as daringly activist as *The Miracle of Life* and, once more under Pollard's direction, gave Margarita one of the strongest roles of her career. In this anti-drug film, she played the young wife Marta, who, under a malicious course of treatment by a rejected doctor suitor, becomes slowly addicted to morphine after her baby dies. She experiences hellish hallucinations and is nearly driven insane by her cravings for the drug. Her bewildered husband almost leaves her to the devices of the insinuating doctor, but in the end he rescues her from the doctor's kidnap attempt, and the married couple is reunited — though presumably with a long recovery ahead of them.[55]

The picture was called "spectacular and sensational," "as weird as any fevered fancy from Edgar Allen [sic] Poe, as bizarre as a cruel dream," and "probably the most ambitious feature production which Pollard Picture Plays studios have made for Mutual release."[56] This was undoubtedly the case, especially in terms of what was required from its star. Margarita played the disturbed, mentally tortured Marta with an emotional fervor that elicited favorable

Wealthy wife Marta (Margarita) is haunted by the vision of a demon (at left) as drug addiction begins to claim her sanity. *The Devil's Assistant* (Pollard, 1917) gave Margarita one of her most challenging roles (courtesy the Margarita Fischer Papers, Special Collections and University Archives, Wichita State University Libraries).

comparisons to her similarly impassioned performance in *The Miracle of Life*. One critic mused poetically, "The eyes of Margarita Fischer — the large, expressive eyes, in which all the horror of a mind deranged by poison are mirrored — are haunting.... She has plunged, with decided success, into the depths of the most powerfully dramatic and direst tragedy."[57] Pollard, ever experimenting with technique, also won praise for his "unusual camera work and technical perfection."[58]

The variety and careful production of the Pollard Picture Plays films won international fame and respect for Margarita. She received especially fervent support from Japanese fans, who seemed to admire both her style of beauty and her carefully crafted films. One man described himself as "one of your great admirers, especially after seeing the film 'Devil's Assistant,' in which you appear with such charming grace."[59] A more poetic devotee wrote, "I always think of you when I look at the moon. And I love your art," also assuring her, "At present your popularity is better than your imagination in Japan."[60] A less fluent but no less enthusiastic fan wrote of *The Pearl of Paradise*, "Its fineness is beyond all description. That clear! That elegant! That charming! Unparalleled in all spot.... I was indeed very thankful for you that you have given us such a great film [sic]."[61] Another fan of that film wrote, "Though there was a rainstorm [when he went to see the film], the theatre overflowed with the admirers and it was greeted with the most enthusiastic applause.... This shows how you are popular in Japan.... I hope your films come to Japan as quickly as they can."[62] Fan adoration did not stop with letters and ticket sales; as the fashionable Margarita recalled, "They sent me a fur coat from Japan. Of course I had to have it made over, but I wore it."[63] Margarita appreciated and responded to this support; one fan wrote gratefully that "it was very kind of you to write me personally in spite of you being very busy."[64] She remained a favorite in Japan for years; in 1919 her photos won a beauty contest for American movie stars, and her Japanese fans voted her "the most beautiful woman in America."[65]

Domestically, a fan of the actress chose this time to rejuvenate Margarita's American Beauty image of a few years before. For the covers of the sheet music for the swelling "The Roses Have Nothing on You" ("Dedicated to Miss. Margarita Fischer") in 1916 and "You're My Rose in the Garden of Love" the following year, songwriter and music publisher Ernest Orne chose portraits of Margarita that invoked her Beauty publicity portraits: flowing white gowns, armfuls of roses, faraway looks.[66] Only Margarita's slimmed-down figure revealed the more recent vintage of the photographs, which may have been a deliberate choice on the part of this artistically inclined fan. Margarita's recent Pollard Picture Plays films were gaining her great critical respect, but due to their variety, her rosy "American Beauty" image was still the most strongly imprinted upon the public consciousness. Of course, besides providing a creative outlet to a fan, the publication of sheet music had a much more pragmatic motivation. In the days before film scoring and theme songs, as film historian Anthony Slide points out, "the sale of [star-associated] sheet music was mutually beneficial to the composer and lyricist, to the publisher and to the featured star."[67] As the roles of composer, lyricist, and publisher were all played by Ernest Orne, he stood to gain significantly from his "dedication" to Margarita — which may well have been unauthorized by the actress, as most such dedications were.[68]

Despite the strength of *The Devil's Assistant* and the high profile of the Pollard Picture Plays' leading lady and films around the world, such ambitious filmmaking placed immense demands on the couple, and the resulting tension was beginning to erode the Pollards' marriage. The financial responsibilities of running a production company put great strain on both director and actress, while Pollard's role as the head of a production company required him to devote resources and attention towards the marketing aspects of filmmaking, for which he had never had much use. The unusual films the pair had made over the past eighteen months had drained them emotionally and put their professional reputations at stake. When, in March 1917, American offered the husband and wife a joint long-term contract, they must have been tempted to return to the security of studio employment. The proposed terms, laid out in a letter to Harry Pollard by studio president Samuel Hutchinson, were fairly generous: $1,000 weekly for six months, $1,250 weekly for six months after that, and an option for a further full year at a salary of $1,500 per week.[69] However, Hutchinson offered the couple only ten days to make a decision, and as *The Devil's Assistant* was already in the works at that time, they turned the contract down.

Margarita became severely ill shortly before the April release of *The Devil's Assistant*, which forced the production company to a financially crippling halt. A brief reassurance was published, stating:

> Marguerite [*sic*] Fischer, the charming and much loved little actress whose acting always pleases the fans, is in the hospital at Los Angeles recovering from an operation. She will be out again in another week and will start work again with the Pollard Picture Plays Company soon after. Miss Fischer has received all sorts of condolences from all sorts of people, for she is dearly loved by all the photoplay fans. Harry Pollard, her director husband, is getting a feature in shape pending her return.[70]

Margarita was jovial during her hospitalization. Though the nature of her operation was not revealed (that would have been quite indelicate), she remained in communication with the press during her recovery, even selecting the next of her beloved cars by peering through the window of her hospital room.[71] Despite her cheerful recovery, Pollard began to exhibit more serious signs of alcoholism under the strain of her absence. Along with his ambitious production methods, this served as a warning sign to the vigilant studio heads at American.[72]

In late May, after seeing *The Devil's Assistant* safely through to release, Margarita took a much-needed vacation from filmmaking and her burgeoning marital difficulties by returning to her childhood home state of Oregon for the first time in years. The official reason for her return was to attend a film convention and the closing Oregon Movie Ball, held in Portland on May 29 and 30, 1917, as an honored guest and leader of the ball's "grand march." And the Movie Ball certainly provided plenty of distraction for Margarita.[73] The Oregonians eagerly welcomed their hometown-girl-made-good. Her presence was gleefully awaited, as "she is one of the best 'mixers' and one of the most congenial of all camera notables." When the doors were opened to the public, three thousand people crammed into the Multnomah Hotel to "mix" with their beloved Margarita and lesser luminaries Dorothy Dalton and J. Warren Kerrigan.[74]

"Miss Fischer is delaying her latest production in order to come to Portland," noted one article triumphantly.[75] Following her visit, the delay grew longer than anyone could have imagined. Around the time she returned home to San Diego, Margarita became unexpectedly ill for an extensive period of time and "did not don studio makeup for months."[76] Unlike her recuperation from previous illnesses — when she cheerfully selected cars from a hospital bed and communicated with the press about her recovery — this time she simply withdrew from the public eye.

It is likely that this period of "illness" represented a time during which Margarita had an abortion and recovered from the procedure. During her years in film, Margarita Fischer had at least one abortion, though the fact was certainly not publicized at the time and was closely guarded within the actress's household even in the decades following the end of her career.[77] Although the exact date of the terminated pregnancy is not known, Margarita Fischer's extended private illness following the Oregon movie ball, as well as a sharp shift in the direction of her career following this withdrawal from public life, are indications that the procedure probably took place at this time. Despite Lois Weber's — and the Pollards'— efforts to demystify and eliminate abortions, they remained the birth control method of last resort for actresses, and a risky, fairly major surgery with the potential to ruin Margarita's health and a guarantee to ruin her career if her public learned of the procedure.

Within the Hollywood community, the termination of unwanted (or wanted) pregnancies was a long-used method for safeguarding the precious commodity of stardom by cloaking premarital or extramarital liaisons, or by preventing an actress's possibly career-debilitating absence from the screen due to pregnancy. Mary Pickford may have had an abortion in 1910, as D.W. Griffith's actress wife Linda Arvidson revealed circumspectly in a memoir that Pickford was pregnant during the filming of the early Griffith picture *The Call to Arms*, released in July 1910. Although the young actress married fellow player Owen Moore in January of the following year, the couple never had a child.[78] Pickford biographer Eileen Whitfield does not recount this suggestive series of events, but instead thinks it likely that Pickford had an abortion in 1913, while still married to the volatile, alcoholic Moore, under the guise of an appendectomy. If the actress did have an abortion, the crude methods used could certainly explain her inability to have much-wanted children during her later marriages to Douglas Fairbanks and Charles "Buddy" Rogers. This turn of events soberingly corresponds to the plot of Lois Weber's *Where Are My Children?*, though Pickford did eventually adopt.[79]

Actresses still made the same decision more than a decade later, often with great difficulty. Silent star Gloria Swanson's extremely candid autobiography begins with an account of her difficult decision to terminate a pregnancy, which was two months along at the time she married her third husband in 1925. At that time — which was morally permissive in comparison to 1917 — she knew that "if I had [my husband's] child in seven months, my career would be finished. The industry and the public would both reject me as a morally unsound character, unfit to represent them.... The very idea [of an abortion] horrified me, but I was convinced that I had no choice."[80] The procedure was botched, and Swanson developed a terrible infection. "For weeks I lay between life and death in a Paris hospital, having nightmares about the child I had killed, wishing I were dead myself."[81] Swanson felt incredible resentment toward the public and the studio heads who clamored for her return, blaming them for the loss of her health and her child. Although her popularity was greater than ever when she returned to Hollywood, "once it was over, I could never view my life or my career in the same way again."[82]

Although Margarita Fischer's own thoughts and reactions are not known, she was in a similar position to Swanson regarding the priority of her career; and the physical toll, if not the psychological, was probably similar as well. The public knew her to be married, and therefore no scandal would have attached to her pregnancy, but it would have temporarily ended her career and permanently changed its nature. She would have been unable to make any films while visibly pregnant, and the knowledge that she had a child would have forever aged her in the public mind. In addition, Dorothy's harrowing childbirth experience and permanently compromised health may have terrified the similarly petite Margarita, on whose continued good health the family finances depended. Most importantly, the financial and emotional dependence of her mother, sister, niece, and husband made it impossible, in Margarita's mind, for her to take any action that would prevent her from supporting her family as she had for the past nineteen years. As Margarita Kotselis explained, "My grandmother [Dorothy] never worked. She [Margarita] took care of her. And she pretty much took care of my mother [Kathie] until my mother married later. And she took care of her own mother.... She supported all of those people.... She really never wanted children."[83] The actress believed that if she had a child, she could not keep working as she had been, and she therefore would not be able to support her family — so she could not have a child. Her decision to have an abortion had to be kept secret from the public and from the filmmaking world as well, since, apart from the usual scandal, Margarita's personal motivations would not be taken into account. She would simply be judged as hypocritical after making the anti-abortion *The Miracle of Life*, and her credibility as an artist would be undermined.

While Harry Pollard must have gone along with the decision to terminate his wife's pregnancy — after all, as her director, he was affected by the status of her career as well — it probably bothered him more than it bothered Margarita. The actress, her great-niece remembered, "went through so many things growing up that she wanted everybody to be tough like she was, and not everybody was tough like she [was]."[84] Her husband, by contrast, was retiring and sensitive —"the kindest, most gentle soul. [Kathie] loved him. She was very close to him."[85] Maintaining such a close connection with his niece may have been a way for him to feel fatherly in the absence of his own children. However, his wife's extended recovery hung over him personally and professionally, and his ever-present drinking problem began to escalate. When Margarita was fully recovered, neither she nor her husband had the heart to embark upon another soul-searching Pollard Picture Plays production. To return the actress to the public eye, Harry Pollard eventually began drafting the scenario for a light romantic comedy, which came to be titled both *The Girl Who Couldn't Grow Up* and *Putting It Over*.

As production wrapped up on that film in August 1917, a further blow fell upon Pollard when the American Film Manufacturing Company, now renamed the American Film Company, Inc., re-extended the offer of a contract (again with a demand for a quick decision) to Margarita alone at the same impressive salary they had previously offered the pair, one thousand dollars weekly. The couple's friendly agents, Richard Willis and Gus Inglis, formally communicated the news:

> Dear Folks:
> Mr. Hutchinson is here.
> He makes Miss Fischer the following offer:
> He will give her one-thousand dollars a week, work to start next Monday.
> Mr. Hutchinson says that he must make an immediate decision as the position rests between Miss Fischer and another star. He will make a positive decision on Wednesday.
> This offer just embraces Miss Fischer and does not include Harry.
> We make it just as he made it, without any comment.
> With all good wishes, we remain,
>   Yours sincerely,
>   Willis and Inglis[86]

Enclosed with this "official" letter of August 13 was a more personal note, assuring the couple that "We DO want things to turn out satisfactorily for you both," but that

6. The Dangerous Talent

Even as Harry Pollard and Margarita Fischer (at right) began to have marital trouble, he remained close to their niece Kathie (center). She thought him "the kindest, most gentle soul," Kathie's daughter remembered (courtesy the Margarita Fischer Papers, Special Collections and University Archives, Wichita State University Libraries).

> He says he only wants Miss Fischer and nothing we can say will alter this we are afraid. It seems so much up to you people; we hardly know what to say.... We had things going so nicely until they started to make investigations and badly as you may feel about it, the fault does NOT lie with us.[87]

It seemed that, since extending his previous offer of a contract to the Pollards in March, American's president Samuel Hutchinson had learned of Harry Pollard's escalating alcohol problem, and he was firmly refusing to re-extend the offer of employment to one who now seemed an unreliable prospect.

The next salvo again came from American, only two days later, by way of the couple's beleaguered agents. "Dear Lady," began the letter to Margarita, "... I wish you would send us a line, making some fixed appointment [to see Hutchinson].... Of course I know how both you and Harry would feel about someone else directing you, but [that] being seemingly impossible, I do think they are only getting good directors at Santa Barbara."[88] The following day, it became apparent that Hutchinson was really putting the screws to the agents, as Richard Willis somewhat desperately contacted Margarita: "I can't tell you exactly in a letter, but there is outside pressure being brought to bear to get the other star and I know that it will be quite advisable for you to be here on Monday, so thought it better to write you again."[89]

As she had been advised, Margarita went to the meeting with Samuel Hutchinson. With Pollard deemed unemployable, and with the demands of Pollard Picture Plays weighing heavy on her, she took the step that had at first seemed unthinkable and decided to accept a contract with a studio that had rejected her husband and director. The decision was bitter; more than fifty years later, she still remembered Hutchinson as "a skunk" and "a tightwad."[90] A strained Margarita signed a year-long contract with American on August 27, 1917.[91] Not without its benefits, her contract's start date was manipulated to allow her to work under the direction of her old friend Lloyd Ingraham, who had been the head of the stock company in which she and Pollard had worked during the summer of their marriage.[92] In addition, she was guaranteed one thousand dollars a week and starring roles for a full year — more money than she had ever made in her life, and more exposure than she had been able to gain through Pollard Picture Plays.

Despite his wife's success, Harry Pollard must have been deeply hurt by this series of events. Besides the humiliation of being unwanted by a studio that had once welcomed him, Margarita's departure effectively dissolved Pollard Picture Plays. The light Cinderella-like *The Girl Who Couldn't Grow Up/Putting It Over* was released in mid–September 1917, and the Pollards' production company fell apart soon afterwards. Its final picture displayed no signs of the tensions underlying its production, as it merely involved Margarita's sheltered rich girl prankishly conflicting with a stepmother and stepsisters until she eventually marries a nobleman.[93] Still, it was well-received; as one reviewer blithely wrote, "It seems good to have Margarita Fischer back in a comedy-drama of the happy-go-lucky kind."[94] Following the picture's release, the "happy-go-lucky" Margarita and her troubled husband moved from San Diego to the Santa Barbara home of American, where the actress prepared once again to embark upon a busy studio-set schedule of filmmaking.[95]

7

In Love and War

The American Film Company, Inc., of 1917 was a somewhat different studio from the one Margarita Fischer and Harry Pollard had left behind in 1915. They had seen the leadership changes that ousted Harry Aitken from American's distributor, Mutual, in 1915, and they were aware that Aitken had departed with the distribution rights to American's sister studios. In 1915, American had been the second-largest studio in California; only Universal was larger. In 1916, the still-thriving studio reached the height of its production at 596 reels, with 242 films produced in the Pollards' old Beauty and Masterpicture brands, as well as Westerns and dramas. Mutual, meanwhile, sought to expand its scope by hiring Charlie Chaplin to form his own studio for Mutual distribution at a contract of $670,000. By 1917, however, the fortunes of American and Mutual were changing. Chaplin departed Mutual for First National, and with Pollard Picture Plays's collapse, American again became the major supplier of film product for Mutual, which entered a financial slump. American was inevitably affected by the decline of its distributor, as it was thereby losing the ability to place the studio's films in theaters. In 1917, American would produce only 54 films at a total of 193 reels.[1]

Into this shaky environment returned Margarita Fischer, this time without the support of her troubled but talented husband as director. She was well-compensated for her venture; indeed, she was probably one of the studio's two highest-paid stars, youthful Mary Pickford competitor Mary Miles Minter being the studio's other greatest draw. Still, she perceived a new formality and distance in the studio that had formerly seemed so congenial; the atmosphere of casual camaraderie, of romping around the countryside for location filming, was gone. Margarita was always cordial, though. Of the other stars, she recalled, "I never had any trouble with them or any pleasantries with them. We just always said, 'Good morning,' and we didn't have any contact with Mary Miles Minter. [But] I knew her, and naturally we were friendly."[2]

While Margarita never maintained a personal publicist, she soon discovered that, in exchange for the security of contractual employment, she would nevertheless be required to shape herself into the star the studio wanted. Attempting to concoct box-office success for the studio's new investment, American began at once to redefine her image; the actress was to bridge traditional and vibrantly new female roles with effervescent energy, innocent sensuality, and wholesome glamour. In livelier publicity articles than those with which she had begun her feature film career with American more than two years before (when she had come across as more languidly traditional), she admitted to her love of acting, dance, cars, driving, and "tinkering" with mechanics.[3] At around the same time, Margarita — along with other notable female stars such as Mary Pickford, Marguerite Clark, and Bessie Love — made news in *Motion Picture* magazine for taking the daring step of wearing pants on film.[4] On a more elegant note, the actress offered frank fashion advice for photoplayers, admitting that "I spend a great deal on my clothes, and it is not only that I like to do so, but I am compelled to," for besides having the responsibility of providing her own wardrobe for all modern pictures, "many go so far as to judge an actress by the clothes she wears."[5]

As preparations began for her first starring vehicle under her new contract, the studio's still photographers made modern and daring portraits of their latest acquisition, circulating an attractive publicity shot of a youthful-looking, winsome Margarita clad only in draperies and clutching at her long, tumbling curly hair.[6] "They were all so nice to me. I knew so many of the cameramen," Margarita remembered of the studio's image-makers, joking, "I don't remember them telling me this or that was the right side of me [for lighting]. Probably it was all bad."[7] Modesty aside, her image was indeed effectively updated; the multitude of shots taken in the first few months of her re-employment with American show the slimmed-down star looking more elegant and even more youthful than she had at the beginning of her film career. With light makeup, short hair, floppy hats, and long pearl necklaces, the actress looks years younger than her age, and her faraway smiles give no sign of the difficult circumstances that brought her back to the studio.

A return to the security of a studio contract also offered Margarita a chance for expanded publicity. She posed for many beautiful, modern portraits such as this one when she began working for American for the third time in 1917. Photograph by Witzel (courtesy the Margarita Fischer Papers, Special Collections and University Archives, Wichita State University Libraries).

As Margarita later described American's publicity, "I did little things that attracted the public, perhaps. That seems to be quite the thing, to do something that will make headlines so pictures will go before the public, but I think probably that being in the business when I was so young, in the theatrical business, I had a feeling that it was cheap to do that."[8] Still, Margarita must have approved of some aspects of this glamorous studio publicity, which relieved her of much of the responsibility of promoting herself (or the danger of not receiving publicity, due to Pollard's reluctance to hire a press agent). American's other attempts at constructing her image must have been painful, though. Although the Fischer-Pollard marriage had never been kept secret from the filmgoing public, American now used it for the first time as a publicity tool, and the studio naturally portrayed the couple as romantic paragons. The distressed husband and wife saw a grating article prominently published about Margarita's youthful loves (almost certainly fabricated, considering the frantic pace of her theatrical company's touring schedule) that concluded in a syrupy paragraph about Pollard, "the man who made all the little loves melt into jello and thru the warmth of her heart merge into one great big, all-absorbing love for himself [*sic*]."⁹

Other publicity articles communicated the determined actress's more progressive tendencies even as they continued to play up the marriage. One piece entitled "Women Can Make Happy Homes and Maintain Successful Career" related the ease with which the actress balanced her career and her home life. The piece is written in a somewhat fervent style that cloaks its message: Margarita, a "gay little sprite," blows her husband "a blessed little kiss from the tips of her fingers" as she tells him, "It's a joy to make a happy home for you." However, the article adds that she is "just as successful in being a happy wife and homemaker as she is as a popular screen artist."¹⁰ In other words, the actress was able to continue to succeed in traditional home-oriented roles while maintaining a non-traditional and demanding career. To stress the importance of career over more traditional roles would have been startling for most prominent women of the time, and for the family-focused Margarita in particular. In equating success in both fields, though, the actress demonstrated that she valued professional fulfillment as well as personal.

A more dignified news release, written by Margarita around the time of her studio transfer, reflected her down-to-earth appeal and held the wistful ring of truth about her marriage:

> We see plenty of make-believe heroes on the screen. They are invariably handsome, graceful, clever, reserved and demigods. My hero is not like that. Not at all! He is plain rather than handsome, but his clothes fit him well and are made by the best tailors. His eyes are not maddening in their mystery, but they are kind and have a crinkly smile in them that children love, and his mouth is clean and firm. He is not so clever that everybody talks about it, but he knows just the right thing to say when I am tired or cross or out of sorts. And he knows just the right time to hold my hand — and maybe to give it just the tiniest squeeze. He does not utter impassioned words of love; but he knows how to order a good dinner in a tone that waiters respect.
>
> He does not tell me that I am the only girl he ever loved; but when he is with me he pays no attention whatever to any other girl present, no matter how attractive she is.¹¹

After almost a decade of marriage, and a turbulent career for both parties, Margarita still appreciated her husband's quiet determination and fidelity. Unfortunately, it was ultimately not enough to hold the marriage together. Despite his wife's affectionate words, and the emphasis American was placing on their marriage, Pollard's "very heavy" alcohol use had continuously undermined the couple's relationship.¹² The husband and wife did not formally separate until 1919,¹³ but references to Pollard are almost completely absent from Margarita Fischer's papers and publicity beginning with the release of Margarita's first film under her new contract, *Miss Jackie of the Army*, a companion to the poorly-received Pollard Picture Play *Miss Jackie of the Navy*. This indicates that an informal separation may have occurred as early as December 1917 or January 1918. Over the next few months, the unemployed Pollard attempted to strike out on his own by directing the film *Which Woman?* for the Universal subsidiary Bluebird Photoplays, but "an illness of several weeks" (which may have been related to alcoholism) forced him to turn over the helm of the film to director Tod Browning.¹⁴

Margarita, meanwhile, must have thought her first film inauspicious, as the *Miss Jackie* title boasted name recognition but carried little success. The choice of subject was motivated by studio patriotism, as the United States had entered the "Great War" in April 1917.

To Margarita, the film may have been recommended mainly by the fact that it reunited her with her old friend and former stock employer Lloyd Ingraham, now a director for American.[15] The film retained much of the first *Miss Jackie* film's cast, but all players (even Margarita) played different characters, since the "Miss Jackie" of the earlier picture had been happily settled at its end.

In promoting this picture and its star, the studio quickly about-faced from its earlier marriage-centric publicity pieces. Articles on Margarita's happy domesticity with her husband gave way to pieces touting the pleasant home life she shared with her mother, sister, and niece, who had moved into her Santa Barbara bungalow.[16] The new, publicly single Margarita Fischer was still as energetic and determined as Harry Pollard's lively young wife had been. She was now steelier, though — both younger in image (since unmarried) and, as the head of her household, more capable and self-reliant. The youthful actress was an independent mother hen to her family, a hard-working but cheerful woman who urged a wholesome "early to bed, early to rise" lifestyle and reflected in her capability the Progressive reforms shaping society. She took pride in her accomplishments and expressed "a dominant faith in my own sex," remarking that "men are not any worse husbands and fathers because they have attained a successful career. The very best wives and mothers of my acquaintance are the women who have some interest in life beyond the trivial non-essential things."[17] As for herself, she added, "fifty years from now, it won't make a bit of difference whether or not I could darn a sock without making bunches in it. But it may make a difference that I have been able to furnish wholesome recreation for the entire family several evenings a week." She also offered "Margarita's Maxims" for success. Besides a "belief" in "raw oysters, raw eggs, and raw prunes" she recommended:

> To be healthy, take a cold shower, and exercise every morning at six thirty.
> To be wealthy, get a good, hard job and stick to it.
> And answering questions for two chatterbox nieces will make one as wise as any one need be.[18]

(In a few publicity articles from this time, American unaccountably gifted the actress with a fictitious second, namesake niece.)

Margarita's happily secure pose was deceptive, for Harry Pollard moved to New York after their separation, and reconciliation seemed unlikely.[19] However, she truly did find solace in her private life with her family, enjoying a settled life with her female relatives and perhaps being consoled by their survival of similar losses. During the three years or so that she lived with her mother, sister, and niece in the late 1910s, she expressed a steady, warm, cheerful persona through articles that stressed the "infectious spirit of love and warm sympathy" that pervaded the Fischer household.[20] The lack of a male presence is accepted without question in these pieces; in fact, "the only man around the house is the chauffeur," says one piece — and he is only necessary because "Margarita just can't find the time, what between acting, gardening and designing clothes, to get out and wash the car and keep it in shape."[21] No man is necessary, though, since capable Margarita provides for her family — including paying for Kathie's private education — as she has "ever since she was twelve years old."[22]

Despite her impressive achievements, these articles say, the young star is everywoman: she grows vegetables, takes script advice from her sister and mother, fishes, takes weekly picnics with her relatives, and gets thrown off of bikes by her "husky" niece.[23] She also, like any

Peaceful domestic scenes such as this one came to define Margarita Fischer's persona after her separation from Harry Pollard. From left, mother Kate and sister Dorothy read, while Margarita offers musical instruction to niece Kathie with somewhat dubious results. Photograph by Hoffman (courtesy the Margarita Fischer Papers, Special Collections and University Archives, Wichita State University Libraries).

patriotic citizen in the late 1910s, "[puts] an awfully big sum in Liberty Bonds" and cultivates a war garden.[24] While these stable and heartwarming episodes were no doubt carefully written to appeal to filmgoers, they were actually accurate: Margarita worked extremely hard for American, releasing her first five features under her new contract in a span of five months. She also "relaxed" hard through trips to the nearby beach or other outings with her mother, sister, and niece.[25] She came to love gardening, too; after developing her war garden of produce and flowers, horticulture became a favorite hobby of hers. In the 1920 compilation book *Who's Who on the Screen*, her brief biosketch related that she "still takes a keen interest in her war garden, which though started as a patriotic duty has since been a source of much pleasure."[26] When, in later decades, she owned a historic home with landscaped grounds and an accompanying orchard, gardening still continued to be one of her favorite hobbies.[27]

Margarita's activism on behalf of the American military soon went far beyond tending a war garden or even personally buying war bonds, for which her small household aggressively saved its funds. On April 6, 1917, the United States had declared war on Germany and joined

Margarita's support of the U.S. Navy as "godmother" won the enthusiastic admiration of her "godchildren" even after the war's end. Here, the navy's recruiting band serenades the actress outside the walls of American's studio in June 1919 (courtesy the Margarita Fischer Papers, Special Collections and University Archives, Wichita State University Libraries).

Europe in fighting the "Great War," the world's costliest in terms of money and human life. The California film industry served as a morale booster and patriotic activist through the production of pro–American films, public appearances by stars, and war bond drives. Margarita took part in each of these aspects. She appeared on the August 1917 cover of *Film Fun* magazine in her *Miss Jackie of the Navy* whites, shaking the hand of a grinning military man. "United We Stand," read the caption.[28] Indeed, *Miss Jackie of the Army* (retitled from *A Daughter of Joan*) was chosen for her first feature under her new contract to play off of her previous *Miss Jackie* release and stress the new film's patriotic military message (in it, Jackie becomes a Red Cross nurse, captures spies, and foils a sabotage attempt).[29]

In the spring of 1918, Margarita made an unusual personal sacrifice to the war effort by changing the spelling of her last name to "Fisher" at the insistence of her studio. A series of publicity shots show her pulling the "C" out of a sign displaying her name and throwing the letter into a map of Germany. The accompanying text reads, "Margarita Fischer kicked the 'c' bodily out of her name last week by means of a little ceremony that showed how much in earnest she was. She picked the offending Germanish letter from the center of her last name and tossed it lightly onto the clay map of Germany that had been fashioned on a table."[30] Margarita was not the only star whose Germanic name changed during the Great War; Signe Auen became Seena Owen, Alfred Vosburgh became Alfred Whitman, and dashing Norman Kaiser, not surprisingly, changed his name to Norman Kerry.

The Americanization of Margarita's name was only a symbolic, studio-mandated gesture, however, as her father's family hailed from Switzerland and had no tie to Germany except that of language. One article presented the decision to change her name's spelling as the actress's own, stating that she "does not care to be wrongfully known as of German extraction. Her mother is of Irish descent and her father had Swiss ancestors. Both of her parents were born in the United States, and the well known film star is an American through and through and wishes to be [known as] one to each and every admirer."[31] This effusion smacks of nervous studio publicity, and, in fact, the actress later recalled that she "had no choice" but to perform the action, since she depended on her studio income to support her mother, sister, and niece. The name change and the publicity photos "saddened me for many years" and "broke my dear Uncle Will's [John Fischer's brother] heart — he died shortly after."[32] During the war, she maintained the Anglicized spelling of her name, though articles about her used either spelling of the surname. "After all was quiet" at war's end, she later recalled, the studio bookended the first publicity with a shot of her putting the "C" back into her name, and she reverted to the original spelling.[33]

Other methods of activism were more enjoyable for the actress, and probably more exciting to the public. Living and working near the coast, Margarita saw a flurry of naval activity, especially when she was in the San Diego area. She also encountered a great deal of baseball, San Diego being the home city for the navy's baseball team. In April 1918, she was invited to become a "godmother" to the Naval Baseball Team of Balboa Park, which maintained a custom of selecting a film actress as their patroness. Margarita accepted the honor and welcomed her new "godchildren" in a brief ceremony held during a game against the California Artillery Corps' Grizzlies. She was presented to the adoring team while wearing "some fine photographic clothes and a wonderful smile," received a baseball signed by all, then increased her popularity further by giving cigarettes to all of the team members.[34] She watched the close-fought game from the team's bench, apparently becoming invested in "her" team's eventual victory. When they racked up a 2–2 game tie in an inter-service series, she promised and sent them a silk pennant for winning before the last game was even played — "Because she firmly believes her godsons will win the series," explained one news item.[35]

At the same time she became godmother to the baseball team, Margarita offered to serve in the same role for the Fourteenth Aero Squadron of North Island, San Diego, which, at all of three years old, was then "the oldest aero squadron in the American air service." On the same day she made her inaugural appearance as the Naval Baseball team's godmother, she also visited the Fourteenth, bearing gifts of cigars and cigarettes, and she received a basket of her trademark American Beauty roses in return from the appreciative fliers.[36] As a private wrote after attending her introduction, "[The cigarettes and cigars] were highly appreciated by them and all agreed that Miss Fischer had made good as a godmother right off the reel.... It is hoped that another visit by the little actress will take place in the near future."[37]

To inspire her second group of godsons, Margarita offered a gold medal to the first pilot from North Island's Rockwell Field to shoot down a "Hun aeroplane." In January 1919, the Phoenix Chamber of Commerce presented the medal on the star's behalf to the parents of the winner, Lieutenant Frank Luke, who had been killed in action in September 1918, shortly after his medal-winning accomplishment.[38] The obverse of the hefty piece bore a picture of a combat airplane and read "Margarita Fisher Medal. For Valor In the Great War of 1918"; the reverse read "To the late American hero and aviation ace, Lieut. Frank Luke. The first Rockwell Field aviator to bring down a German airplane as well as 13 others and 25 balloons." Margarita herself later logged some time in an airplane — a full two hours and eighteen minutes — during the summer of 1918, and in June 1919 she took another flight in Phoenix as a special guest at the city's Frank Luke Air Memorial Tournament.[39]

As well as sponsoring these wartime morale-builders, the outdoorsy star joined "San Diego's smart set" in April 1918 for a Sweetwater dam fishing outing in her honor as recognition for her diligent work in support of war efforts. To her surprise, she caught the second fish of the day. This unusual pastime was only the latest in a string of faddish wartime amusements for the wealthy, which over the course of one week had also included "aviation tea dances, morning surf bathing parties, and moonlight evening clambakes."[40] Supporting the war could involve glamour; later in the summer of 1918, Margarita revealed the fact that the elegant gowns she wore in her film *Impossible Susan* — one of which cost a whopping twenty thousand dollars — were designed and made in America.[41] And yet, she admitted on a more down-to-earth note in an article titled "Even a Movie Staress can Conserve Clothes, It Seems," she actually remade clothes from previous seasons into new outfits in order to save money and materials.[42]

The public nature of Margarita's career allowed her to contribute to the war effort in unique and significant ways. In response to an open plea from Secretary of the Treasury William McAdoo, who came stumping to Santa Barbara, she and other stars of American began a Liberty Bond drive for employees of the studio, determined to raise more money than any other studio of the same size (a mid-sized independent, they maintained a staff of about 75–100 actors and 200–300 production personnel in 1916, but had fewer during the war).[43] Studio personnel forecast a bond total of at least $350,000 — thus the Fischer family's determination to contribute every spare cent to the cause.[44] The energetic actress also contributed her acting talents for patriotic purposes; in May 1918 she was one of six American players,

7. In Love and War

and the only female among them, to put on a benefit theatrical performance of Eugene Walter's play *The Wolf* to aid Belgian prisoners of war in Germany.[45] The play itself told a simple story, focusing on one day in the life of a bitter Scotsman who hates the daughter of his late wife and her lover. It was regarded as well staged and well paced—and with Margarita and her fellow stock player-turned-director Lloyd Ingraham both being in the cast, there was plenty of theatrical experience to go around. Margarita's portrayal of the hated daughter, an ingenuous woodland girl, was reviewed as "in every manner a great achievement," while the evening itself was "a gala occasion, [with] beautiful women, sumptuously gowned, excellent music and a crowded theater" which raised $1,400.[46] Margarita shared in the celebratory aspects of the event, for at the end of her bravura performance, her enthusiastic godsons were out in full force. The Fourteenth Aero Squadron gave her a six-foot mass of American Beauty roses, which was too heavy for her even to hold up, and the Naval Baseball Team presented her with a basket of lilies. These were only the most notable among floral offerings so numerous that it was reported that "several autoloads were taken to local hospitals.[47]

The whirl of patriotic activism and gaiety continued as 1918 progressed. The overbooked star came down with severe pneumonia following the exhausting performance of *The Wolf*, the morning after which she had unwisely left for Los Angeles to shoot scenes for her next film.[48] Even before she was completely recovered from this illness, however, she attended a Red Cross benefit dance put on by the Fraternal Order of Eagles in Oxnard, auctioning off dances and photographs. One photo sold for thirty-five dollars, and the actress's highest-selling dance went for twenty-five dollars to a man who "explained that though he could not dance he wanted Miss Fischer just to pass the interval of the dance talking with him."[49] The following month, on July 3, 1918, the sociable actress hosted a patriotic dinner and ball at the Potter Hotel, the location of her recent triumph in *The Wolf*. She clearly had fun with the invitations, which hearkened back to her touring days and playful dinners of "Consomme a la Margarita" and "Banana Fritters a la Dot":

> You're invited, July 3,' 18, to a party at The Potter—
> First a dinner, a la Hoover, in the Moorish room with a lot'er
> Good things to eat;
> Then a dance to dreamy music, in the Palm room's fairy bower—
> Lovely nooks and polished floors, limpid lights and all aflower—
> It's hard to beat!
> Seven o'clock the dinner hour; the dress—just as you wish—er
> All I ask, come be the guest of Margarita Fisher.
> (Hm, let me see,
> It's usual in these matters, an importance it doth lend,
> To add four little letters at the very, very, end:
> R.S.V.P.)[50]

More than half a century later, she remembered this party with great delight as a "very pleasant, very congenial" event attended by all of American's current luminaries.[51]

These worthy—and entertaining—actions filled out the actress's noble public persona, but, ultimately, work provided the greatest personal escape from her faltering marriage. Even illness barely slowed her down: despite a delay of a few days in filming due to a bout of "la grippe" (influenza) in November 1917, her *Miss Jackie of the Army* appeared in December 1917.[52] Even with her springtime bout of pneumonia, there was no appreciable pause in her

A glamorous flag-wrapped Margarita Fischer evokes the Statue of Liberty in this wartime publicity shot for the American Red Cross (courtesy the Margarita Fischer Papers, Special Collections and University Archives, Wichita State University Libraries).

schedule of releases; she made films at an incredible rate following *Miss Jackie of the Army*, starring in nine features in 1918. Aware of competition from Mary Pickford and other younger stars, American marketed Margarita as similarly pure and youthful, but also stressed her talent as a wild comedienne, her characters rich and beautiful but physically chaotic and lighthearted. By doing so, the studio placed her firmly within a tradition of adventurous and attractive female stars of the 1910s, beginning with early serial queens Kathlyn Williams, Pearl White, and Helen Holmes, and continuing with athletically inclined actresses such as dancer Irene Castle and swimmer Annette Kellerman.[53]

Margarita had long been accustomed to strenuous filmmaking, as witnessed by the grueling location shoots of *The Quest* and *The Pearl of Paradise*, as well as the silly snake stunts in *Miss Jackie of the Navy*. For the first time, however, her persona was cemented: no longer would her versatility be stressed; instead, her capability and femininity were marketed as components of her energetic appeal in comedy-romances. By June 1918, she had earned the nickname "the Madcap of the Screen."[54] This accessible but still admirable, glamorous image served Margarita Fischer well during the war years, when her title roles in movies such as *Molly Go Get 'Em*, *Jilted Janet*, *Ann's Finish*, *The Primitive Woman*, and *Impossible Susan* (all 1918) provided escapist relief. These were by no means as complex and demanding as the films she had made with Harry Pollard, however. When the actress returned to the security of contract employment, she also tacitly had agreed to change her image once more.

8

The Lure of the Mask

"After all is said and done," noted contemporary film writer Austin Lescarboura, "persons go to motion-picture theatres to be entertained.... And that is precisely what makes the comedy films so popular these days."[1] Under contract to American, Margarita rode this wave of popularity and provided a distraction from the terrible war still going on overseas. Her first film of 1918, *Molly Go Get 'Em*, appeared in theaters only four weeks after the release of *Miss Jackie of the Army* and cast its star as a rich, impish, hoydenish young woman "whose principal object in life is to have fun," as one review explained. "If other people get in her way while she is having it, who is to blame her?"[2] Another review gave an apt snapshot of the type of comic "hoydenisms" with which the star was already becoming associated:

> Miss Margarita Fischer, "tomboy of the screen," as they call her, is a fascinating little she-rogue in [*Molly Go Get 'Em*], a play that affords full swing for the peculiar comedy genius of the clever star.
>
> Miss Fischer is given a role that keeps her in the picture nearly every minute of the time and is full of the lively action which so well suits her. She hits the high spots in a fast motor car with her sister's best beau, climbs garden walls in dainty lingerie that tears on every projection, creates all sorts of difficult situations and gets out of them with her usual charming insouciance.[3]

Moving Picture World printed advertising aids for theaters running the film, including slogans "For the Program" ("Molly was a good little getter" and "The tribulations of a younger sister"), "Advertising Phrases" ("American girl outwits French count" and "Ten days on bread and water for Margarita Fischer"), and "Stunt Suggestions." The latter included tips on drawing attention to the film, either by reenacting a scene from the movie in the street, or by persuading jewelers to display false pearls along with a sign relating them to the plot of the picture.[4]

The "Molly" type of willful, energetic character caught in some type of (intentionally or not) mistaken identity and romance became Margarita's signature role over the course of the next year, as American attempted to recapture success by making essentially the same film time and again in different settings. As *Jilted Janet*, she was "one of those happy, carefree creatures" who shows up a jilting ex-lover by hosting him and his new bride in an appropriated mansion, then falling in love with the home's true owner.[5] In *Ann's Finish*, Margarita played the "petted daughter of a lumber king" who is sent to finishing school and there gets into a romantic tangle with a novelist pretending to be a burglar. She did "more than ordinarily well" with this scenario, though a reviewer wryly commented that "considerable might be said" about the film's consistency around her character.[6] The following month, in *The Primitive Woman*, she was cast as a "mischievous" and wealthy young woman who tricks a "woman-hating author" into falling in love with her — and also got the chance to demonstrate her old vaudeville skills, such as somersaulting and dancing.[7] Her next picture, *A Square Deal*, satirized intellectualism as her petted, impressionable character married on the condition that either she or her new husband could leave "the shackles" whenever they chose.[8] Then, as *Impossible Susan*, Margarita portrayed "a wild but lovable child" who wreaks romantic havoc among a group of bachelors, including a father and son.[9]

The persona had begun to wear thin with critics by the time this latest film was released in July 1918. *Moving Picture World*'s Margaret I. MacDonald pointed out Margarita's "monotonously" played character, which was nonetheless still the best in a film chock-full of "unconvincing characterization."[10] The reviewer summed up, "If one is looking for big dramatic values or faultlessness of construction, *Impossible Susan* will fail to please. On the contrary those looking for a pretty little photoplay narrative with a tinge of comedy and a sprinkling of romance will find what they are after." American tacitly admitted the sameness of Margarita Fischer's roles in a press release the same month that suggested that reporters describe her as "a distinctively individual actress" whose "acting extends beyond the limits prescribed by the golden-haired, becurled, ingenue. She is vital, living, breathing, and holds her own so firmly as———————that she delights every minute of the way."[11] Her characters were so interchangeable that the press copy simply left the name blank, to be filled in anew with every release.

Part of the problem with Margarita's pictures may have lain in the fact that she was working on an extremely tight schedule — she was releasing a feature-length film every four or five weeks, and appearing onscreen almost constantly in these films. In addition, though, she had won the honor of having "her very own scenario writer," Beatrice Van, a former magazine writer and sometime actress (she had first been featured in Margarita's 1915 *The Girl from His Town* and co-starred with her in several pictures that followed).[12] Van drafted stories for scenarist Elizabeth Mahoney to expand into movie "scenarios," or silent film scripts. The honor may have backfired, though, for the writing team unintentionally pressed Margarita into a mold. While a hopeful news item touted the fact that "Miss Fisher's latest releases ... have given box-office demonstration of the fact that Miss Van's scenarios are exactly fitted to Miss Fisher's requirements," Van was no more able than Margarita Fischer to appear at her best when forced to turn out plots for film after film at a rapid pace. Decades later, Margarita still thought of the younger woman as "a better writer" than many others she worked with. But "most of the stories she wrote were co-ed stories, college life," and Margarita was repeatedly cast in these and other "society pictures," as she called them.[13]

American's high hopes for the actress began to fade shortly after that time, as in late 1918 and early 1919 the film industry suffered severe financial losses due to declining ticket sales during a postwar recession. Even before the end of the Great War in November 1918, stock in film companies was dropping in worth, and in an attempt to recapture patriotic audiences, studios had filmed war pictures, for which the market abruptly disappeared upon armistice.[14] At the same time, the film industry — and the nation as a whole — reeled from the deadly effects of an influenza epidemic of unprecedented seriousness. Margarita Fischer's bout of "la grippe" in November 1917, while reported as quite serious at the time, preceded the lethal strain that swept westward across the country beginning in the fall of 1918, and it may actually have

By the time *Ann's Finish* was released in March 1918, Margarita's wealthy mischief-making character was fully formed. Although she had a talent for energetic comedy, she eventually came to resent the sameness of her roles and the speed at which her films were produced (courtesy the Margarita Fischer Papers, Special Collections and University Archives, Wichita State University Libraries).

provided her with some immunity. The "Spanish influenza," as the virulent epidemic was called, actually originated (by the best guess of many of today's epidemiologists) in rural Kansas. It killed between 50 and 100 million people worldwide, half of them young, healthy adults in their twenties and thirties. More than half of these deaths took place just as World War I was winding down, between September and December 1918, and, in fact, troop movements may have helped spread the virus more quickly.[15]

The effect on the nation was shattering, and the effect on the film industry was as well, in both personal and financial terms. As waves of illness spread across the country in late 1918 and early 1919, many theaters were shut down (a contemporary estimate was as high as eighty percent) for reasons of quarantine, along with other public gathering places like schools and churches, and attendance at movies plummeted. The National Association of Motion Picture Producers actually ordered a four-week halt to production and new releases on October 14, 1918—"not for health reasons," film historian Richard Koszarski explains, "but because economic chaos would have resulted from attempts to release new features while most theaters were under quarantine."[16] Production on the East Coast stopped completely. Comparatively mildly hit California still saw a sixty percent cut in film production, with some studios (mainly small or independent ones, like Griffith, Bruton, and Chaplin) continuing normal operation, and others (including Universal, Metro, Fox, and Lasky) releasing their employees for a four-week unpaid "vacation." Famous victims of the epidemic included handsome thirty-one-year-old Metro star Harold Lockwood and Metro director John Collins, only twenty-eight, the husband of actress Viola Dana, who herself grew quite ill.[17] Lillian Gish caught the "Spanish influenza" as well; though she recovered around the time of the war's end, five others connected with D. W. Griffith's studio died.[18]

The American Film Company shared in the financial woes of the film industry as a whole. The studio continued releasing movies at a steady pace throughout 1918, like other independents, with the exception of the summer months, when the studio began scrambling to find a distribution alternative to Mutual. Mutual had been struggling since Harry Aitken's departure with most of its suppliers in 1915, and the distributor had been still more severely crippled by the dissolution of Charlie Chaplin's supplying studio upon his 1917 departure for First National. In 1917 and 1918, Mutual depended mainly on American to supply it with product, which weakened American through both production pressures and the limited distribution—and thus limited box office receipts—of its films.[19] By mid–1918, Mutual had gone into receivership and was struggling to place American's products in theaters. At first it cut distribution in half, to every other week, providing the excuse that "the public must not be overfed on production in the summer."[20] This was merely a postponement of the inevitable, however. When Mutual went under, as American studio chronicler Timothy James Lyons put it, "American either had to find a new distributor, distribute on its own, or fail."[21]

Left adrift, American first proposed the option of distributing its own films. The studio's president, Samuel Hutchinson, proposed and publicized an "entirely new sales plan" in which American would sell directly to theater exhibitors rather than sending out its pictures through a distributor.[22] In order to ensure the quality of service and projection, studio representatives would be on site at every theater and would send daily reports back to the home office. As a sweetener to theaters, Hutchinson promised that they would receive films from Margarita Fischer, Mary Miles Minter, and William Russell, a popular "athletic star" (the action hero of bygone days). The studio head did note a benefit of the new system to the stars as well: "In the past we have been somewhat dependent on the wishes of our distributing organization and so have occasionally been forced to speed up studio work to meet insistent demands for a picture on a certain date.... In the future ... we will make each picture as a separate unit, taking as long as may be necessary to handle the job properly."[23] This flexible statement carried the promise of relief for the studio's overworked actors.

Hutchinson's plan was revolutionary and would have given unprecedented independence to the studio. Unfortunately, it was all talk, impossible to put into action on any kind of large scale, especially given the immense financial reserves that would be needed to keep studio representatives on the payroll at theaters around the country. After some further searching, American finally arranged to distribute through France-based Pathé Exchanges on a states-rights basis (distribution rights were sold outright rather than contracted out) in July 1918, contracting to deliver a minimum of twenty-four pictures per year.[24] Of this total, eight films were to star Margarita Fischer, and eight to star Mary Miles Minter. Far from implying relief for American's players, the Pathé arrangement put the responsibility for two-thirds of the studio's product on the shoulders of two tiny women, one of whom (Minter) was still only a teenager.

Even after these arrangements were cemented, the studio still suffered from a shortage of funds. Exhibition, production, and profits were all cycling downwards, and American began lagging behind on its payments to employees. American also proved unable to fill the production quotas demanded by Pathé; in 1919, the faltering studio released only seventeen of the promised twenty-four features, six of which starred Margarita. An additional four starred Minter, who then moved to the Realart studio to work under William Desmond Taylor's directorship late in the year—a further blow to American. The studio had indeed been hampered by its distribution troubles, but this former powerhouse was even more limited by its failure to secure its own theaters for screening its films. As more farsighted studios snapped up theaters that then became exclusive vehicles for the exhibition of their product, independents without proprietary theaters became increasingly limited in terms of theaters that would agree to exhibit their films.[25]

Margarita Fischer represented American's last and best hope for solvency, and when her contract came up for renewal in September 1918, the struggling studio would have promised her almost anything in order to keep her under their employ. Her 1917 contract had proposed a second year at a salary of $1,250 per week, but when the time came for the negotiation of terms for this new year, a raise from her weekly salary of one thousand dollars proved impossible. The 1918 contract was only able to guarantee three months of employment at one thousand dollars per week, but it did maintain the clause that the actress be cast only in starring roles.[26]

Instead of a salary increase, the studio offered Margarita a different incentive: her own production brand, to bear her name and be associated exclusively with her work just as the Beauty brand had been when it originated four years before. Margarita Fischer's first eponymous production was also her first to be distributed through Pathé. The film, *Money Isn't Everything* (also known under the title *Beauty to Let*), was released in September 1918 with hopeful publicity. "Comedy dramas are the order of the day just now when the world is demanding lighter thoughts as a relief from the grim news it faces daily in dispatches," stated one article. The film, it continued, cast Margarita as an escort who hired out her company on the condition she not be asked to speak while with her employers, and "almost any exhibitor can imagine for himself the fun possibilities that lie in such a situation."[27] *Motion Picture News* noted the exciting fact that the film would feature Margarita in "almost a score of different gowns, and included is said to have been one made at the cost of eighteen hundred dollars. This film play will no doubt set a new record for expensive wardrobe."[28]

The unfortunate film was developed during the transition between Mutual and Pathé distribution, and despite its new "producer," the film was essentially the same as her earlier releases. The plot was light and contrived, and more attention had been paid to promoting her "gowns" than to providing an outlet for her talent. *Moving Picture World*'s Margaret I. MacDonald reviewed *Money Isn't Everything* with disappointment:

> The production is considerably lacking in the comedy element, and as straight comedy-drama falls short of the "punch" which is usually expected in this class of picture. Whether it is the story that is at fault or the method of presentation, which is unconvincing, is a matter rather difficult of analysis. Margarita Fisher has done better work.[29]

The sameness should have come as no surprise: in her renewed contract, American maintained the right to "select, designate, and produce" her film properties.[30] Margarita had no more control over her pictures than before they bore her brand name, and her next few films were again the same product under a new label. In *The Mantle of Charity*, released in November 1918, she played a rich girl who dresses her dog as a baby in order to sneak it onto a train, thereby meeting a husband, who feels compassion for her unwed motherhood. A news item for her next film, *Fair Enough*, released at the end of December 1918, explained the plot in this way: "If you are a pretty girl, and if you see an attractive automobile, just appropriate it. Then, when you are arrested merely marry the policeman — and you are safe.... [Margarita Fischer] demonstrates how there is a way out of all difficulties — if one is pretty."[31] This slightly misrepresents the plot, which turned upon the chestnut of mistaken identity: the policeman was, of course, actually a millionaire's son who wished to practice some profession.

As she had once enjoyed the stardom American built for her in 1914, so Margarita now felt constrained by it. Technical advances and the maturing of the feature film as an art form had pushed the boundaries of screen storytelling far beyond the capacities of her Beauty days, but she was being forced to repeat the same unrealistic tales over and over. To some degree, this phenomenon was native to the development of stardom rather than the fault of her studio. According to author Sean P. Holmes, the development of the star system actually took power away from the stars, placing it in the hands of studio heads who elevated a few actors to stardom at the expense of others, determining their worth as well as their image.[32] The rare exception was Mary Pickford, who enjoyed almost complete decision-making ability as a producer of her own films — but she found that even she had to answer to the demands of the public, who wanted to see her in youthful, scrappy roles despite her own desire to explore adult characterizations. Expectations from film audiences and the performers themselves were higher than ever in the late 1910s, yet audiences still demanded that their favorite performers continue to present them with familiar product, even as the performers themselves grew impatient with and resentful of this flip side of their fame. Sharp-eyed (and sometimes sharp-tongued) film observer Iris Barry, writing in 1926, observed "the idiot star system" molding talented (or untalented) actors into repeating the same roles in which they became popular. "The stars daren't try to act; no one would recognize them. They just have to go on playing the same type-part they started in."[33]

In *Fair Enough* (1918, American), Margarita (second from right) again played a variation of her "madcap" character. This time, however, she had a chance to tinker with a car, which she probably enjoyed (courtesy the Margarita Fischer Papers, Special Collections and University Archives, Wichita State University Libraries).

Margarita surely chafed in her repetitive roles, especially when their mediocrity began to draw fire from critics. *Moving Picture World*'s Margaret I. MacDonald was neither the first nor the harshest critic to notice that "Margarita Fisher has done better work." As early as the March 1918 release of *Ann's Finish*, a critic had noted that the picture was inconsistent, though admitted that its star did "more than ordinarily well."[34] By early 1919, the *New York Review* critic, Laurence Reid, hardly bothered to address the particulars of Margarita's newest release, *Molly of the Follies*, in which she played a sideshow dancer at Coney Island. "Margarita Fisher Harum Scarums Through Another Five Reel Picture," Reid titled his review, and pointed out that

> It doesn't matter a great deal what the Margarita Fisher pictures are called, as long as they permit the actress to frolic to her heart's content. Therefore, the picture being made for that purpose, it is plainly seen that the title cuts no figure at all except to distinguish one piece from another.
>
> The subject matter is invariably the same and deals principally in the escapades of a willful girl who refuses to conduct herself in a reasonable way until the climax reveals a group of

exasperated characters. When everyone has nearly suffered to the breaking point through her mad impulses, then milady settles down and is seen no more until incorporated as a "harum scarum" in the succeeding Fisher story.[35]

To a degree, Reid was unfairly harsh on Margarita, since a similar spirited child-woman character had won unprecedented success for Mary Pickford. However, Pickford also held an unprecedented degree of creative control over her films and frequently based them on solid literary sources. Margarita was simply assigned studio-drafted scripts in as quick a succession as possible, and although she poured as much energy as she could into her roles, she had neither the production time nor the resources to individualize each part. Without fresh surroundings, the character itself grew tedious, and American's lack of financial resources further hindered its advancement. As contemporary film writer Iris Barry noted, "It is hard for all but the few very best people to act well in an inferior story. For one thing, a perhaps only half-realized air of defeat settles down in the studio, and from the director to the smallest official, confidence (a most inspiring and infectious thing) is lacking."[36] If this was true under ordinary circumstances, it must have been exacerbated by American's shaky condition. Financial uncertainty was daily present, and it is hard to imagine confidence thriving in such an atmosphere.

Still, Reid's trenchant criticism had little effect. One month after *Molly of the Follies* debuted, Margarita's formulaic character incited romance, misunderstandings, and a boxing match in the parlor in *Put Up Your Hands*.[37] Two months after that, in May 1919, her *Charge It to Me* evoked another tepid response.[38] A reviewer bemoaned its "frail plot," which unfolded over the course of five reels as "nothing more than a prank on the part of friend wife to teach her husband that she should have a charge account of her own."[39] *Trixie from Broadway*, which followed in June 1919, was one more comedy of unwitting mayhem and misunderstanding in which Margarita's character married a millionaire in disguise, who then tested her love and nearly drove her away with his stratagems.[40]

As American grimly wrung the last drops of spirit from a formerly fresh characterization, the contract-bound Margarita saw clearly the effect on her career of these too-similar movies. After the release of *Charge It to Me*, the demoralized actress's irritation flashed forth with uncharacteristic bluntness in a brief article entitled "Margarita Fisher Is Mightily Miffed." Hounded by waggish fans who continually repeated the film's title and catchphrase, the usually gracious star huffed, "This charge-it-to-me business is really getting on my nerves. It's worse than ... any of those other overworked slang phrases that give folks the ear-ache. Some day I'll do something rash to the person who throws that expression into my face, and then I'll tell the judge to charge it to 'charge it to me.'"[41]

Still, the many fan letters among the actress's papers attest to her continued power to please audiences despite critical yawns and her own growing frustration. Throughout Margarita's lackluster releases of 1919, missives from admirers of her work continued to pour into the studio. "I admire you for your beauty, girlish winsomeness, unaffectedness, and clever acting," wrote one teenaged fan.[42] Said another young fan of her films, "I need one of your pictures to cheer me up.... I haven't been disappointed once. That's saying something!!"[43] Another admirer wrote of her esteem for Margarita's earlier films as well as new ones, noting, "The reason I like you so well is because you are so absolutely different."[44] Yet another wrote, "Nothing is more desirable to me than to see one of your delightful pictures.... I do enjoy your splendid work so much, you are always so dear and sweet."[45] Margarita's fashion sense received attention, as well as her talent and looks; a teenage fan wrote thrillingly of her admiration of the star's clothes in *Fair Enough* and requested a pattern or "any discarded clothing," as "I am very romantic and I think it would be thrilling to wear an actress's movie clothes." (With her eye on a particular "smock" of the actress's, the girl enclosed a picture of the coveted item, with the admonishment to "please return it.")[46]

Older audiences and men enjoyed Margarita's playing as well; in the ornate script of the nineteenth century, one male admirer wrote to tell the actress of "going out of the motion picture theatre with smiles Wednesday evening, in which I enjoyed the picture *Fair Enough*."[47] Another fan wrote her a long, chatty letter about himself, beginning by saying, "Beauty is certainly a prerequisite for one entering your great field of work. You are beautiful and depict the highest type of womanhood. From what I hear and see you are very popular and there seems to be an ever increasing demand for your productions."[48] A movie theater manager from New York City confirmed this, writing that "I can assure you that you are ... the most likely & admired star [stressing the word with red ink] in my small moving picture theater. Why: they all come and ask when we are going to show a picture in which Miss Margarita Fisher appears."[49] A spicier letter from a male fan, marked "PERSONAL" and addressed to the "Black Eyed Beauty of the Screen," noted after seeing *Trixie from Broadway* that "The compliments paid you were innumerable, some saying that if they could only lay eyes on you in person, they would die of high blood pressure. Others said they would give a thousand dollars to play the part of Collins [the male lead]."[50] (Margarita's secretary nervously scrawled "Don't answer" across the top of this last letter.) In return for such expressions of delight and admiration, the actress remained devoted to her fans, responding conscientiously to their almost universal requests for personal notes and pictures. Many followed up to thank her for "the beautiful autographed picture" they had received from their beloved star.[51]

Although she no doubt appreciated her fans' continuing assurances of her popularity, in May 1919 a news item in the *Los Angeles Times* suggested that Margarita was at last ready to guide her career formally into more challenging channels. The actress's production company, noted the item, was preparing to make "elaborate seven and eight-reel productions adapted from notable novels and plays. Miss Fisher will play highly emotional roles, in place of the delightful little comedies in which she has been appearing."[52] After the release of *Trixie from Broadway*, Margarita stretched her artistic wings somewhat in the romantic drama *The Tiger Lily* by playing a tempestuous Italian peasant girl. The picture itself was a stereotyped love triangle melodrama set in "Little Italy," but at least it represented a change from her hoydenish romantic comedies. A reviewer gave the star credit for the "spirit and color" of her performance, but noticed that the prolific actress "has not been fortunate lately and the impression is gained that she is working on too quick a schedule.... [The picture] leads one to think it was only created to fulfill the order marked 'Rush.'"[53] Even if this were so, the recommended "catch lines" for theaters to advertise the picture were fabulously and creatively melodramatic: "She didn't like her own people. They never knew how to be gentlemen. But a young man, an American, came into her life and instantly her heart responded. But his life was in danger because of her jealous admirer, Giovanni."[54]

American's last major box office draw may finally have been able to leverage her talents into the production of a better picture after the release of *The Tiger Lily*, for a more reasonable three months passed before the release of Margarita's next film, *The Hellion*. Her performance

8. The Lure of the Mask

in this feature required more emotional depth from the actress than she had been asked to deliver since her Pollard Picture Plays days. In a plot that suggested aspects of both *The Devil's Assistant* and *The Dragon*, Margarita played the dual roles of, as she put it, "a girl who is insane from the use of drugs" and "a singer in a cheap café." "Both were very trying," she admitted, but the roles had "great emotional possibilities — it meant terribly hard work — but oh, how I did love it!"[55] In the film, her cabaret singer, Mazie del Mar, closely resembles a young society woman, Blanche Harper, who became unhinged after hearing of her fiancé's presumed death in the Great War. Mazie is persuaded by the wealthy Blanche's embezzling relatives to take Blanche's place when the fiancé is found to be still very much alive. The film allowed Margarita alternately to dance and rave wildly while still giving her audiences the happy ending they had come to expect. Blanche is mistaken for Mazie and tragically killed by the "hellion" of the title, Mazie's malicious cabaret manager; but then Mazie and Blanche's fiancé fall in love and build a new life together.[56]

Margarita welcomed the chance to play difficult dual roles in *The Hellion* (American, 1919). In this still, cabaret singer Mazie del Mar listens astounded to the plans of Helen and Joseph Harper (Lillian Langdon and Henry Barrows) as they concoct a plot based on her uncanny resemblance to their wealthy but insane niece Blanche. Margarita as Mazie holds a picture of Margarita as Blanche (courtesy the Margarita Fischer Papers, Special Collections and University Archives, Wichita State University Libraries).

Margarita's delighted return to more demanding filmmaking may have been motivated by her awareness of her stale screen persona as much as by her personal need for artistic satisfaction. Although she was still very popular with the public, her film career had now lasted almost a decade, and she was aware that new screen players constantly drew audience attention away from even the most established stars unless they kept their work and their image fresh. The movie screens of 1919 were graced by a mixture of luminaries: the exotic Russian actress Alla Nazimova was receiving enormous salaries playing ethnic and literary roles; Gloria Swanson had moved into racy drawing room romantic comedies; smoldering Rudolph Valentino debuted in bit parts; beautiful sisters Norma and Constance Talmadge had, respectively, mastered languid romance and sprightly comedy; Lillian Gish's subtle loveliness and emotional depths still bloomed under D. W. Griffith's direction in the blockbuster melodrama *Broken Blossoms*; and Mary Pickford continued to rule the hearts of filmgoers with childlike spirit.[57] The following year, delicate-featured twenty-eight-year-old screen newcomer Katherine MacDonald became known by Margarita's former nickname of "The American Beauty."[58] Such stars were a sharp departure from the heavy-lidded vamps who had swept the box office a few years earlier. The vamp persona did persist until the end of the silent era, as energetic, exotic sirens from abroad, like Pola Negri and Alla Nazimova, brought freshness to the vamp stereotype and were able to make a name for themselves at the end of the decade. Margarita Fischer's nearer contemporary Theda Bara was floundering, though, despite having her own production company. She had been trapped for too long in the most turgid aspects of the vamp persona and retired in 1919.[59] At the end of the 1910s, "innocence, real or simulated, was still the most highly rewarded quality in the feminine film star," noted film historian Edward Wagenknecht.[60]

Margarita Fischer's solution to professional competition, as always, was to define herself in contemporary terms as the essence of appeal: young, personable, beautiful, and fashionable. She had proved her offscreen worth with her wartime activism and her devotion to her family; she now demonstrated her right to remain on the screen by revising her age and appearance. In 1918 she reported her birth year as 1894, dropping eight years from her actual age, and by the following year she had become younger still, as a fan magazine column reported her age as twenty-two.[61] Taking a cue from the youthful connotations of Pickford's famously golden-haired appearance, it suddenly became important to Margarita to straighten out the issue of her coloring. Articles and star compendiums now referred to her hair as "copper-tinted," which, although an accurate description, may have seemed odd to readers, since she looked very dark on the orthochromatic film still in use (thus the fan letter addressed to the "Black Eyed Beauty of the Screen").[62] One piece tried to explain, "You thought her a brunette, didn't you? She does photograph that way," likening her dark auburn hair color to "a copper tone, nay, like a bronze medal." This was a bit of a stretch, but it made for a poetic comparison. The same piece also described Margarita Fischer's eyes as "grayish green — like the Atlantic Ocean after a storm, when floating sand gives a shimmer to its deep green waves."[63] A modern persona, too, was important; aware of the new image of young womanhood sweeping the country, the star's publicity items casually mentioned that "Margarita Fisher, the 'flapper' ingénue, has finished 'A Square Deal,'" or that "Margarita Fisher ... has been called 'the prettiest flapper in the films.'"[64]

Revise her image though she did, Margarita remained haunted at the end of the 1910s by the uncertain state of her career. Her studio was financially unstable, geographically isolated and distant from the industry's growing center at Los Angeles, and devoted to formulaic filmmaking. One gossip column whispered in July 1919 that "Margarita Fischer, being the only star the American Film Company seems to have left to its name, is spending considerable of her time in Los Angeles. It is said that Miss Fischer may soon have a company of her own."[65] She would not have been alone if she took such a step; film scholar William K. Everson points out that, by 1919, "stars who had been happy to entertain their fans with perhaps four or five medium-length films a year now became impresarios in full charge of their own productions, determined to stagger audiences with only two (and soon, just one) productions annually."[66]

After the release of *The Hellion* in October 1919, Margarita followed the example of these fellow stars and waited five months before releasing her next film, *The Dangerous Talent*, in which she played a forger. At six reels, this was her longest film yet.[67] The long break between releases may actually have been motivated by her studio's inability to pay her steadily. By the year's end in 1919, American had only $73.55 in the bank, and was more than $35,000 in debt. Santa Barbara's stores had learned of the company's shaky finances the hard way and by this time declined to give credit to studio employees.[68] Only a month after *The Dangerous Talent* reached theaters in March 1920, Margarita appeared with her early IMP costar King Baggot, the former "King of the Movies," whose career was now on the wane. Margarita played his wife in *The Thirtieth Piece of Silver*, a drama of marital misunderstanding that Baggot biographer Sally A. Dumaux describes as "an entertaining film with no pretensions to greatness."[69]

Again frustrated by her casting, Margarita refused to accept a role in her next planned vehicle, *The House of Toys*, a cross-class marital drama that was eventually released by American with other players in June 1920.[70] The discouraged Margarita didn't expect approval over her scripts — "I don't think anybody ... at the American Film Company ever had the approval of any part of the script," she later admitted.[71] If she was to be expected to carry a studio, though, she wanted to receive roles that were varied and interesting to play, and that would catch and keep the attention of fans. Since she felt that these would not be offered her at American, she was finally ready to look elsewhere. The actress proved the previous year's rumors true as she began to organize her own production company — not a studio brand this time, but an independent business under her full control. By late 1920 she had traveled to New York to manage and publicize it. The Christmas issue of *Motion Picture News* contained a prominent and, to American, somewhat inflammatory article about the new company. The piece stated firmly that, in Margarita's recent pictures for American, "she, as the star, received the usual commendatory compliments for her individual work. Unfortunately, not all of Miss Fisher's stories have been on a par with her ability. From now on, however, Miss Fisher will devote much time to the careful selection of stories." There is a touch of bitterness in the actress's quoted statement that "Individuality on the screen has not been emphasized nearly enough. At least in the Margarita Fisher Productions it will be."[72]

Not surprisingly, American took issue with the actress's plans and brought a suit against her for breach of contract for refusing the role in *The House of Toys*.[73] The resolution of the suit is not known, and it may have been dropped. The action likely proved fatal to American, as Margarita truly was its last bankable star. The actress signed a contract with Independent

Films Association in February 1921, and soon after her departure, American stopped producing movies.[74] *Payment Guaranteed,* a five-reel love triangle feature released in March 1921, was Margarita's last film for American and one of American's last three new releases. American hung on as an independent studio for three more months, until June 1921, by re-releasing earlier pictures. After that, explains studio chronicler Timothy James Lyons, it became "a mere shell for others' use."[75]

Besides her undeniable desire to be shed of her failing studio, Margarita had a second motive for pursuing her own production company in New York in late 1920: she wanted to reconcile with Harry Pollard.[76] The pair had never legally dissolved their marriage, but Margarita had felt hopeless about it as recently as the 1920 census; the family bungalow in Santa Barbara housed "Margarita Pollard," age "25" (actually 34), with marital status marked "D" for divorced.[77] By the year's end, though, something had evidently changed her mind and given her reason to believe the marriage could be saved. Perhaps this something was Pollard's renewed career and sense of self-worth; in the summer of 1920, after being out of work for nearly two years, he had begun directing the snappy science fiction serial *The Invisible Ray* for the struggling New York–based Frohman Amusement Corporation.[78] The near-bankrupt studio would have been less choosy about its directorial staff and was a logical place for Pollard to restart his career.[79] Margarita intended to give him a further boost and rekindle their former symbiotic working marriage — she tapped him as the director of her planned "society and comedy dramas" under her new contract with the Independent Films Association.[80] She explained, "I want for a director a man who is schooled in the fundamentals of directorial work, but also one who is creative, who can dilate on an original idea and make of it something really worth while. That's my idea of a director."[81] And only one man would do.

Unfortunately, this new chapter in her — and his — career never came to pass. Pollard's ability to work was newfound and fragile, and the troubled director needed full-time support and attention if the marriage was to succeed. Margarita had a difficult decision to make between her personal and professional demands. Was this man, whom she had once called her "hero," worth more than her career? Would her production company truly allow her to revitalize her screen image yet again, and was that promise worth the personal sacrifice it would undeniably involve? Ultimately, Margarita decided, it was not. She chose in 1921, as she had in 1911, to abandon her film career in order to strengthen her relationship with the charming Kansan she had loved for so long. Her independent production company, which had promised her the "individuality" she craved, never made a film.

In May 1921 the actress appeared in a small role in former Vitagraph star Edith Storey's vehicle *Beach of Dreams,* a romantic fish-out-of-water plot similar to *The Quest* and *The Pearl of Paradise,* but with a female rather than a male protagonist.[82] This represented a sharp departure for her, as the film was affiliated with Robertson-Cole, an ambitious but ultimately unsuccessful New York–based independent distributor and studio network (star Edith Storey made only one more film, the last of her career, with Robertson-Cole following *Beach of Dreams*). Robertson-Cole, which had assumed Mutual's former holdings when the distributor dissolved, represented the type of work Margarita valued: a focus on "stars, stories, and directors," and a belief that "[the] only worthwhile production is the best."[83] Still, it is a surprise that she accepted a supporting part rather than angling for the lead, especially considering that the film was actually copyrighted in July 1920, before she decided to retire.

Margarita's role may have been completed even before she formally left American — another possible motivation for the studio's suit against her.

Perhaps the best explanation for Margarita's uncharacteristic behavior — both self-effacing and sly — was the studio's New York location. She probably came to New York to visit Harry Pollard, and while she was there shoehorned the *Beach of Dreams* part in between her roles for American. After this final release and the end of her working relationship with American, she retired from the screen in order to, as Universal Studios publicity later put it, "devote herself exclusively to being Mrs. Harry Pollard."[84] The 1920s proved to be one of the most exciting and changeable times not only in film but in American history, but Margarita Fischer Pollard, who had headed her own theatrical company as a teenager and who had astounded the filmgoing nation with her beauty and talent, planned to spend the remainder of the decade as a housewife.

9

When Queenie Came Back

The 1920s began and ended with a financial whimper, but the years in between were one big bang that changed not only the fabric of American society but also the workings of the film industry. By 1921, the year of Margarita Fischer's retirement from the screen, a postwar recession was beginning to give way to consumerist prosperity that both offered new choices to many Americans and conflicted with their traditional values. Successes and failures were mixed as people struggled to make sense of a new world in which America was a major power, in which some held unprecedented wealth and others struggled to keep up with social changes. Per capita income nearly tripled in the first three decades of the twentieth century; however, the number was brought up sharply by a prosperous few, and less than half of the population earned this average amount.[1] In 1920, the film industry grew to become the nation's fifth largest business, and the Nineteenth Amendment's passage gave women the right to vote. Less positively, farm income plummeted by 1921 to less than one-half of its 1919 level, and a reactionary Red Scare in the decade's first years eroded political freedoms and fostered suspicion of immigrants and "radicals."[2]

Changes in the film industry paralleled those of society. The late 1910s and early 1920s saw the continued conglomeration of independent studios and movie theaters into larger organizations. These included Metro-Goldwyn-Mayer (known as MGM), formed in 1924 from the three individual studios that made up its conglomerate name, and Carl Laemmle's increasingly powerful Universal Studios. This process of merging effectively pushed smaller studios like Selig and American into insolvency and also, according to film historian J. M. Klenotic, resulted in a standardization of film content and production.[3]

A succession of scandals in the early 1920s intensified the process of homogenization. The buoyant, obese comedian Roscoe "Fatty" Arbuckle was tried for rape and manslaughter in 1921; Margarita's director on *The Lonesome Heart*, William Desmond Taylor, was murdered in 1922; and wholesome, handsome leading man Wallace Reid, who had played opposite Margarita in IMP roles ten years before, died as a result of morphine addiction in 1923. The results of all three scandals were dramatic: after two well-publicized trials resulting in hung juries, Arbuckle was eventually found innocent in a third trial, but his career was almost irrevocably ruined (he was able find work as a director under a pseudonym a few years later, and began acting again only after a decade had passed). As police investigated Taylor's still-unsolved murder, they uncovered illicit romantic connections between the director and both comedienne Mabel Normand and innocent Pickford-like actress Mary Miles Minter, Margarita's former fellow player at American four years before. Neither Minter's nor Normand's career ever recovered from the scandal.[4]

Reid's death was perhaps the greatest tragedy of all for the film industry. After a 1919 accident during filming left the likable actor in terrible pain, his studio, Paramount, prescribed him morphine so that he could complete the picture and continue working at the punishing pace expected from a well-paid leading man. Reid soon became addicted to the drug as well as to alcohol, and his health quickly suffered. The weakened star died of influenza at the age of thirty-one in a sanitarium where he was attempting to break his addiction. His widow, the sharply intelligent actress Dorothy Davenport, blamed the studio for her husband's addiction and demise. She took the unusual step of publicizing the unsettling and often undignified circumstances of Reid's death, winning public sympathy for her late husband.[5]

After this rapid succession of scandals, public outcry against the perceived corruption of Hollywood life led the film industry once again to censor itself rather than allowing an outside agency to dictate film content. In 1922, industry leaders organized the Motion Picture Producers and Distributors of America (later renamed the Motion Picture Association of America) under the leadership of former U. S. Postmaster General Will Hays in order to supervise screen content according to nebulously defined standards.[6] Silent film scholar William K. Everson points out that "the 'changes' to Hollywood product resulting from its self-imposed purge were ... more a matter of additions than subtractions." Studios still made suggestive pictures, but they leavened their slate of releases with religious films and light comedies.[7] Such new emphases suited public tastes, for the interest of filmgoers was draining away from the progressive, innovative works of recent years, such as those of Pollard Picture Plays, Lois Weber, and even "the Master," D. W. Griffith.[8] Instead, filmgoers — the majority of whom were women — began to flock to contemporary pictures that more closely reflected the reality of their own lives. In hundreds of 1920s films, young and spirited women known as "flappers" balanced work, college, social expectations, shopping, and romance.

As early as 1918, the flapper (probably known as such because of the unbuckled boots often worn by stylish young women of the time) had blazed her way into the American consciousness, and Margarita Fischer had immediately appropriated the trendy sobriquet for herself. Over the next few years, the flapper image became almost omnipresent in films. This type of characterization, notes historian Mary P. Ryan, was "a glamorous rendition of the social options open to women," which "marked the solidification of a new pattern of female roles characterized by a dynamic equilibrium between work, home, and consumer activities." These new roles, found in pictures such as Gloria Swanson's *Why Change Your Wife?* (1920) and Colleen Moore's *Flaming Youth* (1923), showed women who were vital, confident, ambitious, and alluring. They combined the confidence of the vamp with the sunny spirit of the ingénue. Their attractiveness was material rather than sexual, Ryan explains, and was intended to "train the female audience in fashionable femininity." *Why Change Your Wife?* and similar films demonstrated through the lead female character that modern beauty required stylish, revealing clothes and youthful exuberance. The flapper's energy appealed to men as well as women, and by the middle of the 1920s it was clear, Ryan states, that "to win husband and happiness, women must join the competition on equal terms with the American flapper."[9]

Actresses as well as audiences felt the pull of this new image. In 1921, the public's favorite leading ladies still included perennial sweetheart Mary Pickford, angel-faced Griffith comedienne Dorothy Gish (Lillian's younger sister), and the well-respected, versatile Clara Kimball Young, but flappers were gaining more of the public's attention each year. The list of the public's 1921 favorites was topped by the fashionable young Talmadge sisters, lovely Norma and mischievous Constance, and also included glamorous up-and-coming starlet Gloria Swanson, a former comic actress in Mack Sennett shorts who was building a reputation as a "clotheshorse" in lavish Cecil B. DeMille comedy-dramas.[10] The following year, a seventeen-year-old New Yorker named Clara Bow made her sparkling film debut in the whaling drama *Down to the Sea in Ships*.[11] Within a few years, she came to define the carefree, sensual appeal of the flapper, and her magnetic screen presence won her the nickname "The 'It' Girl." Bow, Swanson, the Talmadges, and other young actresses set American fashions in the 1920s with their large, shadowed eyes, bobbed hair, painted bows of mouths, wispy or exotic costumes, and — above all — their fun-loving energy and confidence. Filmgoers of the 1920s were increasingly fascinated by stardom rather than by storytelling, a preoccupation based on public desire to crack the mystery of an idolized star's personal life.[12] Audiences of the 1920s wanted their idols to have glamorous offscreen personas that tallied with the roles actors played onscreen.[13]

Margarita Fischer had helped to define fashion in the previous decade, and she could easily have assumed the look of a flapper. She had energy to spare, an interest in fashions of all kinds, and a willingness to show her body in stylish clothes (or out of them, as she had proven in *The Pearl of Paradise*), and her youthful features looked lovely in the simple styles of the late 1910s and early 1920s. Her style of facial beauty was still in fashion, too, as evidenced by the popularity of strikingly similar-looking younger stars such as Marguerite Courtot and Alice Joyce, who shared the elder actress's dark hair, oval face, strong nose, and large eyes. Margarita could not so easily, however, adopt the deliberate, worldly screen personality of the flapper. In the years before her retirement, she had developed a signature character notable as much for an asexual naïveté as for wild energy. Even as an expectant mother or a nude islander, her artlessness negated any controversial or carnal aspects of her performance. "Youth and innocence are personified by Miss Margarita Fischer," stated a news item from the mid–1910s.[14] The statement was no less true of her screen persona at the time of her 1921 retirement, and while the former quality had always worked in her favor, the latter was no longer so compelling in the flapper-dominated film world of the early 1920s.

Margarita's figure, too, had fallen out of style by this time. She had slimmed down since her Beauty days and was compact, curvy, strong, and capable; according to the 1920 biosketch compendium *Who's Who on the Screen*, she was "just five feet high" and 117 pounds.[15] Young actresses of the time, however, were required to fit what historian Heather Addison calls a "physical culture" of idealized thinness, encouraged by the insecurity and need inherent in the growing culture of consumption.[16] Addison quotes a 1922 article from *Photoplay*, the magazine that crowned Fischer the "American Beauty" of 1914, which describes a "New American Beauty" of a "softened, feminized ... tiny, childish, girlish type."[17] Now passing her mid-thirties, Margarita was as self-aware as ever, and she probably realized the limitations of her image as she observed younger actresses during her absence from the screen. She had already seen the California film industry grow and change a great deal over the past decade, and she was content for the moment to take everything in from her husband's side as they rebuilt their marriage and he rebuilt his Hollywood career.

Their efforts soon met with success. After reintroducing himself to the world of film with the clever serial *The Invisible Ray*, Harry Pollard teamed in 1922 with Reginald Denny, an aspiring star from England, to film a series of two-reel pictures for an independent

By 1920, Margarita still fit the nation's standards of beauty sufficiently well to serve as an attractive print model for stylish clothing. This June 1920 photo was taken for *Fashion Gossip*. However, her public persona included none of the worldliness of the flapper (courtesy the Margarita Fischer Papers, Special Collections and University Archives, Wichita State University Libraries).

company. This serial, *The Leather Pushers*, cast the elegant, stage-trained Denny as an impoverished heir who becomes a boxer to regain his family fortune. Denny had served Great Britain in the Great War and had won a brigade boxing championship during his military years, so he was plausible in the role. Still, as the actor recollected for film historian Kevin Brownlow, "we had to make them independently because no one would touch them. 'Prize fighting? Who would go and look at it?'"[18] Although the producer soon went bankrupt, the serial drew the attention of Universal, in large part because Laemmle perceived a competitor was interested in the short films. Universal picked up the option, but Laemmle had little interest in the serial. Denny recalled that "[Universal] never thought they had anything [in *The Leather Pushers*], but when they released them — boy, they went over!"[19] The behemoth studio hired Pollard and Denny to finish the 1922 series and to create two more installments in 1923 and 1924 due to its popularity. The series revitalized Pollard's directorial career and brought him back into the folds of the studio system. It also made a star of Denny, who moved into feature films for Universal, and his part in *The Leather Pushers* was then recast with Billy Sullivan (an actual relative of a famous boxer) so the successful serial could continue.[20]

The serial's success held unexpected benefits for others as well. A twenty-year-old print model and aspiring actress named Norma Shearer played the bit part of a flower girl in one of the early episodes of *The Leather Pushers*, causing her to catch the eye of Irving Thalberg, then a young producer at Universal. Margarita later called Thalberg "one of the most brilliant men ever turned out by Hollywood," and he certainly had an eye for screen talent and potential.[21] Thalberg was intrigued by the young Shearer's striking looks, as well as her natural screen presence, and when he developed a reputation as a wunderkind producer and talent scout and moved to Louis B. Mayer's studio in 1923, he offered Shearer her first Hollywood contract. Shearer and Thalberg married in 1927, and their union was extremely successful both personally and professionally.[22] This personal connection would prove to work in Pollard's favor several years later when he made another career change, following Thalberg to the studio by then called MGM.

During and following the successful years of *The Leather Pushers*, Pollard also directed features for Universal. In 1922, he filmed the quirky drama *Confidence* and the Hoot Gibson Westerns *Trimmed* and *The Loaded Door*.[23] Working with Hoot Gibson was a step up and a vote of confidence for Pollard, as Gibson was the studio's most popular Western star at that time. (Part of his drawing power may have come from the realism of his performances; Gibson was a former cowboy who had actually entered films in 1910 as a stuntman before beginning his acting career in 1912.) Gibson had only begun making feature films in 1921; prior to that, he was known for two-reelers that mixed Western actors and storylines with modern settings and technology, such as airplanes. In his feature films, the cowboy star demonstrated an easy comedic style that earned him $14,500 a week at his peak — far more than his director was earning.[24] Gibson's adventurous screen persona allowed Pollard to explore the boundaries of the Western, a genre he had last touched for the IMP almost a decade earlier. Gibson's features were classified as "Universal Jewels," or high-caliber productions, and they eventually fell within their own production company. A scholar of silent screen cowboys noted that Gibson's films "were made with a degree of professionalism which many of the other Westerns of the period lacked.... He was assigned good directors ... [and] above-average stories."[25] For Pollard to be invited to join the company of Gibson was a definite sign that he was back in the game.

The following year, Pollard directed Rockliffe Fellowes, a character actor with a passing resemblance to later star Edward G. Robinson, in a sports picture, *Trifling with Honor*. By the end of 1923, Harry Pollard had established himself as a dependable director for Universal, and the studio had enough confidence in him to assign him to more prestigious projects with Reginald Denny, now a popular leading man. Denny's and Pollard's next collaboration, *Sporting Youth*, was to be a comic action film with a "mistaken identity" plot involving race cars and criminals. With Denny as the male lead, the picture needed a leading lady who could handle the role of a wealthy, exuberant instigator.

Naturally, Margarita Fischer learned from her husband of this latest project, and she thought this sounded like a perfect opportunity to return to the screen now that Pollard's career was back on track. The script of *Sporting Youth* would have offered an excellent vehicle for a comeback; her recent years with American had certainly schooled Margarita in every variation of the mischief-making heiress character, and she would have enjoyed acting under her husband's direction once more. Convinced, Pollard lobbied Universal hard on behalf of his wife, but Reginald Denny persuaded the studio instead to cast rising star Laura La Plante, a nineteen-year-old who had been working in Hoot Gibson films. "Pollard didn't have the real comedy touch," Denny later explained. "Pollard was all for the broad comedy and I was for the lighter. We just couldn't agree."[26] Pollard resented Denny's intervention into the film's casting, and the pair cooled towards each other afterwards; nevertheless, *Sporting Youth* was a hit and cemented Denny's reputation as a comedian.[27]

Universal attempted to recapture this success by reteaming Denny and Pollard immediately. Just as American had limited Margarita's screen roles a few years before, Universal handed Pollard projects over which he had little control, but both he and Denny were professional enough to be able to work together despite their personal distaste for one another. In June 1924, they collaborated on the light romantic comedy *The Reckless Age*, and over the next year they made three more comic-action films together: *Oh, Doctor*; *I'll Show You the Town*; and *California Straight Ahead*. Margarita never did win a part in any of these films; instead, they were cast with high-profile leading ladies, including Mary Astor, Marian Nixon, and Lilyan Tashman. The Pollard-Denny teamings were more financially successful than those of Denny and his other frequent director, William Seiter, who Denny felt shared his own preference for subtle comedy.[28] So great was their appeal to

Harry Pollard cultivated a scholarly image as a successful director for Universal in the mid–1920s (courtesy the Harry Pollard Papers, Special Collections and University Archives, Wichita State University Libraries).

audiences, in fact, that the often-critical film writer Iris Barry devoted a whole page to the quality of the Denny comedies in her 1926 work *Let's Go to the Movies*, describing them as the best pictures put out by Universal:

> ... The comedies of Mr. Reginald Denny are very comic. They are also well photographed, perfectly acted, superbly timed, fast moving and altogether what is called one hundred per cent. box office value. They exhilarate as neatly as they make one laugh.
> ... Universal [makes event films] in order to provide for Mr. Reginald Denny, which is exactly as it should be, for Mr. Reginald Denny is the kind of thing that the cinema most needs.... It is criminal to miss seeing a single one of [his films] and that is that![29]

The financial success of the director's teamings with Denny, meanwhile, caused Carl Laemmle to take notice. "Comedy is King and Pollard His Premier," proclaimed the latest "Straight from the Shoulder" full-page press release by the enthusiastic president of Universal. "Pollard is a serious-minded, serious-appearing chap. He has no twinkle in his eye. But he has something deeper and better. POLLARD HAS A TWINKLE IN HIS HEART: He has to his credit the most amazing list of successful pictures I ever heard of in my whole moving picture career" (a credit that does not necessarily follow from the director's internal twinkle, but no doubt lay close to the studio's own heart). The bombastic item concludes with Laemmle's characteristic excitement: "Mr. Pollard, I salute you: You may get a lot of pleasure out of what you have accomplished, but no matter how much happiness it gives you, it doesn't give you half so much as it gives me. I'M PROUD OF YOU — PROUD TO BUSTIN.'"[30]

Margarita Fischer was undoubtedly just as pleased by her husband's success, but by now she felt she had seen too many changes from the sidelines of the film industry over the past three years. Whether her image was suited for leading roles or not, she wanted to make more films before her formerly devoted public forgot her completely. The *Sporting Youth* disappointment was only a temporary setback. By the middle of 1924, before his series of Denny comedies began, Pollard had signed on with Universal to direct a Virginia Valli vehicle, *K—The Unknown*, and Margarita had lined up a substantive supporting role in the picture. For one of the first times in her film career, she would not play the female lead, but the sacrifice was worth it to get her name in front of film audiences again.

With her unerring eye for a publicity opportunity, Margarita scouted Pasadena for location shots a few weeks before the release of *K—The Unknown* and bought a new car while she was there. As a result, she appeared on the front page of the *Pasadena Star-News*'s Automobile Section under the wordy headline "Former Screen Star of First Magnitude Emerges from Retirement and Is Acclaimed by Critics for Splendid Performance in Late Film Drama." A drawing and three photos of the actress appeared below the headline. In one shot, she sits behind the wheel of another of her beloved vehicles, her "New Rickenbacker Eight Sedan"; in another, she stands next to the car (a driver is visible behind the wheel); in the third, she sits coyly on its front fender. She appears proud and — as always — quite stylish in a loose-fitting dress, several strands of pearls, a long fur coat, and a banded cloche hat over her bobbed hair. The text accompanying these large images was brief, recapping Margarita's career (referring to her as "Margarita Fischer Pollard" and "Miss Pollard") and noting that she, "like other prominent players, has declined to sign a contract with any particular company and she will henceforth do what is known as 'free lancing'— associating herself with any one particular

9. When Queenie Came Back

A chic Margarita Fischer poses with her new car in this 1924 photo, taken as she prepared to make her film comeback (courtesy the Margarita Fischer Papers, Special Collections and University Archives, Wichita State University Libraries).

studio for the duration of one or more productions."³¹ The article places a positive spin on the actress's freelance status, but, in fact, her comeback was in a very uncertain state. A lavish publicity spread for *K—The Unknown* billed her as "Margarita Pollard," a sign of how much her name had been effaced in only three years, while that of her husband had become better known.³² Universal had agreed to employ Margarita only for the one picture, and she would have to begin seeking work at square one again if no further offer was forthcoming. She would surely have welcomed the security of a studio contract.

Unfortunately, her performance in *K—The Unknown* was not notable enough for Universal to sign her on for other projects. It was simply "not a very good film," states writer and film historian F. Gwynplaine MacIntyre.³³ The film, based on the novel *K* by popular mystery writer Mary Roberts Rinehart, occupies itself with the melodramatic romances of nurse Sidney Page, played by Virginia Valli, a slim twentysomething actress who shared clean modern looks and a slightly cleft chin with a still-unknown Swedish actress named Greta Garbo, then just a year away from her first American film contract. Vivacious Sidney is pursued by many men but attracted only to one, surgeon Max Wilson. Sidney's interest in the dashing doctor gives rise to public gossip, when in truth she is practically the only young woman in town with whom the surgeon is not having an affair. A much more suitable partner shows himself in the person of the mysterious "K," who romances Sidney but hides a secret. When one of Sidney's admirers shoots Dr. Wilson, K saves the doctor's life and reveals his true identity as a celebrated surgeon, winning Sidney's heart. Margarita Fischer played the unremarkable third-billed role of Charlotte Harrison, one of the many young women who succumb to Max Wilson's dubious charms.

Margarita must have been disappointed with the lackluster vehicle chosen for her film comeback, but it seems not to have hurt her ability to find employment. Soon after the November 1924 release of *K—The Unknown*, she arranged with Paramount to act in another romantic drama, *Any Woman*, directed by Henry King.³⁴ Margarita again played a supporting role, that of Mrs. Rand, a stockbroker's wife. Her part, while not large, was significant to the plot. When her husband and his business partner proposition and try to compromise their secretary (the leading female role, played by Alice Terry), Mrs. Rand helps the younger woman meet up with her lover and therefore escape the predatory businessmen.³⁵ The film, released in May 1925, was reviewed by the *New York Times*'s Mordaunt Hall as "[not] particularly subtle or original," but with "a number of agreeable stretches which make it enjoyable light entertainment."³⁶

The film's leading lady bore a slight resemblance to Margarita Fischer — and, in fact, Margarita may have felt a kinship in life story as well as appearance to Alice Terry, a slight, brown-haired actress in her mid-twenties. Both actresses were native Midwesterners who were married to directors (Terry to Rex Ingram, best remembered for silent epics such as 1921's *The Four Horsemen of the Apocalypse* and 1925's *Ben-Hur*); both were petite, athletic brunettes (although Terry frequently wore a blonde wig in films) with large, expressive eyes and strong noses; both attempted to downplay their dark complexions in order to gain more mainstream roles.³⁷ The casting of this younger counterpart in *Any Woman*'s ingénue role must have indicated to Margarita that her days as a leading lady were over.

Surprisingly, though, a much more prestigious project followed soon after the release of *Any Woman*. Harry Pollard was by now one of Universal's top directors, thanks in large part

9. When Queenie Came Back

By the time she was cast in *Any Woman* (Famous Players, 1925), Margarita was no longer thought of as a leading lady. Here, female lead Alice Terry (standing) implores Margarita's character for help. Margarita played a supporting but pivotal role in this film (courtesy the Margarita Fischer Papers, Special Collections and University Archives, Wichita State University Libraries).

to the success of his comic films with Reginald Denny, and in 1925 he proposed an ambitious feature-length adaptation of *Uncle Tom's Cabin* to a receptive Carl Laemmle. Laemmle agreed, on the condition that Pollard would continue to direct comedies during the planning stages of the historical epic.[38] Once Pollard received the go-ahead to direct the historical epic, studio director-general Henry McRae suggested (possibly at Pollard's prompting) that Margarita Fischer play the pivotal role of the light-skinned slave Eliza in the proposed Universal film, a part that she had frequently played on stage during her touring years.[39] McRae had the reputation of being one who "could always be depended upon to help a down-and-out actor."[40] The chance to play Eliza again, and to act under her husband's direction as he brought to bear the resources of the world's largest movie studio, seemed to Margarita to be a golden opportunity for her to revitalize her career.

10

Uncle Tom's Cabin

The story of *Uncle Tom's Cabin* was much more familiar in 1927 than it is to a twenty-first century audience. Changing tastes in entertainment, as well as a greater sensitivity to the racial stereotypes often perceived in the story, have caused it to decline as a source of entertainment and instead take on mainly historical interest. In the early decades of the previous century, however, it was a stalwart of both stage and screen. The work began life as Harriet Beecher Stowe's runaway success of an antebellum novel. Published in 1852, the book told the story of two slaves, Uncle Tom and Eliza, who are owned by the Shelby family at the novel's outset. When Mr. Shelby plans to sell Eliza's son to cover debts, Eliza flees northward with her child, hoping to be reunited with her husband in Canada. Uncle Tom, meanwhile, is sent south down the Mississippi River to be sold at a slave market. On his way, he encounters the sympathetic St. Clares, who eventually buy Tom. Upon St. Clare's death, his wife sells Tom to a cruel plantation owner named Simon Legree. Tom withstands Legree's torments by drawing on his strong Christian faith and is eventually martyred.[1] More than just a touching story, however, the novel both expressed and inflamed the tensions between the slaveholding and free portions of the nation in the years before the Civil War. As author Michele Wallace explained, "Uncle Tom's Cabin was one of the most influential texts of the latter half of the 19th century and the first half of the 20th century.... Critics and fans alike credit the book with having provided the first easily exportable image-text for immediate and popular consumption depicting the plight of the slave in the U.S. South."[2]

Of course, it was also just a plain good story, with a wide variety of colorful sympathetic and unsympathetic characters of all ages and races; the slave characters as well as the upper-class whites were portrayed as three-dimensional humans. After the Civil War, the antebellum text was a natural for adaptation to the stage. Productions of *Uncle Tom's Cabin* became a staple of touring companies in the late 1800s and early 1900s; Margarita herself had played the part of Eliza as the youthful head of the Fischer players. The work was a natural fit for film as well, since the story was so familiar to audiences that they would understand it even in a silent, truncated form. Its first adaptation was a ten-minute 1903 Edison version that predates even the more famous *The Great Train Robbery* as an example of narrative feature filmmaking. Other film versions appeared in 1903 (Lubin), 1910 (Vitagraph, Thanhouser), 1913 (IMP, Kalem), 1914 (World, the first version in which an African American actor played Uncle Tom), and 1918 (Famous Players–Lasky). The 1913 IMP three-reel version of the tale, now lost, had cast Harry Pollard as Uncle Tom and Margarita Fischer as Topsy.[3] *Uncle Tom's Cabin* could hardly have seemed a more auspicious choice for Margarita to cement her return to film, and she was surely optimistic when Pollard began scouting for location shots in mid–1925. Not only would she be working once again under her husband's directorship — a closeness that had been of great importance since her return to the screen — but she was very familiar with the story and the role, due to her own career history.

Several factors combined at once to undermine the planned film's production speed and quality, though. As film historian David Pierce points out, "Universal did not have the expertise or the management controls for large scale productions."[4] Production began with more zeal than practicality on *Uncle Tom's Cabin*, as the script was still bloated and unfocused, hampered in its development by Pollard's and Laemmle's joint desire not to offend Southern filmgoers. Perhaps as a result of the script's nebulous structure, Pollard and his location crew wasted a great deal of time and money looking for the most historically accurate settings and the perfect conditions under which to film. The film's dramatic high point, Eliza's river crossing with her child over fractured ice in order to escape the bloodhounds of slave traders, required more than three weeks of scouting before filming, and the inclement weather during which the crew filmed took a toll on their health. Pollard caught a cold which infected his teeth, a subsequent dentist visit broke his jaw, and he was hospitalized in New York with blood poisoning. He eventually required six operations on his jaw, and his recovery was so lengthy that he resigned as the film's director and was replaced by Margarita's one-time IMP director Lois Weber (by now one of the only women directors in male-dominated, conglomerated Hollywood), who began rewriting the script. To add insult to literal injury, the hard-won ice-crossing footage was eventually discarded, and the scene was later refilmed on a studio set.[5]

After a five month hospitalization, a scarred and haggard Pollard had regained his strength. He was ready and eager to resume control of the film, and Weber graciously stepped aside. "It has been Mr. Pollard's lifelong desire to make this film, and I feel that it should be given back to him," she explained in a news item.[6] Although cordial, the transition was by no means smooth. After more than half a year, Pollard was still at the beginning of the filmmaking process, not yet having finished casting the film. "'Uncle Tom's Cabin' has sheltered a lot of grief in its time," stated the same news item, "and when Universal started out to film the picture they seem to have forgotten to hang the horseshoe over the door."

Controversy arose over whether to cast black actors or have white actors in blackface play pivotal roles, which would improve the film's reception in the South. Ultimately, Pollard pleased no one but himself by casting both races. James Lowe, a distinguished African-American actor known for his work in Westerns, was to play Uncle Tom (after an initial battle of wills with the originally cast African-American actor Charles Gilpin, which resulted in his firing). While it is tempting to attribute progressive ideals to Pollard for casting a black actor to play Uncle Tom, it is more likely that this historical stickler simply thought it would be the most accurate way to present the story.

He was, however, not averse to crossing racial lines when casting exigencies demanded it. The mischievous role of the young slave Topsy that Margarita had so coveted a decade and a half before was similarly desired by the teenaged Mona Ray, a diminutive white vaudeville actress. After Pollard initially refused to audition her, thinking her too old, she wheedled her way into a blackface role (asking no salary) in the live theatrical prologue of a film premiere Pollard attended at one of Sid Grauman's famous theaters. Grauman, who appreciated a practical joke, watched in delight as Ray strutted forward in the middle of her act, quoting Topsy's most famous lines—"I wasn't born! I just growed!" The rest of the audience may have been confused, but Pollard got the message, reevaluated his opinion and cast her as Topsy.[7] She played the role in blackface (though extremely convincing blackface; as author Michele Wallace notes, her true race is undetectable).[8] The light-skinned slaves—Eliza, her mother Cassie, and her husband George—were simply played by white actors with appearances unaltered (except for, in Margarita's case, a long black wig). Pollard could in no way have overlooked the convenience of having an experienced portrayer of Eliza in his own home, and it would at the time have been unthinkable to cast a black actor as her love interest. According to film historian David Pierce, the decision to fill these central roles with white actors was supported by Universal's sales department in New York, which sent a memo to the California production facility stating that "white audiences are not likely to find negroes' love affairs attractive or interesting. However [due to the casting of white actors as George and Eliza], the audience will no doubt lose sight of the fact that they are not white."[9]

Harry Pollard faced difficult racial issues in casting *Uncle Tom's Cabin*, especially if the film were to succeed in the South. He finally decided to cast African-American actor James Lowe (right) in the title role. At left is longtime supporting and character actress Virginia Grey, here in her film debut as Little Eva at age ten (courtesy the Harry Pollard Papers, Special Collections and University Archives, Wichita State University Libraries).

Pollard also changed the film's plot by making Eliza a much more significant character and by placing the story's action during the Civil War, which eliminated the source novel's original abolitionist message. This decision was probably made with fiscal motivations — box office would be significantly decreased if the film were not accepted in the South — but some sources gave it much loftier motivations. Stated a fan magazine article about the film's release, "Mrs. Stowe's book has always been misunderstood, particularly below the Mason and Dixon line.... Pollard is presenting a true, sympathetic story of the South in ante-bellum days, in other words, doing the Stowe novel [theatrically] as it should have been done and as she would have done it herself had she had any control over the dramatic rights."[10] Despite Pollard's efforts at placation, however, Southerners remained hostile to the film. A November 1926 article in the Memphis, Tennessee, *News Scimitar* recounted the anger of the local chapter of United Daughters of the Confederacy over Pollard's decision to film portions of the picture in the city. The chapter president, the granddaughter of Confederate general and Ku Klux Klan founder Nathan Bedford Forrest, stated that "The story is false, and is a direct insult to the old true South."[11]

As production continued, the film's cost spiraled. Production costs on *Uncle Tom's Cabin* eventually reached almost $1.8 million, making it one of the most expensive silent films ever. Besides the costs of location shooting and discarded footage (977,000 feet, or 977 full reels were exposed), Universal had spent tens of thousands to achieve the realism needed to accommodate Pollard's production methods. As enumerated in a souvenir book's list, "Fascinating Facts and Figures on the Making of *Uncle Tom's Cabin*," the cast and extras eventually swelled to more than 2,400 people, and the company traveled more than 26,000 miles scouting for location shots. After all this travel, most of the shooting was actually done in Universal's sunny California studios, which made additional artifice necessary, such as snow made from 400 tons of gypsum and 12 carloads of breakfast cereal. The wintry fog was achieved by "the burning of two hundred tons of lowly, worn out automobile tires; the picture results are most artistic but the aesthetic efforts during the actual filming of these scenes were not so pleasantly received by the nostrils of the brave players."[12]

The epic production also required sixty bales of Spanish moss, 200 barrels of paint, 65 sets (compared to an average of eight or nine), 1,000 live adult trees, and 66,000 individual props.[13] As Pollard wanted to give the impression of shooting on location, sets were fully constructed and furnished so they could be approached and filmed from any angle. In addition, the studio refurbished a historic riverboat for Mississippi scenes, paying more than four thousand dollars weekly in rent, as well as reconstruction costs. Finally, Eliza's chase and ice-crossing scene had to be recreated in the studio, a feat which required three acres, the diversion of the Los Angeles river, and an additional 37 shooting days.[14]

Production dragged on for so long that, once the film was finally complete, the cast threw a "Reunion Dinner Party." The party invitation was charming, poking hilarious fun at the lengthy process in a "Foreword":

> With all due modesty we admit that there have been auspicious occasions before. Columbus discovered America; we'll grant that. Washington crossed the Delaware; we'll even agree on that point. Lindbergh flew over the Atlantic; who are we to take credit from him.
> But [of] all the auspicious occasions of the past, this, tonight, is the auspiciousest, marking as it does, the announcement that the world's greatest motion picture is officially finished.

> Hail, ye historians! Mark ye! Write it on your tablets and indite it in your scrolls, "Uncle Tom's Cabin" is in the box! After nineteen months of intensive, extensive and expensive labor, many of us now have to look for jobs.
>
> History has been made this past year and seven months. Automobiles have been bought and paid for; first payments have been made on property with sidewalks, gas, telephone, lights and sewers in; many anemic wardrobes have been amply replenished; hitherto unblemished vocabularies have been enriched with the ultimate in profanity; and, oh, yes, a picture has been made.[15]

Following the cheeky Foreword came a menu reminiscent of Margarita's "nineteenth" birthday party and her patriotic party at the Potter. The film's leading lady clearly had a hand in its drafting, as the menu included "Fruit Cocktail a la Margarita," "Olives Ethiope," "Celery, 10 Per Cent Cut Effective Immediately," "Salade St. Clare," and, of course, "Eliza-Crossing-the-Ice Cream."[16]

As the cast and crew enjoyed their fun, Carl Laemmle was optimistic before the November 1927 release of his "Universal Super-Jewel," one of the studio's most prestigious and

This image from *Uncle Tom's Cabin* (Universal, 1927) provides an example of the film's grand scale. A historic riverboat was completely refurbished for the picture. In the foreground, Margarita Fischer as Eliza tries by any possible method to escape from George Siegmann as the cruel Simon Legree (courtesy the Harry Pollard Papers, Special Collections and University Archives, Wichita State University Libraries).

expensive productions. "The picture will go forth from Universal City as the most faithful reproduction of characters, settings, and the spirit of the times, ever put into celluloid," trumpeted a press release.[17] In March 1927, the studio replaced Pollard's annual contract (the most recent of which was signed in October 1926) with a new five-year contract, assuring, as a press release stated, "the exclusive services of a man who has risen to exceptional heights in the directorial field ... and who now is acknowledged as one of the foremost directors in the industry."[18] Under this new contract, Pollard would earn a phenomenal $100,000 per film.[19] At the time, all but the largest star salaries still usually hovered between five hundred to two thousand dollars weekly, while a Hollywood secretary got by on a weekly salary of forty dollars.[20] Universal's practice of hyping high costs and salaries was widely emulated at the time, as high figures were regarded as a mark of quality and of a production's or performer's worth.[21]

Other publications picked up on the hype; the film was the major focus of the "Pre–View" section of the *Los Angeles Sunday Times* in March and May 1927.[22] A news item excitedly touted the real-life romance between director Pollard and his leading lady, sentimentalizing the couple's road to fame and cheering that "today they are still the happy couple they were in the days when jobs were scarce, meals ditto, the future bleak."[23] (The most notable statement made in the entire article is Margarita's uncharacteristic hint at her true age in saying she had been married for fifteen years — which, the author noted, she only revealed "after much teasing.") The director–leading actress marriage was a fascinating topic for the press's discussion, just as it had been in the late 1910s. A major article in *Motion Picture Classic* breathlessly recalled the couple's 1913 foray as Uncle Tom and Topsy for IMP — "and fourteen years later Pollard has become a famous director and — more remarkable from some points of view in the movie world — is still married to the same wife."[24]

Universal itself unleashed the full force of its publicity department by distributing "Sixteen pages of Proven Press copy for the Universal masterpiece 'Uncle Tom's Cabin'" for use by the media. Among the flamboyant claims made within these pages was the statement in a brief biography of Margarita that her father had been a minstrel star and that she owed her Beauty contract to her performance as Topsy in the 1913 three-reel film version of the same story. The sixteen pages also included five template reviews of the film — naturally, all raves.[25] In addition, an article in *Universal Weekly* stressed the accuracy not of props or sets, but of Margarita's scuttle across the ice in the film's most iconic scene. "When Eliza eludes the bloodhounds ... you can be sure that she does it in the most approved fashion of the best criminals.... [Margarita Fischer] took pains, when the company was on location in the East last winter, to visit Dannemora Prison and there learn from a 'lifer,' who has many escapes on his record, exactly how this should be done."[26]

Unfortunately, even after such flamboyant publicity and a nearly two-million-dollar, nineteen-month investment on the part of Universal, Pollard failed to make a hit film. The seams of the lengthy and troubled patchwork picture show, and the difficult production, coupled with Pollard's single-minded pursuit of realism in sets and locations, cost the film its entertainment value. The movie's static staging, and Pollard's use of superimpositions and irising, would have seemed dated even at the time of the picture's release, and the characters look neither historically accurate nor fashionably contemporary. The actors wear heavy makeup, and some performances are stagey and old-fashioned, especially that of the leering Simon Legree (George Siegmann, who had given a similar performance in Griffith's 1915 *Birth of a Nation*). To audiences of the late 1920s, *Uncle Tom's Cabin* looked instantly outmoded, despite its high production values.

The appearance of the film was probably the greatest handicap to the film's box office success. In the late 1920s, film audiences — assumed by fan magazines to be female-dominated — were turning away from historical dramas to modern subject matter. They were interested in stars who could serve as role models for behavior and dress, and appeal in a way that was relevant for modern life. In response, "in marketing the star, the studios understood that the real connection between performer and audience occurred when the fan took on, in the dream space of the movie theater, the star's intangible qualities of personality and style."[27] (Margarita Fischer's late–1910s fan letters complimenting her clothing and friendly persona are examples of the development of this type of interest.) Of course, historical films were still made, but modern style and relevance had to be maintained. Glamorous female film stars, especially, provided a bridge between the modern and historical by introducing contemporary fashion and design into period style (a practice that continues today). "If a period

This still from *Uncle Tom's Cabin* shows the film's odd costumes and theatricality. Simon Legree (George Siegmann, right) threatens his slave mistress Cassie (Eulalie Jensen, center), while Eliza (Margarita Fischer) prepares to escape out of the window (courtesy the Harry Pollard Papers, Special Collections and University Archives, Wichita State University Libraries).

picture suddenly appeared depicting women correctly attired for that period, the shock for the uninitiated would be great," explains silent film historian Kevin Brownlow.[28] Margarita Fischer — as leading lady, the bridge between filmgoers and the film — is unflatteringly made up and dressed in *Uncle Tom's Cabin*, which probably further lessened its appeal. Her 1920s-style makeup is combined with hairstyles and clothing that are neither modern nor historically accurate. By contrast, her husband's compulsive quest for accuracy in design, sets, and props ensured that they were scrupulously appropriate to the 1860s and thereby eliminated some of the film's visual appeal for 1920s audiences.

Although they did not explicitly draw attention to the film's unstylish look, contemporary critics noticed its oddities of casting, scripting, and performance. The *Los Angeles Times* stated that "it is a relief to see the old drama beautifully done," but that the story itself "is outmoded. It belongs to another day in the theater, yet its power and significance will never be entirely lost."[29] However, "much of the picture is sketchy. The thread of one plot is dropped and another taken up. In view of the wealth of material already at hand, it hardly seems necessary to drag in bodily Sherman's march to the sea." The critic did give Margarita herself credit for "an unforgettable characterization as Eliza," and for "fine dramatic work ... when her child is taken from her and sold to a Georgian planter. This perhaps is the most moving scene in the picture." The Los Angeles audience also loved the film's dramatic ice-crossing scene and actually applauded its presentation. Still, the critic thought, "Harry Pollard's direction throughout is workmanlike and good, but only in one or two instances is it really inspired.[30]

Such mixes of praise and criticism became familiar from reviewers, though they could not always agree on which details of the film impressed or bothered them. "I remember a critic in New York saying, 'Why did they pick Margarita Fischer to play Eliza? She looks about as much like a Creole as....'— they compared me with some other girl that was so blonde, very, very, blonde," Margarita recalled indignantly, wounded at the slight to her famously chameleon-like looks. In fact, she had dyed her auburn hair black for the role.[31] *New York Times* reviewer Mordaunt Hall was more moderate. He first noted that "Mr. Pollard has presented some scenes with unusual skill, particularly those scenes in which Topsy and Eva are beheld," and also singled out for praise Eliza's ice-crossing scene, Pollard's riverboat scenes, the overall performances of Mona Ray and Virginia Grey as Topsy and Eva, and the "excellent performance" of James Lowe as Uncle Tom. In addition, "Margarita Fischer, with the merest suspicion of an Ethiopian on her countenance, does very well as Eliza." However, "There is always an unremitting effort to make this picture tearful, which is possibly to be expected. Here, however, the hardships and cruelty are never depicted with the slightest idea of restraint." Hall names the death of Little Eva, the scourging of Uncle Tom, and the brutishness and death of Simon Legree as examples of this characteristic (Legree "has never been pictured as possessing any virtues, but here his presence is repugnant, especially when he storms about the room with food drueling [sic] from his mouth").[32]

Filmgoers found some of the same faults with the film: due to complaints from the premiere audience and from censors, *Uncle Tom's Cabin* was hastily re-edited just after its premiere in order to tone down its perceived brutality. After being trimmed by nearly half an hour, it entered general release in late 1928 some ten months after its New York premiere. By that time, synchronized sound had begun reshaping filmmaking methods, and Universal also added a track of synchronized sound effects and music, but no dialogue, to the film for use by theaters with sound equipment. The cuts improved the film's clarity, and it did very good business in rural America. It still came half a million dollars short of breaking even, though, thus hurting the studio, Pollard's career, and Margarita's attempt at a comeback.[33]

Still, some aspects of the problem-riddled picture are very appealing. James Lowe is dignified and subtle as Uncle Tom, and future character actress Virginia Grey, making her film debut at age ten as the angelic Little Eva, plays her brief part with great maturity and sweetness. Margarita, billed as the picture's star, is quite effective as Eliza, despite any unlikeliness in her appearance. Her performance is generally understated and believable, and her mobile face is heartfelt. She laughs with delight as children dance around her on her wedding day; she gasps in terror as dogs chase her and her child across ice floes over a wintry river; she tenses as Legree lustfully paws her, using only her eyes to communicate her loathing and horror; tears of joy stream down her quiet, uplifted face as she is reunited with her mother, and later with her child and husband.[34]

Although she did not suspect it at the time, *Uncle Tom's Cabin* was to be Margarita Fischer's last film. Her final retirement from the screen was probably due to a combination of personal and professional factors. Although she looked a decade younger than her carefully concealed forty-one years, her outmoded appearance in *Uncle Tom's Cabin*, combined with its failure at the box office, might have turned studio heads against her. It certainly provided no impetus for Universal to offer her a contract. Audience tastes were inclined towards the modern or recent, not the overtly historical. In 1927, Margarita again saw her former title pass to a more youthful star when lovely twentysomething actress Billie Dove appeared in a contemporary romance called *American Beauty* for First National studio, and the studio began promoting her with that nickname.[35] The top-grossing films of 1927 gave further hints as to changing audience tastes: two of the greatest money-makers were the Mary Pickford romantic comedy *My Best Girl* and the ground-breaking part-talkie Al Jolson picture *The Jazz Singer*. *Love*, a Greta Garbo-John Gilbert vehicle based on *Anna Karenina*, was also a high-grossing film that year, sharing literary roots and a period setting with *Uncle Tom's Cabin*.[36] In contrast to Pollard's film, however, *Love* was well-paced and elegantly stylish, and its financial returns were no doubt assisted by the fact that it starred two of the silent era's most attractive players, who were currently engaged in a torrid and aggressively publicized romance. When the Academy Awards were established as a political and social force within the film industry in the late 1920s, the most powerful figures in movies recognized flapper star Clara Bow's World War I romance and battle epic, *Wings*, as the best dramatic picture of the 1927–1928 year.

Looking back in later decades, when Margarita was asked why she had retired from filmmaking, the actress laughed ruefully, "I guess I wasn't wanted any longer."[37] She maintained, however, that she truly "retired at the request of my husband ... who wanted me to be with him always, and this I could not do unless I gave up my career."[38] Pollard's health struggles and professional roller coaster of the past few years had led him to depend on the full-time support of his wife—a support not given entirely without regret, as she added, revealingly, that "At the beginning I missed my work terribly and it took me some time to get used to being without it."[39] Margarita had also enjoyed and began to miss her fame and her fans—aspects of filmmaking that Pollard had never liked and could never appreciate.

Pollard's wishes aside, Margarita was swept into retirement as the film industry underwent a whirlwind conversion to sound filmmaking. The reproduction of natural sound had long been a goal of the film industry; in 1919, technical film writer Austin Lescarboura described prototypical sound systems and noted, "images and sound waves being in perfect synchronization ... describes, in brief, the eventual goal of cinematography.... [E]verything that does not quite come up to the ideal is but temporary and can only be considered as a milestone in the steady progress of the art."[40] Over the next eight years, steady progress indeed occurred; the invention of the audion tube permitted sound to be amplified sufficiently to fill a theater, while sound recording itself became dominated by more accurate electrical methods (recording into a microphone) rather than the earlier acoustic techniques (recording into an amplifying horn, cutting into a malleable medium such as a wax cylinder with a stylus). Before these advances, studios, theater owners, and audiences had rejected sound filmmaking processes as too limited, complex, or expensive.[41] By the mid–1920s, however, two distinct processes were being refined that would allow film audiences to enjoy true-to-life sound fully: the Warner Brothers' Vitaphone system, which recorded sound onto large records which were synchronized with film play via belts, and the Fox Movietone system, which adapted a German technology of converting recorded sound into light beams onto a strip of film next to the corresponding image.[42]

In 1926, the Warners publicly demonstrated the success of their sound-on-disc Vitaphone process with talking shorts and the feature film *Don Juan*, which starred John Barrymore and featured synchronized sound effects but no dialogue. The film was accompanied at its August 6 premiere by eight Vitaphone shorts, the first of which featured Will Hays, president of the Motion Picture Producers and Distributors of America, introducing not only the following shorts but the concept of talking pictures as the next phase of filmmaking development:

> Far indeed have we advanced from that few seconds of shadow of a serpentine dancer thirty years ago when the motion picture was born....
> The future of the motion picture is as far-flung as all the tomorrows, rendering greater and still greater service as the chief amusement of all our people and the sole amusement of millions and millions, exercising an immeasurable influence as a living, breathing thing.[43]

Although delivered in a stagy, over-rehearsed manner, Hays's florid speech could hardly have overstated the "immeasurable influence" that sound technology would exercise on the filmgoing public and, more slowly, on the film studios themselves.

The following year, *The Jazz Singer*, starring the charismatic, eager Al Jolson (who had already made his sound debut in the 1926 Vitaphone short *A Plantation Act*), became the first feature film with synchronized dialogue segments. The film was mainly silent — only about fifteen percent of the footage was sound — but its few dialogue and song sequences were electrifying to 1927 audiences. Critics lauded the film, and audiences applauded enthusiastically as beloved entertainer Jolson commanded the screen as well as the stage. Despite the limited number of theaters that had installed Vitaphone sound equipment (only 157 nationwide by the end of 1927), the film eventually grossed $2.6 million, six times its production cost.[44] "Talking pictures" were an immediate hit, and studios quickly began the process of conversion to the new form.

The final years of silent film were, ironically, the greatest years for artistic freedom since the beginnings of the studio system. Studios in a state of technological flux were desperate for products to fill theaters, and relaxed their control over filmmakers as a result.[45] (Harry Pollard's financial carte blanche from Universal in filming *Uncle Tom's Cabin* is an example of this phenomenon.) During the period of conversion, from 1927 to 1930, such diverse silent gems as King Vidor's poetic romance *Sunrise* (1927), the boisterous Hollywood insider comedy *Show People* (1928), and Greta Garbo's mature drama *A Woman of Affairs* (1928) were released. After a short period of adjustment and innovation, though, studios were anxious to associate themselves solely with sound film and with stars who could perform well in this new medium. As early as February 1927, five studios without a proprietary sound system — Universal, MGM, Paramount, First National, and Producer's Distributing Corporation — convened to discuss converting to sound. They agreed to study the competing sound on disc and sound on film systems for a year, then select an industry standard.[46] The future of film lay in sound.

11

Beach of Dreams

The new art form of film, barely more than three decades old but already mature and sophisticated, was suddenly and fundamentally changed with the introduction of synchronized sound. As film historian Kevin Brownlow eloquently summarized this period, "When sound arrived, it not only brought the silent era to a close. It wrecked the careers of many stars and of many directors, who, while expert with silent pictures, were lost when it came to dialogue. Like sculptors forced suddenly to take up painting, they found themselves working in the same studios, in the same business, but in a completely different medium."[1] Louise Brooks, a whip-smart silent ingénue who soon turned her back on Hollywood, later became one of the most unblinking chroniclers of the 1920s in film and explained the studio thought processes that came to define this transitional time: "Old pictures were bad pictures. Pictures were better than ever. An actor was only as good as his last picture. These three articles of faith were laid down by the producers, and business was conducted in a manner to prove them."[2]

Not surprisingly, the careers of many of the most popular silent stars did not survive the transition to sound. No spoken words could sustain John Gilbert's impossibly romantic silent screen image, especially when paired with the dashing actor's overly proper elocution and a slightly nasal voice that did not record well on the primitive technology.[3] Quintessential flapper Clara Bow was thrust quickly into sound filmmaking with no time to prepare, and though her husky Brooklyn accent suited her brash, working-class screen persona well, she was cripplingly intimidated by on-set sound equipment. Lillian Gish's fragile onscreen image was irrevocably linked with a virginal innocence that now seemed to belong to bygone days. Her greatest successes were behind her, though she was able to segue into strong character parts in later decades.[4]

Sometimes careers foundered because of a performer's image rather than vocal unsuitability. Reginald Denny had built his stardom mainly in energetic middle-class comedies of American life, many of which were directed by Harry Pollard, but the actor himself hailed from England and had the cultured accent to prove it. Although his voice was pleasant, it was actually too refined for his roles. Unable suddenly to switch his image—or, apparently, to retrain his accent—he eventually transitioned into supporting roles as a stock Englishman character.[5] Norma Talmadge was less successful. She made a few sound films, but "she had one foot in the 1890s and the other in the 1920s," says film historian Jeanine Basinger, and her meltingly dramatic roles did not adapt well to sound. After a few consecutive flops, her career was over in 1930. Her younger sister Constance, known for light, modern comedies, took her own career more casually; she happily retired in 1927 and left her audiences behind in the silent era, coaxing Norma to join her with the famous telegram, "Quit pressing your luck, baby. The critics can't knock those trust funds Mama set up for us."[6] The seemingly indestructible Mary Pickford, Margarita's nearest contemporary who was still making consistently successful films, lopped her famous long curls into a chic bob (an event which made the front page of the *New York Times*) for her first sound picture, 1929's *Coquette*, in an attempt to appeal to Jazz-Age audiences. Her performance was a success and won her an Academy Award, but "in going modern," as biographer Robert Windeler notes, "Mary Pickford lost her uniqueness and became just another leading lady in her thirties." She made three more films of decreasing financial success, then retired in 1933 at the age of forty-one.[7]

Margarita Fischer did not at once know what to make of all these changes, but she took them in stride. In August 1928, she visited her paternal aunt Anna Fischer, a school principal in Salem, and offered a "hometown" interviewer her thoughts on the changes sweeping the film industry. As the reporter paraphrased, "Mrs. Pollard says that the invasion of the movietone and the vitaphone [sic] is the biggest factor in the moving picture industry at present although no one is prepared to say exactly how far the talking movies will be carried. Mrs. Pollard thinks there will always be some silent movies."[8] In this she was not alone; Carl Laemmle implemented a policy for Universal as late as 1929 that all the studio's feature films were to have a silent version (which could easily be adapted for a foreign market by substituting intertitles in a different language) as well as a sound version.[9] Margarita herself was not opposed to the new technology. She was pragmatic about the cinema player's responsibility to "study and work constantly to keep up with the advancing industry."[10] Harry Pollard was willing to go even further when asked about the significance of talking pictures. "It's the biggest thing that has happened in the motion picture industry," he opined. "We had gone about as far as we could go in silent pictures.... I predict bigger things for talking pictures and will say that I think they will come to supplant the legitimate stage before very long."[11] Whether or not this "typical legit" (as his wife described him) was happy about that is debatable, but certainly it offered new storytelling opportunities to one so well versed in spoken word performance.

Although Margarita was also open to the idea of making a sound film, she never had the chance. She would probably have adapted to the new style quickly, since her long professional history and stage training had endowed her with great stylistic flexibility and an uncommonly fine speaking voice. A film fan who recalled her early stage career wrote affectionately, "Oh, how I would like to hear your voice again, it is very pretty. I have never heard anything like it."[12] A 1928 article, written before Margarita's retirement became final, describes her "beautiful English" and "easy and quiet" voice, adding that "'Talkies' should hold no fear for her."[13] The actress herself never tested this confident statement, but neither did she ever express bitterness about the end of her film career. Despite her wistful statements about "[missing] it terribly," she insisted that she "never" felt regret about giving up her work.[14] Instead, she remained supportively at Pollard's side, lighting his pipe in publicity photos for his next Universal film, a part-talking version of the Edna Ferber novel *Show Boat*, in which Pollard would again test Universal's resources and the limits of his own filmmaking ability.[15]

At about this time, a face from the past grabbed headlines around the country. Charles C. "Cash and Carry" Pyle, Dorothy's former husband (he had by now remarried), had used the theatrical and managerial techniques honed through his years with the Fischer family's touring company and the Theatre Margarita to develop himself into "the P. T. Barnum of professional sports." He had solidified his reputation by promoting and organizing endorsements for football star Harold "Red" Grange beginning in 1925, thereby also gaining publicity and attention for himself. He organized and promoted a transcontinental footrace from Los Angeles to New York City, lasting from March to May 1928, with the winner to receive a $25,000 prize. A condition of entering the race was that its management — that is, Pyle — would receive fifty percent of the money earned by runners in appearances and endorsements resulting from their participation. In a turn of events that would not for a moment have surprised the Fischer women, the race was beset throughout with financial troubles, including multiple lawsuits against Pyle for unpaid debts. By the time the race neared New England, it was still $60,000 in the red. Pyle did, however, manage to pay the prize-winning runners, and even planned a second transcontinental race to be run in the opposite direction the following year.[16] Twenty-year-old Kathie, her father's only child, visited Pyle in New York around this time and got to meet the handsome, single "Red" Grange, a memorable event for a young woman. Still, this was no fresh start for the father and daughter; Pyle was always "in and out of her life" and "didn't treat her very well," Kathie's daughter recalled in later years.[17]

The rest of the Fischer family remained in California, where another person had joined the family circle. The Pollards had moved into the elegant Country Club Manor apartments in Los Angeles following the complex's construction in 1926, probably around the time the couple began work on *Uncle Tom's Cabin*. As a Christmas present for his wife, Pollard had bought his wife a luxurious Packard car, surprising her with it by telling her to look out of their sixth-floor apartment window into the apartment complex driveway. "There was the Packard Town Car with a great big bow ribbon on top — oh boy, I fled out!" Margarita remembered.[18] Unfortunately, the chauffeur the couple was then using was "a terrible drunkard," whom Pollard refused to let drive his wife any longer. He applied to Universal for a reliable chauffeur, and an energetic young man named Arthur Field interviewed for the job as a temporary position. He cautioned the Pollards that he would take the job for only three months, but quickly became an integral part of the family circle.[19] He remained in service to the family for nearly fifty years, as driver, handyman, helper, and friend, until the end of his life.

In the meantime, Harry Pollard prepared to embark upon the production of another epic film. The planned scope of *Show Boat* was to be as grand as that of *Uncle Tom's Cabin*, and it represented a significant financial outlay from Universal, coming as it did immediately after the hemorrhaging costs of *Uncle Tom's Cabin*; Carl Laemmle paid author Edna Ferber $65,000 in 1926 for the film rights to the Mississippi River–set novel. The book's transformation to film became complicated, however, when Ferber sold the stage rights to Florenz Ziegfeld, who enlisted the songwriting team of Jerome Kern and Oscar Hammerstein II to turn the book into a musical. When the musical stage show immediately became a big hit, Laemmle and Pollard had a dilemma on their hands: should they simply adapt the novel for the screen, or should they nod to the popular stage show and adapt *Show Boat* using its songs?[20]

The dilemma arose in part because of the length of time that had elapsed since Laemmle had purchased the novel's screen rights. Over the two years that passed before production finally began in 1928, at least ten different scripts were developed, and these were all for silent pictures.[21] Indeed, *Show Boat* actually began filming as a silent in mid–1928, but, as during the casting of *Uncle Tom's Cabin*, Pollard soon decided on a storytelling compromise: the film would also contain dialogue segments and original songs, thus avoiding any royalties to Ziegfeld.[22] This part-talkie approach was not uncommon; it had been used to great success by *The Jazz Singer* as a way of punching up important scenes with expensive, picky sound technology while keeping costs relatively low by filming less flashy or more action-oriented scenes without sound. Once again, the youthful Laura La Plante was to play the leading role in a Pollard film; she was cast as Magnolia Ravenal in this first screen adaptation of the Edna Ferber story about life and love between an innocent young riverboat performer and the charming wastrel who becomes her husband. Norman Kerry was originally indicated for the role of the husband, Gaylord Ravenal, though the part eventually went to Joseph Schildkraut.[23]

Once filming was complete, however, Pollard and Laemmle recognized the futility of creating a competing musical version to the wildly popular stage show, and in January 1929 Laemmle inked a deal with Ziegfeld for use of the stage songs in exchange for a share of the film's profits plus an additional payment (probably around $100,000). A musical prologue was then added to the film in which the current stage stars sang five of the show's Kern-Hammerstein hits.[24] In addition, songs from the stage musical were shoehorned in for Laura La Plante, using the best available methods of the day. Since sound dubbing was not yet possible, Pollard creatively worked around his non-singing leading lady; La Plante simply stood in front of a curtain and mouthed the words to her songs ("Ol' Man River" and "Can't Help Lovin' Dat Man"), while a singer behind the curtain actually recorded the film's soundtrack.[25]

Harry Pollard must have been grateful for his wife's support during the challenging shoot. This was a risky time to embark upon the production of an epic, falling as it did during the transition between the silent and sound eras, and once again, as with *Uncle Tom's Cabin*, there was a great deal of tricky location and water shooting. Pollard had relished technical innovation since his earliest days behind the camera, though, and proved himself entirely up to the challenge. During an era when many directors found themselves pigeonholed as only suited for silents, the bespectacled Kansan won Carl Laemmle's public approval by capably directing *Show Boat*'s musical and sound portions, as well as the silent sequences, and even co-writing the dialogue.[26]

Unusually, the new picture was to premiere in Florida to take advantage of the sunny state's winter status as "society's playground"—and possibly to gain a little extra press due to the lack of competition from other films. The film's planned Miami premiere on March 15, 1929, was marred by union protesting unrelated to *Show Boat*, but which culminated in projector sabotage that completely prevented the film from being shown. It successfully rolled out in Palm Beach the following day and in New York in April.[27] On the day of the Palm Beach premiere, a full-page "Straight from the Shoulder" ad for the film appeared under tireless promoter Carl Laemmle's byline in *Motion Picture News*. "Harry Pollard, I Salute You!" shouted the headlines, while the text evoked the "Straight from the Shoulder" ad in support

Opposite: Harry Pollard's follow-up to *Uncle Tom's Cabin* was *Show Boat* (Universal, 1929)—a return to the Mississippi River, but this time with dialogue and musical segments. This page from *Greater Show World* offered information about the cast, the *Cotton Blossom* itself, and the film's April premiere in Florida (courtesy the Harry Pollard Papers, Special Collections and University Archives, Wichita State University Libraries).

HARRY POLLARD
Director of "Show Boat"

LAURA LA PLANTE
as "Magnolia" in "Show Boat"

JOSEPH SCHILDKRAUT
as "Ravenal" in "Show Boat"

OTIS HARLAN
*as "Capt. Andy" in "Show Boat"
The Show Boat*

THE SHOW BOAT

Silent Versions for All Universal Films

Every feature-length picture made at Universal City will have a silent version, is announced by Carl Laemmle, president.

This policy is the result of a determination that neither the foreign market nor the theatres unwired for sound shall be neglected in the enthusiasm for talking pictures.

The Universal policy is in marked contrast with that of certain other producers who have announced that they will make no more silent pictures.

Universal, it was stated, will go out stronger than ever for the foreign market, regarded as menaced, as far as American producers are concerned, by the change to talking pictures. Abandonment of silent pictures is regarded as an extreme short-sighted policy by Carl Laemmle.

Show Boat Premiere in Florida

The million-dollar picturization of Edna Ferber's novel, "Show Boat," opened simultaneously March 17th at the Capitol Theatre in Miami and the Paramount Theatre in Palm Beach. The usual custom of having the world premieres in New York, Chicago or Los Angeles was broken by Universal, following conferences with the officials of the Florida cities who were anxious to bring such an important event to their localities. Miami and Palm Beach, society's playground, were crowded with winter visitors who were enthusiastic about this colorful spectacle of show boat life on the Mississippi in the early '90s. Reports from Miami are very encouraging. The Capitol Theatre with a seating capacity of only 700, is averaging $2,500 a day. In the first two weeks 48,000 people have seen the stupendous production. This represents more than 70 per cent of the total white population of the city.

The movietone prologue to "Show Boat" comprises the hits of Florenz Ziegfeld's stage production of the same name.

of Pollard's comic direction that had appeared a few years earlier. After lauding the director's comic successes and *Uncle Tom's Cabin*, the excited copy called *Show Boat* "the topmost peak in all his high peaks of achievement."[28] Audiences agreed: a month later, the film was still playing to capacity crowds in Miami and taking in $2,500 daily in box office receipts for a 700-seat theater. A trade journal estimated that 48,000 people saw it in that city in the first two weeks of exhibition — that is, "more than 70 per cent of the total white population."[29]

In general, critics shared Laemmle's and viewers' enthusiasm, though they were understandably more analytical of *Show Boat*'s shortcomings. The reviewer for Hollywood's *Film Mercury* found it to be "not without its faults," especially in the slow-moving first half of the film. However, "over and above these the picture carries a powerful human appeal that completely sways the audience and surmounts minor weaknesses.... The latter half of 'Show Boat' is so excellent that the audience should never be allowed to gain an impression from the early reels that the picture is not an outstanding achievement." This critic also found the sound recording and dialogue to be skillfully executed.[30] When the film opened in New York two weeks later, *World* critic Quinn Martin concurred with the overall impression of the film as "noteworthy, and, for the greater part, ... superbly managed." This reviewer found the actors' performances and the film's staging compelling, taking issue only with "no end of unnecessary, pointless material grafted into the running story" which he recommended Universal trim out.[31] The studio may, in fact, have done so; while a contemporary review says the film lasted "nearly three hours," it survives in a version of just over two.[32]

Criticisms of the film were perhaps unavoidable in New York, where the beloved stage show still played and inevitably invited comparisons. *New York Times* film critic Mordaunt Hall, clearly enamored of the stage show's tunes, thought "the melodies in this well-staged lachrymose tale are so fine that they atone for some of the prolonged melodramatic stretches.... It is a pity that [Pollard] has such a passion for pathos, for he does not realize where misfortunes on the screen become tedious to the onlooker."[33] He allowed that the actors' performances were respectable, but found the dissolution of the Ravenals' marriage to be overlong. Hall also was disappointed in the film's sound recording — "sometimes the incidental sounds are too pronounced."[34] Pollard himself admitted to the jarring nature of the part-talkie structure, attributing it to a holdup in the song rights and allowing that the finished product was "a bit patchy ... we tried to make it as presentable as we could."[35]

Comparing *Show Boat* to the popular live show is somewhat unfair, as the filmmakers were working in an entirely different, unfamiliar, and rapidly changing medium. Film writer Victor Oscar Freeburg, a connoisseur of what he referred to as "pictorial beauty," had written trenchantly in 1926:

> If I look upon a motion picture as a kind of substitute for some state play or novel, it seems to me a poor thing, only a substitute for something better; but if I look at it as something real in itself, a new form of pictorial art in which things have somehow been conjured into significant motion, then I get many a glimpse of touching beauty, and I always see a great range of possibilities for richer beauties in future examples of this new art.[36]

It is as if he had been able to look forward three years to the completion of *Show Boat*. In its transitional sound-silent combination, it would indeed be a disappointment to lovers of the stage musical's songs. But on its own terms, in its performances and pacing, it is buoyed by moments of touching beauty.

In fact, the entire film was, states Universal historian I. G. Edmonds, "a beauty to behold."³⁷ In it, Pollard remedied all the directorial faults that plagued the troubled *Uncle Tom's Cabin* and demonstrated an artistic sensibility he had not expressed since his days with Pollard Picture Plays. His *Show Boat* boasts carefully created sets and costumes, and fine, subtle performances from the cast. Joseph Schildkraut is appropriately dashing and self-centered as the leading man, La Plante's Magnolia is fresh-faced but dignified and strong, and sad-eyed former vamp Alma Rubens is touching in her small role as the world-weary Julie (although all references to her interracial marriage are removed) in one of the actress's final performances before her premature death from heroin addiction.³⁸

The film's Vitaphone soundtrack was recorded onto a series of discs that accompanied the film's original release; unfortunately, some of these have since been lost, including those that contained the film's most famous songs and all of Alma Rubens's dialogue.³⁹ Nonetheless, *Show Boat* survives as a powerful and accomplished film, and it represents the high point of Pollard's directorial career with Universal. In its wistful final scene, in which a trembling "Lonesome Road" plays while a chastened Schildkraut returns at twilight to the show boat and to the wife he left so many years ago, *Show Boat* achieves a mature and unsentimentalized artistry, perhaps given greater resonance by its director's own experience with marital trouble and reconciliation.

Unlike *Uncle Tom's Cabin,* the film was a box office success, largely due to its popularity in the Midwest and small towns.⁴⁰ The very success of the film reawakened some of the issues that had caused the Pollards' marital trouble in the first place: Harry Pollard reentered the spotlight of the press, a position with which he was acutely uncomfortable. For the first time in their marriage, Pollard was much better-known than Margarita Fischer, which was probably the preference of neither spouse. A long article with the crowing title "Shy Harry Pollard, Film Director, Has Never Been to a Hollywood Party" held the ring of truth: when the beleaguered Pollard was taxed by the reporter for the reasons for his absence from the Hollywood social scene, he replied, "I've never had time and, besides, nothing I can say will prove of interest to you. Interview Mrs. Pollard."⁴¹ While Margarita would no doubt have cheerfully obliged, her contributions to the article were limited to her presence in the article's attractive photos and in the autobiography dragged out of the unwilling subject. Although Pollard "struggled quite ... hard to escape" from the interview — and proved himself "one of the best listeners this writer ever interviewed"— he eventually unbent enough to recount his career path. His personality was summarized as "a shy, reticent and retiring individual who works eighteen hours a day and never plays," and is "noted among his fellows as a stickler for accuracy."⁴²

This was indeed correct; Pollard was in the habit of spending several hours each evening planning his next day's work in detail.⁴³ But he may have disagreed with the description of himself as shy; he instead comes across, as would be expected for a man too impatient with his own fame to hire a press agent, as businesslike but with a wry sense of humor. He stated that his favorite of his own films was *Show Boat,* but thought star Joseph Schildkraut had a "terrible name." He was excited about his planned next picture, a personal project called *The Barnstormer* that was to be "written around my own youthful experiences" with touring stage companies and would again feature La Plante and Schildkraut. Displaying deep gratitude, he fondly recalled the theatrical managers who had been generous at the start of his career, as well as his good fortune in meeting and serving as the "leading man" for his "beautiful" wife.⁴⁴

The planned *Barnstormer* film was to make up one of the episodes in a Pollard-directed trilogy recounting American regional entertainment, of which *Show Boat* stood as the first film. Unfortunately, it was soon scrapped, as the other proposed film in the trilogy (*The Minstrel Show*) had been tentatively built on the box-office draw of the Jolson name — Al's brother Harry. As casting of the leading role wavered between Jolson and another former vaudevillian, Eddie Leonard, the plans for both films fell apart.[45] Pollard's next film was instead *Tonight at Twelve*, released in late September 1929 — only about five months after *Show Boat* was completed. This was his first "all talking" picture, but he was again unfazed by the challenge. "Ever since I started directing some years ago I have written dialogue into my scripts," he revealed matter-of-factly. "I never could quite see the sense of having an actor say one thing when he meant something else."[46]

On the surface, this new film was quite a departure from the epic productions with which the Pollards had spent the last several years of their lives. *Tonight at Twelve* was a romantic farce of tangled relationships, loves, and misunderstandings that was admirably suited to the infant sound industry in its snappy, dialogue-driven plot and stage-bound structure (in fact, it was adapted from a play of the same name), which made set design and sound recording easier. However, as one reviewer noted, "Plays of this sort require a great deal of planning and working out in order to get the action under way properly and keep the tempo accelerating up to the grand climax and blow-off."[47] While some might have argued that Pollard did not achieve the ideal tempo in his previous epics, he had at least learned from their technical demands, and the same reviewer found the pacing of his latest film "very well achieved," as well as "productive of a great quantity of laughter ranging from small titters to deep belly roars."[48] The director deserved some of the credit for the comic success, as once again he co-wrote the dialogue.

Pollard then immediately moved into the production of *Undertow*, which boasted promising leads in John Mack Brown, who had made a name for himself as Joan Crawford's love interest in 1928's *Our Dancing Daughters*, and stunning blonde Mary Nolan, a former Ziegfeld showgirl with equal talents for acting and self-destruction. Featuring the pair as a blind lighthouse keeper and his isolated, discontented wife, the plot revolves around the development of their relationship from courtship to hardship to reentry upon the scene of Nolan's former love. The film ends with the reconciliation of the married pair and the restoration of the husband's sight. While entertaining enough for an average moviegoer, the film cannot have tested Pollard's skill very much, and it did not impress critics. Certainly it did not meet the high standards of *New York Times* critic Mordaunt Hall, who found much of the difficulty to be in interpreting the story from stage to screen: "The dialogue is so faulty and ill written, the scenery so pasteboard-like and the photography for the most part so indifferent, that any attempt to make of this simple tale the bit of O'Neill-like realism that it might easily be would necessitate a revision of everything."[49] Hall had found much the same fault with *Tonight at Twelve*, noting that "it follows, without regard for all that has been done with the camera before, the customs of the theatre."[50] In this, Pollard was technology-bound and training-bound, like many other directors of the early sound era. At least he was not culpable for *Undertow*'s poor dialogue, not having taken part in scripting that film.

After the filmmaking whirlwind of 1929, Harry Pollard and Margarita Fischer took a rare vacation together to the Territory of Hawaii (it was not yet one of the United States) in

11. Beach of Dreams

The Pollards took a much-needed vacation to Hawaii in January 1930. Like any other enthusiastic tourists, they found the tropical scenery "indescribable" in its beauty. Here they pose with the rocky aftermath of a volcanic eruption: "8 tons hurled over one mile high during eruption May 1924" (courtesy the Margarita Fischer Papers, Special Collections and University Archives, Wichita State University Libraries).

January 1930. The couple enjoyed their first trip to the islands together, enjoying a brief respite from the deadlines and dialogue of the film industry. They simply soaked in the scenery, which seemed breathtaking even to eyes accustomed to the beauties of the California coast, and they posed cheerfully with leis and landmarks like any other tourist couple. "We had expected to be disappointed in Hawaii after all the wonderful things we had heard about it," Pollard, typically blunt, confided in a phone interview, but "truthfully, our wildest hopes have been exceeded. The train ride along the coastline was indescribable."[51] Even here, however, the exhausted director could not relax as he wished to. The couple's trip was brief and frequently interrupted by unscheduled interviews and appeals for personal appearances from the renowned filmmaker, most of which Pollard declined due to his limited time and great fatigue. Looking aged but cheerful in newspaper photos, he confided to the press that his next planned film for Universal was "a talking picture version of Booth Tarkington's *The Flirt*."[52] Intended to feature "an all-star cast," he confided that "we plan to do it on a larger scale than ever before." He had to be back in Los Angeles by February 1 for the beginning of production.[53]

In fact, although the couple returned on schedule, the planned film was never made by Pollard or any other director (though two earlier silent versions of the tale had already been filmed). Pollard's career at Universal was effectively over at the time he and Margarita vacationed in Hawaii, though he had no awareness of that fact at the time. The melodramatic *Undertow*, released in February 1930 after his return to California, was Pollard's last film for the studio. The stock market crash of October 1929 touched off the Great Depression, the worst economic recession in the history of the United States. The nation had weathered a recession as recently as ten years before, when the end of the Great War knocked the economy into a temporary dive before the "Roaring Twenties" of peacetime consumerism set in. No previous recession had been so severe, so long-lasting, or so widespread as the one that began in 1929, though. By December 1930, almost one-fourth of working adults in major cities were unemployed, while some schools closed due to lack of funding from local tax bases. An estimated one-third of school-aged children not attending school (more than three million nationwide in 1930) went to work instead, many in sweatshops, to supplement family incomes.[54] Most film studios were hit as hard as the public, since people with no money to spare were understandably hesitant to shell out for a movie ticket, and studio heads who had thought to make a bundle in the stock market were instead saddled with huge losses. In 1930, Universal's operating budget was only $12 million, an amount intended to finance twenty films, as well as pay star and staff salaries. Even with limitations on expensive productions — no more *Uncle Tom's Cabin*s, no more *Show Boat*s — the studio would post a loss of $1.2 million in 1932.[55]

Although Pollard had a five-year contract with Universal that should have lasted until 1932, the studio could no longer afford his $100,000-per-film salary after the Depression began — particularly after two prestigious epics in four years had bled dollars from its coffers, and especially when the ambitious director's next planned property was to be another "all-star" treatment that seemed likely to break the studio's strained budget. A studio contract was a guarantee of a performer's services, but it was not a guarantee to the performer that those services would be retained. Although Carl Laemmle was good-hearted, he may not have been anxious to keep such a high-salaried and detail-oriented director during lean times. It is likely that the parting of the ways was mutual, however, since Pollard recognized his opportunities at Universal would henceforth be limited to films like *Undertow* and *Tonight at Twelve*.

Instead, Pollard prepared to make a career move that had been made several years earlier by Irving Thalberg, and then by Thalberg's future wife, former *Leather Pushers* bit actress Norma Shearer: he moved to the wealthier MGM studio. Louis B. Mayer's eponymous studio had merged with Metro Pictures and Goldwyn Pictures, incorporating under the familiar name in 1924, and "boy wonder" Irving Thalberg, barely thirty years old, was now the head of production of this studio. MGM had some of the deepest pockets in Hollywood, as well as the broadest array of talent, boasting "more stars than there are in heaven." Ironically, these unprecedented filmmaking resources also meant a lessening of the role of the director. At MGM, the frail genius Thalberg held near-complete creative control of the entire filmmaking process, and he believed that the secret of a good film lay in a good script. "He searched for the right stimulants among Broadway plays, Book-of-the-Month club novels, magazine fiction, and the occasional classic, then worked with screenwriters, as in a laboratory, to package and administer them," explained Shearer biographer Gavin Lambert. With script in place, MGM directors needed only to ensure that the scenario was capably translated to the silver screen, to be "dependable rather than independent."[56]

It is a surprise, perhaps, that Pollard chose to move to a prestigious studio which would require him to sublimate his talent and verve to suit the tastes of administration — or that the studio itself would be interested in a filmmaker who tended to be "independent" rather than "dependable" in both his production methods and his recurrent alcoholism. However, there is no sign that Pollard's productivity was affected in 1929–1930; in fact, with Margarita's full-time support, he was able to see through to completion more films than he had in more than a decade. This very pace probably exhausted him, though, and he may have welcomed the chance to turn over the creative reins, so to speak, to a younger and more energetic man. With the Depression affecting even the wealthy, this was no time to stop working simply because of artistic pride (although to hedge their bets, the Pollards also began investing successfully in blue-chip stocks).[57] If he was going to make films in a mold, Pollard may have reasoned, he might as well make them for the most prestigious and financially sound studio in existence. MGM was, in fact, the only American studio that consistently ran in the black during the Great Depression.

As her husband's career moved in a new direction that promised continued financial stability without overly taxing his tenuous health, Margarita Fischer again grew restless in her retirement. Around the same time her husband moved to MGM, she sought out work on local stages as an outlet for her talents that would not detract from her ability to "caretake" Pollard. The first performance of which she kept a record was a supporting role in *The Romantic Young Lady*, a light, comic Spanish play dealing progressively with the proper place of women. Margarita would surely have enjoyed the colorful, spirited leading female role, but at age forty-four she was simply too old to play ingénues anymore. The last few years of her film career had inured her to smaller roles, and she performed her lesser part with her customary flash and spirit. Her reputation apparently preceded her; respected theatrical critic Florence Lawrence (not the same as the silent film actress) noted that "Marguerita [*sic*] Fischer, former screen star, was given an ovation as she appeared stunningly gowned, and stormy in her tempestuous scene with a reluctant lover."[58]

"No Permanence to Retirement: Marguerita [*sic*] Fischer Back in Limelight," trumpeted a *Los Angeles Times* headline a few days later. The accompanying article profiled Margarita as she prepared for the "colorful role of the Spanish dancer" in *The Romantic Young Lady*. "I always enjoyed filling a foreign characterization because of the glamour that inevitably surrounds it," the actress remarked. "I am so happy to be back in the theater once more that, even though my part is small, I sit through the hours of rehearsal, cherishing every minute."[59] Besides offering information about the play, the article attempted to address the puzzling issue

Margarita Fischer posed for this portrait in 1930, the year she returned to the local stage. At age forty-four, she was considered too old in acting circles to be cast in leading roles (courtesy the Margarita Fischer Papers, Special Collections and University Archives, Wichita State University Libraries).

of such a popular actress's retirement and reappearance. "Quite some time back, when she relinquished stardom to become Mrs. Harry Pollard, she thought she would forever forget the limelight in the light of the home fires," stated the article. "That proved impossible." Margarita herself offered the mystifying, ultra-feminine excuse of a "timidity complex which causes her many struggles in the process of self-assertion.... [A]fter she had been steeped a while in domesticity she lacked the positiveness essential to putting one's self over in Hollywood."[60] While she may have lost the drive to pursue a Hollywood career, the declaration of a "timidity complex," from a woman who had negotiated her own contracts since her early twenties, was almost certainly a face-saving cover-up for other, perhaps less flattering, reasons for retirement, such as her husband's alcoholism or her own age.

Regardless of the reason for her retirement, the glamorous interviewee stated that she hoped "she [was] back to stay," and she soon began to look on the stage as her renewed profession. In the federal census of 1930, she reported her occupation as "theatre actress," while Pollard's was "motion picture director." Mindful of her image as always, Margarita listed her age as thirty-five rather than forty-four, and even Pollard sliced a few years off his true age by listing himself as forty-six rather than fifty-one.[61] Through late fall in 1930, Margarita continued to appear in supporting roles on different local stages and was always well-reviewed by the critic Florence Lawrence, who had clearly come to admire the actress. Lawrence called the former star's performance in the "racy" Moliere comedy *The Imaginary Invalid* "stunning," and in *Dancing Days*, the critic noticed that "Beautiful Margarita Fischer, charmingly gowned, lends a brief but brilliant note to the drama."[62]

Margarita's "brilliant" performance in *Dancing Days* in October 1930 is the last one of which she kept a record, and it might well have been the last one of her revived theatrical career. In 1931, she and Pollard moved from their rented condominium in Los Angeles to the historic Rancho Buena Vista adobe house in Vista, California, about ninety miles southeast of Los Angeles. Pollard was looking for an escape from the Hollywood scene, but "what triggered them to go to this house, I don't know," mused Margarita Fischer's namesake great-niece Margarita Kotselis. "They just fell in love with it, and decided to buy it, and put the money in to restore it."[63] Although Pollard was still directing films for MGM, the eighty-year-old Rancho was a longed-for getaway within driving distance of the studio, as well as the couples' first permanent home together since their marriage twenty years before. Pollard considered this home "a haven where he could rest between his labors," Margarita Fischer later explained. "He spent years in searching for such a place."[64]

The renovations occupied Margarita's attention for a time, since the historic house had become so run down that "you could fall through the floors."[65] The home's structure was still solid, though, and its stone foundation and thick adobe walls were intact. The retired actress lavished attention on rehabilitating the low-slung, winding adobe house in keeping with its architectural character. The Pollards eventually spent more than $150,000 to renovate the building and its 50-plus acres of grounds, on which the couple grew avocado and citrus trees. They also began putting their own Hollywood stamp on the property; they had a garage built, and chauffeur and handyman Arthur Field laid out and took care of the grounds, and oversaw the addition of walkways, a patio, a swimming pool, and a fountain outside. More practically, the Pollards added closets and modernized the home's bathroom, adding complete indoor plumbing and installing then-unheard-of double sinks.[66] This oldest house in Vista took six months to restore aesthetically and structurally.[67] Once the structure of the home was secured, Margarita began to fill it with exquisite antiques, also embellishing many of the adobe's eleven rooms with colorful Mexican tiles. "She kept it as historical and as true to what it should be as she could," recalled her great-niece, and "it was just really a beautiful place"—though the actress's greatest pride was the library that she built up in her endless quest for self-education.[68] She and her husband loved the house, and Margarita in particular seemed to feel that she had found a true home there. An employee at the adobe later recalled to Margarita how "you would appear suddenly down the walk by the side of your house on the garden side, so ready for the new day, smiling" in the midst of the peaceful surroundings.[69]

Once settled in their retreat, the couple began to involve themselves once more in Hollywood society through the rarefied atmosphere of the MGM studio. Pollard got off to an inauspicious start when his first picture for MGM, an adaptation of the stage musical *Great Day*, was shut down in August 1930 after ten days of production. The fault belonged mainly to the overzealous studio, too eager to put the talented director of *Show Boat* to work on a musical as soon as possible without developing a solid script, and just at a time when the musical was falling out of fashion due to a spate of too many mediocre pictures. As Joan Crawford, the film's intended leading lady, explained, "The part wasn't well defined, I had never played an ingénue and I went into the picture with grave misgivings."[70] Crawford, touted by MGM as "the personification of youth and beauty and joy and happiness,"[71] was eager to shed her hard-partying jazz-baby image and feared that one more musical would instead cement it. As one biographer described it, Crawford had "a will to succeed at any cost" and might simply have refused to continue in a role that she felt would limit her career.[72] She impatiently told studio head Louis B. Mayer, "Southern drawl I can do, but I just can't talk baby talk!" The picture was scrapped, despite the loss of $280,000 in accrued production costs.[73]

Crawford certainly did not have the power to dictate studio decision-making, but any resistance on her part may have just served to convince Thalberg and Mayer that continuing the ill-planned production would simply be throwing good money after bad due to the decline of the musical genre's popularity. This setback might have been embarrassing for Margarita's husband, but the older actress herself could certainly have understood Crawford's sentiments; she had been at a similar career crossroads ten years earlier when she had refused to act in American's frivolous *House of Toys*. Out of this failed cinematic endeavor grew a friendship between the two actresses; Joan Crawford became a frequent visitor at the Rancho and gave the Pollards a magnolia tree that still stands in the home's courtyard.[74]

Margarita probably got to know other MGM stars through her husband's connection at this time as well. She later recounted details of the career of Norma Shearer, Irving Thalberg's wife, who became the "First Lady of MGM" as a powerful and talented star in her own right. Always positive, Margarita commented that "Miss Shearer deserves every bit of her success, for she is a very lovely and wonderful person."[75] (She probably refrained from making this comment around her friend Joan Crawford, however, who considered Shearer an undeserving and unfairly advantaged rival for MGM's best female roles.)

Pollard, meanwhile, had mixed luck with his next directorial efforts for his new studio. Following a preview screening, *Hollywood Reporter* could hardly say enough to the good about his January 1931 musical film *The Southerner*. The picture was described as "a real treat ... for sheer entertainment, for audience reaction, for comedy and music that are so entrancing that they excite, this picture must rank at the top of the list for this or any other year. It is SWELL!"[76] *Hollywood Daily Screen World* was more moderate in its enthusiasm; the critic thought it "charming, and well directed, but not a picture for the masses," as it is a "satire on family and society hypocrisy."[77] This second reviewer also enjoyed one of baritone star Lawrence Tibbett's songs, but recommended that another be cut, as it did not fit smoothly into the plot. MGM, still wary of musicals since taking a loss on *Great Day*'s production, took this advice a step further. Always willing to recut a film to increase its appeal, MGM withdrew the film after its previews, sliced out almost all of its songs, and rereleased it as *The Prodigal*—in which form it actually lost the studio money.[78] This is perhaps no surprise, since even the *Hollywood Reporter* admitted that "there doesn't seem to be much" plot; rather, "it is a comedy of situation and dialog."[79] With the songs clipped away, the woodenness of Tibbett's performance was revealed, and the singer's film career proved to be short-lived and sporadic.

Pollard's follow-up film, *Shipmates*, quickly followed on *The Southerner/Prodigal*'s heels (it was released only two months later) and was a bona fide hit. Starring witty, smooth-faced new leading man Robert Montgomery, the maritime comedy-drama focused on John Paul "Jonesy" Jones (Montgomery), a brash, arrogant navy sailor who humorously conflicts with officers, and, first dishonestly, then sincerely, courts an admiral's daughter. At film's end, Jonesy has come to a respectful truce with his superiors, saved the naval fleet from explosion, and been accepted to the U. S. Naval Academy. The film boasted a fine supporting cast, with silent film veteran Hobart Bosworth as the aging admiral; Ernest Torrance as Jonesy's Scottish nemesis-turned friend, Chief Bosun's Mate MacTavish; Cliff Edwards as the grim-faced, glib-tongued comic relief; and lovely Dorothy Jordan as the wry, forgiving admiral's daughter who decides the brash Jonesy is worth waiting for.[80]

Shipmates was praised for its acting, direction, and "clever dialogue," and it became one of the top five box office successes of May 1931.[81] "Harry Pollard has given the picture plenty of pep and the numerous writers engaged in the task of making this into a picture have done their job right well," approved *Hollywood Reporter*. "MGM continues its line of 1931 successes and offers another box-office attraction and will send them away smiling and satisfied."[82] Viewed today, *Shipmates* is slight but still clever, visually interesting, and entertaining. Pollard puts no particular directorial stamp on the film (not a surprise for Thalberg-era MGM films), but he capably handles a gamut of scenes ranging from romance at a rugged seaside to comedy in a ship latrine to life-threatening adventure in artillery practices and the film's explosive finale. A few intertitles are injected to set the scene—a soon-to-fade holdover from the silent era—but apart from these there is no sign that the director had any difficulty adapting to sound filmmaking.

Following the release of *Shipmates*, Pollard was absent from the screen for thirteen months, perhaps for reasons of health. He made two final films for MGM in 1932: *When a Fellow Needs a Friend* and *Fast Life*. The former of these films (alternately called *When a Feller Needs a Friend*), released in April, starred popular child actor Jackie Cooper as "Limpy" Eddie Randall, a boy with a brace on his leg. The film was scripted by Sylvia Thalberg, sister of Irving. The picture came in for a moderately positive review from the *New York Times*. As the critic observed, "It is a piece with plenty of hokum ... needless to say, the old man and the boy elicited heaps of sympathy from the audience." Also praising the "old-fashioned humor" in the movie, and Jackie Cooper's "undeniably interesting" performance, the critic nonetheless believed that "he has not been directed with the same skill he was in 'Skippy' or 'The Champ,'" both Academy Award–winning films of the previous year.[83]

Pollard again had a few months' rest with Margarita at their renovated adobe before beginning production on his next and last film, *Fast Life*, in late September 1932.[84] This output was certainly less than that of 1929, when he embarked on a post–*Show Boat* whirlwind for Universal, but it was fairly typical of the sound filmmaking process at MGM for directors, although actors usually worked at a more prolific pace. After completing production in early November, *Fast Life* was released in December 1932. The picture returned Pollard to watery sets, like in *Shipmates*— even, in its opening scenes, to the Navy — as it focused on the efforts of two young sailors-turned-unsuccessful entrepreneurs (William Haines and comic sidekick Cliff Edwards) to develop and sell an engine modification that will help a speedboat go faster. They catch the eye of a softhearted but financially precarious boat manufacturer who is determined to win the prestigious International Cup — and who has a beautiful daughter (Madge Evans) who provides the love interest for the film. After several plot twists, including piracy, a love triangle, and a last-minute kidnapping of Evans to subvert her wedding to a stuffed shirt (Conrad Nagel), the engine is perfected just in time for the pair to win the Cup and the girl, and ensure the financial success of all.[85]

Pollard handled the film's frequent action scenes well, and although *Hollywood Reporter* judged the film to have "a senile story that any fan could recite by rote after the first fifty feet," the periodical still thought it "great entertainment for every class of audience."[86] Even the *New York Times* liked "the pleasing performances of the two principals.... Although the story is shallow, the amusement afforded by many of the incidents is keen."[87] It was not, however, a financial success; it lost money for MGM, and, in fact, the story behind the scenes is more compelling than the film itself. *Fast Life* was a vehicle for waning star William Haines, whose wit and boyish good looks had made him one of the studio's most popular leading men by the late silent era. His *Alias Jimmy Valentine*, released in 1929, represented MGM's first foray into sound filmmaking, albeit only in its final reel. Haines had a wonderful voice for sound, moderately deep and with a hint of roughness that suited his smart-aleck character. A top box office draw in 1930, his popularity had decreased by 1932 due to the aging of his boyish image, Haines's conflicts with studio heads, his association with the silent era, and the press's growing awareness of Haines's homosexuality.[88] *Fast Life*, notes Haines biographer William J. Mann, "was treated as a B film, distributed poorly. There was little ad campaign for it; it doesn't appear prominently in any MGM press book. The odds were stacked against it from the start."[89] *Fast Life* was Haines's final MGM film; the studio had him under contract for nearly another year but chose never again to cast him.[90]

Fast Life was also the final film of Harry Pollard's career, though almost certainly not for reasons of personal conflict with MGM leadership. Pollard may have retired due to waning health, or his contract may not have been renewed due to bad timing. In December 1932, at the time of the release of *Fast Life*, MGM was in a financial squeeze due to a second consecutive year of falling profits, and the studio was cutting costs on film productions and personnel salaries.[91] The director of a "B picture" like *Fast Life* would probably have been among the first to experience a cut. In addition, the frail Irving Thalberg, producing for Louis B. Mayer since 1923 and working at the time as MGM's head of production, worked himself into a heart attack in December 1932. During Thalberg's extended recovery he was eased out of his position by Louis B. Mayer in favor of Mayer's son-in-law, David O. Selznick.[92] Thalberg, who had overseen the entire stable of directors and shepherded fifty films a year from story to release, had represented a significant ally and guide for the studio's directors, so his (temporary) departure, combined with Pollard's own growing health problems, may have provided additional motivation for Pollard to retire or for Mayer not to renew his contract at this time. The completion of *Fast Life* marked the close of a chapter in Pollard's life, as well as that of his wife's. Though Margarita maintained social relationships in Hollywood in the years to follow, the end of her husband's employment at MGM also, after twenty-two years, represented the end of her professional connection to the film industry.

The fiscally cautious Pollards were financially secure even in this worst year of the Great Depression, and Harry Pollard may not have regretted the end of his career, for despite his cinematic talents, he had never felt as much delight or respect for film as he had for his career on the stage. Yet, over the course of the quarter century he had spent with Margarita Fischer, this charming, determined descendant of Kansas farmers had helmed lastingly important films as well as crowd-pleasers. From the beginning of his self-made career, he had been "ambition and energy personified," as he described himself, constantly searching for accuracy and perfection in his movies just as he had in his early stage performances. His films for MGM represent a more limited type of filmmaking than that with which he had built his reputation, but even here he proved capable and creative. Throughout his cinematic career he sought to push the technical and moral boundaries of filmmaking, even as this compulsion destroyed his health by bringing him to alcoholism and illness.

The "ambition and energy" that the Pollards had created on the silent screen, and that the director had then brought to MGM, were all over now, for the film industry was changing once more. The Pollards watched from their beloved Vista retreat as the Academy of Motion Picture Arts and Sciences, organized by MGM head Louis B. Mayer, continued to handed out "Oscars" each year for accomplishments in film; as brazen platinum blonde Jean Harlow revised standards of beauty for a new generation of filmgoers; as the Great Depression motivated snappier, grittier plots; and as questions of censorship again intruded into the industry and required a stringent revision of the lax Production Code. The film industry was quite different now from the almost bucolic environment in which Margarita Fischer and Harry Pollard had first made films in California for the IMP twenty years before. If they regretted leaving the new Hollywood behind, they never said so.

In Vista, however, retirement may not have agreed with Harry Pollard—or, alternatively, he may have finally determined to kick his alcoholism and enjoy his retirement years. Either way, after a few years of peace at the adobe house, and after much prodding from his wife, he entered a nearby sanatorium for treatment.[93] He was too far advanced in his illness, though, and he died in Pasadena on July 6, 1934, at the age of fifty-five. The death was publicly attributed to a heart attack—which indeed may have been the direct cause.[94] The *New York Times* stated only that the "veteran motion picture actor and director" had passed away "after a short illness."[95]

Besides his legacy of performances, direction, and cinematic innovation, Pollard left a solid $145,000 in assets. He left $10,000 to each of his three surviving siblings, and the remainder to Margarita—which, along with her own money, was enough to ensure her lifelong financial security.⁹⁶ In her immediate sorrow, this was little consolation to the grieving widow, of course; more than three decades later she referred wistfully to 1934 as "the year I lost my beloved husband.... Life changed for me at that time."⁹⁷ For a while, she contemplated selling the Rancho that she and Pollard had bought as "a haven where he could rest between his labors," but she eventually came to regard the home as a place of happy memories, telling a reporter in 1936, "Now I feel that I can never let it go."⁹⁸

12

Her Heritage

In the years following her husband's death, the still sociable Margarita Fischer developed a busy, comfortable life for herself. The year following Harry Pollard's retirement, 1933, Margarita occupied herself by becoming involved with the Dominos Club, a social organization for actresses that put out a breezy monthly bulletin of gossip and news about acting jobs. Margarita never used this club as a way to find jobs, but probably instead enjoyed the chance to keep up with old friends from her years in the film industry. She maintained her connection with this organization until 1937, even inviting the entire membership to a picnic at her Vista home.[1]

Without her husband, however, the retired actress felt "desperately lonely," and she built a life that brought her increasingly farther away from the world of Hollywood.[2] Tied to her own filmmaking schedule for seventeen years, and then that of her husband for an additional five, she had had little flexibility for time-consuming hobbies or travel. However, the judicious investments made during her and her husband's careers ensured her lifelong financial comfort, as well as that of her sister and niece.[3] In retirement, she therefore had the resources, as well as the freedom, to pursue anything she wished, and she decided to try to escape her loneliness by traveling at length and broadly. Margarita's travels began in June 1936, pushing her over the next few weeks from California through the Panama Canal and around the North American continent to New York.[4] As her unprecedented solo journey began, she wrote brave letters to her aunt Anna Fischer. In early July, from New York, Margarita wrote of seeing Rockefeller Center, the NBC studio, and Radio City Music Hall, and of being invited to attend the Major Bowes Amateur Hour (she lucked into that one through an acquaintance, as usually "it takes from three to four months to get an invitation"). "It is wonderful — I thot [*sic*] of you many times and wished for you to be here too.... I've been desperately lonely up to now. But — the trip was interesting and I am glad to have made it."[5]

From New York, she left for an extended world tour in two legs. The first swept her across the Atlantic on the *Queen Mary*, and then through France, Italy, Switzerland, Germany, Holland, and England in seven weeks before returning her to New York on August 31, 1936.[6] Although awed by the sights she saw in Europe, she still could not shake her feeling of unwanted solitude, writing to her "Auntie dear" frequently. She briefly joined up with "a group of college girls, 16 in all," in France, but traveled alone after she and the young women parted itineraries in London. "I am thrilled over all these romantic places," she wrote from Nice, "but I am lonely for my loved ones."[7] The very speed of her travel kept her occupied, though; she wrote with the determined cheer of the touring traveler that "Paris is just as I had always wanted it to be — wonderfully interesting — but the stay was all too short and

12. Her Heritage

hurried," while in Milan, "we had only a few hours.... But what glorious hours they were."[8] Later, upon reflection, she thought that her expectations for Paris, the "fashion centre of the world," had been too high not to occasion disappointment—"perhaps because one saw in Hollywood so many beautiful women, perfectly gowned and groomed."[9]

While still touring through Europe, she corresponded with another travel agent about the details of the second leg of her "'Round the World" trip. "I have sketched out roughly the inclusive price and it comes to about $3000," warned her travel agent. "Your steamship ticket alone costs much over $1000. This figure ($3000) does not include any expenses before Sept. 4."[10] This cost represented more than double the per capita annual income of most workers in 1936; the Pollards had indeed invested well.[11] (Margarita could not quite leave Hollywood habits behind as yet; when she began her travels, she had to pay an extra luggage charge for bringing four bags, when only one was permitted.[12]) The expansive itinerary came to include ports and nearby cities around the world, including (using modern names) London, Tangier, Gibraltar, Marseilles, Naples, Rhodes, Beirut, Damascus, Nazareth, Jerusalem, Cairo, Calcutta, Mumbai, Singapore, Hong Kong, Manila, Shanghai, Beijing, Nagasaki, Kobe, Kyoto, Tokyo, Yokohama, Honolulu, and finally home to California in time for Christmas.

Margarita indulged her desire for travel in 1936, journeying all the way around the world. She visited Egypt and the Middle East prior to seeing Asia and then heading home across the Pacific (courtesy the Margarita Fischer Papers, Special Collections and University Archives, Wichita State University Libraries).

As a distraction, the trip was not entirely successful. The exotic sights passing before Margarita's eyes drew her attention, but as soon as she was alone, she grew pensive again. "I should be home about Dec 19th," she guessed in a note written from shipboard on her way to Egypt. "And oh what a joyous day that will be."[13] She was unexpectedly caught by the press in Shanghai, who squeezed an interview out of the former actress in her hotel as she prepared to leave for Japan. Her response was characteristically polished, gracious, and slightly self-deprecating. She met with the admiring reporter in "an exquisite three-quarter length coat of grey kidskin, worn over a smart black, tailored suit, with black toreador hat."[14] For the star-struck interviewer, Margarita recalled marrying her "leading man for life" at the age of seventeen (some eight years distant from the truth, but her old habit of hiding her age was still with her), and also joked about modern films: "They are so much better than the silents which seem so funny now. In those days our makeup and even posing were quite different."[15] More interested in turning the conversation away from herself, she commented on the recent death of her husband's former production supervisor, Irving Thalberg, who had passed away of pneumonia in September 1936 at the age of only thirty-seven. She recalled the "brilliant" young man fondly and recounted her late husband's role in bringing him and his wife together. She closed by explaining that she was "glad to be going home" soon.[16] When she returned to Vista just in time for Christmas, she still kept her love of travel, though she would never again travel so extensively or so far from home.

Perhaps because of her lengthy absence, which intensified her feeling of isolation, Margarita spent the remainder of her first decade of widowhood reconnecting with her family in California. Following Harry Pollard's death, Dorothy had moved in with her. In 1945 the household grew still further when Kathie, her nine-year-old son Charles (named for his grandfather) and her toddler daughter, Margarita Dorothy, moved in with the elder Margarita and Dorothy, building a multigenerational household of Fischers akin to that of Margarita's days with American. Arthur Field—hired as a chauffeur, but by now like a member of the family—remained in his own quarters at the Rancho as the property's caretaker, with his job eased when Margarita sold off all but eight and a half of its more than fifty acres of produce ranchland.[17]

Sorrow touched the family in 1950, when Charles, who had had a heart condition since birth, died at the age of fourteen.[18] The four Fischer women and Arthur Field continued to live in the historic adobe until the following year, when Margarita sold it for the respectable price of $85,000 in favor of a smaller hilltop home in Vista.[19] She reconstructed her comprehensive library in this second Vista house, which remained her home for the rest of her life. Kathie and her daughter moved from this new family home to Westmoreland, a morning's drive away, upon Kathie's remarriage in 1955, but young Margarita returned to visit her great-aunt, grandmother, and beloved "Uncle Arthur" over school vacations and holidays. As the older generation aged, they traveled frequently, but trips were within driving distance—Yosemite, the Grand Tetons, Jackson Hole—rather than to the exotic overseas locales Margarita had visited in the 1930s.[20]

Even in retirement, the former actress stayed active with a variety of hobbies and issues that she found important. During World War II, much younger stars like Betty Grable played the pinup role Margarita had played a generation earlier, while the silent star herself volunteered for the Red Cross and acted as a plane spotter.[21] She also remained socially involved;

12. Her Heritage

Aboard the *Chichibu Maru* on the final leg of Margarita's 1936 world tour, which brought her from Yokohama to California. The former actress (fifth from right) had a gift for making friends, and she forged connections on this journey that lasted for years (courtesy the Margarita Fischer Papers, Special Collections and University Archives, Wichita State University Libraries).

her interest piqued by her former historic home, she joined the local historical society.[22] She enjoyed hosting parties, too, maintaining a formal living room in her adobe home just for the social gatherings to which she invited friends from Vista and, less often, connections from her Hollywood days. Dorothy, who did all the family's cooking on an everyday basis, had developed gourmet skills and took pride in catering the formal parties hosted by her sister.[23]

In private life, decades after she had first stepped onto a stage, Margarita retained the charm that had won audiences over throughout her career. When she moved into her smaller Vista home in 1951, she quickly made friends with her new neighbors, a couple with grown children who referred to the former actress as "The Fairy Princess" and admired her lovely home and antiques. "You must have heard it, time and again — that your house is so very beautiful!... The artistry with which you have assembled everything — makes it the most interesting and attractive house," warmly wrote her neighbor after an evening at the silent star's home.[24] "She had a lot of friends, and everybody loved her," her great-niece Margarita Kotselis recalled. Even her former staff from the adobe Rancho remained devoted to the "Good and Kind and True" actress, sending heartfelt, affectionate letters and Christmas cards into the 1960s.[25]

The retired star also encountered many admirers. She made devoted friends across Europe during her travels, and she continued to receive dedicated fan letters a full four decades after her final screen appearance.[26] She never remarried, however; and, to her family's knowledge, she never entered into a serious relationship with another man in the decades following Harry Pollard's death.[27] However, as she entered her eighties, she cemented what was at the very least a warm, affectionate friendship with a man of about her own age, J. B. "Jimmie" Sunderland, who lived in Washington state but frequently traveled to California. In between visits, he sent affectionate cards from "Your Jimmie" to "My Margarita!!!," writing upon one occasion that he was "bubbling over with pent-up affection" for his "one & only very warm admirer"—and that he was "waiting for our next meeting which I do hope will be soon, and *alone*."[28] He also praised her "usual happy mood" and encouraged her practically to "Keep well and strong and look to Him daily."[29] Age took its toll on the relationship, as one or the other of the pair experienced ill health. As Jimmie wrote with a touch of impatience upon one indisposition, "As soon as I have recovered sufficiently to make myself relevant I will again offer to you all the admiration and adulation that I can muster."[30] Margarita's side of the correspondence has not been preserved, but she seems to have provided him with encouragement

Visiting the Mexican province of Ensenada with friends, probably around 1960. Margarita (center) always retained her love of travel and frequently took trips around the United States with family members. The woman to her left is unidentified; Arthur Field is to her right (courtesy the Margarita Fischer Papers, Special Collections and University Archives, Wichita State University Libraries).

enough to continue corresponding with and pursuing her. A hint at her own feelings was jotted in broken lines on one of her admirer's final preserved envelopes: "Thank him for cards/beautiful cards with their heartwarming sentiment/I treasure them."[31]

This brief flowering of romance represented an intensification of the peaceful, comfortable sociability that marked the former star's decades out of the spotlight. Within Margarita's family circle, her preferred pastimes still included gardening, a hobby first nurtured during the lean, victory-gardening days of World War I. While she still lived at the adobe ranch, its large grounds required a great deal of care from the entire family, even after Margarita sold off the greater portion of her acreage. Her admiration for elegant automobiles, also fostered during her early career, stayed with her into retirement as well. Arthur Field now did the driving, but the former daredevil who had decades earlier selected her shiny Winton from a hospital bed still carefully chose a new car every three years (her preferences ran to Lincoln Town Cars, then to Cadillacs). Reading remained another favorite diversion; the desire for knowledge that had dogged her as a shy, unschooled teenaged performer had stayed with her into her confident adulthood. "She was very much into reading," stated Margarita Kotselis. "Her library had everything you could think of.... She was just so knowledgeable."[32]

Her thirst for knowledge, and her expectations about it, were transferred to her young namesake relative, for whom she, Dorothy, and Kathie shared the task of parenting, not always smoothly. "My aunt ... could be hard on you. She was caring and loving, but she could be difficult. She was the one that I probably was a little more afraid of. She was the one that you're constantly trying to impress, and constantly trying to do everything right [for]. And if you didn't do it right, she would be the first one to tell you."[33] Herself a high achiever, the self-made former actress had equally high expectations for her family members, and she believed her sister and niece had not lived up to their potential (both had troubled personal lives, and Kathie was eventually to marry five times). As Margarita's namesake great-niece explained, "She wanted the best for me ... she didn't want me to go down that road, so she probably was a little harder on me." The equally strong-willed Kathie and her aunt Margarita conflicted at times, but the younger Margarita recalled that, despite her great-aunt's strictness about behavior and academic achievement, "she was never a mean person. She was always a loving person."[34] Regardless of their conflicts, Kathie and Margarita Fischer remained very close until the end of Margarita's life.[35]

Religion also became a more important part of the retired star's life as she aged. Although their Scotch-Irish mother had raised her and her sister as Catholics, Margarita became experimental with her faith in her late middle age. She considered herself a Seventh-Day Adventist for a time, but eventually began practicing as a Catholic again.[36] Dorothy, by contrast, remained devoutly Catholic throughout her lifetime, making time daily to say rosaries and repeatedly offering a novena of holy masses as a Christmas gift to her younger sister.[37] At the age of seventy-two, on April 4, 1958, Margarita affirmed her Catholic faith by becoming a "member in perpetuity" of the Congregation of the Benedictine Sisters of Perpetual Adoration in San Diego through a membership offered her by the devout Dorothy.[38]

As the years passed, Margarita eventually became concerned with her long-forgotten image and her professional reputation. For years after her husband's death, she had not discussed her remarkable career, even within her family, though her sister and niece had happily shared stories of the family's years in Hollywood with young Margarita. The former actress had instead built herself a full, prosperous, and positive life entirely apart from the glamour of the film industry. In 1958, however, her final film, *Uncle Tom's Cabin*, was re-released after thirty years in the Universal Studios vault. Despite the picture's mediocre 1920s box office take, Colorama Features bought the rights from Universal. They updated the picture for mid-century audiences by filming a prologue with, and narration by, cadaverous character actor Raymond Massey, who was known for portraying Abraham Lincoln.[39] The Massey version of the film, including music and sound effects, was re-released for television in 1961 to mark the hundredth anniversary of the beginning of the Civil War.[40]

This may have provided the spark that brought the actress Margarita Fischer back to life in the retired Mrs. Pollard. She began reaching out to past contacts, responding to film historians, and visiting sites at which she had built her career decades before. The elder actress kept up sporadic contact with Virginia Grey, who enjoyed a long career as a sweet-faced supporting and character player after making her film debut as a child in *Uncle Tom's Cabin* in 1927. In 1965, Margarita sent the younger actress some photos and "'presents' of yesteryear," which Grey received with great affection. "What a darling you are, and what a beautiful surprise you gave me," enthused the former Little Eva. "I can see how well and happy you are, and the years have treated my beautiful lady kindly."[41] The same year, Margarita's niece Kathie — now Kathrine Havens — contacted famed former gossip columnist Hedda Hopper about the possibility of donating some of her elderly aunt's possessions to the Motion Picture Museum, including a lace table runner and place-doily set that Margarita noted had been "made to order in France" at an original cost of $2,500. (Hopper suggested the Hollywood Museum instead.)[42]

In 1967 and 1968, Margarita responded quickly and as completely as she could to the queries of film historians, though they often sought information about co-stars rather than about herself. Having worked at so many studios over a period of almost two decades, Margarita was a living link to almost every notable figure of early Hollywood, and she was frequently asked to comment on personalities who were now more well-known than herself but who had not survived the passing decades.[43] She was happy to stand as a representative of the young film industry, and in 1969, at the age of eighty-three, the venerable actress attended a festival of early films made in San Diego.[44] Her 1916 *The Pearl of Paradise* might well have been among the movies screened for audiences. At about the same time, she went back to Santa Barbara to visit her old studio and found American's former production center greatly changed from the days when her own small shoulders and those of a frail teenager had carried the responsibility for the studio's fortunes. "I went to my old dressing room, which is now occupied by a husband and wife who have a store, and they sell various articles, and there was the same old room. And right across the hall was Mary Miles Minter. It brought back many, many memories."[45]

Having been intimately connected with the film industry for nearly two decades, Margarita always remained interested in film for its own sake. She asserted in 1936 that "I am a great movie fan and think the present day sound pictures are marvelous," and in the late 1960s that "I am still interested in film — and think present day actors are excellent."[46] She did, however, feel sympathy for the new stars whose scandals and tribulations were gleefully covered by the press: "My niece takes so many of the motion picture magazines, and there's so much gossip about them and, oh, I regret it.... [Film fans] all like to read about people's private lives. I'm terribly against that; I don't believe in exposing people's private lives."[47]

She was at last ready to reflect on her own career as well. Around 1970 she enthusiastically gave an oral interview about her life on stage and screen to film historian Robert S. Birchard. After the passage of decades, the difficulties of her former career had receded in her memory: the financial struggles, the quest for good scripts, the jealousies and politics, the hardships and difficulties of a life in front of the camera had largely dissolved away. She frankly enjoyed herself throughout the interview, recalling her lengthy film career, especially her time with American, as "very, very pleasant ... that was such a happy time" (though she did refer to studio head Hutchinson, who had declined to hire her husband in the midst of his troubles with alcoholism, as a "skunk"). "I'm enjoying this so much," she stated. "I love to just drive through the memories that come to me."[48] She mentioned at that time that she had spoken recently with her old scenarist Beatrice Van, who had helped to turn her into American's "Madcap of the Screen" in the late 1910s. The writer, she noted, was planning a book of memoirs, though nothing seems to have come of Van's intentions.

The elderly former actress was somewhat vague and wandering during parts of the interview, and she recognized this, excusing herself on the grounds of age and ill health. (She also made a joke of her advanced age, exclaiming laughingly over old photos, "Gosh, it must be wonderful to have your own teeth. Look at my mouth! With real teeth in it."[49]) In fact, since the 1960s began, the health of Margarita and her sister had been waning. Dorothy's constitution, never strong throughout adulthood, had declined quickly, and she moved in with her daughter Kathie in 1962 for her final few years of life. To sum up their relationship as her health grew increasingly frail, Dorothy painstakingly wrote her beloved sister and lifelong companion this note [*sic*]:

My love one—
 Just a little note. I can't write what want to write, but you know how I feel in my heart. I love you, and forgive me all I have don't hurt you in my life. But I love you. Lovingly, Dottie[50]

Dorothy passed away in February 1964 at the age of seventy-nine, at Queen of Angels Hospital in Los Angeles, "after a long illness."[51]

Margarita's own health declined in small ways through the 1960s, as she aged from her seventies into her eighties. Her small frame swelled by sixteen pounds (from 120 to 136, or fifteen percent of her weight) between 1965 and 1968, and she eventually required a hearing aid and prescriptions for sleep, kidney and bladder infections, cramps, throat infections, "stomach distress," high blood pressure, heart palpitations, her circulation, dizziness, and her thyroid.[52] In general, these conditions did not affect her way of life, and she enjoyed independence and fairly good overall health until shortly before her death.[53] In 1967 and again in 1969, though, she grew seriously ill.[54] Increasingly aware of her mortality, she began to organize and notate her numerous papers. "Keep for future information," she wrote in her spiky, clear hand; "Write a brief of article for papers on my death and photos."[55] Perhaps feeling the end of her life drawing near, she mused in a letter to an old friend from her touring days on the stage about the blessings of "peace of mind (the priceless possession)."[56]

Margarita Fischer lived in her Vista home until nearly the end of her life, assisted by longtime faithful friend Arthur Field. Always independent, in 1974 she fell in her kitchen while standing on a chair to try to reach into a high cabinet. She hit her head when she fell, and "she was never the same after that," recalled her great-niece.[57] She lived at home for a few months after her fall, but when her need for help grew greater than what Arthur Field could provide, she entered a nursing home in the nearby coastal town of Encinitas.[58] Shortly afterwards, she died there of a stroke on March 11, 1975, one month past her eighty-ninth birthday.[59] Like many other past and present members of Hollywood royalty, including her husband, she was buried in Forest Lawn cemetery in Glendale, California.[60] Arthur Field passed away peacefully in the Vista home only two months later, at the age of seventy-six, and was found by Kathrine Havens when she went to visit her old friend.[61]

After Margarita Fischer's death, Kathrine Havens inherited her aunt's estate, as well as her papers and memorabilia. She safeguarded them for a time, but she was in failing health herself in the late 1970s. James H. Thomas, a professor at Wichita State University in Wichita, Kansas, contacted her in the process of researching a book about her father, C.C. Pyle, and his role in promoting the "Bunion Derby" of the late 1920s. Havens assisted him with his work and then offered the university her late aunt's and uncle's papers, making only one request. "I must have copies of all pictures … for my grandchildren," she appealed, for "it's really their heritage."[62] Before her death in 1988, she saw the Margarita Fischer and Harry Pollard papers organized, preserved, and secured for researchers.[63] Their lives and careers, thus laid out, are the extraordinary legacy not only of one family, but also of a changing industry, a society, and a time departed.

13

Conclusion: *Any Woman*

As the nineteenth century gave way to the twentieth, complex shifts in attitude were at work, changing American society in general and views of women and acting in particular. Margarita Fischer, born in 1886, saw this shift from Victorian to modern attitudes, and incorporated them both into her acting career. She put forth varied but wholesome images even as she masterminded much of her own stage and film work, battling social strictures and exceeding expectations throughout her long and successful career in theater and silent film. She headlined her own touring company before the age of twenty; *Photoplay* readers voted her America's favorite actress in 1914; thirteen years later, she starred under her husband Harry Pollard's direction in one of the most expensive films ever made at that point, Universal's two-million dollar version of *Uncle Tom's Cabin*. While she was a talented and enthusiastic performer, the path of her career was actually defined by the needs of her family: financial requirements motivated the beginning of her career on the stage as a child, encouraged her movement into film, and eventually brought it to a close when her personal support was more necessary than the monetary returns of her career.

Margarita Fischer's adaptability and image-consciousness made her the nation's most beloved actress in the mid–1910s, although these same qualities caused her stardom to vanish quickly after her retirement. After honing her acting skills onstage in her youth, she combined them with an eye for glamour and publicity, and brought them to bear in the film industry. She maintained her film stardom throughout the 1910s by tapping into the country's fascination with youth, beauty, glamour, and warmth. As views of these qualities altered, so did Margarita's image, and her careful attention to public tastes kept her popular with fans even when her pictures were weak.

Her malleability on film kept her from creating any strong persona besides that of a hoydenish heiress, though, and her high artistic standards led her to reject this characterization. As film writer Iris Barry observed in 1926, "The mere ability to act tends at first to lessen the actor's hold on the public, because he offers them something variable."[1] Margarita never created an image that stood on its own, apart from her roles, as strongly as did Theda Bara's heavy-lidded vamp or Mary Pickford's spunky golden-curled persona. In addition, her limited personal publicity also lessened her ability to imprint herself on a public that craved personal information about their screen idols. Responsible for promoting herself due to her lack of a publicist, she was reluctant to speak about anything but her career and the wholesome aspects of her family relationships. As she explained late in life, "I've had a lot of experiences but they're a little too personal to reveal."[2] With her fame therefore resting on the constant presence of her movies in theaters, Margarita's 1921 retirement at her husband's behest abruptly severed her from the moviegoing public and the connections that had kept her professional reputation intact. Despite her undeniable talent as an actress, she never truly recaptured the attention and esteem that had made her a star. She graciously took smaller roles, playing the most colorful of these with relish, and probably could have maintained a film career of supporting roles and character parts as she moved into middle age. Once she had grown too old to play the leading roles she had always prided herself upon, though, she was less committed to her vocation and relinquished it (though not without a pang) when the demands of her marriage dictated it.

After her final retirement from stage and screen, Margarita chose to live quietly while the film industry changed cataclysmically, and she became further and further removed from the public eye. Near the end of her life, she made private connections and reintroduced herself to figures from her past, but she and her works had been forgotten for so long that few people could connect with her screen image of a half-century earlier. Even before her death in 1975, she had been forgotten by many film historians and preservationists. Margarita Fischer is therefore, in a sense, a case study of the importance of image to fame and the ephemerality of celebrity. Her personal choices, the professional environment in which she worked, and the society in which she lived all contributed to shape her career, bring her to prominence, and then remove her from the public eye. Understanding the path of Margarita Fischer's career fosters an understanding of the social values that led to this process.

The stardom of the 1910s and early 1920s mattered little once the film industry began to focus on sound film, and before her death in 1975 Margarita Fischer saw her name virtually effaced. It seems incredible that such a popular, innovative actress could have vanished, along with so many others, from the pages of film history, but such was often the case. The groundwork for the silent era's disappearance was laid during its heyday. As novelist and silent film scenarist Anita Loos recalled, in the 1910s and 1920s, "we had little respect for a métier that we looked down on as a mere passing fad. Nobody ever dreamed that those images would one day start to speak.... Those of us whom the movies were making rich were bent only on cashing in before the craze died out."[3] Although the craze never did die out, the constant demand for new product meant pictures that had completed their release schedule had no more usefulness.

Once yet another craze arose for sound filmmaking, silent films had hardly a chance. As Louise Brooks later wrote, "Old pictures were bad pictures." Studios concerned with the transition to sound no longer valued their earlier silent output or the work of stars who failed to succeed in sound films, and silent film stock was recycled for its silver content, burned unintentionally (the nitrate stock used almost exclusively until mid-century was highly flammable), destroyed to free up shelf space, or simply allowed to deteriorate. In the absence of preservative measures, all nitrate film stock decomposes over time, first bubbling and then melding into a stiff, fragile coil of reddish-brown dust — a process that can take as little as one or two decades, depending on storage conditions.

Sometimes destruction was mandated; films that were remade in sound versions were often systematically destroyed except for a single archived print, while films based on literary works were sometimes destroyed following release so the author could contract for a new interpretation of the work. Some silent films vanished in an even more dramatic fashion; MGM and Universal experienced vault fires and explosions that destroyed thousands of reels of film.⁴ Fox's New Jersey storage vault of nitrate films exploded, too, in 1937. All of the studio's silent films were destroyed, including those of 1910s superstar Theda Bara. Only four of Bara's forty-two screen performances exist today, preserved by chance or collectors, but these do not represent her best work in the opinion of critics or of Bara herself.⁵ For studios that did not outlast the silent era, such as Selig and American, or even Pollard Picture Plays, the likelihood of a film having been preserved is even lower. With such cards stacked against their survival, the existence of any silent films into the preservation era is a blessing, and it is almost more amazing that any survive than that so many have crumbled out of existence.

Of course, the loss of such work is still devastating, especially given the glimpses into studios and career paths that are granted through the sampling of works that survive. Margarita Fischer's career output has been decimated in the decades since her retirement from film. She held prints of some of her movies in the years following the end of her career — her great-niece remembers seeing the characteristic cans — but these vanished following the former actress's death in 1975. Today, only two of her more than 175 films and shorts are available on video: the 1913 short *How Men Propose* and her cinematic swan song, the 1927 version of *Uncle Tom's Cabin*. Still, she has been fortunate in comparison to Bara, as additional work survives in film archives around the world. The Library of Congress holds several other pictures, one in a fragmentary state: the one-reelers *The Merry Wives of Windsor* (1910) and *Draga, the Gypsy* (1913); a single damaged reel of her first feature film, *The Quest* (1915); and, deep in their uncatalogued archives, the features *The Pearl of Paradise* (1916) and *Put Up Your Hands* (1919). The Library of Congress also holds paper prints (essentially long photographs) of random portions from American Film Manufacturing Company movies, which were deposited with the Library for the purposes of copyright. This step, made purely for fiscal reasons, may have had the artistic consequence of preserving at least parts of Margarita's extensive work for the studio, although not in an intelligible form.⁶ Other archives around the world possess copies of *A Midsummer's Love Tangle* (1914), a Beauty film in which she acted with her niece Kathie, and *Robinson Crusoe* (1913), the actress's first three-reeler.⁷ At least two other films may survive in private collections.⁸

Autographed studio portrait of Margarita Fischer. The spelling of her name as "Fisher" dates this to 1918. Photograph by Witzel (courtesy the Margarita Fischer Papers, Special Collections and University Archives, Wichita State University Libraries).

While this is cause for celebration, the reduction of a seventeen-year film career to such a short list of pictures is still a significant loss. Margarita's most innovative or unusual works, including the socially conscious *The Miracle of Life*, her early turn as Topsy in the 1913 version of *Uncle Tom's Cabin*, and her dual roles in *The Dragon* and *The Hellion*—probably do not survive and can be known only from stills. As a very small silver lining, the quality of such stills is excellent, as set photographers generally used a very large negative which captured all of the film's carefully constructed detail.[9] In the absence of the films themselves, these do provide an inkling of the style and structure of the majority of Margarita Fischer's screen work.

With nearly all of Margarita Fischer's career output inaccessible to film fans, her fame declined into obscurity. Not all silent stars suffered the same fate, however. Those fortunate or ambitious enough to create a strong image — or to have others create one for them — have stayed in the nation's consciousness to the present day, regardless of the accessibility of their films. Although Theda Bara's unrelenting vamp image eventually destroyed her career, its power has kept her in the public's memory for ninety years. Mary Pickford oversaw preservation efforts on her own films, and she introduced herself to a new generation when her autobiography, *Sunshine and Shadow*, appeared in 1955. The Talmadge sisters, Norma and Constance, were immortalized in a chatty tell-all 1978 biography by Anita Loos, who intended, in irreverent but affectionate fashion, to remedy the fact that they "exist for the most part only in the memories of those old enough to have seen their silent films."[10]

Of 1920s actresses, Clara Bow may remain the best known today; her difficult life and unlikely career have been examined in a thoughtful, sympathetic documentary and biography in the past few years. Contemporaries of Louise Brooks, a bitingly intelligent flapper starlet in Hollywood in the late 1920s, knew her more for her fast lifestyle and her trend-setting severe black pageboy than for her acting ability, which lay largely untapped in cheesecake roles for Paramount. In later decades, however, she saw her fame grow to unprecedented heights when film buffs discovered her sparkling performances in two German films: *Pandora's Box* and *Diary of a Lost Girl* (both 1929). Before her death in 1985, Brooks built a renewed reputation as an incisive essayist on film history and published the memoir *Lulu in Hollywood*.

Margarita Fischer's comparative obscurity is, unfortunately, much more common. By one estimate, less than 10 percent of silent films survived into the 1970s (thus the survival of Margarita's films is actually below average).[11] The 1914 *Photoplay* poll that named the young star as America's favorite actress is only one of many cases in which a now-forgotten star won popularity polls in silent-era film magazines.[12] Margarita Fischer is one of fifty "lost players" briefly studied by Billy H. Doyle in his *Ultimate Directory of the Silent Screen Performers*, and Doyle could easily have profiled dozens more. Her eclipse was especially quick, though. In 1914, Robert Grau wrote one of the earliest film histories, *The Theatre of Science*, and included material about Margarita Fischer as an important young star, but later film historians neglected Margarita — and many other former luminaries — as early as the 1920s, when film industry veteran Terry Ramsaye's 1926 *A Million and One Nights* first dismissed her as merely "[the] wife of Harry Pollard."[13]

In recent decades, the growing interest in historical specialization, particularly in issues relating to race, class, and gender, has led many authors to mine undocumented areas of film history for inspiration, resulting in a reclamation of early cinematic figures who, like

Margarita, were significant in their time but faded from memory in subsequent decades. For example, an impressive literature exists dealing with women in the early years of film. *Without Lying Down: Frances Marion and the Powerful Women of Early Hollywood*, by Cari Beauchamp, looks most particularly at influential women behind the camera, but also depicts the historical and geographic context for female empowerment within which popular and influential actresses like Margarita Fischer were able to flourish. Anthony Slide's *The Silent Feminists* also stays behind the camera to examine this context through the careers of several significant female directors. Slide concludes that such unprecedented female power came about because film, like theater before it, suffered from a lack of respectability in its developing years. Having women in prominent roles lent the industry a sense of legitimacy while it became established with the public. As profits grew and companies combined into conglomerations, male leadership forced these trailblazing women into less important and creative roles.

In front of the camera, though, female stars were the greatest box office draws throughout the silent era. Actresses often fit into specific types and gained public followings for repeating a certain type of role. Richard Dyer's *Stars* and Richard DeCordova's *Picture Personalities: The Emergence of the Star System in America* examine the development of film stardom and the nature of fame over the course of the twentieth century, phenomena that had their origins in the early silent era. In 1910, the budding star system began to flourish when an elaborate publicity stunt resulted in the revelation to the public of the name of one of their favorite actresses. One year later, the first fan magazine was founded; the next year, narratives grew more complex with the invention of the serial; another two years later, feature-length films were becoming more popular, and California was virtually entrenched as the center of film production in the United States. As film historian Diane Negra points out, "the critical analysis of stardom [is a] necessary and inevitable component of any efforts to understand aesthetic, industrial, and ideological film history."[14] According to Dyer, the very idea of stardom reveals something significant about our nation's values and preoccupations. If this is so, then the development of the film industry, and of Margarita Fischer's career, is a case study in American desires.

These desires were by no means static throughout the silent era. The silent films of the 1910s are very different in content and construction from those of the 1920s, and those of the early 1910s are just as different from those of the late 1910s. While nearly every film historian devotes considerable attention to familiar and undeniably significant figures like Lillian Gish and D. W. Griffith, they tend to neglect the directors, performers, and studios from film's earlier years who were just as important in their time but whose work and reputations did not survive the passage of time. Jeanine Basinger's recent *Silent Stars*, which profiles "a group of silent film stars who are somehow forgotten, misunderstood, or underappreciated," excludes performers, like Margarita, with few surviving works, "since I wanted to see as many movies starring the same person as possible."[15] Anthony Slide seconds her opinion that lost films undermine modern-day ability to judge professional reputation, asking, "Can we really judge [a career] on the basis of one film?"[16]

Modern film historians understandably find it difficult to evaluate an actor whose work does not survive in large quantity, yet the example of Theda Bara demonstrates that stardom can persist even in these cases. Although only four of her films exist today (and these not her best work), she remains the definitive vamp ninety years after the release of *A Fool There Was*, and her lost film *Cleopatra* is longed for and speculated about by film historians. It is unrealistic to expect silent actors to have the same reputation in our time as in their own, but stars like Theda Bara, Florence Lawrence, Mary Pickford, and Clara Bow are appreciated as much for their significance to their contemporary fans as they are for the significance of their surviving work to film history.

Margarita Fischer deserves similar consideration, for a multitude of pictures and articles show how admired she was and how completely she fit into, defined, and was defined by the time in which she lived. The most popular actress in the country in the mid–1910s, she reflected both the nation's preoccupation with modernity and its ties to traditional morals. Her life was unusual on its glamorous surface but familiar in its choices, informed by commonly held personal values. A determined and talented actress with high artistic standards, she nevertheless depended on her popularity enough to create inferior work that appealed to the public. She was also greatly influenced by the expectations put on women at the turn of the twentieth century. Raised according to the principles of the late Victorian era, and accustomed to close family ties fostered by a decade of theatrical touring, she valued these ties and felt a particular duty to meet the needs of her husband even at the expense of the career she prized so highly. She took on the role of "Mrs. Harry Pollard" as seamlessly as she had taken on so many hundreds of others over the course of her career. She is, therefore, important not only as an actress but as a woman of her time, and her film career is as notable for what it demonstrates about the importance of image and the changing nature of public tastes as it is for the work that she created.

In Margarita Fischer's opinion, her films were both her greatest accomplishment and merely one of many chapters in the family story to which she devoted decades of care and attention. Once she left the world of film, and once her husband died, she turned her back on the cinematic world for years and focused her considerable energy and will instead on building and caring for her family. And once they were grown, or had died, and these latest accomplishments had come to a natural close, she found strength and pride in everything she had achieved across her lifespan, and welcomed the opportunity to speak of her work and bring it back into the public consciousness.

Sadly, she outlived almost all of her films, and we may never truly be able to judge the depth and breadth of her talent. The evidence that survives, though, is tantalizing, hinting at work that was fascinating, creative, artistic, and risky, and through her work in movies as much as her carefully preserved papers, she truly comes alive. Seen today, her screen presence is powerful and natural enough to overcome dated fashions or degraded film. In both comedy and drama she is engaging and magnetic, as her face — winking, desperate, or heartfelt — tells us exactly what she feels across the silence of decades. Her most interesting work is now just a series of stilled images — a butterfly girl, a Spanish hellcat, a cabaret singer, an opium addict, a tormented mistress, a conflicted pregnant woman, an innocent South Seas princess — but in every persona, in every picture, her wide eyes capture the viewer. She wants to be seen and known; she created everything for that reason.

Filmography

This filmography is arranged in chronological order. The initial version was compiled by film historian J.B. Kaufman for the Department of Special Collections, Ablah Library, Wichita State University, which holds Margarita Fischer's and Harry Pollard's papers. That document has been expanded using information from additional primary and secondary sources. Still, the resulting filmography is almost certainly incomplete as a result of the anonymous nature of many of Margarita Fischer's early performances.

Listings take the form of: *Title* (Studio/Distributor). Film length. Release date. Director: name. Source text and script information. Cast: actor (character name) [MF being Margarita Fischer].

1 reel of film is equal to 1,000 feet. Where no cast member besides Margarita Fischer has been confirmed, or where other information is not known, the relevant portion of the listing has been omitted. Cast listings include all confirmed cast members.

There, Little Girl, Don't Cry (Selig). 1 reel. May 12, 1910.
The Trimming of Paradise Gulch (Selig). 1 reel. May 30, 1910. Director: Francis Boggs. Cast: MF, Tom Mix.
After Many Years (Selig). 1 reel. May 30, 1910.
Romeo and Juliet in Our Town (Selig). 1 reel. June 13, 1910.
The Red Man's Way (alt.: *The Way of the Red Man*) (Selig). 1 reel. July 7, 1910. Director: Otis Turner.
The Cowboy's Stratagem (Selig). 1 reel (995 feet). July 28, 1910.
Her First Long Dress (Selig). 640 feet; split reel of 960 feet with *Shrimps*. August 1, 1910.
The Road to Richmond (Selig). 1 reel. September 1, 1910.
Big Medicine (Selig). Split reel with *Bertie's Elopement*. September 19, 1910.
The Kentucky Pioneer (Selig). 1 reel (990 feet). September 29, 1910.
For Her Country's Sake (Selig). 1 reel. October 6, 1910.
Settled Out of Court (Selig). 1 reel. October 31, 1910.
The Early Settlers (Selig). 1 reel. November 3, 1910.
The Vampire (Selig). 1 reel. November 10, 1910. Based on a poem by Rudyard Kipling. Cast: Charles Clary, MF.
The Merry Wives of Windsor (Selig). 1 reel. November 24, 1910. Director: Francis Boggs [?]. Cast: MF (Mrs. Page), Kathlyn Williams (Mrs. Ford).
In the Wilderness (Selig). 1 reel. December 8, 1910.
Two Lucky Jims (American/Motion Picture Distributors and Sales Co.). 955 feet. December 8, 1910. Director: Sam Morris.
The County Fair (Selig). 1 reel. December 15, 1910. Based on a play by Neil Burgess.
The Squaw and the Man (American/Motion Picture Distributors and Sales Co.). 1 reel. December 29, 1910.
An Arizona Romance (American). 1 reel. January 9, 1911.
Bertie's Bandit (American). 1 reel. January 26, 1911.
The Mission in the Desert (American). 1 reel. February 2, 1911.
Over the Hills (to the Poorhouse) (IMP). November 30, 1911. Cast: King Baggot, MF.

The Girl and the Half-Back (IMP). 700 feet. December 18, 1911. Cast: King Baggot (Victor Fisher), MF (Alice), William E. Shay.

A Pair of Gloves (IMP). 600 feet; split reel with *Niagara Falls*. December 23, 1911.

The Portrait (IMP). 1 reel. December 28, 1911.

A Lesson to Husbands (IMP). 400 feet; split reel with *Broke* or *How Timothy Escaped*. December 30, 1911. Cast: King Baggot, MF.

The Trinity (IMP). January 4, 1912. Cast: King Baggot, MF ("Baby" Lena).

In the Northern Woods (IMP). January 12, 1912.

The Worth of a Man (IMP). 1 reel. January 25, 1912. Cast: Harry Pollard (young hunchbacked surgeon), MF (his sweetheart).

Mrs. Matthews, Dressmaker (IMP). 1 reel. February 8, 1912.

Who Wears Them? (IMP). 600 feet; split reel with *The Tea Industry in the United States*. February 10, 1912. Cast: Harry Pollard (Harry French), MF (Mrs. French).

The Rose of California (IMP). February 29, 1912.

A Melodrama of Yesterday (IMP). March 7, 1912. MF, Harry Pollard.

The Call of the Drum (IMP). March 7, 1912. MF, Harry Pollard.

Better Than Gold (IMP). 1 reel. March 21, 1912. Cast: MF (dual role: mother and daughter), Harry Pollard (Parson Jim), Myrtle Green, Harry Green.

The Baby (IMP). Split reel with *Squnk City Fire Company*. March 30, 1912. Director: Francis J. Grandon. Scenario: Alice Mellor. Cast: MF (Mrs. Noel Grantley), Harry Pollard (Mr. Noel Grantley), Miss Angelis (Nurse Edna), Little Wilbur (the baby).

Squnk City Fire Company (IMP). Split reel with *The Baby*. March 30, 1912. Director: Francis J. Grandon. Scenario: J.W. Culbertson. Cast: Harry Pollard (Bob Summers), Ben Horning (Doc Smizely), Edward Lyons (Zeke Stoely), MF (Mary Harding), Miss Crolius (Mrs. Harding), E.J. LeSaint (Mr. Harding).

Where Paths Meet (IMP). April 1, 1912. Cast: MF (Alice), Harry Pollard (young lover), B.J. LeSaint (father), H.S. Mack.

The Dove and the Serpent (IMP). April 4, 1912. Cast: MF (Tortola, the dove), Edward Lyons (Luis, the serpent), Harry Pollard, Ben Horning, Miss Bennett, E. J. LeSaint.

On the Shore (IMP). May 6, 1912.

The Land of Promise (IMP). May 9, 1912. Cast: Harry Pollard (poor Mexican), MF (his wife), Ben Horning (rancher).

Jim's Atonement (IMP). May 13, 1912.

The Return of Captain John (IMP). 1 reel. June 6, 1912. Director: Francis J. Grandon. Story: Francis J. Grandon. Cast: Louise Crolius, Harry Pollard, MF, Ben Horning, Edward J. Le Saint, Dolly Larkin.

Nothing Shall Be Hidden (IMP). 1 reel. June 10, 1912. Director: Harry Pollard. Cast: MF, Harry Pollard.

Love, War, and a Bonnet (IMP). 1 reel. July 1, 1912. Director: Harry Pollard. Cast: MF, Harry Pollard, Eugene Kelly, Louise Crolius, William Bertram.

The Parson and the Medicine Man (IMP). 1 reel. July 8, 1912. Director: Edward J. LeSaint. Cast: MF, Edward Lyons, Harry Pollard, William Bertram.

Hearts in Conflict (IMP). 1 reel. July 15, 1912. Director: Edward J. Le Saint. Cast: MF, Harry Pollard, Gordon Sackville, Gertrude Short, William Bertram.

The Hand of Mystery (Rex). 2 reels. July 25, 1912. Cast: Robert Z. Leonard (new foreman), MF, Malcolm MacQuarrie (Mexican), Harry Tenbrook (discarded foreman).

Big Hearted Jim (IMP). 1 reel. August 12, 1912. Director: Harry Pollard. Cast: Harry Pollard, Edward Lyons, MF, Mr. Kelly.

On the Border Line (Nestor). 1 reel. September 2, 1912. Director: Harry Pollard. Cast: Harry Pollard, MF, William Clifford, Lloyd Ingraham, Gertrude Claire, G. Tempest.

The Exchange of Labels (IMP). Split reel. September 21. 1912. Cast: MF, Harry Pollard, Eugene Kelly.

The Employer's Liability (Nestor). 1 reel. October 7, 1912. Director: Henry Otto. Cast: William Clifford, MF, Harry Pollard, Eugenie Forde, Dorothy Livingston, Dale Merwin, Bobby Strand, Henry Otto, Gordon Sackville, Howard Lindsay, Arthur Forde.

Betty's Bandit (Nestor). 1 reel. October 21, 1912. Director: Henry Otto. Cast: Harry Pollard (Harry

Parsons), Lloyd Ingraham (Rancher Cole), Henry Otto (Farmer Allen), Gertrude Claire (Mrs. Allen), MF (Betty Allen, their daughter), William Clifford (Mexican Pete), Frank G. Rice (sheriff).

The Tribal Law (101 Bison). 2 reels. November 16, 1912. Director: Otis Turner. Cast: Wallace Reid, MF, Charles Inslee.

A Fight for Friendship (Nestor). 1 reel. November 18, 1912. Director: Henry Otto. Cast: Harry Pollard, William Clifford, Henry Otto, Gertrude Claire, MF, Louis Fitzroy, George Rice.

Trapped by Fire (101 Bison). 1 reel. November 19, 1912. Cast: MF, Charles Inslee, E.H. Philbrook.

An Indian Outcast (101 Bison). 1 reel. November 29, 1912. Cast: Charles Inslee, Wallace Reid, Chief Harvey, William Gittenger, MF, Harry Tenbrook.

Romance and Reality (Nestor). 1 reel. December 2, 1912. Director: Harry Pollard.

The Rights of a Savage (101 Bison). 1 reel. December 7, 1912. Director: Harry Pollard.

The Old Folks' Christmas (IMP). 1 reel. December 23, 1912. Director: George Loane Tucker. Scenario: Herbert Brenon, George Loane Tucker. Cast: Robert Z. Leonard, MF, J. Farrell MacDonald.

The Great Ganton Mystery (alt.: *The Great Canyon Mystery*) (Rex). 2 reels. March 27, 1913. Director: Robert Z. Leonard. Cast: Robert Z. Leonard, Edward Alexander, Lillian Herbert, Charles W. Travis, MF.

Until Death (Rex). 2 reels. April 10, 1913. Directors: Lois Weber, Phillips Smalley. Scenario: Lois Weber. Cast: Phillips Smalley, Lois Weber, Harry Pollard, MF.

A Friend of the Family (Rex). 1 reel. April 17, 1913. Story: F.W. Randolph. Cast: Iva Shepard, MF.

The Wayward Sister (Rex). 1 reel. April 27, 1913. Director: Otis Turner. Cast: Robert Z. Leonard, MF.

The Turn of the Tide (Rex). 1 reel. May 1, 1913. Cast: Robert Z. Leonard, MF.

In Slavery Days (Rex). 2 reels. May 22, 1913. Director: Otis Turner. Scenario: Otis Turner, Allan Dwan. Story: James Dayton. Cast: Robert Z. Leonard, MF, Jane Ainsley, Edna Maison, Iva Shepard.

Draga, the Gypsy (Rex). 1 reel. June 29, 1913. Cast: Robert Z. Leonard (Jack Harlow), MF (Draga).

A Woman's Folly (Rex). 1 reel. July 3, 1913. Director: Robert Z. Leonard. Cast: MF, Robert Z. Leonard, Joseph Singleton, Iva Shepard, Mr. Bogangi.

The Wrong Road (Rex). 1 reel. July 17, 1913. Cast: MF, Robert Z. Leonard, Harry Tenbrook, Joseph Singleton, Miss Tafft.

How Men Propose (Crystal). Split reel. July 20, 1913. Directors: Lois Weber, Phillips Smalley. Cast: MF (Grace Darling), Chester Barnett.

Robinson Crusoe (101 Bison). 3 reels. July 29, 1913. Director: Otis Turner. Scenario: Allan Dwan. Based on a novel by Daniel Defoe. Cast: MF (daughter of Captain Harvey), Robert Z. Leonard (Robinson Crusoe), Edward Alexander, Charles Travis.

The Power of Heredity (Rex). 1 reel. July 31, 1913. Cast: Robert Z. Leonard, MF (Marie), Stella Adams, Joseph Singleton.

When the Prince Arrived (Rex). 1 reel. August 7, 1913. Director: Robert Z. Leonard. Cast: Robert Z. Leonard, MF, Joseph Singleton, Frank Borzage.

Sally Scraggs, Housemaid (Rex). 1 reel. August 14, 1913. Director: Robert Z. Leonard. Cast: Robert Z. Leonard (Frank Norcross), MF (Doris Lowrey), Laura Oakley (Mrs. Shackleton).

Uncle Tom's Cabin (IMP). 3 reels. August 25, 1913. Director: Otis Turner. Cast: MF (Topsy), Harry Pollard (Uncle Tom), Gertrude Short, Edward Alexander, Iva Shepard.

The Evil Power (Rex). 2 reels. September 4, 1913. Director: Otis Turner. Scenario: Otis Turner.

The Light Woman (Rex). 1 reel. September 7, 1913. Directors: Lois Weber, Phillips Smalley. Scenario: Lois Weber. Story: Lois Weber. Based on a poem by Robert Browning. Cast: Eddie Polo, Lois Weber, Phillips Smalley, MF.

The Diamond Makers (Rex). 2 reels. September 11, 1913. Story: Stella Machefert. Cast: MF (Shedah, Oriental princess), Robert Z. Leonard (Westerly, a detective), James McQuarrie, Joseph Singleton.

The Fight Against Evil (Rex). 1 reel. September 14, 1913. Director: Otis Turner. Cast: MF (Mary), Robert Z. Leonard (doctor), Laura Oakley (adventuress), Iva Shepard, Mrs. W. O'Connor, Grace Carlyle, Joseph Singleton.

Paying the Price (Rex). 1 reel. September 28, 1913. Director: Otis Turner. Cast: MF (Jane), Robert Z. Leonard (Robert), William Walters, Mrs. William O'Connell.

Shon, the Piper (101 Bison). 2 reels. September 30, 1913. Director: Otis Turner. Camera: William

Foster. Subtitle verses: James Dayton. Cast: Robert Z. Leonard (Shon, a Duke disguised as a piper), MF (Madge), Joseph Singleton, John Burton, Lon Chaney.

Like Darby and Joan (Rex). 1 reel. October 5, 1913. Cast: Robert Z. Leonard, MF, Marcia Moore, William McDonald, Ed Brady.

The Thumb Print (Rex). 2 reels. October 23, 1913. Directors: Lois Weber, Phillips Smalley. Scenario: Lois Weber. Cast: Robert Z. Leonard (Clayton), MF (Dolores), John Burton, Harry Tenbrook, Malcolm MacQuarrie.

The Primeval Test (Rex). 2 reels. November 6, 1913. Director: Otis Turner. Scenario: Allan Dwan. Cast: Robert Z. Leonard (Bob Stannard), MF (Margery Stannard), Reese Gardner (Dick Thompson), John Burton (Dr. Harrison).

The Boob's Dream Girl (Rex). 1 reel. November 9, 1913. Director: Otis Turner. Cast: Robert Z. Leonard (Bob Hicks, the Boob), John Burton (Mr. Van Zant, a bogus count), MF (Margarita, the Dream Girl), Malcolm MacQuarrie (Count Alberti), Jane Saunders (his wife), Harry Fisher (Roland Long, a detective), Fanny Stockbridge.

The Missionary Box (Rex). 1 reel. November 13, 1913. Director: Robert Z. Leonard. Cast: Robert Z. Leonard, MF, Joseph Callahan, Joseph Singleton, John Burton, Mrs. W. McConnell.

His Old-Fashioned Dad (Rex). 1 reel. November 16, 1913. Cast: MF (Peggy), Robert Z. Leonard (Bob), Harry Fisher (his pal), John Burton (Bob's father), Joseph Callahan.

Fires of Fate (Rex). 2 reels. November 20, 1913. Directors: Wallace Reid, Willis Robards. Scenario: Wallace Reid. Cast: Wallace Reid, Dorothy Davenport, Ed Brady, Robert Z. Leonard, MF.

The Tale of a Lonely Coast (Rex). 1 reel. November 27, 1913. Director: Otis Turner. Cast: Robert Z. Leonard (Ben), MF (the girl).

Withering Roses (American [Beauty]/Mutual). 1 reel (966 feet). January 14, 1914. Director: Harry Pollard. Story: Marc Edmund Jones. Cast: MF (dual role: Mary Wood and fairy in vision), Harry Pollard (John Everett), Joe Harris (the evil spirit), Kathie Fischer (crippled child), Fred Gamble (her father), Adelaide Bronti (maid).

Fooling Uncle (American [Beauty]/Mutual). 1 reel. January 21, 1914. Cast: MF (Peggy), Kathie Fischer (her sister), Harry Pollard (Harry), Fred Gamble (Uncle), Joseph Harris (valet).

Bess, the Outcast (American [Beauty]/Mutual). 1 reel (934 feet). January 28, 1914. Cast: MF (Bess), Harry Pollard (schoolmaster), Nettie Beatrice (Gladys), Adelaide Bronti (gossip), Joseph Harris (the actor).

Sally's Elopement (formerly *Peggy's Elopement*) (American [Beauty]/Mutual). 1 reel. February 4, 1914. Director: Harry Pollard. Cast: MF, Harry Pollard (storekeeper's son), Kathie Fischer (naughty little girl), Mary Scott.

The Wife (American [Beauty]/Mutual). 1 reel. February 11, 1914. Cast: Harry Pollard (Harry Gordon), MF (Margaret Turner Gordon), Joseph Harris (Harvey).

The Sacrifice (American [Beauty]/Mutual). 1 reel. February 18, 1914. Director: Harry Pollard. Cast: Harry Pollard (Harry, a fisherman), MF (Marie, an Italian girl), Kathie Fischer (their son), Joseph Harris (Antonio).

The Professor's Awakening (American [Beauty]/Mutual). 1 reel. February 25, 1914. Director: Harry Pollard. Cast: MF (fisherman's daughter), Harry Pollard (Professor Blake).

Italian Love (American [Beauty]/Mutual). 1 reel. March 4, 1914. Cast: MF (Italian girl), Harry Pollard, Fred Gamble.

Closed at Ten (American [Beauty]/Mutual). 1 reel. March 11, 1914. Director: Harry Pollard. Cast: Harry Pollard (Jack Bandle), MF (Marjorie Holmes), Fred Gamble (Mr. Evans), Perry Banks (Professor Dow).

The Girl Who Dared (American [Beauty]/Mutual). 1 reel. March 17, 1914.

The Peacock Feather Fan (American [Beauty]/Mutual). 1 reel. March 24, 1914. Director: Harry Pollard. Cast: MF (Polly Bainbridge), Harry Pollard (John Keith), Julius Frankenburg (Billy Mayberry), Joseph Harris (Martin Courtland), Gladys Kingsbury (Widow Willing).

Sweet Land of Liberty (American [Beauty]/Mutual). 1 reel. March 31, 1914. Cast: MF, Harry Pollard.

Retribution (American [Beauty]/Mutual). 1 reel (996 feet). April 7, 1914.

Mlle. La Mode (American [Beauty]/Mutual). 1 reel (977 feet). April 14, 1914. Cast: MF (Margaret Lee), Fred Gamble (Harry Lee), Harry Pollard (Paul Knox Jr.), Joseph Harris (Paul's father).

The Man Who Came Back (American [Beauty]/Mutual). 1 reel (980 feet). April 21, 1914. Cast: Harry Pollard (Donald Baxter), MF (Mabelle Arnold), Adelaide Bronti.

A Flurry in Hats (American [Beauty]/Mutual). 1 reel. April 28, 1914. Cast: MF (Hattie Hood Dunlap), Harry Pollard (Knox Dunlap), Fred Gamble (Captain Hood), Mary Scott (Mother Hood), Jane Schafer (Bridget Stetson, the cook).

Eugenics versus Love (American [Beauty]/Mutual). 1 reel. May 5, 1914. Cast: MF, Harry Pollard, Fred Gamble.

Her Heritage (American [Beauty]/Mutual). 1 reel (986 feet). May 12, 1914. Director: Harry Pollard. Cast: MF (Mrs. Van Arsdale), Harry Pollard (Dr. Van Arsdale), Joseph Harris (J. Preston Warren), Gladys Kingsbury (Mrs. Warren).

The Courting of Prudence (American [Beauty]/Mutual). 1 reel. May 19, 1914. Cast: MF (Prudence Benton), Harry Pollard (Larry Neil).

Jane, the Justice (American [Beauty]/Mutual). 1 reel. May 26, 1914. Cast: MF (Jane Higgins), Fred Gamble (her father, the constable), Joseph Harris (Zeb Cobb), Scott Beal (Harry).

Drifting Hearts (American [Beauty]/Mutual). 1 reel. June 2, 1914. Cast: MF, Harry Pollard, Frank Cooley, Kathie Fischer, Agnes Childs.

Nancy's Husband (American [Beauty]/Mutual). 1 reel. June 9, 1914. Director: Harry Pollard. Cast: MF, Harry Pollard, Fred Gamble.

The Dream Ship (American [Beauty]/Mutual). 1 reel (968 feet). June 16, 1914. Based on a poem by Eugene Fields. Cast: MF (Mary Baxter), Harry Pollard ("Jeune Coeur"), Fred Gamble (beggar), Frank Cooley (king).

The Tale of a Tailor (American [Beauty]/Mutual). 1 reel. June 23, 1914. Cast: MF, Harry Pollard, Joseph Harris, Fred Gamble.

Via the Fire Escape (American [Beauty]/Mutual). 1 reel (980 feet). June 30, 1914. Cast: MF (Anita Bowen), Joseph Harris (Richard Harding), Fred Gamble (Edward Harding), Mary Scott (Mrs. Harding).

The Other Train (American [Beauty]/Mutual). 1 reel (943 feet). July 7, 1914. Director: Harry Pollard. Cast: MF (Mary Baxter), Harry Pollard (Rev. John Gordon), James Harris (Harold Preston), Fred Gamble (Freddy Harvey), Perry Banks (station agent), Frank Cooley (circus manager).

A Joke on Jane (American [Beauty]/Mutual). 1 reel. July 14, 1914. Cast: Harry Pollard (Joseph Rich), MF (Jane Rich), Frank Cooley (the slugger).

Her "Really" Mother (American [Beauty]/Mutual). 1 reel (1,006 feet). July 21, 1914. Director: Harry Pollard. Story: Hettie Grey Baker. Cast: MF (Mary), Kathie Fischer (Kathie Stanton).

A Midsummer's Love Tangle (American [Beauty]/Mutual). 1 reel. July 28, 1914. Director: Harry Pollard. Story: Isabel M. Reynolds. Cast: MF (Trixy Lynn), Kathie Fischer (Buddy), Fred Gamble (Judge Lynn), Harry Pollard (Jack Weston).

A Suspended Ceremony (American [Beauty]/Mutual). 1 reel (985 feet). August 4, 1914. Director: Harry Pollard. Cast: MF (Trixy Lynn), Harry Pollard (Jack Weston), Kathie Fischer (Buddy), Joseph Harris (Archibald Tendervery), Fred Gamble (Judge Lynn), Mary Scott (Mrs. Lynn), Perry Banks (justice of the peace). Sequel to *A Midsummer's Love Triangle*.

Susanna's New Suit (American [Beauty]/Mutual). 1 reel (990 feet). August 14, 1914. Director: Harry Pollard. Scenario: James Edward Hungerford. Cast: MF (Susanna Van Dusen), Harry Pollard.

The Silence of John Gordon (American [Beauty]/Mutual). 1 reel. August 18, 1914. Director: Harry Pollard. Cast: MF, Harry Pollard, Kathie Fischer, Fred Gamble, Joseph Harris.

Susie's New Shoes (American [Beauty]/Mutual). 1 reel (976 feet). August 25, 1914. Cast: MF (Susanna Van Dusen), Harry Pollard (William Van Dusen), Joseph Harris (fake blind man), Fred Gamble, Mary Scott (Mrs. Riley). Possible sequel to *Susanna's New Suit*.

A Modern Othello (American [Beauty]/Mutual). 1 reel. September 1, 1914. Cast: MF, Harry Pollard (Mr. Mason), Mary Martin, Harry Wulze, Kathie Fischer.

The Motherless Kids (American [Beauty]/Mutual). 1 reel. September 8, 1914. Cast: MF (Betty), Kathie Fischer, Buddy Powers.

The Only Way (American [Beauty]/Mutual). 1 reel (993 feet). September 15, 1914. Director: Harry Pollard. Cast: MF, Harry Pollard.

Caught in a Tight Pinch (American [Beauty]/Mutual). 1 reel. September 22, 1914. Director: Harry Pollard. Cast: MF, Harry Pollard, Joseph Harris.

The Taming of Sunnybrook Nell (American/Mutual). 1 reel (990 feet). September 25, 1914.

The Legend of Black Rock (American [Beauty]/Mutual). 1 reel. September 29, 1914. Director: Harry Pollard. Cast: MF (Carmelita), Joseph Harris (Joe Thornton), Mary Scott (his mother), Gladys Kingsbury (Mona Reaves), Kathie Fischer and Albert Cavens (children).

Nieda (American [Beauty]/Mutual). 1 reel. October 6, 1914. Director: Harry Pollard. Cast: MF (Nieda Graham), Harry Pollard (Jean, a trapper), Joseph Harris (Nieda's father).

The Divinity of Motherhood (alt.: *Motherhood*) (American [Beauty]/Mutual). 1 reel. November 10, 1914. Director: Harry Pollard. Scenario: Olga Pritzlau Clark. Cast: MF (Marjorie, the Woman), Kathie Fischer (Cupid), Harry Pollard (the Man), Joseph Harris (the son).

When Queenie Came Back (American [Beauty]/Mutual). 1 reel (989 feet). November 17, 1914. Cast: MF (Isabel Van Dyke), Joseph Harris (Henry Van Dyke).

Cupid and a Dress Coat (American [Beauty]/Mutual). 1 reel. December 1, 1914. Director: Harry Pollard. Cast: MF (Ethel Peyton), Harry Pollard (Henry Warner), Joseph Harris (Sam Reynolds).

The Quest (American/Mutual [Masterpicture]). 5 reels. March 22, 1915. Director: Harry Pollard. Story: F. McGrew Willis. Cast: MF (Nai), Harry Pollard (John Douglas), Joseph Singleton (De Villiers/Chief Neto), Robyn Adair (Sub-chief Kaura), Lucille Ward (Mrs. Chalmers), William Carroll (tribal priest), Nan Christy (Helen Carruthers), Kathie Fischer.

The Lonesome Heart (American/Mutual [Masterpicture]). 4 reels. June 3, 1915. Director: William Desmond Taylor. Cast: MF (Samanthy, an orphan), Lucille Ward (Sara Prue), William A. Carroll (Tom), Robyn Adair (George Stuart), Joseph Singleton (James Stuart), Kathie Fischer.

The Girl from His Town (American/Mutual [Masterpicture]). 4 reels. August 5, 1915. Director: Harry Pollard. Scenario: May Futrelle and Richard Willis, based on a novel by Marie Van Vorst. Cast: MF (Sarah Towney), C. Elliott Griffin (Dan Blair), Beatrice Van (Duchess of Breakwater), Joseph Harris (Prince Ponitowsky), Joseph Singleton (Lord Galore), Fred Gamble (Joshua Ruggles), Robyn Adair (Blair the elder), William Carroll, Lucille Ward.

Infatuation (American/Mutual [Masterpicture]). 4 reels. September 2, 1915. Director: Harry Pollard. Scenario: Mary O'Connor, based on a novel by Lloyd Osbourne. Cast: MF (Phyllis Ladd), Harry Pollard (Cyril Adair), Joseph Singleton (John Ladd), Lucille Ward (Mrs. Fensham), William Carroll, Robyn Adair.

The Miracle of Life (American/Mutual [Masterpicture]). 4 reels. October 21, 1915. Director: Harry Pollard. Cast: MF (Grace Catherwood), Joseph Singleton (John Catherwood), Lucille Ward.

The Dragon (Equitable/World). 5 reels. January 3, 1916. Director: Harry Pollard. Story: Perley Poore Sheehan. Scenario: Russell E. Smith. Cast: MF (dual role: Messalla, the child, and Elizabeth, the mother), Katherine Calhoun (Mayme), Bennett Southard (Moberly Trail), Joseph Harris (Fred Carrollton), Harry Leighton (A. Biskany), Thomas J. McGrane (Tanner, a millionaire), Sheridan Block (Grashaw).

The Pearl of Paradise (alt.: *Tropic Love*) (Pollard Picture Plays/Mutual [Star]). 5 reels. November 2, 1916. Director: Harry Pollard. Story: Harry Pollard. Cast: MF (dual role: Yulita, Alice in flashback), Harry Pollard (dual role: Lt. John Weldon, Alice's first husband in flashback), Joseph Harris (Gomez), J. Gordon Russell (Captain Piete Van Dekken), Beatrice Van (Denise, Weldon's fiancée).

Miss Jackie of the Navy (Pollard Picture Plays/Mutual [Star]). 5 reels. November 30, 1916. Director: Harry Pollard. Scenario: Alfred Sloman. Cast: MF (Jackie Holbrook), John Steppling (Silas Holbrook), Mrs. M. McCuire (Mrs. Holbrook), Jack Mower (Captain Robert Crowne), J. Gordon Russell (Bill Blount), Joseph Harris (Lord Cashless), Louis Fitzroy (Professor Dusenberry), Beatrice Van (Kate, his daughter), Helene Miers (Bridget), Pete the dog.

The Butterfly Girl (Pollard/Mutual [Star]). 5 reels. January 8, 1917. Director: Henry Otto. Cast: MF ("Pep" O'Mally), Jack Mower (Robert Whipple, Jr.), J. Gordon Russell (Marcus Renshaw), Della Pringle (Trixie Louella Boniface), Marie Kiernan (Little Sister Bess), Joseph Harris (Robert Whipple, Sr.), John Steppling (Heinie, the Weinie Man).

The Devil's Assistant (Pollard/Mutual [Star]). 5 reels. April 2, 1917. Director: Harry Pollard. Scenario: J. Edward Hungerford. Cast: MF (Marta), Monroe Salisbury (Dr. Lorenz), Kathleen Kirkham (Marion Dane), Joseph Harris (butler), J. Gordon Russell, Jack Mower (John Lane).

The Girl Who Couldn't Grow Up (alt.: *Putting it Over*) (Pollard/Mutual). 5 reels. September 17, 1917. Director: Harry Pollard. Scenario: Harry Pollard. Cast: MF (Peggy Brockman), Jack Mower (Lord George Raleigh), John Steppling (Herbert Brockman), Jean Hathaway (Mrs. Brockman), Joseph Harris (Wiggens, the butler), Lule Warrenton (Tia Ana), Leota Lorraine (Iris Stanley), Marjorie Blinn (Bertha Stanley).

Filmography

Miss Jackie of the Army (formerly *A Daughter of Joan*). (American/Mutual [Star]). 5 reels. December 10, 1917. Director: Lloyd Ingraham. Story: Beatrice Van and William Parker. Scenario: Chester B. Clapp. Cast: MF (Jackie), Jack Mower (Lt. Adair), L.C. Shumway (Lt. Wilbur), Hal Clements (Col. Kerwood).

Molly Go Get 'Em (American/Mutual [Star]). 5 reels. January 7, 1918. Director: Lloyd Ingraham. Story: Beatrice Van. Scenario: Elizabeth Mahoney. Cast: MF (Molly Allison), Jack Mower (Billy Wilcox), Hal Clements (Robert Allison), Margaret Allen (Julia Allison), David Howard (Gordon Gilbert), True Boardman (Count Renaud), Emma Kluge (Mrs. Vanderverr), Alfred Ferguson.

Jilted Janet (American/Mutual [Star]). 5 reels. February 11, 1918. Director: Lloyd Ingraham. Story: Beatrice Van. Scenario: Elizabeth Mahoney. Camera: Frank J. Urson. Cast: MF (Janet Barnes), Jack Mower (Jules Graham), Edward Peil (Ernest Morgan), Golda Madden (Suzette Sparks), David Howard (Pratt Barnes), Jean Robbins (Mercedes), Fred Smith (Leon).

Ann's Finish (American/Mutual [Star]). 5 reels. March 11, 1918. Director: Lloyd Ingraham. Story: Beatrice Van. Scenario: Elizabeth Mahoney. Camera: Frank J. Urson. Cast: MF (Ann Anderson), Jack Mower (Robert Chappell), Adelaide Elliot (Madame D'Arcy), David Howard (Teddy Barnes), John Gough (the Rat), Robert Klein (the Weasel), Perry Banks (the Fox).

The Primitive Woman (American/Mutual [Star]). 5 reels. April 15, 1918. Director: Lloyd Ingraham. Story: Henry Albert Phillips. Scenario: William Parker. Cast: MF (Nan Graythorpe), Jack Mower (Professor Learned [Stephen Graves]), Millard Wilson (Ned Graythorpe), Emma Kluge (Mrs. T. Ashbury Graves), Helen Howard (Nell Graves), Molly McConnell (Ida), Edward Peil (Edward Burnham).

A Square Deal (American/Mutual [Star]). 5 reels. June 10, 1918. Director: Lloyd Ingraham. Scenario: Elizabeth Mahoney. Based on a story by Albert Payson Terhune. Cast: MF (Alys Gilson), Jack Mower (Thurston Bruce), Val Paul (Peyton LeMoyne), Constance Johnson (Marion Hamilton), Louis M. Wells (John Gilson), Nanine Wright (Mary Gilson).

Impossible Susan (American/Mutual [Star]). 5 reels. July 22, 1918. Director: Lloyd Ingraham. Story: Joseph Poland. Scenario: Elizabeth Mahoney. Cast: MF (Susan Gaskell), Jack Mower (Bernard Marshall), Lloyd Hughes (Ted Marshall), Hayward Mack (Henri Delafaire), Beverly Travers (Eva Thornton), Louis M. Wells (Leon Gaskell), Anne Schaefer (Martha Brown).

Money Isn't Everything (alt.: *Beauty to Let*) (American/Pathé). 5 reels. September 29, 1918. Director: Edward Sloman. Scenario: William Parker. Based on a story by Fred Jackson. Cast: MF (Miss Margery Smith), Jack Mower (Franklyn Smith), J. Morris Foster (Henry Rockwell), Wedgewood Nowell ("Diamond Tim" Moody), Kate Price (Betty Nan).

The Mantle of Charity (American/Pathé). 5 reels. November 17, 1918. Director: Edward Sloman. Story: Edward Sloman. Scenario: Stephen Fox. Cast: MF (Norah McDonald), Jack Mower (Paul Howell), Dan Gilfether (Judge Kerr), Louella Maxam (Anna Houlahan), J. Gordon Russell (Tom Houlahan), Kate Price (Mrs. Malone).

Fair Enough (American/Pathé). 5 reels (4,800 feet). December 29, 1918. Director: Edward Sloman. Story: J. Anthony Roach. Scenario: Elizabeth Mahoney. Cast: MF (Ann Dickson), Eugenie Forde (Mrs. Ellen Dickson), Alfred Hollingsworth (James Dickson), Harry McCoy (Frederick Pierson), Alice Knowland (Madame Ohnet), Jack Mower (Carey Phelan), Bull Montana ("Happy" Flannigan), J. Farrell MacDonald (Chief of Police Morgan).

Molly of the Follies (American/Pathé), 5 reels. February 16, 1919. Director: Edward Sloman. Based on a story by Peter Clark Macfarlane. Cast: MF (Molly Malone), Jack Mower (Joe Holmquist, human submarine), Lule Warrenton (Kate Malone, Molly's mother), J. Farrell MacDonald (Swannick), Mary Lee Wise (Emily Ewing/Aunt Henrietta), Millard L. Webb (Milton Wallace).

Put Up Your Hands (alt.: *Hold Up Your Hands*) (American/Pathé). 5 reels. March 16, 1919. Director: Edward Sloman. Story and Scenario: L.V. Jefferson. Cast: MF (Olive Barton), George Periolat (Peter Barton, her father), Emory Johnson (Leonard Hewitt), Hayward Mack (Alvin Thorne), William Mong ("Highball" Hazelitt), J. Gordon Russell ("Three Gun" Smith), Kate Price (Bridget), Marion Lee (Aunt Abigile), Bull Montana.

Charge It to Me (American/Pathé). 5 reels. May 4, 1919. Director: Roy William Neill. Story and Scenario: L.V. Jefferson. Cast: MF (Winnie Davis), Emory Johnson (Elmer Davis), Augustus Phillips (Howard Weston), L.S. McKee (Col. Godfrey Hibbard), Budd Post (Archie Gunn), Bull Montana ("Corkscrew" McCann), George Swann (Hercules Strong), J. Farrell MacDonald (Officer Hennessey), Sophie Todd (Maggie).

Trixie from Broadway (American/Pathé). 5 reels (4,850 feet). June 15, 1919. Director: Roy William Neill. Assistant director: Sherry Hall. Story: Agnes C. Johnston. Scenario: Frank Howard Clark. Cast: MF (Trixie Darling), Emory Johnson (John Collins), George Periolat (Broadway Benham), Frank Clark (Jim Brown), Olga Grey (Gertie Brown), J. Farrell MacDonald ("Slim" Hayes).

The Tiger Lily (American/Pathé). 5 reels (4,784 feet). July 27, 1919. Director: George L. Cox. Scenario: Joseph Franklin Poland. Cast: MF (Carmina), Emory Johnson (David Remington), George Periolat (Luigi), E. Alyn Warren (Giovanni), J. Barney Sherry (Philip Remington), Rosita Marstini (Mrs. Philip Remington), Beatrice Van (Dorothy Van Rensselaer), Frank Clark (Antonio).

The Hellion (American/Pathé). 5 reels. October 1919. Director: George L. Cox. Story and Scenario: Daniel F. Whitcomb. Cast: MF (dual role: Mazie Del Mar, Blanche Harper), Emory Johnson (George Graham), Charles Spere (Larry Lawson), Henry Barrows (Joseph Harper), Lillian Langdon (Helen Harper), George Periolat (Signor Enrico), Frank Clark, Bull Montana.

The Dangerous Talent (alt.: *The Golden Gift*) (American/Pathé). 6 reels (5,460 feet). March 20, 1920. Director: George L. Cox. Scenario: Lois Zellner. Based on a novel by Daniel F. Whitcomb. Cast: MF (Leila Mead), Harry Hilliard (Gilbert Ellis), Beatrice Van (Mildred Shedd), Harvey Clark (Horton), Neil Hardin (Bob Ames), George Periolat (Peyton Dodge), Mary Talbot (a derelict).

The Thirtieth Piece of Silver (American/Pathé). 6 reels. April 1920. Director: George L. Cox. Assistant director: Sidney H. Algier. Scenario: Daniel F. Whitcomb. Based on a novel by Albert Payson Terhune. Cast: MF (Leila Cole), King Baggott (Tyler Cole), Forrest Stanley (Capt. Peyton Lake), Lillian Leighton (Mignon Brunner).

The Week-End (American/Pathé). 6 reels. July 1920. Director: George L. Cox. Assistant director: Sidney H. Algier. Story: Cosmo Hamilton. Scenario: George L. Cox and Arthur J. Zellner. Cast: MF (Vera Middleton), Milton Sills (Arthur Tavenor), Bertram Grassby (Spencer Jardine), Harvey Clark (Watt Middleton), Mary Lee Wise (Mrs. Watt Middleton), Mayme Kelso (Mrs. Grace Maynard), Beverly Travers (Mrs. Clara Churchill), Harry Lonsdale (James Corbin), Lillian Leighton (Mrs. James Corbin).

The Gamesters (American/Pathe). 6 reels. November 1920. Director: George L. Cox. Assistant director: Sidney H. Algier. Story: Lois Zellner. Cast: MF (Rose), Hayward Mack (Jim Welch), L.C. Shumway (Marshall Andrews), P. Dempsey Tabler (Brad Bascom), Evans Kirk (Paul Rosson), Joseph Bennett (Harvey Blythe).

Their Mutual Child (American/Pathé). 6 reels. December 1920. Director: George L. Cox. Assistant director: Sidney H. Algier. Scenario: Daniel F. Whitcomb. Based on a novel by P.G. Wodehouse. Cast: MF (Ruth Bannister), Joseph Bennett (Bailey Bannister), Margaret Campbell (Mrs. Lora Delane Porter), Nigel Barrie (Kirk Winfield), Harvey Clark (George Pennicut), Andrew Robson (John Bannister), Beverly Travers (Mamie), Pat Moore (Baby William Bannister Winfield), Thomas O'Brien (Steve Dingle), William Lloyd (Hank Jardine), William Marion (Percy Shanklyn), Stanhope Wheatcroft (Basil Milbank).

Payment Guaranteed (American/Pathé). 5 reels. March 1921. Director: George L. Cox. Story and Scenario: Lois Zellner. Cast: MF (Emily Heath), Cecil Van Auker (Stephen Strange), Hayward Mack (Harry Fenton), Harry Lonsdale (Jim Barton), Harvey Clark (reporter), Marjorie Manners (Myrtle), Alice Wilson (Gertie).

Beach of Dreams (Haworth Studios/Robertson-Cole Distributing). 5 reels (5,005 feet). May 8, 1921. Director: William Parke. Scenario: E. Richard Schayer and Nan Blair. Based on a novel by Henry de Vere Stacpoole. Cast: Edith Storey (Cleo de Bromsart), Noah Beery (Jack Raft), Sidney Payne (La Touche), Jack Curtis (Bompard), George Fisher (Maurice Chenet), Joseph Swickard (Monsieur de Brie), MF (Madame de Brie), F. Templar Powell (Prince Selm), Gertrude Norman (La Comtesse de Warens), Cesare Gravina (Professor Epnard).

K—the Unknown (Universal). 9 reels (8,146 feet). November 23, 1924. Director: Harry Pollard. Scenario: Hope Loring, Raymond L. Schrock, and William Leighton. Based on a novel by Mary Roberts Rinehart. Cast: Virginia Valli (Sidney Page), Percy Marmont ("K" Le Moyne), MF (Charlotte Harrison), Francis Feeney (George "Slim" Benson), John Roche (Dr. Max Wilson), Maurice Ryan (Joe Drummond), Myrtle Vane (Aunt Harriet Kennedy), William Carroll (Dr. Ed Wilson).

Any Woman (Famous Players-Lasky/Paramount). 6 reels (5,963 feet). May 4, 1925. Director: Henry King. Story: Arthur Somers Roche. Scenario: Jules Furthman and Beatrice Van. Cast: Alice Terry (Ellen Linden), Ernest Gillen (Tom Galloway), MF (Mrs. Rand), Lawson Butt (James Rand), Aggie Herring (Mrs. Galloway), James Neill (William Linden), De Sacia Mooers (Mrs. Phillips), Henry Kolker (Egbert

Phillips), Thelma Morgan (Alice Cartwright), George Periolat (Robert Cartwright), Lucille Hutton (Agnes Young), Arthur Hoyt (Jones), Malcolm Denny (Lord Brackenridge).

Uncle Tom's Cabin (Universal). 13 reels. November 4, 1927. Director: Harry Pollard. Scenario: Harvey Thew and Harry Pollard. Based on the novel by Harriet Beecher Stowe. Cast: James Lowe (Uncle Tom), Virginia Grey (Eva St. Clare), George Siegmann (Simon Legree), MF (Eliza), Eulalie Jensen (Cassie), Arthur Edmund Carew (George Harris), Adolph Milar (Haley), Jack Mower (Mr. Shelby), Vivian Oakland (Mrs. Shelby), J. Gordon Russell (Tom Loker), Skipper Zeliff (Edward Harris, a slave owner), Lassie Lou Ahern (Little Harris), Mona Ray (Topsy), Aileen Manning (Miss Ophelia), John Roche (St. Clare), Lucien Littlefield (Lawyer Marks), Gertrude Astor (Mrs. St. Clare), Gertrude Howard (Uncle Tom's wife), Geoffrey Grace (the doctor), Rolfe Sedan (Adolph), Marie Foster (Mammy in St. Clare house), Francis Ford (lieutenant), Martha Franklin (landlady), Nelson McDowell (Phineas Fletcher), Grace Carlisle (Mrs. Fletcher), C.E. Anderson (Johnson), Dick Sutherland (Sambo), Tom Amardares (Quimbo), Bill Dyer (auctioneer).

Inconclusive Releases

Selig

Rival Dramatists. Margarita Fischer lists this as a Selig release in an early attempt at reconstructing her filmography. Unlike the other Selig titles she lists, this film is not possible to identify with any catalogued release. Selig did release a film called *Rival Cooks* on April 18, 1910, as a split reel with *Mr. A. Jonah*, but it is not known whether Margarita Fischer appeared in this film.

American (Beauty)

The Mysterious Telegram

Forbid Them Not. Director: Harry Pollard. No other production information is available for these films (planned for 1914); they almost certainly never materialized.

Universal

The Pill Doctor (Imp).

His Better Half (Imp).

In a Strange Land (Powers). No additional information is available for these three films; they may never have been produced.

In Society. This was planned for around 1913. No other production information is available, though a photo credited to this film appears in the article "Margarita Fischer: The American Beauty" in the Fischer Papers, Box 13, green scrapbook.

The Boob Detective. Director: Robert Z. Leonard. This was planned for around 1913 but was never completed with Margarita Fischer. Robert Z. Leonard released *The Sherlock Boob* in 1914 with Ella Hall, which may represent the completion of this project.

The Diamond Thieves (Universal IMP). 1 reel. February 1, 1917. Director: Robert Z. Leonard. Cast: MF, Robert Z. Leonard.

Robinson Crusoe (Universal Laemmle). 3 reels. February 18, 1917. Director: Robert Z. Leonard. Author: Daniel Defoe. Cast: MF, Robert Z. Leonard.

A Sin Unatoned (Universal Laemmle). 1 reel. February 21, 1917. Director: Robert Z. Leonard. Cast: MF, Robert Z. Leonard.

Human Flames (Universal Laemmle). 1 reel. March 8, 1917. Director: Robert Z. Leonard. Scenario: Lois Zellner. Cast: MF, Robert Z. Leonard.

The Brand of Death (Universal Big U). 1 reel. May 18, 1917. Director: Wallace Reid. Cast: Wallace Reid, Dorothy Davenport, MF.

Defiance (Universal Big U). 1 reel. May 31, 1917. Cast: MF. The release of the above six films is not confirmed. These may all represent rereleases of otherwise undocumented 1913 films, as ROBINSON CRUSOE is almost certainly a rerelease of the 101 Bison film of July 29, 1913. The 1913 film was directed by Otis Turner rather than Robert Z. Leonard, however, so the film may have been "recredited" upon release.

Equitable

The Big Play. Announced in September 1915 but never produced.

American

High Heels. Director: Lloyd Ingraham. Story: Helen Starr. Scenario: James E. Hungerford. (From another source: Story: Beatrice Van. Adaptation: Elizabeth Mahoney.) Cast: MF, Jack Mower, David Howard, Golda Madden, Edward Peil, Jean Robbins, Fred Smith, Perry Banks. This may be an alternate title for *Jilted Janet*.

The Rose of Hell. Director: George L. Cox. Scenario: Dorothy Yost, based on a story by Lois Zeilner.

The Angel of the House. Scenario: Olga Pritzlau Clark. There is no indication that the above two films were ever produced.

Pollard Picture Plays

The Knight Of Tarquizzi. January 25, 1917.

Birds of Passage. February 22, 1917.

The Light of Heaven. March 22, 1917. These titles were announced for release on the above dates, but the projects never materialized.

Chapter Notes

Introduction

1. See Jerry Breitigam, "A Home Town Girl," source unknown, 1918, Margarita Fischer Papers, MS 81–4 [hereafter Fischer Papers], Department of Special Collections, Ablah Library, Wichita State University, Wichita, Kansas, Box 14, green *Pearl of Paradise* scrapbook.

Chapter 1

1. Thomas J. Schlereth, *Victorian America: Transformations in Everyday Life, 1876–1915* (New York: HarperCollins, 1991; HarperPerennial, 1992), 7.
2. Crandall Shifflet, *Victorian America, 1876 to 1913*, Almanacs of American Life, ed. Richard Balkin (New York: Facts on File, 1996), 36, 54, 56, 64–66, 70.
3. Fifteenth Census of the United States, 1930: Los Angeles County, California Population Schedule, and Marion County, Oregon Population Schedule. Available from Ancestry.com [database online]. 1998–2006. Indexed by Ancestry.com from microfilmed schedules of the 1930 U.S. Federal Decennial Census. Data imaged from National Archives and Records Administration. 1930 Federal Population Census. Washington, D.C.: National Archives and Records Administration. John Fischer was long deceased in 1930; information about his family background is gleaned from the census data offered by his sister Anna, Margarita Fischer's aunt, who remained unmarried and is thus traceable through the family surname. Author Billy H. Doyle asserts in his brief essay on Margarita Fischer that Kate Fischer's maiden name was "Hagney," and that John Fischer was born with the surname "Ficher." Both seem unlikely, though, as Kate's father Dominic Heagney's military record confirms the spelling of the surname, and as Margarita Fischer discussed in her later life her ascendants' disappointment when she altered the spelling of her family name. See Billy H. Doyle, *The Ultimate Directory of the Silent Screen Performers: A Necrology of Births and Deaths and Essays on 50 Lost Players* (Metuchen, N.J.: Scarecrow Press, 1995), 21; Margarita Fischer to Roi Uselton, [December 3?, 1967], Fischer Papers, Box 1, folder 22. Dominic Heagney's military record available from Ancestry.com; courtesy of Geoff Williams.
4. Biographical Note to the Fischer Papers, available from <http://specialcollections.wichita.edu/collections/ms/81-04/81-4-A.HTML>; Margarita Fischer, interview by Robert S. Birchard, [1970?], tape recording. (Margarita interviewer Robert Birchard estimates the year of this interview as 1970 or 1971, when the actress was about eighty-five years old.)
5. Biographical Note to the Fischer Papers.
6. "Marguerita Fischer, Star of Movieland Here to Visit Old Scenes of Childhood [sic]," *Capital Journal* (Salem, Oregon), August 16, 1928, Fischer Papers, Box 18, folder 12. Information about Anna Fischer's teaching career is found in Fifteenth Census of the United States, 1930: Marion County, Oregon Population Schedule.
7. Margarita Fischer interview; Biographical Note to the Fischer Papers; Ruth [Kingsley?], "It's a Long Lane That Has No Turning," source unknown, Fischer Papers, Box 14, green *Pearl of Paradise* scrapbook.
8. Adolphe D'Ennery and Fernand Cormon, *A Celebrated Case: A Drama in Prologue and Four Acts* (New York: Samuel French, n.d.), 3–25.
9. Margarita Fischer interview.
10. "Margarita Fischer: Playing Leads with the Rex Company," source unknown, [1913?], Fischer Papers, Box 13, personal scrapbook.
11. Fischer to Uselton.
12. Biographical Note to the Fischer Papers.
13. Margarita Fischer interview.
14. "It's a Long Lane That Has No Turning." High school-educated women were not uncommon by the turn of the twentieth century, but this level of education still tended to be sought only for vocational purposes. The family might therefore have felt formal education unnecessary, since their daughters had already settled on a career on the stage.
15. John Hanners, *"It Was Play or Starve": Acting in the Nineteenth-Century American Popular Theater* (Bowling Green, Ohio: Bowling Green State University Popular Press, 1993), 2–3.
16. Claudia D. Johnson, *American Actress: Perspective on the Nineteenth Century* (Chicago: Nelson-Hall, 1984), 13–15.
17. Ibid., 10, 18.
18. Andrew L. Erdman, *Blue Vaudeville: Sex, Morals and the Mass Marketing of Amusement, 1895–1915* (Jefferson, N.C.: McFarland & Company, 2004), 1–4, 7.
19. Charles W. Stein, ed., *American Vaudeville as Seen by Its Contemporaries* (New York: Alfred A. Knopf, 1984), xi–xiii.
20. Douglas Gilbert, *American Vaudeville: Its Life and Times* (New York: Whittlesey House, McGraw-Hill Book Company, 1940), 3–6.
21. Johnson, 24–29.
22. Hanners, 1.
23. Fischer and Van Cleve's Players advertising playbill, 1901–02 season, Fischer Papers, Box 13, personal ledger.
24. "A Home Town Girl"; "It's a Long Lane That Has No Turning."
25. Margarita Kotselis, interview by author, May 25,

2006, Wichita, Kansas [via telephone], tape recording. Margarita Dorothy Kotselis is the only surviving child of Dorothy and Charles Pyle's only child, Kathrine. She lived with Margarita Fischer and Dorothy Fischer Pyle for a large portion of her youth, and graciously consented to share her family memories with the author.

26. Margarita Fischer interview.
27. See Fischer Papers, Box 13, personal ledger. Most of these plays were adapted into films at least once in the 1910s. *East Lynne* alone was filmed at least nine times before 1920, including a 1916 version starring Theda Bara, best known as a vamp, in the role of Lady Isabel.
28. Mrs. Henry Wood, *East Lynne*, in *S.R.O.: The Most Successful Plays in the History of the American Stage*, ed. Bennett Cerf and Van H. Cartmell (Garden City, N.Y.: Doubleday, Doran, & Company, 1944).
29. "Well Done," source unknown, [1906?], Fischer Papers, Box 13, personal scrapbook.
30. "Margarita Fischer: The American Beauty," source unknown, [1914?], Fischer Papers, Box 13, personal scrapbook.
31. "Amusements: Sonna Family Theater," *Idaho Daily Statesman* (Boise, Idaho), May 22, 1902. Courtesy of Geoff Willams.
32. Margarita Fischer to Mrs. William E. Borah, August 28, 1966, Fischer Papers, Box 1, folder 20.
33. Mrs. William E. Borah to Margarita Fischer, [1966?], Fischer Papers, Box 1, folder 20.
34. "The Margarita Fischer Co.," *Coquille Herald* (Coquille, Ore.), December 6, 1905, Fischer Papers, Box 13, personal ledger.
35. Margarita Kotselis interview.
36. "Marguerita Fischer, Star of Movieland Here to Visit Old Scenes of Childhood."
37. "It's a Long Lane That Has No Turning."
38. "Margarita Fischer: The American Beauty."
39. "Margarita Fischer Co.: This Popular Company Now Here with Strong Caste [sic]," *Heppner Gazette* (Heppner, Ore.), August 11, 1904, Fischer Papers, Box 13, personal ledger; "Miss Fischer a Star," *Pendleton Morning Tribune* (Pendleton, Ore.), July 27, 1904, Fischer Papers, Box 13, personal ledger; "Amusements," *Idaho Daily Statesman* (Boise City, Idaho), July 24, 1904, Fischer Papers, Box 13, personal ledger.
40. "Miss Fischer Company: Starts in This Week with a Side-Splitting Comedy at the Frazer," *Pendleton Morning Tribune* (Pendleton, Ore.), August 2, 1904, Fischer Papers, Box 13, personal ledger.
41. S.J. Kleinberg, *Women in the United States: 1830–1945* (New Brunswick, N.J.: Rutgers University Press, 1999), 38, 146–47.
42. Alice Kessler-Harris, *Out to Work: A History of Wage-Earning Women in the United States* (New York: Oxford University Press, 1982), 116.
43. Lois W. Banner, *Women in Modern America: A Brief History*, 2d ed. (San Diego: Harcourt Brace Jovanovich, 1984), 5–7.
44. Kleinberg, 141.
45. Johnson, 58–59.
46. Margarita Fischer Company advertising pamphlets, [1903? and 1904?], Fischer Papers, Box 13, personal ledger.
47. Margarita Fischer Co. advertising playbill, [1903?], Fischer Papers, Box 13, personal ledger; "Girl Is Star at 19," paper unknown, [1915?], Fischer Papers, Box 13, personal scrapbook.
48. This photo is located in the Fischer Papers, Box 11, folder 1.
49. "Margarita Fischer: Playing Leads with the Rex Company." Throughout her career, Margarita Fischer remained aware of, even self–conscious about, the size and prestige of the parts she played. This is understandable, as lead status was an important part of contractual negotiations for actors in both theater and film. When Margarita took supporting roles late in her acting career, she tended to belabor the desirability of the part in interviews.
50. "Big Crowd at Girton's," *Daily Humboldt Times* (Eureka, California), December 31, 1905, Fischer Papers, Box 13, personal ledger.
51. Geoff Williams, *C.C. Pyle's Amazing Foot Race: The True Story of the 1928 Coast-to-Coast Run Across America* (New York: Rodale, 2007), 69; "Fischer Company Leaves the City," *Evening Capital News* (Boise, Idaho), July 25, 1904, Fischer Papers, Box 13, personal ledger.
52. Margarita Kotselis interview.
53. Margarita Fischer Co. players to Margarita Fischer, February 12, 1906, Fischer Papers, Box 13, personal ledger; "A Packed House at Girton's," source unknown, [February 1906], Fischer Papers, Box 13, personal scrapbook.
54. "Big Crowd at Girton's"; performance invitation, February 12, 1906, Fischer Papers, Box 13, personal ledger; Hotel Grand Dining Room and Café dinner invitation, February 12, 1906, Fischer Papers, Box 13, personal ledger.
55. "A Packed House at Girton's."
56. "Epoch Making Event in Eureka's Welfare," source unknown, [June 1906], Fischer Papers, Box 13, personal scrapbook.
57. Margarita Fischer interview.
58. Theatre Margarita program pamphlet, June 14–19, 1906, Fischer Papers, Box 13, personal ledger. This play was later filmed by D. W. Griffith as *Orphans of the Storm* (1922).
59. Crescent Theatre program, June 20, 1906, Fischer Papers, Box 13, personal ledger.
60. F.W. Parker, of Parker and Pyle, to the Margarita Fischer Co., June 24, 1906, Fischer Papers, Box 13, personal ledger.

Chapter 2

1. Margarita Fischer interview.
2. "Margarita Fischer: Playing Leads with the Rex Company."
3. "W. of W. Endorse Fischer Benefit," source unknown, [1906?], Fischer Papers, Box 13, personal scrapbook.
4. Anonymous fan to Margarita Fischer, September 18, 1907, Fischer Papers, Box 13, personal ledger.
5. *San Francisco Dramatic Review*, September 7, 1907, Fischer Papers, Box 13, personal ledger.
6. Central Theatre, city unknown, to Margarita Fischer, April 1907, Fischer Papers, Box 13, personal ledger; cover portrait, *San Francisco Dramatic Review*, September 7, 1907, Fischer Papers, Box 13, personal ledger; various theatrical engagement telegrams, October 1907, Fischer Papers, Box 13, personal ledger.
7. Walter Sanford to Margarita Fischer, October 24, [1907], Fischer Papers, Box 13, personal ledger.
8. "Theatre Manager Placed Under Arrest," source unknown, [1906?], Fischer Papers, Box 13, personal scrapbook.
9. Ibid.; Margarita Kotselis interview; Kathrine P. Havens record, Social Security Death Index, available from <http://ssdi.rootsweb.com/>.

10. Margarita Kotselis interview.
11. "Mother-in-Law Said to Be Disturbing Element," *Oakland Tribune* (California), March 11, 1908. Courtesy of Geoff Williams.
12. Divorce papers, Dottie vs. Charles Pyle, S-279356, Office of the Clerk of the Circuit Court of Cook County. Courtesy of Geoff Williams.
13. Margarita Kotselis interview.
14. Walter Sanford's Engagement Contract, October 31, 1907, Fischer Papers, Box 13, personal ledger.
15. Unidentified article, [November 1907], Fischer Papers, Box 13, personal ledger.
16. Tenth Census of the United States, 1880: Republic County, Kansas, Population Schedule. Available from Ancestry.com [database online], 2001–2004. Index compiled by the Church of Jesus Christ of Latter-Day Saints; Ninth Census of the United States, 1870: McLean County, Illinois, Population Schedule. Available from Ancestry.com. *1870 United States Federal Census* [database on-line], 2001–2004. Indexed by Ancestry.com from microfilmed schedules of the 1870 U.S. Federal Decennial Census. Data imaged from National Archives and Records Administration. 1870 Federal Population Census. Washington, D.C.: National Archives and Records Administration.
17. "Shy Harry Pollard, Film Director, Has Never Been to a Hollywood Party," *St. Louis Star*, May 1, 1929, Harry Pollard Papers, MS 81–5 [hereafter Pollard Papers], Department of Special Collections, Ablah Library, Wichita State University, Wichita, Kansas, oversized folder.
18. Ibid.; "Harry Pollard: Writer, Director, Actor," *Photoplay*, June 1914, 80–81, Fischer Papers, Box 13, personal scrapbook.
19. Ibid.
20. "Shy Harry Pollard, Film Director, Has Never Been to a Hollywood Party."
21. Ibid.
22. Margarita Kotselis interview; "Shy Harry Pollard, Film Director, Has Never Been to a Hollywood Party."
23. "Timeline of the San Francisco Earthquake, April 18–23, 1906," *Virtual Museum of the City of San Francisco*, 1995–2004, <http://www.sfmuseum.org/hist10/06timeline.html> [March 4, 2007].
24. "Harry Pollard: Writer, Director, Actor."
25. Margarita Fischer interview.
26. Dorothy Herzog, "'Uncle Tom's Cabin' Houses Flicker Romance: Now It Can Be Told!," *Daily Mirror* (location unknown), April 9, 1926, Fischer Papers, Box 3, Folder 1.
27. Gilbert Gardner to Margarita Fischer, April 27, 1908, and May 9, 1908, Fischer Papers, Box 13, personal ledger.
28. Cover image, *Empress Theatre Herald*, September 28, 1908, Fischer Papers, Box 13, personal ledger.
29. "The Empress," [1908], source unknown, Fischer Papers, Box 13, personal ledger.
30. Walter Sanford's Engagement Contract, October 12, 1908, Fischer Papers, Box 13, personal ledger. This contract set Margarita Fischer's term of employment as November 16, 1908, to June 1909.
31. "Ambitious to Become Big Star," *Oregon Daily Journal* (Portland, Oregon), August 26, 1909, Fischer Papers, Box 13, personal ledger.
32. Unidentified article, Fischer Papers, Box 13, personal ledger.
33. Frawley Company playbill for Winnipeg Theatre, week of January 3, 1910, Fischer Papers, Box 13, personal ledger.
34. "It's a Long Lane That Has No Turning."
35. "Margarita Fisher Well Cast in 'The Wolf,'" *Morning Press* (Santa Barbara, California), April 28, 1918, Fischer Papers, Box 14, green *Putting It Over* scrapbook.
36. "Three New Stars of the Screen Just Captured by Equitable," *New York Review*, September 25, 1915, Fischer Papers, Box 18, Folder 12; "Margarita Fischer: Playing Leads with the Rex Company"; "Girl Is Star at 19."
37. "It's a Long Lane That Has No Turning."

Chapter 3

1. C.W. Ceram, *Archaeology of the Cinema* (New York: Harcourt, Brace, & World, [1965]), 85, 148–150.
2. Stephen Herbert and Luke McKernan, eds., *Who's Who of Victorian Cinema* (London: British Film Institute, 1996), 48.
3. William K. Everson, *American Silent Film* (New York: Oxford University Press, 1978; reprint, New York: Da Capo Press, 1998), 24–29 (page citations are to the reprint edition).
4. Kalton Lahue, ed., *Motion Picture Pioneer: The Selig Polyscope Company* (New York: A.S. Barnes, 1973), 11–14, 27; Terry Ramsaye, *A Million and One Nights: A History of the Motion Picture Through 1925* (New York: Simon & Schuster, 1926; Simon & Schuster, 1964), 304–07.
5. F.N. Shorey, "Making a Selig Film," *Film Index* IV (January 30, 1909), 4–5; reprinted in Lahue, 48.
6. Anthony Slide, "Those Elusive Budget Figures," in *Silent Topics: Essays on Undocumented Areas of Silent Film* (Lanham, Md.: Scarecrow Press, 2005), 21.
7. Melvyn Stokes, "Introduction: Reconstructing American Cinema's Audiences," in *American Movie Audiences: From the Turn of the Century to the Early Sound Era*, Melvyn Stokes and Richard Maltby, eds. (London: British Film Institute, 1999), 3–5.
8. Garth S. Jowett, "The First Motion Picture Audiences," in *Film Before Griffith*, John L. Fell, ed. (Berkeley: University of California Press, 1983), 196–206.
9. Richard Hofstadter, ed., *The Progressive Movement, 1900–1915* (Englewood Cliffs, N.J.: Prentice-Hall, 1963), 2–7.
10. Lee Grieveson, *Policing Cinema: Movies and Censorship in Early-Twentieth-Century America* (Berkeley: University of California Press, 2004), 21, 25–26.
11. Ibid., 25, 188–90.
12. Lary May, *Screening Out the Past: The Birth of Mass Culture and the Motion Picture Industry* (New York: Oxford University Press, 1980), 36.
13. Kelly R. Brown, *Florence Lawrence, the Biograph Girl: America's First Movie Star* (Jefferson, N.C.: McFarland & Company, 1999), 70.
14. A. Nicholas Vardac, *Stage to Screen: Theatrical Method from Garrick to Griffith* (Cambridge: Harvard University Press, 1949), 187, 198.
15. Richard Koszarski, *An Evening's Entertainment, 1915–1928. History of the American Cinema*, ed. Charles Harpole, vol. 3 (New York: Charles Scribner's Sons, 1990), 181.
16. Vardac, 24–25.
17. Ramsaye, 441–42.
18. Mrs. D.W. Griffith [Linda Arvidson], *When the Movies Were Young* (New York: Benjamin Blom, 1925; Reprint, New York: Benjamin Blom, 1968), 31–32, 54.
19. Author Richard deCordova notes that Lawrence was not the first actress to have her name publicized in an

attempt to draw audiences into a theater; that honor probably belongs to Elita Proctor Otis, whose name was used to advertise a 1909 Vitagraph version of *Oliver Twist*. The Laemmle publicity surrounding Lawrence was, however, "the most masterful, and probably the most significant, early promotion." See Richard deCordova, *Picture Personalities: The Emergence of the Star System in America* (Chicago: University of Illinois Press, 1990), 41, 55. Kelly R. Brown, Lawrence's biographer, makes the distinction that she "was the first player, male or female, to use her name to advertise not only a single motion picture but also the production company she worked for. The company, in turn, was able to place more films in theaters because the public wanted to see the films that she was in." See Brown, 157.

20. Eileen Bowser, *The Transformation of Cinema, 1907–1915. History of the American Cinema*, ed. Charles Harpole, vol. 2 (New York: Charles Scribner's Sons, 1990), 103.

21. "IMP: We Nail a Lie," 1910 press release, printed in Daniel Blum, *A Pictorial History of the Silent Screen* (New York: Grosset & Dunlap, 1953), 18; "Florence Lawrence," Ken Wlaschin, *The Illustrated Encyclopedia of the World's Great Movie Stars and Their Films: From 1900 to the Present Day* (New York: Salamander Books, 1979), 25.

22. Richard Dyer, *Stars* (London: British Film Institute, 1979), 9–10.

23. Brown, 158.

24. According to film historian Kevin Brownlow, theatrical actors did not truly respect the cinema until after the 1915 release of *The Birth of a Nation* and the subsequent formation of the Triangle Corporation under D.W. Griffith, Thomas Ince, and Mack Sennett. The Triangle at once drew several theatrical notables into its fold, possibly because of connections from Griffith's own former stage career. See Kevin Brownlow, *The Parade's Gone By...* (Berkeley: University of California Press, 1968), 3–4.

25. Paula Marantz Cohen, *Silent Film and the Triumph of the American Myth* (New York: Oxford University Press, 2001), 135–36.

26. Robert Grau, *The Theatre of Science* (New York: Benjamin Blom, 1914), 102.

27. Erie Shepard to Margarita Fischer, December 29, 1918, Fischer Papers, Box 1, folder 11.

28. Hector Ames, "So This Is a Studio, Is It?," source unknown, [1917?], Fischer Papers, Box 14, green *Pearl of Paradise* scrapbook.

29. "Margarita Fischer: Playing Leads with the Rex Company."

30. "Shy Harry Pollard, Film Director, Has Never Been to a Hollywood Party."

31. Margarita Fischer interview.

32. Dan Thomas, "Talkies Don't Bother Pollard — He Always Made His Actors Talk," *NEA Service Cleveland* (wire service), May 6, 1929, Pollard Papers, Box 3, folder 4.

33. "Shy Harry Pollard, Film Director, Has Never Been to a Hollywood Party."

34. Shorey; reprinted in Lahue, 49.

35. "Pointers on Picture Acting," Selig Polyscope Company, 1910, reprinted by Lahue, 63.

36. Ibid., 55.

37. Margarita Fischer filmography, Fischer Papers, index folder. This filmography was developed by film historian J. B. Kaufman, based on the contents of the Fischer Papers. It is quite accurate in what it includes, although it is not exhaustive since Margarita Fischer did not retain production information on all of her films. When cross-referenced with the American Film Institute's silent film database, a more complete filmography can be constructed for the actress. The earliest Margarita Fischer release that can be confirmed is that of *There, Little Girl, Don't Cry* on May 12, 1910 — which would almost certainly have entered production some time in April 1910. Due to the dearth of Selig records, Margarita's own attempt at reconstructing a filmography in 1912 provides a starting point for researching many of her Selig titles. She admits, though, that there are "many more that I have forgotten" which could have had earlier release dates. See unidentified letter, Margarita Fischer, 1912 [?], Fischer Papers, Box 14, black scrapbook.

38. Quoted in Robert Hamilton Ball, *Shakespeare on Silent Film: A Strange Eventful History* (New York: Theatre Arts Books, 1968), 67–68.

39. *The Merry Wives of Windsor* (1910), dir. Francis Boggs, 8 min., Library of Congress, videodisc.

40. Ball, 88, 316.

41. Margarita Fischer filmography.

42. Ball, 66.

43. Unidentified letter, Margarita Fischer, 1912 [?], Fischer Papers, Box 14, black scrapbook. Paul E. Mix, *The Life and Legend of Tom Mix* (Cranbury, N.J.: A.S. Barnes, 1972), 74, 76, 78.

44. Andrew Brodie Smith, *Shooting Cowboys and Indians: Silent Western Films, American Culture, and the Birth of Hollywood* (Boulder: University Press of Colorado, 2003), 38, 60.

45. Ibid., 42–43, 52–53.

46. Margarita Fischer interview.

47. Timothy James Lyons, *The Silent Partner: The History of the American Film Manufacturing Company, 1910–1921* (New York: Arno Press, 1974), 64, 66.

48. Bowser, 149.

49. Margarita Fischer filmography. Stills from *Bertie's Bandit* showing Margarita Fischer and Harry Pollard can be found in the Fischer Papers, Box 2, folder 2.

50. "Margarita Fischer: Playing Leads with the Rex Company"; unidentified newspaper articles, Fischer Papers, Box 13, personal ledger.

51. Margarita Fischer interview.

52. Margarita Fischer to Roi Uselton, 1968(?), Fischer Papers, Box 1, folder 22; Biographical Note to the Fischer Papers; Marriage announcement, paper unknown, 1912(?), Fischer Papers, Box 13, personal ledger.

53. Evelyn F. Scott, *Hollywood When Silents Were Golden* (New York: McGraw-Hill Book Company, 1972), 20.

54. Robert L. Greene to Margarita Fischer, June 21, 1911, Fischer Papers, Box 13, personal ledger.

55. "At the Gayety," unidentified newspaper, [1911], Fischer Papers, Box 13, personal ledger.

56. This play was co-written by Beulah Marie Dix, the mother of Hollywood memoirist Evelyn F. Scott. Dix, who went on to write for the screen in the mid–teens and into the sound era, demonstrating — like Margarita and her husband — the fluidity with which careers in "the legitimate" transitioned back and forth to film at this time.

57. Scott, 152–53.

58. "At the Theaters: 'The Road to Yesterday' at the Gayety," unidentified newspaper, [June 1911], Fischer Papers, Box 13, personal ledger.

59. "Problem of Miss Fischer: No Fashion Guide for Costume of 'Eve' in Garden," unidentified newspaper, [1911], Fischer Papers, Box 13, personal ledger; "'Return of Eve' Draws Big Crowd at Gayety," unidentified newspaper, [1911], Fischer Papers, Box 13, personal ledger.

60. "New System of Keeping Down the Temperature," unidentified newspaper, [1911], Fischer Papers, Box 13, personal ledger.

61. Keene Abbott, "Plays and Players," unidentified newspaper, [1911], Fischer Papers, Box 13, personal ledger.

62. Independent Film Co. [sic] contract, November 27, 1911, Fischer Papers, Box 1, folder 26. The Pollards remained friends with Lloyd Ingraham after leaving his company; he eventually moved into film as well, and directed Margarita in several features in 1917 and 1918.
63. Margarita Fischer interview.
64. Sally A. Dumaux, *King Baggot: A Biography and Filmography of the First King of the Movies* (Jefferson, N.C.: McFarland & Company, 2002), 193. Margarita Fischer's role in this short film is unidentified; uncharacteristically, she does not play the female lead.
65. Margarita Fischer filmography.

Chapter 4

1. I.G. Edmonds, *Big U: Universal in the Silent Days* (New York: A.S. Barnes, 1977), 18–22.
2. Sanford to Fischer.
3. Dumaux, 194. The plot played out concisely in 700 feet of film — only about nine or ten minutes.
4. Ibid., 5, 7, 42.
5. Edmonds, 23–24.
6. Grau, 207.
7. Margarita Fischer filmography; Dumaux, 194.
8. Unidentified letter, Margarita Fischer, 1912 [?]. Contemporary references to the IMP often capitalized it in this manner.
9. Edward Wagenknecht, *The Movies in the Age of Innocence* (Norman: University of Oklahoma Press, 1962), 33–34.
10. Daniel Blum, *A Pictorial History of the Silent Screen* (New York: Grosset & Dunlap, 1953), 31; Blair Miller, *American Silent Film Comedies: An Illustrated Encyclopedia* (Jefferson, N.C.: McFarland & Company, 1995), 114–15.
11. Everson, 369.
12. Lahue, *Motion Picture Pioneer*, 14–15, 223–24.
13. Bowser, 151.
14. Dumaux, 42–43.
15. Dorothy Schneider and Carl J. Schneider, *American Women in the Progressive Era, 1900–1920* (New York: Facts on File, 1993), 16–17.
16. Anthony Slide, *The Silent Feminists: America's First Women Film Directors* (Lanham, MD: Scarecrow Press, 1996), 3–4.
17. Ibid., 5–12.
18. Cari Beauchamp, *Without Lying Down: Frances Marion and the Powerful Women of Early Hollywood* (Berkeley: University of California Press, 1997), 9–11.
19. Robert Windeler, *Sweetheart: The Story of Mary Pickford* (London: W.H. Allen, 1973), 58, 70, 88.
20. Beauchamp, 39; Blum, 118.
21. Slide, *Silent Feminists*, 29–39, 41. Weber has been largely neglected by modern-day feminist scholars, possibly because of her firm opposition to abortion — a viewpoint Margarita Fischer shared.
22. Carolyn Lowrey, *The First One Hundred Noted Men and Women of the Screen* (New York: Moffat, Yard, & Co., 1920), 190.
23. Kalton Lahue, *Continued Next Week: A History of the Moving Picture Serial* (Norman: University of Oklahoma Press, 1964), 6–9.
24. Nan Enstad, "Dressed for Adventure: Working Women and Silent Movie Serials in the 1910s," *Feminist Studies* 21, no. 1 (1995): 67–90.
25. Blum, 21, 32–33.
26. Miriam Hansen, *Babel and Babylon: Spectatorship in American Silent Film* (Cambridge: Harvard University Press, 1991), 120.
27. Grau, 254.
28. Brown, 69.
29. Grau, 255.
30. Ibid., 246–47. Grau asserts that *Moving Picture World* was actually founded in 1910, but a search of the WorldCat database of library holdings confirms the 1907 date.
31. Brownlow, *The Parade's Gone By...*, 2.
32. Anthony Slide, *Aspects of American Film History Prior to 1920* (Metuchen, N. J.: Scarecrow Press, 1978), 102–3.
33. Grau, 249–51.
34. Ibid., 103–04.
35. deCordova, 73, 9.
36. Gaylyn Studlar, "The Perils of Pleasure? Fan Magazine Discourse as Women's Commodified Culture in the 1920s," in *Silent Film*, Richard Abel, ed. (New Brunswick, N.J.: Rutgers University Press, 1996), 267–70.
37. Robert Dance and Bruce Robertson, *Ruth Harriet Louise and Hollywood Glamour Photography* (Berkeley: University of California Press, 2002), 205.
38. *A Movie Star*, dir. Fred Fishback, 25 min., *Slapstick Encyclopedia*, vol. 2: *Keystone Tonight!: Mack Sennett Comedies*, Image Entertainment, 2002. Videodisc.
39. Margarita Kotselis interview.
40. Margarita Fischer interview.
41. Margarita Fischer filmography.
42. "Actress of Silent Days Visits Shanghai," *Vista Press* (Vista, California), December 31, 1936, Fischer Papers, oversized folder.
43. Banner, 22–23.
44. Margarita Kotselis to author, e-mail of February 19, 2007.
45. Austin Lescarboura, *Behind the Motion Picture Screen* (New York: Scientific American Publishing Company, 1919; reprint, New York: Benjamin Blom, 1971), 42–44 (page citations are to the reprint edition).
46. Margarita Fischer filmography.
47. Stephen Railton, "Harry Pollard and Uncle Tom, Act 1: The Imp Film, 1913," *Uncle Tom's Cabin in American Culture*, 1998–2007, < http://www.iath.virginia.edu/utc/onstage/films/imphp.html > [April 22, 2007].
48. Margarita Fischer interview.
49. "Girl Is Star at 19."
50. Cohen, 140.
51. *Draga, the Gypsy* (1913), dir. unknown, 15 min., Library of Congress, videodisc.
52. Margarita Fischer filmography.
53. "Shy Harry Pollard, Film Director, Has Never Been to a Hollywood Party."
54. Universal's member studios initially included the IMP, Powers, Champion, Nestor, Éclair, and Rex. Richard E. Braff's *The Universal Silents: A Filmography of the Universal Motion Picture Manufacturing Company, 1912–1929* (Jefferson, N.C.: McFarland & Company, 1999) provides production information on more than 9,000 fiction films distributed by Universal from its formation to the end of the silent feature era and was a helpful resource in supplementing Margarita Fischer's filmography.
55. Margarita Fischer filmography.
56. David Robinson, *From Peep Show to Palace: The Birth of American Film* (New York: Columbia University Press, 1995), 161–62. Robinson quotes an October 1913 Universal advertisement in *Moving Picture World* that listed 13 actors and 13 actresses, and stated, "The photograph of any star on

this wonderful list if displayed in your lobby with the words 'Here Today' is positively bound to boost your receipts.... Every one of these favorites has a big following. Take advantage of it and *turn their popularity into increased profits for yourself.*"

57. *How Men Propose* (1913), prod. and dir.(?) Lois Weber, 6 min., *America's First Women Filmmakers*, vol. 6, *The Origins of Film (1900–1926)*, Unapix Consumer Products, 1995, videocassette. Despite this film's impressive credentials, it, like *Draga the Gypsy*, does not appear on the Fischer filmography, probably because Margarita Fischer's performance is uncredited. Both are indexed as Margarita Fischer performances by library and film archive databases, however.

58. Margarita Fischer interview.
59. Lyons, 11, 106.

Chapter 5

1. Margarita Fischer interview.
2. Lyons, 76.
3. See Stirling Macoboy, "American Beauty," in *The Ultimate Rose Book* (New York: Harry N. Abrams, Inc., [1993]), 49. The rose was first bred in 1875 as the "Madame Ferdinand Jamin" but was introduced to the United States as the "American Beauty" in 1885, and for the next several decades was the most popular rose in the nation. This contradicts any publicity that implies that the rose was named for Margarita's image — as the rose had been around since before her birth, the naming rather went the other way.
4. Margarita Fischer interview.
5. "Margaret Fischer," source unknown, [December 1913 or January 1914], Fischer Papers, Box 13, personal scrapbook.
6. Ibid.; unidentified article, [December 1913 or January 1914], Fischer Papers, Box 13, personal scrapbook.
7. Unidentified article, [December 1913?], Fischer Papers, Box 13, personal scrapbook.
8. Unidentified article, [January 1914?], Fischer Papers, Box 13, personal scrapbook.
9. Unidentified article, [January 1914], Fischer Papers, Box 13, personal scrapbook.
10. Unidentified articles, [December 1913 or January 1914], Fischer Papers, Box 13, personal scrapbook; Margarita Fischer filmography.
11. "Margarita Fischer (Beauty)," [1914?], Fischer Papers, Box 13, personal scrapbook.
12. Unidentified article, [1914?], Fischer Papers, Box 13, personal scrapbook.
13. "Fits Formula for Beauty Model," source unknown, [December 1914?], Fischer Papers, Box 13, personal scrapbook.
14. Lyons, 107, 155.
15. Margarita Fischer filmography; Lyons, 227–30.
16. Grau, 375.
17. "Victory on the Last Lap!" popularity poll, *Photoplay*, June 1914, 140, Fischer Papers, Box 13, personal scrapbook.
18. Kevin Brownlow, *Mary Pickford Rediscovered: Rare Pictures of a Hollywood Legend* (New York: Harry N. Abrams, 1999), 90–93.
19. Paul C. Holmes to Margarita Fischer, June 18, 1914, Fischer Papers, Box 1, folder 11.
20. Leona Hyacinth Peters to Margarita Fischer, March 27, 1914, Fischer Papers, Box 1, folder 11.
21. Anna E. Williams to Margarita Fischer, October 29, 1913, Fischer Papers, Box 1, folder 11.
22. A. Davis to Margarita Fischer, January 26, 1914, Fischer Papers, Box 1, folder 11.
23. Margarita Fischer interview.
24. E.S. Stark to Margarita Fischer, August 12, 1914, Fischer Papers, Box 1, folder 11.
25. E.S. Stark to Margarita Fischer, November 10, 1914, Fischer Papers, Box 1, folder 11.
26. Schneider and Schneider note that the "companionate marriage" grew out of the increased independence and social equality won by the "New Woman," and that it required a redefinition of traditional masculine as well as feminine roles. See Schneider and Schneider, 147–48.
27. Margarita Fischer filmography.
28. Ball, 201.
29. Margarita Fischer interview.
30. Ibid.
31. Ibid.
32. Unidentified clipping, [1914], Fischer Papers, Box 13, personal scrapbook; "Popular Actress Never Saw Moving Picture Until After She Had Played in Several Productions," *Daily Capital Journal* (Salem, Oregon), [1914?], Fischer Papers, Box 13, personal scrapbook.
33. Margarita Fischer interview.
34. "The American Studio," *Moving Picture World*, July 10, 1915, 255, Fischer Papers, Box 14, black scrapbook.
35. Margarita Fischer interview.
36. Ibid.
37. "Little Kathie Fischer," source unknown, [1914], Fischer Papers, Box 13, personal scrapbook; "Harry Pollard with Margarita Fischer" clipping, [1914], Fischer Papers, Box 13, personal scrapbook.
38. Unidentified article, [January 1914], Fischer Papers, Box 13, personal scrapbook; Margarita Fischer filmography.
39. "Kathie Fischer with Beauty Films," source unknown, [February 1914], Fischer Papers, Box 13, personal scrapbook.
40. Unidentified articles, [July? 1914], Fischer Papers, Box 13, personal scrapbook.
41. Margarita Kotselis to author, e-mails of February 20, 2007, and February 21, 2007.
42. Margarita Kotselis interview.
43. Ibid.
44. Margarita Fischer filmography; Grau, 374.
45. Margarita Fischer filmography.
46. "C.C. Pyle Resigns Position with Commonwealth," source unknown, [1918], Fischer Papers, Box 13, personal scrapbook.
47. Quoted in Dumaux, 120.
48. Lillian Gish, *The Movies, Mr. Griffith, and Me* (Englewood Cliffs, N. J.: Prentice-Hall, 1969), 90.
49. Response to "Bessie R., Hobart, Iowa," source unknown, [1914], Fischer Papers, Box 13, personal scrapbook.
50. "Girl Is Star at 19."
51. Lyons, 84–85.
52. Al P. Nelson and Mel R. Jones, *A Silent Siren Song: The Aitken Brothers' Hollywood Odyssey, 1905–1926* (New York: Cooper Square Press, 2000), 146–47.
53. Gish, 143, 153.
54. Nelson and Jones, 116.
55. Ibid., 117, 152–53.
56. *The Birth of a Nation* (1915), dir. D.W. Griffith, 180 min., Madacy Entertainment, 2001, videodisc.
57. Review of *The Birth of a Nation*, *New York Dramatic Mirror*, March 10, 1915, 28, collected in George C. Pratt, *Spellbound in Darkness: A History of the Silent Film* (Greenwich, Connecticut: New York Graphic Society, 1973), 208.

58. Gish, 156.
59. Brownlow, *The Parade's Gone By...*, 26.
60. Everson, 368.
61. Ramsaye, 717–19.
62. Lyons, 81–82, 88–89.
63. Stuart Oderman, *Lillian Gish: A Life on Stage and Screen* (Jefferson, N.C.: McFarland & Company, 2000), 59, 67, 69–70.
64. Lescarboura, 20.
65. See record for *The Quest* (American Film Manufacturing Company, 1915) [database online]; available from WorldCat. Of *The Quest*'s original five reels, 861 feet of one (probably the second reel) survives in the Library of Congress.
66. "A Home Town Girl."
67. "'Flying A' Sidelights," source unknown, [1915], Fischer Papers, Box 14, black scrapbook; unidentified clipping, [1915], Fischer Papers, Box 14, black scrapbook.
68. James S. McQuade, review of *The Quest*, *Moving Picture World*, March 27, 1915, 1940, Fischer Papers, Box 14, black scrapbook.
69. Ibid.; review of *The Quest*, source unknown, [1915], Fischer Papers, Box 14, black scrapbook.
70. *The Quest* (1915), dir. Harry A. Pollard, 15 min. [fragment], Library of Congress, videodisc.
71. McQuade, review of *The Quest*.
72. Richard Willis, "Margarita Fischer," *Movie Pictorial*, July 1915, 8–9, Fischer Papers, Box 14, black scrapbook.
73. Ibid.
74. Alexander Walker, *Stardom: The Hollywood Phenomenon* (New York: Stein & Day, 1970), 51–52.
75. *A Fool There Was* (1915), dir. Frank Powell, 66 min., Kino Video, 2002, videocassette.
76. Eve Golden, *Vamp: The Rise and Fall of Theda Bara* (Vestal, N.Y.: Emprise Publishing, 1996), 27, 40–41, 44, 55.
77. Janet Staiger, *Bad Women: Regulating Sexuality in Early American Cinema* (Minneapolis: University of Minnesota Press, 1995), 147–48.
78. Sumiko Higashi, *Virgins, Vamps, and Flappers: The American Silent Movie Heroine* (St. Albans, VT: Eden Press Women's Publications, 1978), 62–75.
79. Windeler, 212–13.
80. Ad for *The Lonesome Heart*, *Moving Picture World*, May 29, 1915, 1382–83, Fischer Papers, Box 14, black scrapbook.
81. "Margarita Fischer Proud of Being First Masterpicture Star," source unknown, [May? June? 1915], Fischer Papers, Box 14, black scrapbook.
82. Margarita Fischer filmography.
83. "Theater A Studio," source unknown, [1915], Fischer Papers, Box 14, black scrapbook; "Some Remarkable Mutual Interiors," source unknown, [1915], Fischer Papers, Box 14, black scrapbook.
84. Ad for *The Girl from His Town*, *Moving Picture World*, August 7, 1915, Fischer Papers, Box 14, black scrapbook; "New Double Exposure," source unknown, [1915], Fischer Papers, Box 14, black scrapbook.
85. James S. McQuade, review of *The Girl from His Town*, *Moving Picture World*, [August? 1915], Fischer Papers, Box 14, black scrapbook.
86. Gaylyn Studlar, "Oh, 'Doll Divine': Mary Pickford, Masquerade, and the Pedophilic Gaze," *Camera Obscura* 16, no. 3 (2001): 197–227.
87. Windeler, 83–84, 88.
88. Margarita Fischer's exact salary in 1915 is unknown, but it was certainly less than one thousand dollars per week, as in 1917 American offered her an improved contract at that weekly salary. Kelly R. Brown notes that five hundred dollars was an average weekly salary in 1916 for "a solid leading lady." See Brown, 104.
89. Iris Barry, *Let's Go to the Movies* (New York: Payson & Clarke, 1926. Reprint, New York: Arno Press, 1972), 58–59 (page citations are for the reprint edition).

Chapter 6

1. Hugo Münsterberg, *The Film, A Psychological Study: The Silent Photoplay in 1916* (New York: D. Appleton, 1916. Reprint, New York: Dover Publications, 1970), 92–93, 100.
2. Ibid., 96.
3. "Motherhood: Striking 'Beauty' Film with Margarita Fischer," source unknown, [November 1914], Fischer Papers, Box 14, green *Putting It Over* scrapbook. The film was known by the title *Motherhood*, as well as the longer title.
4. Stills from *The Divinity of Motherhood* (November 1914), Fischer Papers, Box 2, folder 11.
5. Schneider and Schneider, 151–55.
6. "Achievements in Public Health, 1900–1999: Family Planning," *MMWR* 48 (December 1999): 1073–80.
7. American Film Institute, 2002, *AFI Catalog: Silent Films: Infatuation* (1915), <http://www.afi.com/members/catalog/DetailView.aspx?s=1&Movie=16551> [November 13, 2004]; "Special Engagement" ad from Ye Liberty Theatre, [September? 1915], Fischer Papers, Box 14, black scrapbook.
8. "Playing 'Imaginary' Mother Sure Cure for the Blues, Says Little Film Star," source unknown, [September? 1915], Fischer Papers, Box 14, black scrapbook.
9. "Margarita Fisher Here," *Los Angeles Times*, July 30, 1919, Fischer Papers, Box 14, green *Pearl of Paradise* scrapbook.
10. Plot summary of *The Miracle of Life*, source unknown, [October 1915], Fischer Papers, Box 14, black scrapbook.
11. Louis Reeves Harrison, review of *The Miracle of Life*, [*Moving Picture World*], [October 1915], Fischer Papers, Box 14, black scrapbook.
12. "National Has Unusual Play," source unknown, [1915], Fischer papers, Box 14, black scrapbook.
13. Review of *The Miracle of Life*, source unknown, [October 1915], Fischer Papers, Box 14, black scrapbook. "Race suicide," a term used by Theodore Roosevelt, among others, refers to the idea that middle-class whites were not reproducing in sufficient numbers to outpace the growth of the country's immigrant population. The concept encompasses abortion and other forms of birth control.
14. Vachel Lindsay, *The Art of the Moving Picture* (New York: MacMillan Company, 1922, 2nd ed. Reprint, New York: Liveright Publishing Corporation, 1970), 253 (page citations are for the reprint edition).
15. *Where Are My Children?* (1916), dir. Lois Weber, 62 min., Turner Classic Movies broadcast, videocassette.
16. The National Board of Censorship had existed to police film content since 1909, but it proved unable to regulate controversial films effectively, and state boards, with their own standards, organized to fill its place. A bill proposing federal censorship of films was first introduced to Congress in 1914; although it died, divisive exploitation and social message films inspired its (unsuccessful) reintroduction in 1916. The same year, the film industry–friendly NAMPI replaced the National Board of Censorship in function and negated its power so that filmmakers wishing to

deal with controversial subjects received at least a temporary reprieve. See Grieveson, 25, 188–90, 204–06.

17. Annette Kuhn, *Cinema, Censorship, and Sexuality, 1909–1925* (London: Routledge, 1988), 30.

18. "Margarita Fischer in 'The Devil's Assistant,'" source unknown, [April 1917], Fischer Papers, Box 14, green *Pearl of Paradise* scrapbook.

19. "Essanay's New Studios," source unknown, [mid-1915], Fischer Papers, Box 14, black scrapbook.

20. Jeffrey Vance, *Chaplin: Genius of the Cinema* (New York: Harry N. Abrams, [2003]), 38–42.

21. Ibid., 42.

22. Brownlow, *The Parade's Gone By...*, 499.

23. Unidentified news item, [summer 1915], Fischer Papers, Box 14, black scrapbook. By coincidence, comedian Harry "Snub" Pollard also worked for Essanay, making at least one film (*By the Sea*) with Chaplin in 1915. He was, at this time, using the professional name of Harry Pollard, which must have made things quite confusing at the studio — but the future Snub, just beginning his film career, had more success there than his opinionated name-alike.

24. Margarita Kotselis interview.

25. Vance, 98, 157–58.

26. Margarita Kotselis interview.

27. Unidentified article, [August? 1915], Fischer Papers, Box 14, black scrapbook.

28. Lyons, 88.

29. Vance, 40.

30. "Three New Stars of the Screen Just Captured by Equitable."

31. Equitable Motion Pictures Corporation advertisement, *Moving Picture World*, September 11, 1915, 1784, Fischer papers, Box 14, green *Pearl of Paradise* scrapbook.

32. "Three New Stars of the Screen Just Captured by Equitable."

33. Michael Slade Shull, *Radicalism in American Silent Films, 1909–1929: A Filmography and History* (Jefferson, N.C.: McFarland & Company, 2000), 202.

34. Plot summary of *The Dragon*, source unknown, [December 1915], Fischer Papers, Box 14, green *Pearl of Paradise* scrapbook.

35. News item about *The Dragon*, *Moving Picture World*, December 18, 1915, Fischer Papers, Box 14, green *Pearl of Paradise* scrapbook.

36. George Blaisdell, review of *The Dragon*, source unknown, [January 1916?], Fischer Papers, Box 14, green *Pearl of Paradise* scrapbook.

37. Benjamin B. Hampton, *History of the American Film Industry from Its Beginnings to 1931* (New York: Dover Publications, 1970. Reprint of *A History of the Movies*, New York: Covici, Friede, 1931), 167.

38. Brownlow, *The Parade's Gone By...*, 430.

39. Blum, 155.

40. Gregory L. Williams, "Filming San Diego: Hollywood's Backlot, 1898–2002," *Journal of San Diego History* 48, 2 (Spring 2002): par. 18. <http://www.sandiegohistory.org/journal/2002-2/filming.htm> [September 24, 2004].

41. "New Studio to Make Mutual," source unknown, [1916], Fischer Papers, Box 14, green *Pearl of Paradise* scrapbook.

42. "Wanted — Handsome Men," source unknown, [September? 1916], Fischer Papers, Box 14, green *Pearl of Paradise* scrapbook.

43. News item in *Moving Picture World*, September 2, 1916, Fischer Papers, Box 14, green *Pearl of Paradise* scrapbook.

44. Unidentified article and schedule, [September? 1916], Fischer Papers, Box 14, green *Pearl of Paradise* scrapbook.

45. "Seen in Silhouette," source unknown, [November 1916], Fischer Papers, Box 14, green *Pearl of Paradise* scrapbook; "Los Angeles Film Brevities," source unknown, [1916], Fischer Papers, Box 14, green *Pearl of Paradise* scrapbook. Images of Fischer's silhouetted nude scenes survive in her collection of papers; see Fischer Papers, Box 19.

46. "Pollard Players Marooned," source unknown, [October? 1916], Fischer Papers, Box 14, green *Pearl of Paradise* scrapbook. Dorothy again recounted this event in the article "A Home Town Girl" of a few years later, indicating that it was not merely publicity.

47. Lyons, 166–68. Lyons used an 8mm print of the film found through Blackhawk Films for his analysis. Although the company still exists, it has changed ownership and dropped *The Pearl of Paradise* from its offerings since the publication of Lyons's book. The picture still survives in the holdings of the Library of Congress but is publicly unavailable.

48. Plot summary of *The Pearl of Paradise*, source unknown, [November 1916], Fischer Papers, Box 14, green *Pearl of Paradise* scrapbook; Lyons, 166. Pollard's filmography lists this as his final starring role, but he might have appeared as an extra in additional films. He appears as an unidentified partygoer in a still from *The Devil's Assistant*, which he directed in 1917. See stills of *The Devil's Assistant*, Fischer Papers, Box 2, folder 10.

49. "Mutual releases," *Moving Picture World*, December 16, 1916, Fischer Papers, Box 14, green *Pearl of Paradise* scrapbook.

50. "Miss Margarita Fischer Thinks 'Jackie of the Navy' Is Her Best Photodrama," source unknown, [December 1916], Fischer Papers, Box 14, green *Pearl of Paradise* scrapbook.

51. Ad for *Miss Jackie of the Navy*, source unknown, [December 1916?], Fischer Papers, Box 14, green *Pearl of Paradise* scrapbook.

52. Unidentified article, [December 1916?], Fischer Papers, Box 14, green *Pearl of Paradise* scrapbook.

53. Review of *Miss Jackie of the Navy*, source unknown, [December 1916?], Fischer Papers, Box 14, green *Pearl of Paradise* scrapbook.

54. Margarita Fischer filmography; "Cabrillo," source unknown, [January 1917?], Fischer Papers, Box 14, green *Pearl of Paradise* scrapbook.

55. "Drama Billed at Peoples: Margarita Fischer Is Appearing in 'The Devil's Assistant,'" source unknown, [April 1917?], Fischer Papers, Box 14, green *Pearl of Paradise* scrapbook.

56. Ibid.; "Margarita Fischer in 'The Devil's Assistant.'"

57. "Margarita Fischer in 'The Devil's Assistant'"; unidentified news item, [March 1917], Fischer Papers, Box 14, green *Pearl of Paradise* scrapbook. Perhaps confused by comparisons with *The Miracle of Life*, one news item reported that *The Devil's Assistant* was to be a "birth control picture" itself. See "Margarita Fischer in Birth Control Picture," source unknown, [1917], Fischer Papers, Box 14, green *Pearl of Paradise* scrapbook.

58. "Margarita Fischer Has Strong Role in 'Devil's Assistant,'" source unknown, February 17, 1917, Fischer Papers, Box 14, green *Pearl of Paradise* scrapbook.

59. Hirosaburo Endo to Margarita Fischer, April 26, 1917, Fischer Papers, Box 1, folder 1.

60. Knoll Tsutadar to Margarita Fischer, August 5, 1917, Fischer Papers, Box 1, folder 1.

61. Kiyoshi Shibui to Margarita Fischer, September 11, 1917, Fischer Papers, Box 1, folder 1.

62. Kanenori Nakata to Margarita Fischer, September 18, 1917, Fischer Papers, Box 1, folder 1.

63. Margarita Fischer interview.

64. Kazuo Takeda to Margarita Fischer, August 19, 1917, Fischer Papers, Box 1, folder 1.
65. "She's America's Queen of Beauty, Japan's View," *Los Angeles Evening Express*, May 17, 1919, Fischer Papers, Box 14, green *Putting It Over* scrapbook.
66. Ernest B. Orme, sheet music, Fischer Papers, Box 19, folder 1.
67. Anthony Slide, "Sheet Music of the Silent Stars," in *Silent Topics: Essays on Undocumented Areas of Silent Film* (Lanham, MD: Scarecrow Press, 2005), 86.
68. Ibid., 88.
69. S.S. Hutchinson to Harry Pollard, March 12, 1917, Fischer Papers, Box 1, folder 26.
70. "Marguerite Fischer Recovering from Operation," source unknown, [April 1917], Fischer Papers, Box 14, green *Putting It Over* scrapbook.
71. "Film Star of Pollard Picture Plays Quickly Chooses Winton," *San Diego Union*, April 8, 1917, Fischer Papers, Box 14, green *Pearl of Paradise* scrapbook; "Star," source unknown, [October 1917], Fischer Papers, Box 14, green *Pearl of Paradise* scrapbook.
72. Biographical Note to the Fischer Papers; Margarita Kotselis interview.
73. "Famous Stars Will Attend Movie Ball," *Oregon Sunday Journal* (Portland, Oregon), May 27, 1917, Fischer Papers, Box 14, green *Pearl of Paradise* scrapbook; unidentified article, [May 1917], Fischer Papers, Box 14, green *Pearl of Paradise* scrapbook.
74. Ibid.
75. "Famous Stars Will Attend Movie Ball."
76. "Star."
77. Margarita Kotselis interview.
78. Arvidson, 176.
79. Eileen Whitfield, *Pickford: The Woman Who Made Hollywood* (Lexington: University Press of Kentucky, 1997), 124–25.
80. Gloria Swanson, *Swanson on Swanson: An Autobiography* (New York: Random House, 1980), 4.
81. Ibid., 5.
82. Ibid., 3.
83. Margarita Kotselis interview.
84. Ibid.
85. Ibid.
86. Willis and Inglis to Mr. and Mrs. Harry Pollard, August 13, 1917, Fischer Papers, Box 1, folder 26.
87. Willis and Inglis to Pollards (personal), August 13, 1917, Fischer Papers, Box 1, folder 26.
88. Richard Willis to Margarita Fischer, August 15, 1917, Fischer Papers, Box 1, folder 26.
89. Richard Willis to Margarita Fischer, August 16, 1917, Fischer Papers, Box 1, folder 26.
90. Margarita Fischer interview.
91. American Film Co. contract, August 27, 1917, Fischer Papers, Box 1, folder 26.
92. Willis and Inglis to Margarita Fischer, August 23, 1917, Fischer Papers, Box 1, folder 26.
93. Margarita Fischer filmography; "'Putting It Over' at Star," source unknown, [October 1917], Fischer Papers, Box 14, green *Pearl of Paradise* scrapbook. Billy H. Doyle states that the company broke up in 1918; if so, it made no films for the final months of its existence, for *The Girl Who Couldn't Grow Up* was the last film for the production company as well as for Margarita as its star. See Doyle, 22.
94. "Star."
95. "Women Can Make Happy Homes and Maintain Successful Career," source unknown, [December 1917], Fischer Papers, Box 14, green *Pearl of Paradise* scrapbook.

Chapter 7

1. Lyons, 82, 84–85, 87–89.
2. Margarita Fischer interview.
3. "So This Is a Studio, Is It?"
4. Anthony Slide, "The Silent Closet: Gays, Lesbians, and Silent Film," in *Silent Topics: Essays on Undocumented Areas of Silent Film* (Lanham, MD: Scarecrow Press, 2005), 54.
5. Unidentified article, [1917 or early 1918], Fischer Papers, Box 14, green *Pearl of Paradise* scrapbook.
6. "So This Is a Studio, Is It?"; Roberta Courtlandt, "Kid Love Affairs," *Motion Picture Classic*, [1917], Fischer Papers, Box 14, green *Pearl of Paradise* scrapbook.
7. Margarita Fischer interview.
8. Ibid.
9. "Kid Love Affairs."
10. "Women Can Make Happy Homes and Maintain Successful Career."
11. Unidentified article, [1917?], Fischer Papers, Box 14, green *Pearl of Paradise* scrapbook.
12. Margarita Kotselis interview.
13. Biographical Note to the Fischer Papers.
14. Unidentified news item, [1918], Fischer Papers, Box 14, black scrapbook.
15. Margarita Fischer filmography; review of *Miss Jackie of the Army*, source unidentified, [December 1917], Fischer Papers, Box 14, green *Pearl of Paradise* scrapbook.
16. "Margarita Fischer Urges System," source unknown, [December 1917], Fischer Papers, Box 14, green *Pearl of Paradise* scrapbook. This article refers to a second niece, the actress's namesake Margarita. She was undoubtedly a complete fiction, as she was mentioned only a few more times in minor publicity articles over the next year and never afterwards. Kathie was Charles and Dorothy Pyle's only child, and census records from 1920 show Kathie as the only child in the household.
17. Ibid.; Margarita Fischer, "Careers: The Modern Woman and the World of Movies," source unknown, [December 1917], Fischer Papers, Box 14, green *Pearl of Paradise* scrapbook.
18. "Margarita's Maxims," *Picture Play Magazine*, May 1918, Fischer Papers, Box 14, green *Pearl of Paradise* scrapbook.
19. Biographical Note to the Fischer Papers. Pollard found little work during his separation from his wife; see Harry Pollard filmography, Fischer Papers, index folder.
20. "It's a Long Lane That Has No Turning."
21. "Margarita Fisher," *Semi-Tropic California*, April 1919, Fischer Papers, Box 14, green *Putting It Over* scrapbook.
22. "It's a Long Lane That Has No Turning."
23. "A Home Town Girl."
24. Ibid.
25. Some photographs from these family outings are held in the Fischer Papers, Box 11, folder 6.
26. Charles D. Fox and Milton L. Silver, eds., *Who's Who on the Screen* (New York, Ross Publishing Co., 1920; reprint, New York: Gordon Press, 1976), 226 (page citations are for the reprint edition).
27. Margarita Kotselis interview.
28. *Film Fun* cover, Fischer Papers, Box 14, August 1917, green *Pearl Of Paradise* scrapbook.
29. "Mutual Star Productions: Miss Jackie of the Army," source unknown, [December 1917], Fischer Papers, Box 14, green *Pearl of Paradise* scrapbook.
30. "Putting Over a Ramble," *Moving Picture World*, May

11, 1918, Fischer Papers, Box 14, Green *Pearl of Paradise* scrapbook.
31. Unidentified news item, *Photoplay Art*, April 1918, Fischer Papers, Box 14, green *Putting It Over* scrapbook.
32. Fischer to Uselton.
33. Margarita Fischer interview.
34. "Margarita Fischer Becomes Godmother of Navy Ball Team," source unknown, [April 8, 1918], Fischer Papers, Box 14, green *Putting It Over* scrapbook; George H. White, "Navy Nine Wins Spectacular Contest," source unknown, [April 8, 1918], Fischer Papers, Box 14, green *Putting It Over* scrapbook.
35. "Pennant Donated," *San Diego Union*, [1918], Fischer Papers, Box 14, green *Putting It Over* scrapbook.
36. "First Aviator to Down Enemy Will Win Medal," *San Diego Union*, April 8, 1918, Fischer Papers, green *Putting It Over* scrapbook; "Aero Squadron Now Boasts a Godmother," *Los Angeles Times*, April [8?], 1918, Fischer Papers, Box 14, green *Putting It Over* scrapbook.
37. Jones, Dayton E. (Pvt.), "Film Actress Adopts 14th," [*Rockwell Flight*?], [April 1918], Fischer Papers, Box 14, green *Putting It Over* scrapbook.
38. "Fisher Gold Medal Given to Airman's Father and Mother," source unknown, [late January or early February 1919], Fischer Papers, Box 14, green *Putting It Over* scrapbook. Luke died on September 29, 1918, and his parents received the medal on January 29, 1919.
39. "A Real Aviatrix," Grace Kingsley, [*Los Angeles Sunday Times*?], [June 1919], Fischer Papers, Box 14, green *Pearl of Paradise* scrapbook. Other stars from American were also interested in the military's aerial activities — as soon as combat was over, Mary Miles Minter began taking flying lessons from handsome veteran and barnstormer-turned-actor Ormer Locklear until her protective mother put a stop to this potentially life-threatening hobby. Minter's mother was right to be concerned; Locklear died in a plane crash while filming an aerial stunt in 1920. See Scott, 108.
40. "Fishing Outings a Fad in San Diego Society," *Los Angeles Examiner*, April 14, 1918, 918, Fischer Papers, Box 14, green *Putting It Over* scrapbook.
41. "Pretty Miss Fisher Wears A $20,000 Gown in Photoplay," source unknown, [July 1918], Fischer Papers, Box 14, green *Pearl of Paradise* scrapbook.
42. "Even a Movie Staress can Conserve Clothes, It Seems," *San Diego Sun*, April 6, 1918, Fischer Papers, Box 14, green *Putting It Over* scrapbook.
43. Lyons, 88.
44. Unidentified news item, source unknown, [May 1918?], Fischer Papers, Box 14, green *Pearl of Paradise* scrapbook.
45. "Performance of 'The Wolf' Is Gala Affair," *Santa Barbara News* (Santa Barbara, California), May 8, 1918, Fischer Papers, Box 14, green *Putting It Over* scrapbook.
46. Ibid.; "American Players Give Benefit Performance," source unknown, [May 1918], Fischer Papers, Box 14, green *Pearl of Paradise* scrapbook.
47. "Performance of 'The Wolf' Is Gala Affair"; unidentified article, [May 1918], Fischer Papers, Box 14, green *Pearl of Paradise* scrapbook.
48. Ibid.
49. "Marguerita Fischer Assists Red Cross," *Santa Barbara Daily News*, June 8, 1918, Fischer Papers, Box 14, green *Putting It Over* scrapbook.
50. "Miss Fisher Issues 'Fire Crackers,'" *Los Angeles Examiner* (Los Angeles, California), July 3, 1918; Invitation, Fischer Papers, Box 18, folder 10.
51. Margarita Fischer interview.
52. Untitled news item, *Moving Picture World*, November 10, 1917, Fischer Papers, Box 14, green *Pearl of Paradise* scrapbook.
53. Jennifer M. Bean, "Technologies of Early Stardom and the Extraordinary Body," *Camera Obscura* 48 (2001): 11–12.
54. "Some Gowns Worn by Margarita Fisher," *Oxnard Daily News* (Oxnard, California), June 9, 1918, Fischer Papers, Box 14, green *Putting It Over* scrapbook.

Chapter 8

1. Lescarboura, 52.
2. Review of *Molly Go Get 'Em*, source unknown, [January 1918], Fischer Papers, Box 14, green *Pearl of Paradise* scrapbook.
3. "March, 1918," source unknown, March 1918, Fischer Papers, Box 14, green *Pearl of Paradise* scrapbook.
4. "Molly, Go Get 'Em," *Moving Picture World*, [January 1918], Fischer Papers, Box 14, green *Pearl of Paradise* scrapbook.
5. "Miss Fischer to Be Present," *San Diego Tribune*, April 5, 1918, Fischer Papers, Box 14, green *Putting It Over* scrapbook.
6. Margaret I. MacDonald, review of *Ann's Finish*, *Moving Picture World*, [March 1918], Fischer Papers, Box 14, green *Pearl of Paradise* scrapbook.
7. Margaret I. MacDonald, review of *The Primitive Woman*, *Moving Picture World*, [April 1918], Fischer Papers, Box 14, green *Pearl of Paradise* scrapbook.
8. "'A Square Deal' from Mutual," *Motion Picture News*, June 15, 1918, Fischer Papers, Box 14, green *Putting It Over* scrapbook.
9. Plot summary of *Impossible Susan*, source unknown, Fischer Papers, Box 14, green *Pearl of Paradise* scrapbook.
10. Margaret I. MacDonald, review of *Impossible Susan*, [*Moving Picture World*], August 3, 1918, Fischer Papers, Box 14, green *Pearl of Paradise* scrapbook.
11. "Margarita Fisher," *Motion Picture News*, July 20, 1918, Fischer Papers, Box 14, green *Putting It Over* scrapbook.
12. Unidentified news item, [1918], Fischer Papers, Box 14, green *Pearl of Paradise* scrapbook.
13. Margarita Fischer interview.
14. Gertrude Jobes, *Motion Picture Empire* (Hamden, Connecticut: Archon Books, 1966), 149, 190.
15. John M. Barry, *The Great Influenza: The Epic Story of the Deadliest Plague in History* (New York: Viking, 2004), 4–5, 92–93.
16. Richard Koszarski, "Flu Season: *Moving Picture World* Reports on Pandemic Influenza, 1918–19," *Film History* 17, no. 4 (2005): 466–85.
17. Ibid.
18. Gish, 218–19.
19. Lyons, 88–89.
20. "Sheldon Announces Summer Schedules," [*Moving Picture World*?], [May? 1918], Fischer Papers, Box 14, green *Pearl of Paradise* scrapbook.
21. Lyons, 91.
22. "American Film Company Outlines Plans," [*Moving Picture World*], [May-June? 1918], Fischer Papers, Box 14, black scrapbook.
23. Ibid.
24. "American to Release Through Pathe," *Moving Picture World*, July 20, 1918, Fischer Papers, Box 14, black scrapbook.

25. Lyons, 90–92, 94, 127.
26. American Film Co. contract, September 4, 1918, Fischer Papers, Box 1, folder 26. Following the end of this contract on January 1, 1919, the actress may have signed another contract, or — due to the uncertain state of the studio's finances — she may simply have worked from film to film. She did not retain any additional contracts, so the security of her employment for American in 1919 is not known.
27. "'Money Isn't Everything' First Fisher Production," source unknown, Fischer Papers, Box 14, green *Pearl of Paradise* scrapbook.
28. "Wardrobe Features in Mutual Subject," *Motion Picture News*, July 20, 1918, Fischer Papers, Box 14, green *Putting It Over* scrapbook.
29. Margaret I. MacDonald, review of *Money Isn't Everything*, *Moving Picture World*, [September 1918], Fischer Papers, Box 14, green *Pearl of Paradise* scrapbook.
30. American Film Co. contract.
31. "Riylhour Monday," source unknown, [December 1918?], Fischer Papers, Box 14, green *Putting It Over* scrapbook.
32. Sean P. Holmes, "The Hollywood Star System and the Regulation of Actors' Labour, 1916–1934," *Film History* 12 (2000): 99.
33. Iris Barry, 109, 120.
34. Review of *Ann's Finish*.
35. Laurence Reid, review of *Molly of the Follies*, *New York Review* (New York, N.Y.), February 8, 1919, Fischer Papers, Box 14, green *Putting it Over* scrapbook.
36. Iris Barry, 96.
37. American Film Institute, 2002, *AFI Catalog: Silent Films: Put Up Your Hands* <http://www.afi.com/members/catalog/AbbrView.aspx?s=1&Movie=15700> [September 24, 2004].
38. Margarita Fischer filmography.
39. Review of *Charge It to Me*, *Motion Picture News*, May 3, 1919, 2906, Fischer Papers, Box 14, green *Putting It Over* scrapbook.
40. American Film Institute, 2002, *AFI Catalog: Silent Films: Trixie from Broadway* <http://www.afi.com/members/catalog/AbbrView.aspx?s=1&Movie=15570&bhcp=1> [May 11, 2007].
41. "Margarita Fisher Is Mightily Miffed," source unknown, [mid-1919], Fischer Papers, Box 14, green *Pearl of Paradise* scrapbook.
42. Marie Kieding to Margarita Fischer, January 16, 1919, Fischer Papers, Box 1, folder 16.
43. Erie Shepard to Margarita Fischer.
44. Doris Soohen to Margarita Fischer, October 1, 1919, Fischer Papers, Box 1, folder 16.
45. Daphne Hall to Margarita Fischer, February 12, 1919, Fischer Papers, Box 1, folder 16.
46. Helen E. Strauss to Margarita Fischer, January 20, 1919, Fischer Papers, Box 1, folder 16.
47. Samuel D. Margolis to Margarita Fischer, February 7, 1919, Fischer Papers, Box 1, folder 16.
48. Roswell Vassar Varno to Margarita Fischer, May 1, 1919, Fischer Papers, Box 1, folder 16. This folder also holds Varno's initial note to the star, dated March 5, 1919, in which he requests an autographed photo.
49. Victor Lanz to Margarita Fischer, August 16, 1919, Fischer Papers, Box 1, folder 16.
50. Rupert W. Harrison to Margarita Fischer, August 12, 1919, Fischer Papers, Box 1, folder 16.
51. Roswell Vassar Varno to Margarita Fischer.
52. News item in "Flashes" column, *Los Angeles Times* (Los Angeles, California), May 16, 1919, Fischer Papers, Box 14, green *Putting It Over* scrapbook.
53. "*The Tiger Lily*: Conventional Picture of 'Little Italy,'" *Motion Picture News*, July 26, 1919, 939, Fischer Papers, Box 14, green *Putting It Over* scrapbook.
54. Ibid.
55. "Speaking of Stars," *California Life*, June 21, 1919, 15, Fischer Papers, Box 14, green *Putting It Over* scrapbook.
56. American Film Institute, 2002, *AFI Catalog: Silent Films: The Hellion*, <http://www.afi.com/members/catalog/AbbrView.aspx?s=1&Movie=15423&bhcp=1> [May 11, 2007].
57. Blum, 171–81.
58. Ibid., 199; Doyle, 237.
59. Ibid., 201; Golden, 187. Bara eventually returned to the screen to parody her earlier image in *The Unchastened Woman* (1925) and the short *Madame Mystery* (1926).
60. Wagenknecht, 176.
61. "Who's Who in Pictures," source unknown, [1918], Fischer Papers, Box 14, green *Pearl of Paradise* scrapbook; "Moving Picture Editor" column, source unknown, February 22, 1919, Fischer Papers, Box 14, green *Putting It Over* scrapbook. The former article reports her still married to Pollard, though the couple may have separated by that time.
62. "A Home Town Girl"; Fox and Silver, 226.
63. "It's a Long Lane That Has No Turning."
64. Unidentified clipping, [May? 1918], Fischer Papers, Box 14, green *Pearl of Paradise* scrapbook; "Making Margarita Graceful," source unknown, [1919?], Fischer Papers, Box 14, green *Pearl of Paradise* scrapbook.
65. News item, *It*, July 1919, Fischer Papers, Box 14, green *Putting It Over* scrapbook.
66. Everson, 4.
67. Margarita Fischer filmography.
68. Lyons, 92–93.
69. Dumaux, 114.
70. Biographical Note to the Fischer Papers; Lyons, 249.
71. Margarita Fischer interview.
72. "Margarita Fisher," *Motion Picture News*, Christmas Number [1920], 230, Fischer Papers, Box 18, folder 12.
73. Biographical Note to the Fischer Papers.
74. Lyons, 94.
75. Margarita Fischer filmography; Lyons, 94, 249.
76. Biographical Note to the Fischer Papers.
77. The household also included the divorced Dorothy (calling herself Mary, her stage name), age "28," who, like Margarita, identified herself as an actress; niece Kathrine, 12; and mother Kate, who is listed as the head of the household. See Fourteenth Census of the United States, 1920: Santa Barbara County, California Population Schedule. Available from Ancestry.com [database on-line], 2001–2004, indexed by Ancestry.com from microfilmed schedules of the 1920 U.S. Federal Decennial Census. Data imaged from National Archives and Records Administration, 1920 Federal Population Census, Washington, D.C.: National Archives and Records Administration.
78. Lahue, *Continued Next Week*, 83–84, 206. Lahue mentions that this serial of fifteen episodes was created as a "state-right release," which meant that a small studio sold its distribution rights rather than contracting with its own distributor, a system that required much less of an investment from the studio. See Lahue, *Continued Next Week*, xvi, for an explanation of the state-right release system.
79. According to Blair Miller, the Frohman Amusement Corporation was founded in 1914 and closed its doors in 1920; *The Invisible Ray* must have been one of its last projects. See Miller, 95.

80. "Margarita Fischer Signs," [1921] source unknown, Fischer Papers, Box 14, black scrapbook.
81. "Margarita Fisher."
82. Margarita Fischer filmography.
83. Fox and Silver, 201.
84. "Sixteen pages of Proven Press Copy for the Universal Masterpiece 'Uncle Tom's Cabin,'" 1927, 7, Fischer Papers, Box 19, oversized folder.

Chapter 9

1. May, 201.
2. Ronald Allen Goldberg, *America in the Twenties* (Syracuse, NY: Syracuse University Press, 2003), 4, 9–13, 20.
3. J.F. Klenotic, "Class Markers in the Mass Movie Audience: A Case Study in the Cultural Geography of Moviegoing, 1926–1932," *Communication Review* 2, no. 4 (1998), 461–95.
4. Everson, 296–97.
5. See James Robert Parish, *The Hollywood Book of Scandals* (New York: McGraw-Hill, 2004), 26–32, for an account of Wallace Reid's addiction and death.
6. Parish, 26.
7. Everson, 297.
8. Griffith's career suffered as other filmmakers adopted his innovations, and public tastes shifted to new subjects. His 1920s works, according to Kevin Brownlow, were "modest in both theme and execution, and have led historians to complain of an artistic decline." See Brownlow, *The Parade's Gone By...*, 93.
9. Mary P. Ryan, "The Projection of a New Womanhood: The Movie Moderns in the 1920s," in *Our American Sisters: Women in American Life and Thought*, 2nd ed., Jean E. Friedman and William G. Shade, eds. (Boston: Allyn and Bacon, 1976), 366–84.
10. Blum, 205.
11. Bow actually played a role in the movie *Beyond the Rainbow* before appearing in *Down to the Sea in Ships*, but her part was cut before release. Once she achieved major stardom, the picture was re-released with her scenes included. See David Stenn, *Clara Bow: Runnin' Wild* (New York: Cooper Square Press, 2000), 22, 26.
12. P. David Marshall, *Celebrity and Power: Fame in Contemporary Culture* (Minneapolis: University of Minnesota Press, 1997), 81–82.
13. Joshua Gamson, *Claims to Fame: Celebrity in Contemporary America* (Berkeley: University of California Press, 1994), 25–27, 29.
14. "'The Dragon' (Equitable)," source unknown, [January 1916], Fischer Papers, Box 14, green *Pearl of Paradise* scrapbook.
15. Fox and Silver, 226.
16. Heather Addison, "Capitalizing Their Charms: Cinema Stars and Physical Culture in the 1920s," *Velvet Light Trap* no. 50 (2002): 15–35.
17. Adela Rogers St. Johns, "New American Beauty," *Photoplay*, June 1922, 26–27; quoted in Addison.
18. Brownlow, *The Parade's Gone By...*, 449, 451.
19. Ibid., 449.
20. Edmonds, 118–19.
21. Wu Ai-Lien, "Former 'American Beauty Girl,'" *North-China Daily News*, November 28, 1936, 3, Pollard Papers, oversized folder. This article is an extended version of "Actress of Silent Days Visits Shanghai" and was evidently truncated and altered to suit local newspapers. Margarita recounted the anecdote about Shearer and Irving Thalberg in this article. Shearer's performance in *The Leather Pushers* is confirmed in the biography *Norma Shearer*, which even includes a still of Reginald Denny with Shearer as flower girl. See Gavin Lambert, *Norma Shearer* (New York: Alfred A. Knopf, 1990), 30.
22. Roland Flamini, *Thalberg: The Last Tycoon and the World of M-G-M* (New York: Crown Publishers, Inc., 1994), 47, 81–82.
23. Harry Pollard filmography. The filmography lists the release date of *The Loaded Door* as 1923, but the databases of the American Film Institute list it as August 14, 1922.
24. Buck Rainey, "Hoot Gibson," *The Strong, Silent Type: Over 100 Screen Cowboys, 1903–1930* (Jefferson, NC: McFarland & Company, 2004), 263–76.
25. Ibid., 267.
26. Brownlow, *The Parade's Gone By...*, 449.
27. Edmonds, 131.
28. Brownlow, *The Parade's Gone By...*, 449.
29. Iris Barry, 208.
30. "Comedy Is King and Pollard His Premier," *Filmograph*, September 5, 1925, 2, Pollard Papers, Box 3, folder 5.
31. "Former Screen Star of First Magnitude Emerges from Retirement and Is Acclaimed by Critics for Splendid Performance in Late Film Drama," *Pasadena Star-News*, Automobile Section, October 30, 1924, Fischer Papers, Box 18, folder 12.
32. Publicity photo spread for *K—the Unknown*, *Wid's Weekly* 2, no. 24 (1924), Pollard Papers, Box 3, folder 6.
33. F. Gwynplaine MacIntyre has viewed a partially deteriorated print of the film that survives in a private collection in Europe. He was generous enough to correspond privately with the author via e-mail, but a public summary of the film's plot and his opinion of its quality may be found on the Internet Movie Database. See Internet Movie Database, 1990–2006, F. Gwynplaine MacIntyre, review of *K—the Unknown*, May 28, 2003, <http://www.imdb.com/title/tt0015030/> [September 3, 2004].
34. Adolph Zukor had formed Famous Players in 1912, and Jesse Lasky had founded his eponymous studio in 1914. The two merged their studios (and one other, Bosworth) under a new distributor, Paramount, later in 1914. Zukor headed Paramount and continued to sweep smaller studios and stars into its sphere of influence. In 1919 he was the most powerful man in the film industry—though by the time Margarita Fischer signed on for a Paramount film, that honor might have belonged instead to Carl Laemmle of Universal. See Blum, 27, 53, 54, 169.
35. American Film Institute, 2002, *AFI Catalog: Silent Films: Any Woman*, <http://www.afi.com/members/catalog/AbbrView.aspx?s=1&Movie=2605> [September 30, 2004].
36. Review of *Any Woman*, Mordaunt Hall, *New York Times*, May 27, 1925, *New York Times* online archive 1851–1980 < http://query.nytimes.com/search/query?srchst=p> [June 25, 2006].
37. Charles Donald Fox, *Famous Film Folk* (New York: George H. Doran Co., 1925), 28.
38. David Pierce, "'Carl Laemmle's Outstanding Achievement': Harry Pollard and the Struggle to Film *Uncle Tom's Cabin*," *Film History* 10, no. 4 (1998): 459–76.
39. Margarita Fischer interview.
40. Edmonds, 70.

Chapter 10

1. Harriet Beecher Stowe, *Uncle Tom's Cabin* (New York: Random House, 1996).
2. Michele Wallace, "*Uncle Tom's Cabin*: Before and After the Jim Crow Era," *TDR* 44 (Spring 2000): 137–56.
3. Stephen Railton, "*Uncle Tom's Cabin* on Film," *Uncle Tom's Cabin & American Culture*, 1998–2005, <http://www.iath.virginia.edu/utc/onstage/films/fihp.html> [November 14, 2006].
4. Pierce, "'Carl Laemmle's Outstanding Achievement.'"
5. Ibid.
6. "Pollard Shifts Back to Uncle Tom," *Los Angeles Daily Times*, July 14, 1926, Pollard Papers, Box 3, folder 1.
7. Edmonds, 149.
8. Wallace.
9. Undated carbon from *Uncle Tom's Cabin* file, Billy Rose Theater Collection; quoted in Pierce, "'Carl Laemmle's Outstanding Achievement.'"
10. Paul Thompson, "Uncle Carl Sells Uncle Tom Down the Movie River," *Motion Picture Classic*, September [1927], 35, Pollard Papers, Box 3, folder 1.
11. "'Uncle Tom' Gets Walloped," *News Scimitar* (Memphis, Tennessee), November 5, 1926, Pollard Papers, Box 3, folder 1.
12. "Fascinating Facts and Figures on the Making of Uncle Tom's Cabin," *Souvenir Book: Carl Laemmle Presents Uncle Tom's Cabin, A Harry Pollard Production*, Pollard Papers, Box 3, folder 2.
13. Ibid.
14. Pierce, "'Carl Laemmle's Outstanding Achievement.'"
15. Invitation to *Uncle Tom's Cabin* Reunion Dinner Party, July 15, 1927, Pollard Papers, Box 3, folder 2.
16. Ibid.
17. "Universal Signs Pollard for Five Years," *Universal Weekly*, March 26, 1927, Pollard Papers, Box 3, folder 1.
18. Ibid.
19. Pierce, "'Carl Laemmle's Outstanding Achievement.'"
20. Valeria Belletti, *Adventures of a Hollywood Secretary*, edited and introduced by Cari Beauchamp (Berkeley: University of California Press, 2006), 83–84, 116.
21. Slide, "Those Elusive Budget Figures," 22.
22. "'The Pre-View' Weekly Film Pictorial Section," *Los Angeles Sunday Times*, March 20, 1927, and May 1, 1927, Pollard Papers, oversized folder.
23. "'Uncle Tom's Cabin' Houses Flicker Romance: Now It Can Be Told!"
24. "Uncle Carl Sells Uncle Tom Down the Movie River."
25. "Sixteen pages of Proven Press copy for the Universal Masterpiece 'Uncle Tom's Cabin.'"
26. "The Lady Who Crosses the Ice," *Universal Weekly*, March 12, 1927, 13, Pollard Papers Box 3, folder 1.
27. Dance and Robertson, 4, 99, 107.
28. Brownlow, *The Parade's Gone By...*, 245.
29. "Novel Makes Notable Film," *Los Angeles Times*, March 29, 1928, Pollard Papers, Box 3, folder 1.
30. Ibid.
31. Margarita Fischer interview.
32. Review of *Uncle Tom's Cabin*, Mordaunt Hall, *New York Times*, November 5, 1927, 16, *New York Times* online archive 1851–1980, http://query.nytimes.com/search/query?srchst=p [August 2, 2006].
33. Pierce, "'Carl Laemmle's Outstanding Achievement.'"
34. *Uncle Tom's Cabin* (1927), dir. Harry Pollard, 112 min., Kino Video, 1999, videodisc. Not everyone agrees with this assessment of Margarita's performance, of course. In his article "Annus Mirabilis: The Film in 1927," Kevin Brownlow states, "The basic error of the director, Harry Pollard, in casting his wife, Margarita Fisher, in the lead is mitigated by an unexpectedly spectacular production." He, like others, singles out the ice-crossing scene for particular praise. See Kevin Brownlow, "Annus Mirabilis: The Film in 1927," *Film History* 17 (2005): 173.
35. Michael G. Ankerich, "Billie Dove," *The Sound of Silence: Conversations with 16 Film and Stage Personalities Who Bridged the Gap Between Silents and Talkies* (Jefferson, NC: McFarland & Company, 1998), 84.
36. WorldwideBoxoffice.com. <http://worldwideboxoffice.com/index.cgi?order=domestic&start=1927&finish=1927> [May 14, 2007].
37. Margarita Fischer interview.
38. "Actress of Silent Days Visits Shanghai," *Vista Press* (Vista, California), December 31, 1936, Fischer Papers, oversized folder.
39. Ibid.
40. Lescarboura, 290.
41. Ron Hutchinson, "The Vitaphone Project. Answering Harry Warner's Question: 'Who the Hell Wants to Hear Actors Talk?'" *Film History*, 14, no. 1 (2002), 40–41.
42. Scott Eyman, *The Speed of Sound: Hollywood and the Talkie Revolution, 1926–1930* (New York: Simon & Schuster, 1997), 65, 77.
43. *Introduction by Will Hays*, (1926), director unknown, 4 minutes, Turner Classic Movies broadcast, videocassette.
44. Eyman, 139–41, 145, 160.
45. Everson, 334–36.
46. Eyman, 115.

Chapter 11

1. Brownlow, *The Parade's Gone By...*, 3.
2. Louise Brooks, *Lulu in Hollywood* (New York: Alfred A. Knopf, 1982), 86.
3. Eyman, 300–04.
4. Ken Wlaschin, *The Illustrated Encyclopedia of the World's Great Movie Stars and Their Films: From 1900 to the Present Day* (New York: Salamander Books, 1979), 20, 21; *Clara Bow: Discovering the "It" Girl*, prod. Elaina B. Archer and dir. Hugh Munro Neely, 65 minutes, Timeline Films, 1999, videodisc.
5. Brownlow, *The Parade's Gone By...*, 448.
6. Jeanine Basinger, *Silent Stars* (New York: Alfred A. Knopf, 1999), 143, 157, 171–72.
7. Windeler, 156–57, 217–18. Besides *Coquette*, for which she won an Oscar, Pickford's sound films were *The Taming of the Shrew* (1929), which co-starred Douglas Fairbanks and which was also released as a silent; *Kiki* (1931); and *Secrets* (1933). The Shakespeare adaptation was the only one of the three to turn a profit, although Pickford professed herself unsatisfied with it.
8. "Marguerita Fischer, Star of Movieland Here to Visit Old Scenes of Childhood."
9. "Silent Versions for All Universal Films," *Greater Show World*, April 15, 1929, 11, Pollard Papers, Box 3, folder 4.
10. "Marguerita Fischer, Star of Movieland Here to Visit Old Scenes of Childhood."

11. "Harry Pollard Enthusiastic Over Islands," *Hilo Tribune-Herald*, January 16, 1930, 4, Pollard Papers, Box 3, folder 4.
12. Holmes to Fischer.
13. "Marguerita Fischer, Star of Movieland Here to Visit Old Scenes of Childhood."
14. "Actress of Silent Days Visits Shanghai."
15. "Shy Harry Pollard, Film Director, Has Never Been to a Hollywood Party."
16. James H. Thomas, *The Bunion Derby: Andy Payne and the Great Transcontinental Footrace* (Oklahoma City: Southwestern Heritage Books, 1980), v–vi, 4, 9, 14, 67, 87, 112, 127–28. The second race was an even bigger financial disappointment than the first.
17. Margarita Kotselis interview.
18. Margarita Fischer interview.
19. Ibid. Before Arthur Field came to work for the Fischer family (which he virtually became a part of), recalled Margarita Kotselis, Field had been married and had two children. The marriage had ended in divorce. Margarita Kotselis to author, e-mail of May 10, 2007.
20. Richard Barrios, *A Song in the Dark: The Birth of the Musical Film* (New York: Oxford University Press, 1995), 81–82.
21. Eyman, 316.
22. Barrios, 82.
23. "Universal Signs Pollard for Five Years," dated March 26, 1927, named Kerry as the intended actor of the Ravenal role.
24. Barrios, 82, 90.
25. Edmonds, 154; Barrios, 90.
26. "Harry Pollard, I Salute You!," *Motion Picture News*, March 16, 1929, Pollard Papers, Box 3, folder 4.
27. Barrios, 90.
28. "Harry Pollard, I Salute You!"
29. "Show Boat Premiere in Florida," *Greater Show World*, April 15, 1929, 11, Pollard Papers, Box 3, folder 4.
30. Review of *Show Boat*, *Film Mercury* (Hollywood, California), March 29, 1929, 15, Pollard Papers, Box 3, folder 4.
31. Quinn Martin, review of *Show Boat*, *The World* (New York City), April 19, 1929, Pollard Papers, Box 3, folder 4.
32. "Uncle Carl Gives Us a Real Contribution to Screen Art," *Film Spectator*, April 20, 1929, 6, Pollard Papers, Box 3, folder 4.
33. Mordaunt Hall, review of *Show Boat*, *New York Times*, April 18, 1929, *New York Times* online archive 1851–1980 <http://query.nytimes.com/search/query?srchst=p> [June 25, 2006].
34. Ibid.
35. "Harry Pollard Enthusiastic Over Islands."
36. Victor Oscar Freeburg, *Pictorial Beauty on the Screen* (New York: n.p., 1923. Reprint, New York: Benjamin Blom, 1972), ix.
37. Edmonds, 154.
38. *Show Boat* (1929), dir. Harry A. Pollard, 125 minutes, Turner Classic Movies broadcast, videocassette. Pollard's middle name is not known, and, in fact, he may not have had one. He probably adopted the middle initial as a means of distinguishing himself from Harry "Snub" Pollard.
39. Klepper, 525.
40. Barrios, 90.
41. "Shy Harry Pollard, Film Director, Has Never Been to a Hollywood Party."
42. Ibid.
43. "Talkies Don't Bother Pollard — He Always Made His Actors Talk."
44. "Shy Harry Pollard, Film Director, Has Never Been to a Hollywood Party."
45. Barrios, 152.
46. "Talkies Don't Bother Pollard — He Always Made His Actors Talk."
47. Review of *Tonight at Twelve*, *The Film Mercury* (Hollywood, California), August 23, 1929, 19, Pollard Papers, Box 3, folder 5.
48. Ibid.
49. Mordaunt Hall, "'Undertow' Falls Short: Defects Prevent Screen Play from Being Fully Effective," *New York Times*, March 1, 1930, *New York Times* online archive 1851–1980 <http://query.nytimes.com/search/query?srchst=p> [June 25, 2006].
50. Mordaunt Hall, "An Unimaginative Film: 'Tonight at Twelve' Provides Much Mystery — Melodrama," *New York Times*, September 23, 1929, *New York Times* online archive 1851–1980 <http://query.nytimes.com/search/query? srchst=p> [June 25, 2006].
51. "Harry Pollard Enthusiastic Over Islands."
52. News item, *Honolulu Advertiser*, January 9, 1930 (morning), Pollard Papers, Box 3, folder 4.
53. "Harry Pollard Enthusiastic Over Islands."
54. Milton Meltzer, *Brother, Can You Spare a Dime?: The Great Depression 1929–1933* (New York: Facts on File, 1991), 19, 28, 30–31.
55. Bernard F. Dick, *City of Dreams: The Making and Remaking of Universal Pictures* (Lexington: University Press of Kentucky, 1997), 74–75. Dick points out that Universal's 1932 loss was actually minor compared to that of other studios: Paramount, for example, lost $21 million; and Fox, Warners, and RKO all lost more than $10 million. Only MGM posted a profit ($8 million), but even this was down by one-third from the profit of 1931.
56. Lambert, 152–53.
57. Margarita Kotselis interview.
58. Florence Lawrence, review of *The Romantic Young Lady*, *Los Angeles Examiner*, March 11, 1930, Fischer Papers, Box 18, folder 12. Kelly R. Brown, biographer of the actress Florence Lawrence, describes a meeting in mid-1921 "between Florence and her name-alike, Florence Lawrence, a very popular and successful critic for the *Los Angeles Examiner*. The resulting article was hilarious. The newspaper critic complained that people were always telling her that she did not photograph well, and the 'Biograph beauty' told her about how people were always letting her have it for not giving them better coverage for pictures." See Brown, 121–22, 141. The critic Lawrence's success persisted at least until the 1930s, when she reviewed Margarita Fischer; by that time the actress Lawrence was eking out an unhappy living playing bit roles and extra parts.
59. "No Permanence to Retirement: Marguerita [sic] Fischer Back in Limelight," *Los Angeles Times*, March 16, 1930, sec. III, p. 13, 20, Fischer Papers, Box 18, folder 12.
60. Ibid.
61. Fifteenth Census of the United States, 1930: Los Angeles County, California Population Schedule. The census also lists a servant, a fifty-eight-year-old woman of Irish descent named Nello W. Wallie, living with the pair. A different Los Angeles population schedule shows the household of Dorothy Pyle (reporting her age as thirty-seven, but actually about forty-six) and Kate Fischer, sixty-seven (also untrue, if she truly was married at twenty-four as she reported). The elderly Kate was not working; Dorothy was employed as a secretary to a private family, but the two were probably both still supported at least partially by Margarita. The family's continual revision of their ages has created

confusion about their birthdates, especially Harry Pollard's. When referred to in works of film history, his year of birth is often listed as 1883, rather than as the correct 1879.

62. Florence Lawrence, review of *The Imaginary Invalid, Los Angeles Examiner*, April 23, 1930, sec. II, p. 2, Fischer Papers, Box 18, folder 12; Florence Lawrence, review of *Dancing Days, Los Angeles Examiner*, October 4, 1930, Fischer Papers, Box 18, folder 12.

63. Margarita Kotselis interview.

64. "Actress of Silent Days Visits Shanghai."

65. Margarita Kotselis interview.

66. Information about Fischer's and Pollard's life at the Rancho is available on-site; the house is today owned by the City of Vista and operated as a historic site.

67. "Actress of Silent Days Visits Shanghai."

68. Margarita Kotselis interview.

69. Betty Lopez to Margarita Fischer, October 18, 1969, Fischer Papers, Box 1, folder 24.

70. Joan Crawford with Jane Kesner Ardmore, *A Portrait of Joan: The Autobiography of Joan Crawford* (Garden City, NY: Doubleday & Company, 1962), 69.

71. *Hollywood Revue of 1929* (1929), dir. Charles Reisner, 116 minutes, *The Dawn of Sound*, sides 1 and 2, MGM/UA Home Video, 1992, videodisc.

72. Alexander Walker, *Joan Crawford: The Ultimate Star* (New York: Harper & Row, 1983), 64.

73. Crawford, 69.

74. Rancho tour information and article "Margarita Fischer Pollard and Harry Pollard."

75. "Former 'American Beauty Girl.'"

76. "'Southerner' a Real Treat," *Hollywood Reporter*, January 9, 1931, 3, Pollard Papers, Box 3, folder 5.

77. "'The Southerner' Charming, but Not Great Entertainment for the Masses," *Hollywood Daily Screen World*, January 9, 1931, Pollard Papers, Box 3, folder 5.

78. Barrios, 331. Barrios attributes the film's lack of success to Pollard's direction, which he finds stultifying. However, the abrupt cutting, star Lawrence Tibbett's limited acting ability, and (as Barrios admits) poorly developed script were probably the major causes, as they undermined the sense of the film.

79. "'Southerner' a Real Treat."

80. *Shipmates* (1931), dir. Harry A. Pollard, 72 minutes, Turner Classic Movies broadcast, videocassette.

81. Review of *Shipmates, Hollywood Daily Screen World*, March 26, 1931, 2, Pollard Papers, Box 3, folder 5; news item, *Hollywood Reporter*, June 5, 1931, Pollard Papers, Box 3, folder 5.

82. "'Shipmates' Adds Another to MGM's List of B.O. Hits," *Hollywood Reporter*, March 20, 1931, 3, Pollard Papers, Box 3, folder 5.

83. Mordaunt Hall, review of *When a Feller Needs a Friend, New York Times*, May 14, 1932, *New York Times* online archive 1851–1980 <http://query.nytimes.com/search/query?srchst=p> [June 25, 2006].

84. William J. Mann, *Wisecracker: The Life and Times of William Haines, Hollywood's First Openly Gay Star* (New York: Penguin Books, 1998), 205.

85. *Fast Life* (1932), dir. Harry A. Pollard, 82 minutes, Turner Classic Movies broadcast, videocassette.

86. Review of *Fast Life, Hollywood Reporter*, November 30, 1932, 3, Pollard Papers, Box 3, folder 5.

87. Mordaunt Hall, review of *Fast Life, New York Times*, December 24, 1932, *New York Times* online archive 1851–1980 <http://query.nytimes.com/search/query?srchst=p> [June 25, 2006].

88. Mann, 200–02, 206–08.

89. Ibid., 208.

90. Ibid., 214.

91. Charles Higham, *Merchant of Dreams: Louis B. Mayer, MGM, and the Secret Hollywood* (New York: Donald I. Fine, 1993), 195.

92. Flamini, 174–75.

93. Margarita Kotselis interview.

94. Pierce, "'Carl Laemmle's Outstanding Achievement.'"

95. Obituary for Harry Pollard, *New York Times*, July 7, 1934, 13, *New York Times* online archive 1851–1980 <http://query.nytimes.com/search/query?srchst=p> [August 2, 2006].

96. "Harry A. Pollard Left $145,000," *New York Times*, August 13, 1934, 9, *New York Times* online archive 1851–1980 <http://query.nytimes.com/search/query?srchst=p> [August 2, 2006].

97. Fischer to Uselton.

98. "Actress of Silent Days Visits Shanghai."

Chapter 12

1. *Dominos Monthly Bulletin*, sporadic issues from November 1933 to September 1937, Fischer Papers, Box 18, folder 10. Margarita's picnic was described in an undated news item clipped to the June 1937 Dominos bulletin.

2. Margarita Fischer to Anna Fischer, July 5, 1936, Fischer Papers, Box 1, folder 18.

3. Margarita Kotselis interview.

4. "Former 'American Beauty Girl.'"

5. Margarita Fischer to Anna Fischer, July 5, 1936.

6. Travel itinerary, Mrs. Annette Brock Private European Tours, [1936], Fischer Papers, Box 1, folder 18.

7. Margarita Fischer to Anna Fischer, letter of July 20, 1936, Fischer Papers, Box 1, folder 18.

8. Margarita Fischer to Anna Fischer, postcard of July 20, 1936, Fischer Papers, Box 1, folder 18; Margarita Fischer to Anna Fischer, [July 31?], 1936, Fischer Papers, Box 1, folder 18.

9. "Former 'American Beauty Girl.'"

10. George B. Brownell to Margarita Fischer, August 12, 1936, Fischer Papers, Box 17, folder 2.

11. Robert R. Nathan, "National Income Gain in 1936 Largest in Recovery Period," *Survey of Current Business*, June 1937, 11–17, <http://library.bea.gov/cgibin/showfile.exe?CISOROOT=/SCB&CISOPTR=3018&CISOMODE=print> [March 8, 2007].

12. Invoice from Annette Brock, [May] 1936, Fischer Papers, Box 17, folder 8.

13. Margarita Fischer to Anna Fischer, September 5, 1936, Fischer Papers, Box 1, folder 18.

14. "Actress of Silent Days Visits Shanghai."

15. Ibid.

16. "Former 'American Beauty Girl.'"

17. "Margarita Fischer Pollard and Harry Pollard"; "Historic Vista Ranch Sale Announced," *Los Angeles Times*, October 28, 1951, courtesy of Geoff Williams; Margarita Kotselis interview.

18. Ibid.; Margarita Kotselis to author, e-mail of February 5, 2007.

19. "Margarita Fischer Pollard and Harry Pollard"; "Historic Vista Ranch Sale Announced," *Los Angeles Times*, October 28, 1951, courtesy of Geoff Williams; Fischer to Uselton.

20. Margarita Kotselis interview.
21. Biographical Note to the Fischer Papers.
22. "Margarita Fischer Pollard and Harry Pollard."
23. Margarita Kotselis interview.
24. Kay Latson to Margarita Fischer, September 25, 1966, Fischer Papers, Box 1, folder 25.
25. Christmas card from Jim Oyler to Margarita Fischer, [1965?–1969?], Fischer Papers, Box 1, folder 24; Betty Lopez to Margarita Fischer.
26. Margarita Kotselis interview; Emeline Koslik to Margarita Fischer, January 4, 1967, Fischer Papers, Box 1, folder 24.
27. Margarita Kotselis interview.
28. J.B. "Jimmie" Sunderland to Margarita Fischer, [1966], Fischer Papers, Box 1, folder 25.
29. Ibid.; J.B. "Jimmie" Sunderland to Margarita Fischer, July 11, 1966, Fischer Papers, Box 1, folder 25.
30. J.B. "Jimmie" Sunderland to Margarita Fischer, June 18, 1966, Fischer Papers, Box 1, folder 25.
31. Note from Margarita Fischer on envelope of July 17, 1966, Fischer Papers, Box 1, folder 25.
32. Margarita Kotselis interview.
33. Ibid.
34. Ibid.
35. Margarita Kotselis to author, e-mail of May 16, 2007.
36. Margarita Kotselis interview.
37. Personal cards, Fischer Papers, Box 1, folder 18.
38. Personal cards, Fischer Papers, Box 1, folder 18.
39. "View From a Local Vantage Point: Comeback," A. H. Weiler, *New York Times*, October 5, 1958, X7, *New York Times* online archive 1851–1980 <http://query.nytimes.com/search/query?srchst=p> [August 2, 2006].
40. "News of TV and Radio: *Uncle Tom*," Val Adams, *New York Times*, February 5, 1961, X15, *New York Times* online archive 1851–1980 *http://query.nytimes.com/search/query?srchst=p* [August 2, 2006].
41. Virginia Grey to Margarita Fischer, June 23, 1965, Fischer Papers, Box 18, folder 21.
42. Undated description of table runner set by Margarita Fischer, Box 1, folder 18; Kathrine Pyle Havens to Hedda Hopper, [April? 1965]; Hedda Hopper to Kathrine Pyle Havens, April 20, 1965, Fischer Papers, Box 1, folder 19.
43. Roi Uselton to Margarita Fischer, October 10, 1967, to April 27, 1968, Fischer Papers, Box 1, folder 22; Frank Flack to Margarita Fischer, July 3, 1968, to July 12, 1968, Fischer Papers, Box 1, folder 16.
44. Gregory L. Williams, par. 21.
45. Margarita Fischer interview.
46. "Former 'American Beauty Girl'"; Fischer to Uselton.
47. Margarita Fischer interview.
48. Ibid.
49. Ibid.
50. Dorothy Fischer Pyle to Margarita Fischer, [early 1960s], Fischer Papers, Box 1, folder 18.
51. Dorothy Fischer Pyle obituary, *Los Angeles Times*, February 10, 1964. Courtesy of Geoff Williams.
52. Undated note regarding hearing aid from Joseph Small Office, Fischer Papers, Box 1, folder 18; Prescription envelope, 1962–68, Fischer Papers, Box 18, folder 13.
53. Margarita Kotselis to author, e-mail of May 16, 2007.
54. Kay Latson to Margarita Fischer, July 13, 1967, Fischer Papers, Box 1, folder 24; Betty Lopez to Margarita Fischer.
55. Personal note, [1965?], Fischer Papers, Box 1, folder 18.
56. Margarita Fischer to Mrs. William E. Borah.
57. Margarita Kotselis to author, e-mails of May 16, 2007, and May 18, 2007.
58. Margarita Kotselis interview.
59. Doyle, 22. Oddly enough, several sources consulted list the year of Fischer's death as 1973, but the later date is confirmed by the Social Security Death Index.
60. Because Margarita's remains were cremated, she was not interred next to her husband. For the curious, Pollard's grave lies in the Great Mausoleum's Sanctuary of Praise, crypt 5350, while Margarita is buried in the Freedom Mausoleum's Columbarium of Independence, niche 33782. Both graves list the correct birthdates for the pair—1879 and 1886.
61. Margarita Kotselis interview. Kotselis recalled that Field had passed away shortly after Margarita Fischer; the Social Security Death index (accessed via http://ssdi.rootsweb.com/) provides the month and year of death.
62. Kathrine Fischer Havens to James H. Thomas, September 22, 1980, Fischer Papers, donor file.
63. Kathrine P. Havens record, Social Security Death Index.

Chapter 13

1. Iris Barry, 94.
2. Margarita Fischer interview.
3. Anita Loos, *The Talmadge Girls: A Memoir* (New York: Viking Press, 1978), 6.
4. David Pierce, "The Legion of the Condemned—Why American Silent Films Perished," *Film History* 9, no. 1 (1997): 6, 7, 10, 12.
5. See Golden, 238–39, for an account of the destruction of Fox's vault and an analysis of Bara's legacy.
6. The *Catalog of Copyright Entries, Motion Pictures 1912–1939* lists 409 copyright applications for the American Film Manufacturing Company and 97 for the American Film Company. It is very likely that some of Margarita Fischer's work survives in the paper prints deposited in association with these copyright applications. However, author Timothy James Lyons states that the paper prints are "relatively useless" for the viewer who would like to get a sense of film narrative. He explains, "The paper prints submitted by American contained only stills from various scenes, mostly in an illogical order, possibly the order in which they were developed. These can serve only to offer some idea of the 'look' of the films rather than any analytical possibilities." See Lyons, 133.
7. *A Midsummer's Love Tangle* is held by the Museum of Modern Art in New York City, and *Robinson Crusoe* survives in London's Cinema Museum. The condition of these films is not known.
8. A partially deteriorated print of *K—the Unknown* (1924) survives in a private collection in Europe, and at least a portion of *The Devil's Assistant* (1917) may also survive in a private collection.
9. Cameras today, when they are not altogether digital, use either a 35mm or a 2¼ × 2¼ inch negative. In Margarita Fischer's day, a still photographer used an 8 x 10 inch negative, which permits the image to be blown up very large with no loss of quality. Most film stills in the Fischer papers are themselves 8 x 10 inches at most, and do not "show off" the capability of the large negative. However, the Fischer Papers do contain large portraits of the actress which are of beautiful quality. See Brownlow, *Mary Pickford*

Rediscovered, 55, for further detail on silent film portraiture and set photography.

10. Loos, 1.

11. Everson, 14–15.

12. Everson, 5. Everson offers Bessie Barrisdale and Dorothy Dalton as examples of such once popular but "now almost forgotten" actresses. The former actress's surname was actually Barriscale, according to other sources — a true testament to how much her star has faded.

13. Ramsaye, 717.

14. Diane Negra, "Introduction: Female Stardom and Early Film History," *Camera Obscura* 48 (2001): 2.

15. Basinger, 3, 4.

16. Slide, *Silent Feminists*, xi.

Bibliography

Primary Sources

Belletti, Valeria. *Adventures of a Hollywood Secretary*, edited and introduced by Cari Beauchamp. Berkeley: University of California Press, 2006.

The Birth of a Nation (1915). Directed by D. W. Griffith. 180 min. Madacy Entertainment, 2001. Videodisc.

Brooks, Louise. *Lulu in Hollywood*. New York: Alfred A. Knopf, 1982.

Crawford, Joan, with Jane Kesner Ardmore. *A Portrait of Joan: The Autobiography of Joan Crawford*. Garden City, NY: Doubleday & Company, 1962.

D'Ennery, Adolphe, and Fernand Cormon. *A Celebrated Case: A Drama in Prologue and Four Acts*. New York: Samuel French, n.d.

Draga, the Gypsy (1913). Director unknown. 15 min. Library of Congress. Videodisc.

Fast Life (1932). Directed by Harry A. Pollard. 82 min. Turner Classic Movies broadcast. Videocassette.

Fifteenth Census of the United States, 1930: Los Angeles County, California Population Schedule and Marion County, Oregon Population Schedule. Available from Ancestry.com. 2001–2004. Database online. Indexed by Ancestry.com from microfilmed schedules of the 1930 U.S. Federal Decennial Census. Data imaged from National Archives and Records Administration, 1930 Federal Population Census, Washington, D.C.: National Archives and Records Administration.

Fischer, Margarita. Interview by Robert S. Birchard, [1970?]. Tape recording.

A Fool There Was (1915). Directed by Frank Powell. 66 min. Kino Video, 2002. Videocassette.

Fourteenth Census of the United States, 1920: Santa Barbara County, California Population Schedule. Available from Ancestry.com. 2001–2004. Database online. Indexed by Ancestry.com from microfilmed schedules of the 1920 U.S. Federal Decennial Census. Data imaged from National Archives and Records Administration, 1920 Federal Population Census, Washington, D.C.: National Archives and Records Administration.

Gish, Lillian. *The Movies, Mr. Griffith, and Me*. Englewood Cliffs, NJ: Prentice-Hall, [1969].

Griffith, Mrs. D.W. [Linda Arvidson]. *When the Movies Were Young*. New York: Benjamin Blom, 1925. Reprint, New York: Benjamin Blom, 1968.

Harry Pollard Papers. MS 81-5. Department of Special Collections, Ablah Library, Wichita State University, Wichita, Kansas.

Hollywood Revue of 1929 (1929). Directed by Charles Reisner. 116 min. *The Dawn of Sound*, sides 1–2. MGM/UA Home Video, 1992. Videodisc.

How Men Propose (1913). Produced and directed(?) by Lois Weber. 6 min. *America's First Women Filmmakers*, vol. 6, *The Origins of Film (1900–1926)*. Unapix Consumer Products, 1995. Videocassette.

Introduction by Will Hays (1926). Director unknown. 4 min. Turner Classic Movies broadcast. Videocassette.

Kotselis, Margarita Dorothy. Interview by author, May 25, 2006, Wichita, Kansas [via telephone]. Tape recording.

Margarita Fischer Papers. MS 81-4. Department of Special Collections, Ablah Library, Wichita State University, Wichita, Kansas.

The Merry Wives of Windsor (1910). Directed by Francis Boggs [?]. 8 min. Library of Congress. Videodisc.

A Movie Star (1916). Directed by Fred Fishback. 25 min. *Slapstick Encyclopedia*, vol. 2. *Keystone Tonight!: Mack Sennett Comedies*. Image Entertainment, 2002. Videodisc.

Ninth Census of the United States, 1870: McLean County, Illinois Population Schedule. Available from Ancestry.com. 2001–2004. Database online. Indexed by Ancestry.com from microfilmed schedules of the 1870 U.S. Federal Decennial Census. Data imaged from National Archives and Records Administration, 1870 Federal Population Census, Washington, D.C.: National Archives and Records Administration.

The Quest (1915). Directed by Harry A. Pollard. 15 min [fragment]. Library of Congress. Videodisc.

Shipmates (1931). Directed by Harry A. Pollard. 72 min. Turner Classic Movies broadcast. Videocassette.

Show Boat (1929). Directed by Harry A. Pollard. 105 min. Turner Classic Movies broadcast. Videocassette.
Stowe, Harriet Beecher. *Uncle Tom's Cabin* (New York: Random House, 1996).
Swanson, Gloria. *Swanson on Swanson: An Autobiography*. New York: Random House, 1980.
Tenth Census of the United States, 1880: Republic County, Kansas Population Schedule. Available from Ancestry.com. 2001–2004. Database online. Index compiled by The Church of Jesus Christ of Latter-day Saints.
Uncle Tom's Cabin (1927). Directed by Harry A. Pollard. 112 min. Kino Video, 1999. Videodisc.
Where Are My Children? (1916). Directed by Lois Weber. 62 min. Turner Classic Movies broadcast. Videocassette.
Wood, Mrs. Henry. *East Lynne*. In *S.R.O.: The Most Successful Plays in the History of the American Stage*, ed. Bennett Cerf and Van H. Cartmell. Garden City, NY: Doubleday, Doran, & Company, 1944.

Secondary Sources

"Achievements in Public Health, 1900–1999: Family Planning." *MMWR* 48 (December 1999): 1073–80.
Addison, Heather. "Capitalizing Their Charms: Cinema Stars and Physical Culture in the 1920s." *Velvet Light Trap* 50 (2002): 15–35.
American Film Institute. *AFI Catalog: Silent Films*. 2002. <http://www.afi.com/members/catalog/silentHome.aspx?s=1&bhcp=1>.
Ankerich, Michael G. "Billie Dove." In *The Sound of Silence: Conversations with 16 Film and Stage Personalities Who Bridged the Gap Between Silents and Talkies*. Jefferson, NC: McFarland & Company, 1998.
Ball, Robert Hamilton. *Shakespeare on Silent Film: A Strange Eventful History*. New York: Theatre Arts Books, 1968.
Banner, Lois W. *Women in Modern America: A Brief History*, 2nd ed. San Diego: Harcourt Brace Jovanovich, 1984.
Barrios, Richard. *A Song in the Dark: The Birth of the Musical Film*. New York: Oxford University Press, 1995.
Barry, Iris. *Let's Go to the Movies*. New York: Payson & Clarke, 1926. Reprint, New York: Arno Press, 1972.
Barry, John M. *The Great Influenza: The Epic Story of the Deadliest Plague in History*. New York: Viking, 2004.
Basinger, Jeanine. *Silent Stars*. New York: Alfred A. Knopf, 1999.
Bean, Jennifer M. "Technologies of Early Stardom and the Extraordinary Body." *Camera Obscura* 48 (2001): 9–56.
Beauchamp, Cari. *Without Lying Down: Frances Marion and the Powerful Women of Early Hollywood*. Berkeley: University of California Press, 1997.
Blum, Daniel. *A Pictorial History of the Silent Screen*. New York: Grosset & Dunlap, 1953.
Bowser, Eileen. *The Transformation of Cinema, 1907–1915. History of the American Cinema*, ed. Charles Harpole, vol. 2. New York: Charles Scribner's Sons, 1990.
Braff, Richard E. *The Universal Silents: A Filmography of the Universal Motion Picture Manufacturing Company, 1912–1929*. Jefferson, NC: McFarland & Company, 1999.
Brown, Kelly R. *Florence Lawrence, The Biograph Girl: America's First Movie Star*. Jefferson, NC: McFarland & Company, 1999.
Brownlow, Kevin. "Annus Mirabilis: The Film in 1927." *Film History* 17 (2005): 168–78.
_____. *Mary Pickford Rediscovered: Rare Pictures of a Hollywood Legend*. New York: Harry N. Abrams, 1999.
_____. *The Parade's Gone By....* Berkeley: University of California Press, 1968.
Ceram, C.W. *Archaeology of the Cinema*. New York: Harcourt, Brace, & World, [1965].
Clara Bow: Discovering the 'It' Girl. Directed by Hugh Munro Neely. 65 min. Timeline Films, 1999. Videodisc.
Cohen, Paula Marantz. *Silent Film and the Triumph of the American Myth*. New York: Oxford University Press, 2001.
Dance, Robert, and Bruce Robertson. *Ruth Harriet Louise and Hollywood Glamour Photography*. Berkeley: University of California Press, 2002.
DeCordova, Richard. *Picture Personalities: The Emergence of the Star System in America*. Chicago: University of Illinois Press, 1990.
Dick, Bernard F. *City of Dreams: The Making and Remaking of Universal Pictures*. Lexington: University Press of Kentucky, 1997.
Doyle, Billy H. *The Ultimate Directory of the Silent Screen Performers: A Necrology of Births and Deaths and Essays on 50 Lost Players*. Metuchen, NJ: Scarecrow Press, 1995.
Dumaux, Sally A. *King Baggot: A Biography and Filmography of the First King of the Movies*. Jefferson, NC: McFarland & Company, 2002.
Dyer, Richard. *Stars*. London: British Film Institute, 1979.
Edmonds, I.G. *Big U: Universal in the Silent Days*. New York: A.S. Barnes, 1977.
Enstad, Nan. "Dressed for Adventure: Working Women and Silent Movie Serials in the 1910s." *Feminist Studies* 21, no. 1 (1995): 67–90.
Erdman, Andrew L. *Blue Vaudeville: Sex, Morals and*

the Mass Marketing of Amusement, 1895–1915. Jefferson, NC: McFarland & Company, 2004.

Everson, William K. *American Silent Film*. New York: Oxford University Press, 1978. Reprint, New York: Da Capo Press, 1998.

Eyman, Scott. *The Speed of Sound: Hollywood and the Talkie Revolution, 1926–1930*. New York: Simon & Schuster, 1997.

Flamini, Roland. *Thalberg: The Last Tycoon and the World of M-G-M*. New York: Crown Publishers, Inc., 1994.

Fox, Charles Donald. *Famous Film Folk: A Gallery of Life Portraits and Biographies*. New York: George H. Doran Co., 1925.

_____, and Milton L. Silver, eds. *Who's Who on the Screen*. New York: Ross Publishing Co., 1920. Reprint, New York: Gordon Press, 1976.

Freeburg, Victor Oscar. *Pictorial Beauty on the Screen*. New York: n.p., 1923. Reprint, New York: Benjamin Blom, 1972.

Gamson, Joshua. *Claims to Fame: Celebrity in Contemporary America*. Berkeley: University of California Press, 1994.

Gilbert, Douglas. *American Vaudeville: Its Life and Times*. New York: Whittlesey House, McGraw-Hill Book Company, 1940.

Goldberg, Ronald Allen. *America in the Twenties*. Syracuse, NY: Syracuse University Press, 2003.

Golden, Eve. *Vamp: The Rise and Fall of Theda Bara*. Vestal, NY: Emprise Publishing, 1996.

Grau, Robert. *The Theatre of Science*. New York: Benjamin Blom, 1914.

Grieveson, Lee. *Policing Cinema: Movies and Censorship in Early-Twentieth-Century America*. Berkeley: University of California Press, 2004.

Hampton, Benjamin B. *History of the American Film Industry from Its Beginnings to 1931*. New York: Dover Publications, 1970. Reprint of *A History of the Movies*, New York: Covici, Friede, 1931.

Hanners, John. *"It Was Play or Starve": Acting in the Nineteenth-Century American Popular Theater*. Bowling Green, Ohio: Bowling Green State University Popular Press, 1993.

Hansen, Miriam. *Babel and Babylon: Spectatorship in American Silent Film*. Cambridge: Harvard University Press, 1991.

Herbert, Stephen, and Luke McKernan, eds. *Who's Who of Victorian Cinema*. London: British Film Institute, 1996.

Higashi, Sumiko. *Virgins, Vamps, and Flappers: The American Silent Movie Heroine*. St. Albans, VT: Eden Press Women's Publications, 1978.

Higham, Charles. *Merchant of Dreams: Louis B. Mayer, MGM, and the Secret Hollywood*. New York: Donald I. Fine, 1993.

Hofstadter, Richard, ed. *The Progressive Movement, 1900–1915*. Englewood Cliffs, NJ: Prentice-Hall, 1963.

Holmes, Sean P. "The Hollywood Star System and the Regulation of Actors' Labour, 1916–1934." *Film History* 12 (2000): 97–114.

Hutchinson, Ron. "The Vitaphone Project. Answering Harry Warner's Question: 'Who the Hell Wants to Hear Actors Talk?'" *Film History* 14, no. 1 (2002): 40–46.

Jobes, Gertrude. *Motion Picture Empire*. Hamden, CT: Archon Books, 1966.

Johnson, Claudia D. *American Actress: Perspective on the Nineteenth Century*. Chicago: Nelson-Hall, 1984.

Jowett, Garth S. "The First Motion Picture Audiences," in *Film Before Griffith*, ed. John L. Fell, 196–206. Berkeley: University of California Press, 1983.

Kessler-Harris, Alice. *Out to Work: A History of Wage-Earning Women in the United States*. New York: Oxford University Press, 1982.

Kleinberg, S.J. *Women in the United States: 1830–1945*. New Brunswick, NJ: Rutgers University Press, 1999.

Koszarski, Richard. *An Evening's Entertainment, 1915–1928*. History of the American Cinema, ed. Charles Harpole, vol. 3. New York: Charles Scribner's Sons, 1990.

_____. "Flu Season: *Moving Picture World* Reports on Pandemic Influenza, 1918–19." *Film History* 17, no. 4 (2005): 466–85.

Kuhn, Annette. *Cinema, Censorship, and Sexuality, 1909–1925*. London: Routledge, 1988.

Lahue, Kalton. *Continued Next Week: A History of the Moving Picture Serial*. Norman: University of Oklahoma Press, 1964.

_____, ed. *Motion Picture Pioneer: The Selig Polyscope Company*. New York: A. S. Barnes, 1973.

Lambert, Gavin. *Norma Shearer*. New York: Alfred A. Knopf, 1990.

Lescarboura, Austin. *Behind the Motion Picture Screen*. New York: [Scientific American Publishing Company], 1919; reprint, New York: Benjamin Blom, 1971.

Lindsay, Vachel. *The Art of the Moving Picture*. New York: MacMillan Company, 1922, 2nd ed. Reprint, New York: Liveright Publishing Corporation, 1970.

Loos, Anita. *The Talmadge Girls: A Memoir*. New York: Viking Press, 1978.

Lowrey, Carolyn. *The First One Hundred Noted Men and Women of the Screen*. New York: Moffat, Yard, & Co., 1920.

Lyons, Timothy James. *The Silent Partner: The History of the American Film Manufacturing Company, 1910–1921*. New York: Arno Press, 1974.

MacIntyre, F. Gwynplaine. Review of *K—the Unknown*, May 28, 2003. Internet Movie Database.

1990–2004. <http://www.imdb.com/title/tt0015030/> [September 3, 2004].

Macoboy, Stirling. "American Beauty," in *The Ultimate Rose Book*. New York: Harry N. Abrams, Inc., [1993].

Mann, William J. *Wisecracker: The Life and Times of William Haines, Hollywood's First Openly Gay Star*. New York: Penguin Books, 1998.

Marshall, P. David. *Celebrity and Power: Fame in Contemporary Culture*. Minneapolis: University of Minnesota Press, 1997.

May, Lary. *Screening Out the Past: The Birth of Mass Culture and the Motion Picture Industry*. New York: Oxford University Press, 1980.

Meltzer, Milton. *Brother, Can You Spare a Dime?: The Great Depression 1929–1933*. New York: Facts on File, 1991.

Miller, Blair. *American Silent Film Comedies: An Illustrated Encyclopedia of Persons, Studios and Terminology*. Jefferson, NC: McFarland & Company, 1995.

Mix, Paul E. *The Life and Legend of Tom Mix*. Cranbury, NJ: A.S. Barnes, 1972.

Münsterberg, Hugo. *The Film, a Psychological Study: The Silent Photoplay in 1916*. New York: D. Appleton, 1916. Reprint, New York: Dover Publications, 1970.

Nathan, Robert R. "National Income Gain in 1936 Largest in Recovery Period," *Survey of Current Business*, June 1937, 11–17, <http://library.bea.gov/cgibin/showfile.exe?CISOROOT=/SCB&CISOPTR=3018&CISOMODE=print> [March 8, 2007].

Negra, Diane. "Introduction: Female Stardom and Early Film History." *Camera Obscura* 48 (2001): 1–7.

Nelson, Al P., and Mel R. Jones. *A Silent Siren Song: The Aitken Brothers' Hollywood Odyssey, 1905–1926*. New York: Cooper Square Press, 2000.

Oderman, Stuart. *Lillian Gish: A Life on Stage and Screen*. Jefferson, NC: McFarland & Company, 2000.

Parish, James Robert. *The Hollywood Book of Scandals*. New York: McGraw-Hill, 2004.

Pierce, David. "'Carl Laemmle's Outstanding Achievement': Harry Pollard and the Struggle to Film *Uncle Tom's Cabin*." *Film History* 10, no. 4 (1998): 459–476.

_____. "The Legion of the Condemned—Why American Silent Films Perished." *Film History* 9, no. 1 (1997): 5–22.

Pratt, George C. *Spellbound in Darkness: A History of the Silent Film*. Greenwich, CT: New York Graphic Society, 1973.

Railton, Stephen. "Harry Pollard and Uncle Tom, Act 1: The Imp Film, 1913," *Uncle Tom's Cabin* in American Culture. 1998–2007. <http://www.iath.virginia.edu/utc/onstage/films/imphp.html> [April 22, 2007].

_____. "*Uncle Tom's Cabin* on Film," *Uncle Tom's Cabin* in American Culture. 1998–2005. http://www.iath.virginia.edu/utc/onstage/films/fihp.html [November 14, 2006].

Rainey, Buck. *The Strong, Silent Type: Over 100 Screen Cowboys, 1903–1930*. Jefferson, NC: McFarland & Company, 2004.

Ramsaye, Terry. *A Million and One Nights: A History of the Motion Picture Through 1925*. New York: Simon & Schuster, 1926; Simon & Schuster, 1964.

Robinson, David. *From Peep Show to Palace: The Birth of American Film*. New York: Columbia University Press, 1995.

Ryan, Mary P. "The Projection of a New Womanhood: The Movie Moderns in the 1920s," in *Our American Sisters: Women in American Life and Thought*, 2nd ed., ed. Jean E. Friedman and William G. Shade, 366–84. Boston: Allyn & Bacon, 1976.

Schlereth, Thomas J. *Victorian America: Transformations in Everyday Life, 1876–1915*. New York: HarperCollins, 1991; HarperPerennial, 1992.

Schneider, Dorothy, and Carl J. Schneider. *American Women in the Progressive Era, 1900–1920*. New York: Facts on File, 1993.

Scott, Evelyn F. *Hollywood When Silents Were Golden*. New York: McGraw-Hill Book Company, 1972.

Shifflet, Crandall. *Victorian America, 1876 to 1913*. Almanacs of American Life, ed. Richard Balkin. New York: Facts on File, 1996.

Shull, Michael Slade. *Radicalism in American Silent Films, 1909–1929: A Filmography and History*. Jefferson, NC: McFarland & Company, 2000.

Slide, Anthony. *Aspects of American Film History Prior to 1920*. Metuchen, NJ: Scarecrow Press, 1978.

_____. "Sheet Music of the Silent Stars." In *Silent Topics: Essays on Undocumented Areas of Silent Film*. Lanham, MD: Scarecrow Press, 2005.

_____. "The Silent Closet: Gays, Lesbians, and Silent Film." In *Silent Topics: Essays on Undocumented Areas of Silent Film*. Lanham, MD: Scarecrow Press, 2005.

_____. *The Silent Feminists: America's First Women Directors*. Lanham, MD: Scarecrow Press, 1996.

_____. "Those Elusive Budget Figures." In *Silent Topics: Essays on Undocumented Areas of Silent Film*. Lanham, MD: Scarecrow Press, 2005.

Smith, Andrew Brodie. *Shooting Cowboys and Indians: Silent Western Films, American Culture, and the Birth of Hollywood*. Boulder: University Press of Colorado, 2003.

Staiger, Janet. *Bad Women: Regulating Sexuality in Early American Cinema*. Minneapolis: University of Minnesota Press, 1995.

Stein, Charles W., ed. *American Vaudeville as Seen by Its Contemporaries*. New York: Alfred A. Knopf, 1984.

Stenn, David. *Clara Bow: Runnin' Wild*. New York: Cooper Square Press, 2000.

Stokes, Melvyn, and Richard Maltby, eds. *American Movie Audiences: From the Turn of the Century to the Early Sound Era*. London: British Film Institute, 1999.

Studlar, Gaylyn. "Oh, 'Doll Divine': Mary Pickford, Masquerade, and the Pedophilic Gaze." *Camera Obscura* 16, no. 3 (2001): 197–227.

_____. "The Perils of Pleasure? Fan Magazine Discourse as Women's Commodified Culture in the 1920s," in *Silent Film*. Richard Abel, ed. New Brunswick, NJ: Rutgers University Press, 1996, 263–97.

Thomas, James H. *The Bunion Derby: Andy Payne and the Great Transcontinental Footrace*. Oklahoma City: Southwestern Heritage Books, 1980.

"Timeline of the San Francisco Earthquake, April 18–23, 1906." *Virtual Museum of the City of San Francisco*. 1995–2004. <http://www.sfmuseum.org/hist10/06timeline.html> [March 4, 2007].

Vance, Jeffrey. *Chaplin: Genius of the Cinema*. New York: Harry N. Abrams, [2003].

Vardac, A. Nicholas. *Stage to Screen: Theatrical Method from Garrick to Griffith*. Cambridge: Harvard University Press, 1949.

Wagenknecht, Edward. *The Movies in the Age of Innocence*. Norman: University of Oklahoma Press, 1962.

Walker, Alexander. *Joan Crawford: The Ultimate Star*. New York: Harper & Row, 1983.

_____. *Stardom: The Hollywood Phenomenon*. New York: Stein & Day, 1970.

Wallace, Michele. "*Uncle Tom's Cabin*: Before and After the Jim Crow Era." *TDR* 44 (Spring 2000): 137–56.

Whitfield, Eileen. *Pickford: The Woman Who Made Hollywood*. Lexington: University Press of Kentucky, 1997.

Williams, Geoff. *C.C. Pyle's Amazing Foot Race: The True Story of the 1928 Coast-to-Coast Run Across America*. New York: Rodale, 2007.

Williams, Gregory L. "Filming San Diego: Hollywood's Backlot, 1898–2002." *Journal of San Diego History* 48, 2 (Spring 2002): par. 18. <http://www.sandiegohistory.org/journal/2002-2/filming.htm> [September 24, 2004].

Windeler, Robert. *Sweetheart: The Story of Mary Pickford*. London: W.H. Allen, 1973.

Wlaschin, Ken. *The Illustrated Encyclopedia of the World's Great Movie Stars and Their Films: From 1900 to the Present Day*. New York: Salamander Books, 1979.

WorldwideBoxoffice.com. <http://worldwideboxoffice.com/index.cgi?order=domestic&start=1927&finish=1927> [May 14, 2007].

Index

Abortion 70, 72, 74, 82, 83, 84
Academy Awards 130, 134, 147
Aitken, Harry 61, 62, 63, 87, 101
Alcazar Theatre 23
American Beauty (studio brand) 53, 55, 56, 58, 59, 60, 61, 70, 72, 81, 87, 102, 103, 161
American Film Company, Inc. 84, 85, 86, 87, 88, 90, 92, 94, 95, 97, 98, 99, 101, 102, 103, 105, 109, 110, 111, 112, 145, 156, 161; *see also* American Film Manufacturing Company
American Film Manufacturing Company 35, 40, 42, 51, 52, 53, 55, 56, 59, 61, 62, 63, 73, 74, 82, 84, 161; *see also* American Film Company, Inc.
American Mutoscope and Biograph Company 31, 43
Amy Woman 120
Ann's Finish 97, 98, 104
Arbuckle, Roscoe "Fatty" 112
Arvidson, Linda 30, 83

Baggot, King 39, 40, 42, 51, 61, 109
Bara, Theda 66, 69, 70, 108, 159, 161, 162, 163, 164
Beach of Dreams 110, 111
Belasco, David 17
Biograph Studio *see* American Mutoscope and Biograph Company
Birchard, Robert S. 157
The Birth of a Nation 61, 62, 127, 128
Borah, Mary 13
Borah, William E. 13
Borzage, Frank 48
Bow, Clara 114, 130, 133, 162, 164
Brooks, Louise 133, 160, 162
Brown, John Mack 140
Browning, Tod 89
The Butterfly Girl 77, 79, 80

Caruso, Enrico 34
A Celebrated Case 8, 15
Chaney, Lon 48
Chaplin, Charlie 74, 75, 76, 87, 101
Charge It to Me 105

Chicago 25, 26, 29, 32, 33, 52, 74
The Clansman see *The Birth of a Nation*
Cooper, Jackie 146, 147
Crawford, Joan 140, 145
Crystal Film Co. 51

The Dangerous Talent 109
DeMille, Cecil B. 35, 114
Denny, Reginald 114, 116, 117, 118, 121, 133
The Devil's Assistant 79, 80, 82, 107
The Divinity of Motherhood 60, 70, 72
Don Juan 131
Draga, the Gypsy 46, 48, 51, 52, 63, 161
The Dragon 76, 77, 107, 162

East Lynne 13, 14
Edison, Thomas 28, 29
Edison Studio 30, 40, 122
Equitable Motion Pictures Corporation 76, 77
Essanay Film Manufacturing Company 32, 74, 75, 76
Eureka, California 16, 17, 23

Fair Enough 103, 106
Fan magazines 43, 44, 57, 61, 66, 108, 127, 156, 163
Fast Life 146, 147
Fellowes, Rockliffe 117
Ferber, Edna 134, 135
Field, Arthur 135, 144, 152, 155, 157, 158
Film industry 28, 30, 39, 46, 70, 99, 101, 112, 113, 148, 162, 163; in Arizona 35, 42, 52; in California 29, 33, 34, 42, 43, 48, 63, 77, 87, 93, 101, 124, 125, 163; censorship of 29, 74, 113, 148; in Chicago 26, 29, 32, 33, 42, 52; conversion to sound filmmaking 131, 132, 133, 134, 135, 136, 138, 160; distribution systems within 28, 39, 40, 42, 62, 101, 102; on East Coast 42, 63, 75, 101, 110; stardom within 31, 43, 44, 103, 108, 109, 114, 128, 129, 159, 160, 163
First National Studio 101, 130, 132
Fischer, Anna 8, 134, 150

Fischer, Babe *see* Fischer, Margarita
Fischer, Dorothy *see* Pyle, Dorothy Fischer
Fischer, John 7, 8, 10, 11, 13, 14, 15, 16, 17, 18, 19, 20, 42, 93
Fischer, Kate 7, 8, 11, 16, 18, 19, 20, 21, 84, 90, 92, 93
Fischer, Kathie 16, 20, 21, 42, 55, 59, 60, 61, 64, 67, 84, 90, 92, 135, 150, 152, 155; *see also* Havens, Kathrine
Fischer, Margarita 7, 17, 23, 28, 85, 126, 151; and "American Beauty" nickname 53, 57, 81, 94, 95, 108, 114, 130; appearance of 8, 11, 15, 37, 46, 48, 51, 53, 56, 78, 81, 88, 106, 108, 114, 118, 129, 152; family relationships of 15, 16, 18, 19, 20, 21, 42, 59, 84, 90, 135, 150, 152, 155, 159, 164; fans of 19, 31, 35, 57, 81, 105, 106, 128, 134, 154; as film actress 30, 31, 45, 46, 50, 65, 66, 69, 71, 74, 108, 110, 117, 118, 120, 134, 156, 159, 160, 161, 162, 164; as film actress for American 35, 40, 52, 53, 55, 56, 57, 58, 59, 60, 61, 63, 64, 67, 70, 72, 86, 87, 89, 90, 92, 94, 95, 97, 98, 99, 101, 102, 103, 105, 106, 107, 109, 110, 111, 117, 157; as film actress for Equitable 76, 77; as film actress for Essanay 74, 75; as film actress for IMP/Universal 37, 38, 39, 40, 42, 45, 46, 48, 51, 64, 118, 120, 121, 122, 124, 129, 130; as film actress for Pollard Picture Plays 77, 78, 79, 80; as film actress for Selig 26, 32, 33, 42, 64, 66; films of *see* specific titles; friendships of 13, 145, 152, 154; health of 14, 82, 83, 84, 95, 99, 101, 154, 157, 158; hobbies and community service of 11, 58, 72, 87, 90, 92, 93, 94, 95, 144, 145, 150, 152, 153, 155; legacy of 156, 157, 159, 160, 161, 162, 164; relationship with Harry Pollard 25, 32, 34, 35, 38, 50, 58, 81, 82, 84, 88, 89, 90, 110, 111, 127, 130, 134, 135, 139, 140, 141, 143, 148, 149, 152, 159, 164;

personality of 11, 15, 16, 20, 31, 34, 75, 84, 114, 130, 139, 144; preoccupation with youth of 16, 35, 60, 61, 66, 108, 127, 144; publicity and media relations of 11, 14, 25, 26, 45, 53, 55, 57, 58, 64, 66, 73, 76, 77, 78, 79, 81, 87, 88, 89, 90, 93, 94, 97, 98, 99, 103, 104, 105, 106, 108, 109, 118, 127, 129, 134, 143, 144, 152; religion of 70, 155; salary of 20, 21, 26, 38, 69, 82, 84, 86, 102, 109; as stage actress 8, 10, 11, 13, 14, 18, 19, 21, 25, 26, 35, 37, 95, 122, 143, 144, 159; versatility as performer 13, 14, 46, 47, 69, 159
Fischer, Margaret *see* Fischer, Margarita
Fischer and Van Cleve's Players 11
Flapper as screen type 108, 113, 114
A Fool There Was 33, 66, 67, 163
Fox, William 40, 66
Fox Studio 66, 101, 131, 161
Freuler, John R. 52, 61, 62
Frohman Amusement Corporation 110

Garbo, Greta 67, 120, 130, 132
General Film Company 40, 42
George, Grace 26
Gibson, Hoot 116, 117
Gilbert, John 130, 133
The Girl and the Half-back 39, 40
The Girl from His Town 67, 69, 99
The Girl Who Couldn't Grow Up/Putting It Over 84, 86
Gish, Dorothy 43, 113
Gish, Lillian 43, 61, 62, 63, 101, 108, 113, 133, 163
Grange, Harold "Red" 135
Grauman, Sid 123
Great Day 145, 146
Great Depression 141, 142, 143, 148
Great War *see* World War I
Grey, Virginia 129, 130, 156
Griffith, D.W. 28, 30, 61, 62, 63, 83, 101, 108, 113, 127, 163
Griffith, Mrs. D.W. *see* Arvidson, Linda

Haines, William 147
Harlow, Jean 148
Havens, Kathrine 156, 157, 158
Hays, Will 113, 131
The Hellion 106, 107, 109, 162
The House of Toys 109, 145
How Men Propose 51, 52, 161
Hutchinson, Samuel 52, 61, 62, 63, 82, 84, 85, 86, 101, 102, 157

Impossible Susan 94, 97, 99
Ince, Thomas 63
Independent Films Association 109, 110
Independent Motion Picture Company (IMP) 31, 37, 39, 40, 42, 45, 51, 109, 112, 116, 122, 127, 148

Infatuation 71, 73
Influenza epidemic 99, 101
Inglis, Gus 84, 85
Ingraham, Lloyd 35, 50, 86, 90, 95
The Invisible Ray 110, 114

The Jazz Singer 21, 130, 131, 136
Jilted Janet 97, 98
Jolson, Al 21, 130, 131

K—The Unknown 118, 120
Kerry, Norman 93, 136
Kotselis, Margarita 152, 155

Laemmle, Carl 31, 37, 38, 39, 40, 42, 50, 77, 112, 116, 118, 121, 123, 126, 134, 135, 136, 138, 142
La Plante, Laura 117, 136, 139
Lasky Studio 101, 122
Lawrence, Florence 30, 31, 39, 43, 44, 51, 164
Leah, the Forsaken 14
The Leather Pushers 116, 142
Leonard, Robert Z. 48
A Lesson to Husbands 40, 42, 67
Lloyd Ingraham Stock Company 35, 37
The Lonesome Heart 67, 112
Los Angeles 59, 95, 109, 125, 135, 144
Lowe, James 123, 129, 130
Lumière brothers 28

The Mantle of Charity 103
Margarita Fischer Company 14, 15, 16, 17, 18, 23, 122
Margarita Fischer Productions 102, 109
Marion, Frances 42, 43
Mayer, Louis B. 116, 142, 145, 147, 148
McRae, Henry 121
The Merry Wives of Windsor 32, 33, 161
Metro-Goldwyn-Mayer Studio (MGM) 112, 116, 132, 142, 143, 144, 145, 146, 147, 148, 160
Metro Studio 101
Minter, Mary Miles 87, 101, 102, 112, 156
The Miracle of Life 72, 73, 74, 76, 80, 81, 84, 162
Miss Jackie of the Army 89, 90, 93, 95, 97, 98
Miss Jackie of the Navy 77, 78, 79, 89, 93, 97
Missouri Valley, Iowa 8
Molly Go Get 'Em 97, 98
Molly of the Follies 104, 105
Money Isn't Everything/Beauty to Let 102, 103
Montgomery, Robert 146
Moore, Colleen 113
Motion Picture Association of America 113, 131
Motion Picture Patents Company 28, 29, 31, 39, 40, 43, 59, 74

Motion Picture Producers and Distributors of America *see* Motion Picture Association of America
A Movie Star 44, 45
Movietone sound system ("sound on film") 131, 132, 134
Moving Picture World 44, 64, 65, 69, 73, 77, 98, 99, 103, 104
Mutual Film Corporation 42, 51, 61, 62, 63, 74, 76, 77, 87, 101, 103, 110
Mutual Masterpictures 62, 64, 67, 72, 87
Mutual Star Productions 77

National Association of Motion Picture Producers 101
National Association of the Motion Picture Industry 74
National Board of Censorship 29
Nazimova, Alla 67, 108
Negri, Pola 108
Nehls, R.R. 59
Nestor Studio 51
New York 25, 29, 75, 90, 109, 110, 124, 129, 135, 136, 150
Nolan, Mary 140
Normand, Mabel 57, 112

101 Bison Studio 51
Oregon 8, 11, 82, 83, 134
Over the Hills (to the Poorhouse) 38, 39

Paramount Studio 67, 113, 120, 132
Parker, F.W. 17, 18
Pathé Exchanges 102, 103
Payment Guaranteed 110
The Pearl of Paradise 77, 78, 81, 97, 110, 114, 156, 161
The Perils of Pauline 43
Photoplay 44, 57, 67, 114, 159, 162
Pickford, Mary 43, 44, 57, 67, 69, 70, 83, 87, 97, 103, 105, 108, 113, 130, 134, 159, 162, 164
Pollard, Harry A. 21, 25, 84, 86, 150; alcoholism of 21, 71, 82, 85, 89, 144, 148; as film actor 35, 38, 39, 42, 45, 46, 50, 55, 56, 58, 61, 63, 64, 65, 71, 75, 78, 122; as film director 50, 52, 55, 56, 60, 61, 63, 64, 65, 67, 69, 72, 76, 77, 78, 80, 81, 82, 84, 89, 110, 114, 116, 117, 118, 120, 121, 122, 123, 124, 125, 127, 129, 130, 132, 133, 134, 135, 136, 138, 139, 140, 141, 142, 143, 144, 145, 146, 147, 148, 159; personality of 21, 23, 45, 50, 75, 84, 139, 141; relationship with Margarita Fischer 25, 32, 34, 35, 38, 50, 58, 81, 82, 88, 89, 90, 110, 111, 127, 130, 134, 135, 139, 140, 141, 143, 148, 159; as stage actor 23, 26, 35, 37
Pollard, Harry "Snub" 21
Pollard, Margarita *see* Fischer, Margarita

Index

Pollard Picture Plays 77, 78, 79, 81, 82, 84, 86, 87, 89, 107, 113, 139, 161
Power, Tyrone, Sr. 74
The Primitive Woman 97, 98, 99
The Prodigal 146
Progressivism 29, 74, 90
Put Up Your Hands 105, 161
Pyle, Charles C. 16, 17, 18, 19, 20, 21, 23, 60, 134, 135, 152, 158
Pyle, Dorothy Fischer 8, 11, 15, 16, 17, 18, 19, 20, 21, 42, 55, 59, 60, 83, 84, 90, 92, 134, 150, 152, 153, 155, 157
Pyle, Kathrine *see* Fischer, Kathie

The Quest 61, 62, 63, 64, 65, 67, 69, 78, 97, 110, 161

Rancho Buena Vista adobe 144, 145, 147, 149, 150, 152, 153, 155
Ray, Mona 123, 124, 129
Realart Studio 102
Reid, Wallace 48, 112, 113
Rex Studio 51
The Road to Yesterday 35, 37
Robertson-Cole Distributing Corporation 110
The Rose of California 42, 45
Rubens, Alma 139
Russell, William 101

San Diego 77, 79, 82, 86, 93, 94, 156
San Francisco 20, 21, 23, 25, 58
Sanford, Walter 20, 21, 25
Santa Barbara, California 52, 53, 58, 59, 63, 85, 86, 90, 94, 156
Schildkraut, Joseph 136, 139
Scott, Mary *see* Pyle, Dorothy Fischer
Seigmann, George 127
Seiter, William 117
Selig, William 26, 29, 39
Selig Polyscope Company 26, 28, 29, 32, 33, 35, 40, 42, 43, 58, 66, 112, 161
Selznick, David O. 77, 148
Selznick, Lewis J. 77
Sennett, Mack 44, 63, 114

Serial films 43, 97, 110, 116, 163
Shakespeare, William: adaptations of work 33, 58
Shearer, Norma 116, 142, 145
Shipmates 146, 147
Shon, the Piper 48
Show Boat (1929 film) 134, 135, 136, 138, 139, 140, 142, 147
Show Boat (novel) 134, 135
Show Boat (stage play) 135, 136, 138
The Southerner 145, 146; see also *The Prodigal*
Sporting Youth 117, 118
A Square Deal 99
Storey, Edith 110
Stowe, Harriet Beecher 122, 125
Sunderland, J.B. "Jimmie" 154, 155
Swanson, Gloria 83, 108, 113, 114

Talmadge, Constance 108, 114, 133, 134, 162
Talmadge, Norma 108, 114, 133, 134, 162
Taylor, William Desmond 67, 102, 112
Terry, Alice 120
Thalberg, Irving 116, 142, 145, 146, 147, 148, 152
Theatre Margarita 17, 18, 19, 20, 23, 135
The Thirtieth Piece of Silver 109
Tibbett, Lawrence 146
The Tiger Lily 106
Tonight at Twelve 140, 142
The Trinity 40
Trixie from Broadway 106
"The Trust" *see* Motion Picture Patents Company
Turner, Otis 32, 48

Uncle Tom's Cabin (1927 film) 121, 123, 124, 125, 126, 127, 128, 129, 130, 132, 135, 136, 138, 139, 142, 156, 161
Uncle Tom's Cabin (other film versions) 46, 122, 127, 162
Uncle Tom's Cabin (novel) 122, 125
Uncle Tom's Cabin (stage play) 13, 121, 122

Undertow 140, 141, 142
Universal Film Manufacturing Company/Universal Studios 42, 43, 44, 46, 48, 50, 51, 52, 61, 77, 87, 89, 111, 112, 116, 117, 118, 120, 123, 124, 125, 126, 127, 129, 132, 134, 135, 138, 139, 141, 142, 147, 156, 160
Universal Jewels 116
Universal Super-Jewels 126

Valentino, Rudolph 108
Valli, Virginia 118, 120
Vamp as screen type 66, 67, 69, 108, 163
The Vampire 33, 40, 66, 67
Van, Beatrice 99, 157
Vaudeville 10, 67, 99
Victorian era 7, 14, 15, 43, 159, 164
Vista, California 144, 148, 150, 152, 153, 157, 158
Vitagraph Studios 110, 122
Vitaphone sound system ("sound on disc") 131, 132, 134, 139

Warner Brothers Studio 131
Weber, Lois 43, 48, 51, 74, 83, 113, 123
Westerns 33, 35, 116
When a Fellow Needs a Friend 146, 147
Where Are My Children? 74, 83
White, Pearl 43, 97
Wichita State University 158
Williams, Kathlyn 33, 43, 57, 97
Willis, Richard 84, 85, 86
Withering Roses 53, 55, 60, 63, 64
The Wolf 95
World Film Corporation 77
World War I 89, 92, 93, 94, 95, 99, 101, 108, 116, 142, 155
World War II 152

Young, Clara Kimball 113

Ziegfeld, Florenz 135, 136, 140

201

www.ingramcontent.com/pod-product-compliance
Ingram Content Group UK Ltd.
Pitfield, Milton Keynes, MK11 3LW, UK
UKHW050525150426
5217IPUK00026B/1806